PROGRAMMING
THE Z80

PROGRAMMING
THE Z80

RODNAY ZAKS

THIRD REVISED EDITION

Cover Design by Daniel Le Noury

Every effort has been made to supply complete and accurate information. However, Sybex assumes no responsibility for its use; nor any infringements of patents or other rights of third parties which would result. No license is granted by the equipment manufacturers under any patent or patent rights. Manufacturers reserve the right to change circuitry at any time without notice.

In particular, technical characteristics and prices are subject to rapid change. Comparisons and evaluations are presented for their educational value and for guidance principles. The reader is referred to the manufacturer's data for exact specifications.

Library of Congress Card Number: 80-5468
ISBN: 0-89588-094-6
First Edition published 1979. Third Revised Edition 1982.
Printed in the United States of America
Printing 10 9 8 7 6 5 4 3 2 1

ACKNOWLEDGEMENTS

Designing a programming textbook is always difficult. Designing it so that it will teach elementary programming as well as advanced concepts while covering both hardware and software aspects makes it a challenge. The author would like to acknowledge here the many constructive suggestions for improvements or changes made by: O.M. Barlow, Dennis L. Feick, Richard D. Reid, Stanley E. Erwin, Philip Hooper, Dennis B. Kitsz, R. Ratke, and Jim Crocker.

A special acknowledgement is also due to Chris Williams for his contribution to the instruction-set and the data structures section.

Any additional suggestions for improvements or changes should be sent to the author, and will be reflected in forthcoming editions.

Several tables in Chapter Four showing hexadecimal codes for the Z80 instructions have been reprinted by permission of Zilog Inc. Tables 2.26 and 2.27 have been reprinted by permission of Intel Corporation.

TABLE OF CONTENTS

PREFACE

This book has been designed as a complete self-contained text for learning programming, using the Z80. It can be used by a person who has never programmed before, and should also be of value to anyone using the Z80.

For the person who has already programmed, this book will teach specific programming techniques using (or working around) the specific characteristics of the Z80. This text covers the elementary to intermediate techniques required to start programming effectively.

This text aims at providing a true level of competence to the person who wishes to program using this microprocessor. Naturally, no book will effectively teach how to program, unless one actually practices. However, it is hoped that this book will take the reader to the point where he feels that he can start programming by himself and can solve simple or even moderately complex problems using a microcomputer.

This book is based on the author's experience in teaching more than 1000 persons how to program microcomputers. As a result, it is strongly structured. Chapters normally go from the simple to the complex. For readers who have already learned elementary programming, the introductory chapter may be skipped. For others who have never programmed, the final sections of some chapters may require a second reading. The book has been designed to take the reader systematically through all the basic concepts and techniques required to build increasingly complex programs. It is, therefore, strongly suggested that the ordering of the chapters be followed. In addition, for effective results, it is important that the reader attempt to solve as many exercises as possible. The difficulty within the exercises has been carefully graduated. They are designed to verify that the material which has been presented is really understood. Without doing the programming exercises, it will not be possible to realize the full value of this book as an educational medium. Several of the exercises may require time, such as the multiplication exercise. However, by doing them, you will actually program and *learn by doing*. This is indispensable.

For those who have acquired a taste for programming when reaching the end of this volume, a companion volume is planned: the *Z80 Applications Book*.

Other books in this series cover programming for other popular microprocessors.

For those who wish to develop their hardware knowledge, it is suggested that the reference books *From Chips to Systems: an Introduction to Microprocessors* (ref. C201A) and *Microprocessor Interfacing Techniques* (ref. C207) be consulted.

The contents of this book have been checked carefully and are believed to be reliable. However, inevitably, some typographical or other errors will be found. The author will be grateful for any comments by alert readers so that future editions may benefit from their experience. Any other suggestions for improvements, such as other programs desired, developed, or found of value by readers, will be appreciated.

1
BASIC CONCEPTS

INTRODUCTION

This chapter will introduce the basic concepts and definitions relating to computer programming. The reader already familiar with these concepts may want to glance quickly at the contents of this chapter and then move on to Chapter 2. It is suggested, however, that even the experienced reader look at the contents of this introductory chapter. Many significant concepts are presented here including, for example, two's complement, BCD, and other representations. Some of these concepts may be new to the reader; others may improve the knowledge and skills of experienced programmers.

WHAT IS PROGRAMMING?

Given a problem, one must first devise a solution. This solution, expressed as a step-by-step procedure, is called an *algorithm*. An algorithm is a step-by-step specification of the solution to a given problem. It must terminate in a finite number of steps. This algorithm may be expressed in any language or symbolism. A simple example of an algorithm is:

1—insert key in the keyhole
2—turn key one full turn to the left
3—seize doorknob
4—turn doorknob left and push the door

At this point, if the algorithm is correct for the type of lock involved, the door will open. This four-step procedure qualifies as an algorithm for door opening.

Once a solution to a problem has been expressed in the form of an algorithm, the algorithm must be executed by the computer. Unfortunately, it is now a well-established fact that computers cannot understand or execute ordinary spoken English (or any other human language). The reason lies in the *syntactic ambiguity* of all common human languages. Only a well-defined subset of natural language can be "understood" by the computer. This is called a *programming language.*

Converting an algorithm into a sequence of instructions in a programming language is called *programming.* To be more specific, the actual translation phase of the algorithm into the programming language is called *coding.* Programming really refers not just to the coding but also to the overall design of the programs and "data structures" which will implement the algorithm.

Effective programming requires not only understanding the possible implementation techniques for standard algorithms, but also the skillful use of all the computer hardware resources, such as internal registers, memory, and peripheral devices, plus a creative use of appropriate data structures. These techniques will be covered in the next chapters.

Programming also requires a strict documentation discipline, so that the programs are understandable to others, as well as to the author. Documentation must be both internal and external to the program.

Internal program documentation refers to the comments placed in the body of a program, which explain its operation.

External documentation refers to the design documents which are separate from the program: written explanations, manuals, and flowcharts.

FLOWCHARTING

One intermediate step is almost always used between the *algorithm* and the *program.* It is called a *flowchart.* A flowchart is simply a symbolic representation of the algorithm expressed as a sequence of rectangles and diamonds containing the steps of the algorithm. Rectangles are used for *commands,* or "executable statements." Diamonds are used for *tests* such as: If information

X is true, then take action A, else B. Instead of presenting a formal definition of flowcharts at this point, we will introduce and discuss flowcharts later on in the book when we present programs.

Flowcharting is a highly recommended intermediate step between the algorithm specification and the actual coding of the solution. Remarkably, it has been observed that perhaps 10% of the programming population can write a program successfully without having to flowchart. Unfortunately, it has also been observed that 90% of the population believes it belongs to this 10%! The result: 80% of these programs, on the average, will fail the first time they are run on a computer. (These percentages are naturally not meant to be accurate.) In short, most novice programmers seldom see the necessity of drawing a flowchart. This usually results in "unclean" or erroneous programs. They must then spend a long time testing and correcting their program (this is called the

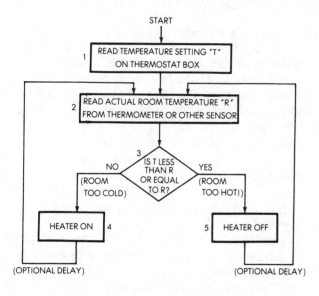

Fig. 1.1: A Flowchart for Keeping Room Temperature Constant

debugging phase). The discipline of flowcharting is therefore highly recommended in all cases. It will require a small amount of additional time prior to the coding, but will usually result in a clear program which executes correctly and quickly. Once flowcharting is well understood, a small percentage of programmers will be able to perform this step mentally without having to do it on paper. Unfortunately, in such cases the programs that they write will usually be hard to understand for anybody else without the documentation provided by flowcharts. As a result, it is universally recommended that flowcharting be used as a strict discipline for any significant program. Many examples will be provided throughout the book.

INFORMATION REPRESENTATION

All computers manipulate information in the form of numbers or in the form of characters. Let us examine here the external and internal representations of information in a computer.

INTERNAL REPRESENTATION OF INFORMATION

All information in a computer is stored as groups of bits. A *bit* stands for a *binary digit*("0" or "1"). Because of the limitations of conventional electronics, the only practical representation of information uses two-state logic (the representation of the state "0" and "1"). The two states of the circuits used in digital electronics are generally "on" or "off", and these are represented logically by the symbols "0" or "1". Because these circuits are used to implement "logical" functions, they are called "binary logic." As a result, virtually all information-processing today is performed in binary format. In the case of microprocessors in general, and of the Z80 in particular, these bits are structured in groups of eight. A group of eight bits is called a *byte*. A group of four bits is called a *nibble*.

Let us now examine how information is represented internally in this binary format. Two entities must be represented inside the computer. The first one is the program, which is a sequence of instructions. The second one is the data on which the program will operate, which may include numbers or alphanumeric text. We will discuss below three representations: program, numbers, and alphanumerics.

Program Representation

All instructions are represented internally as single or multiple bytes. A so-called "short instruction" is represented by a single byte. A longer instruction will be represented by two or more bytes. Because the Z80 is an eight-bit microprocessor, it fetches bytes successively from its memory. Therefore, a single-byte instruction always has a potential for executing faster than a two- or three-byte instruction. It will be seen later that this is an important feature of the instruction set of any microprocessor and in particular the Z80, where a special effort has been made to provide as many single-byte instructions as possible in order to improve the efficiency of the program execution. However, the limitation to 8 bits in length has resulted in important restrictions which will be outlined. This is a classic example of the compromise between speed and flexibility in programming. The binary code used to represent instructions is dictated by the manufacturer. The Z80, like any other microprocessor, comes equipped with a fixed instruction set. These instructions are defined by the manufacturer and are listed at the end of this book, with their code. Any program will be expressed as a sequence of these binary instructions. The Z80 instructions are presented in Chapter 4.

Representing Numeric Data

Representing numbers is not quite straightforward, and several cases must be distinguished. We must first represent integers, then signed numbers, i.e., positive and negative numbers, and finally we must be able to represent decimal numbers. Let us now address these requirements and possible solutions.

Representing integers may be performed by using a *direct binary* representation. The direct binary representation is simply the representation of the decimal value of a number in the binary system. In the binary system, the right-most bit represents 2 to the power 0. The next one to the left represents 2 to the power 1, the next represents 2 to the power 2, and the left-most bit represents 2 to the power $7 = 128$.

$$b_7b_6b_5b_4b_3b_2b_1b_0$$
represents
$$b_7 2^7 + b_6 2^6 + b_5 2^5 + b_4 2^4 + b_3 2^3 + b_2 2^2 + b_1 2^1 + b_0 2^0$$

The powers of 2 are:

$2^7 = 128$, $2^6 = 64$, $2^5 = 32$, $2^4 = 16$, $2^3 = 8$, $2^2 = 4$, $2^1 = 2$, $2^0 = 1$

The binary representation is analogous to the decimal representation of numbers, where "123" represents:

$$
\begin{array}{rl}
1 \times 100 = & 100 \\
+\, 2 \times 10 = & 20 \\
+\, 3 \times 1 = & 3 \\
\hline
= & 123
\end{array}
$$

Note that $100 = 10^2$, $10 = 10^1$, $1 = 10^0$.

In this "positional notation," each digit represents a power of 10.
In the binary system, each binary digit or "bit" represents a power of 2, instead of a power of 10 in the decimal system.

Example: "00001001" in binary represents:

$$
\begin{array}{rll}
1 \times 1 = 1 & (2^0) \\
0 \times 2 = 0 & (2^1) \\
0 \times 4 = 0 & (2^2) \\
1 \times 8 = 8 & (2^3) \\
0 \times 16 = 0 & (2^4) \\
0 \times 32 = 0 & (2^5) \\
0 \times 64 = 0 & (2^6) \\
0 \times 128 = 0 & (2^7) \\
\hline
\end{array}
$$

in decimal: $\quad = 9$

Let us examine some more examples:

"10000001" represents:

$$
\begin{array}{rl}
1 \times 1 = & 1 \\
0 \times 2 = & 0 \\
0 \times 4 = & 0 \\
0 \times 8 = & 0 \\
0 \times 16 = & 0 \\
0 \times 32 = & 0 \\
0 \times 64 = & 0 \\
1 \times 128 = & 128 \\
\hline
\end{array}
$$

in decimal: $\quad = 129$

"10000001" represents, therefore, the decimal number 129.

By examining the binary representation of numbers, you will understand why bits are numbered from 0 to 7, going from right to left. Bit 0 is "b_0" and corresponds to 2^0. Bit 1 is "b_1" and corresponds to 2^1, and so on.

Decimal	Binary	Decimal	Binary
0	00000000	32	00100000
1	00000001	33	00100001
2	00000010	•	
3	00000011	•	
4	00000100	•	
5	00000101	63	00111111
6	00000110	64	01000000
7	00000111	65	01000001
8	00001000	•	
9	00001001	•	
10	00001010	127	01111111
11	00001011	128	10000000
12	00001100	129	10000001
13	00001101		
14	00001110	•	
15	00001111	•	
16	00010000	•	
17	00010001	•	
•			
•			
•		254	11111110
31	00011111	255	11111111

Fig. 1.2: Decimal-Binary Table

The binary equivalents of the numbers from 0 to 255 are shown in Fig. 1-2.

Exercise 1.1: What is the decimal value of "11111100"?

21

Decimal to Binary

Conversely, let us compute the binary equivalent of "11" decimal:

$$11 \div 2 = 5 \text{ remains } 1 \longrightarrow 1 \qquad \text{(LSB)}$$
$$5 \div 2 = 2 \text{ remains } 1 \longrightarrow 1$$
$$2 \div 2 = 1 \text{ remains } 0 \longrightarrow 0$$
$$1 \div 2 = 0 \text{ remains } 1 \longrightarrow 1 \qquad \text{(MSB)}$$

The binary equivalent is 1011 (read right-most column from bottom to top).
The binary equivalent of a decimal number may be obtained by dividing successively by 2 until a quotient of 0 is obtained.

Exercise 1.2: *What is the binary for 257?*

Exercise 1.3: *Convert 19 to binary, then back to decimal.*

Operating on Binary Data

The arithmetic rules for binary numbers are straightforward. The rules for addition are:

$$0 + 0 = \quad 0$$
$$0 + 1 = \quad 1$$
$$1 + 0 = . \quad 1$$
$$1 + 1 = (1) \quad 0$$

where (1) denotes a "carry" of 1 (note that "10" is the binary equivalent of "2" decimal). Binary subtraction will be performed by "adding the complement" and will be explained once we learn how to represent negative numbers.

Example:

$$\begin{array}{cc} (2) & 10 \\ +(1) & +01 \\ \hline =(3) & 11 \end{array}$$

Addition is performed just like in decimal, by adding columns, from right to left:

Adding the right-most column:

$$\begin{array}{c} 10 \\ +01 \\ \hline \end{array}$$

(0 + 1 = 1. No carry.)

Adding the next column:

$$\begin{array}{r} 10 \\ +01 \\ \hline 11 \end{array} \quad (1 + 0 = 1. \text{ No carry.})$$

Exercise 1.4: Compute 5 + 10 in binary. Verify that the result is 15.

Some additional examples of binary addition:

0010	(2)		0011	(3)
+0001	(1)		+0001	(1)
=0011	(3)		=0100	(4)

This last example illustrates the role of the carry.

Looking at the right-most bits: $1 + 1 = (1)\ 0$
A carry of 1 is generated, which must be added to the next bits:

$$\begin{array}{r} 001 - \text{ column 0 has just been added} \\ +000 - \\ +\ \ 1 \quad \text{(carry)} \\ \hline = \ (1)\,0 - \text{where (1) indicates a new} \\ \text{carry into column 2.} \end{array}$$

The final result is: 0100

Another example:

0111	(7)
+0011	+ (3)
1010	=(10)

In this example, a carry is again generated, up to the left-most column.

Exercise 1.5: Compute the result of:

$$\begin{array}{r} 1111 \\ +0001 \\ \hline =? \end{array}$$

Does the result hold in four bits?

With eight bits, it is therefore possible to represent directly the numbers "00000000" to "11111111," i.e., "0" to "255". Two obstacles should be visible immediately. First, we are only representing positive numbers. Second, the magnitude of these numbers is limited to 255 if we use only eight bits. Let us address each of these problems in turn.

Signed Binary

In a signed binary representation, the left-most bit is used to indicate the sign of the number. Traditionally, "0" is used to denote a *positive* number while "1" is used to denote a *negative* number. Now "11111111" will represent −127, while "01111111" will represent +127. We can now represent positive and negative numbers, but we have reduced the maximum magnitude of these numbers to 127.

Example: "0000 0001" represents +1 (the leading "0" is "+", followed by "000 0001" = 1).

"1000 0001" is −1 (the leading "1" is "−").

Exercise 1.6: What is the representation of "−5" in signed binary?

Let us now address the *magnitude* problem: in order to represent larger numbers, it will be necessary to use a larger number of bits. For example, if we use sixteen bits (two bytes) to represent numbers, we will be able to represent numbers from −32K to +32K in signed binary (1K in computer jargon represents 1,024). Bit 15 is used for the sign, and the remaining 15 bits (bit 14 to bit 0) are used for the magnitude: 2^{15} = 32K. If this magnitude is still too small, we will use 3 bytes or more. If we wish to represent large integers, it will be necessary to use a larger number of bytes internally to represent them. This is why most simple BASICs, and other languages, provide only a limited precision for integers. This way, they can use a shorter internal format for the numbers which they manipulate. Better versions of BASIC, or of these other languages, provide a larger number of significant decimal digits at the expense of a large number of bytes for each number.

Now let us solve another problem, the one of speed efficiency. We are going to attempt performing an addition in the signed binary representation which we have introduced. Let us add "−5" and "+7".

+7 is represented by   00000111
−5 is represented by   10000101

The binary sum is: 10001100, or −12

This is not the correct result. The correct result should be +2. In order to use this representation, special actions must be taken, depending on the sign. This results in increased complexity and reduced performance. In other words, the binary addition of signed numbers does not "work correctly." This is annoying. Clearly, the computer must not only represent information, but also perform arithmetic on it.

The solution to this problem is called the *two's complement* representation, which will be used instead of the *signed binary* representation. In order to introduce two's complement let us first introduce an intermediate step: *one's complement.*

One's Complement

In the one's complement representation, all positive integers are represented in their correct binary format. For example "+3" is represented as usual by 00000011. However, its complement "−3" is obtained by complementing every bit in the original representation. Each 0 is transformed into a 1 and each 1 is transformed into a 0. In our example, the one's complement representation of "−3" will be 11111100.

Another example:

$$+2 \text{ is } 00000010$$
$$-2 \text{ is } 11111101$$

Note that, in this representation, positive numbers start with a "0" on the left, and negative ones with a "1" on the left.

Exercise 1.7: *The representation of "+6" is "00000110". What is the representation of "−6" in one's complement?*

As a test, let us add minus 4 and plus 6:

$$-4 \text{ is } 11111011$$
$$+6 \text{ is } 00000110$$

the sum is: (1)   00000001   where (1) indicates a
                                        carry

The "correct result" should be "2", or "00000010".

Let us try again:

$$-3 \text{ is } 11111100$$
$$-2 \text{ is } 11111101$$

The sum is: (1)   11111001

or "−6," plus a carry. The correct result should be "−." The representation of "−5" is 11111010. It did not work.

This representation does represent positive and negative numbers. However the result of an ordinary addition does not always come out "correctly." We will use still another representation. It is evolved from the one's complement and is called the two's complement representation.

Two's Complement Representation

In the two's complement representation, positive numbers are still represented, as usual, in signed binary, just like in one's complement. The difference lies in the representation of *negative numbers*. A negative number represented in two's complement is obtained by first computing the one's complement, and then *adding one*. Let us examine this in an example:

+3 is represented in signed binary by 00000011. Its one's complement representation is 11111100. The two's complement is obtained by adding one. It is 11111101.

Let us try an addition:

$$(3) \quad\quad 00000011$$
$$+(5) \quad +00000101$$
$$=(8) \quad =00001000$$

The result is correct.

Let us try a subtraction:

$$
\begin{array}{rl}
(3) & 00000011 \\
(-5) & +11111011 \\
\hline
& =11111110
\end{array}
$$

Let us identify the result by computing the two's complement:

the one's complement of 11111110 is   00000001

Adding 1   +   1

therefore the two's complement is   00000010 or +2

Our result above, "11111110" represents "-2". It is correct.

We have now tried addition and subtraction, and the results were correct (ignoring the carry). It seems that two's complement works!

Exercise 1.8:   *What is the two's complement representation of "+127"?*

Exercise 1.9:   *What is the two's complement representation of "−128"?*

Let us now add $+4$ and -3 (the subtraction is performed by adding the two's complement):

$$
\begin{array}{l}
+4 \text{ is } 00000100 \\
-3 \text{ is } 11111101 \\
\hline
(1) \quad 00000001
\end{array}
$$

The result is:

If we ignore the carry, the result is 00000001, i.e., "1" in decimal. This is the correct result. Without giving the complete mathematical proof, let us simply state that this representation does work. In two's complement, it is possible to add or subtract signed numbers regardless of the sign. Using the usual rules of binary addition, the result comes out correctly, including the sign. The carry is ignored. This is a very significant advantage. If it were not the case, one would have to correct the result for sign every time, causing a much slower addition or subtraction time.

For the sake of completeness, let us state that two's complement is simply the most convenient representation to use for simpler processors such as microprocessors. On complex processors, other representations may be used. For example, one's complement may be used, but it requires special circuitry to "correct the result."

From this point on, all signed integers will implicitly be represented internally in two's complement notation. See Fig. 1.3 for a table of two's complement numbers.

Exercise 1.10: *What are the smallest and the largest numbers which one may represent in two's complement notation, using only one byte?*

Exercise 1.11: *Compute the two's complement of 20. Then compute the two's complement of your result. Do you find 20 again?*

The following examples will serve to demonstrate the rules of two's complement. In particular, C denotes a possible carry (or borrow) condition. (It is bit 8 of the result.)

V denotes a two's complement overflow, i.e., when the sign of the result is changed "accidentally" because the numbers are too large. It is an essentially internal carry from bit 6 into bit 7 (the sign bit). This will be clarified below.

Let us now demonstrate the role of the carry "C" and the overflow "V".

The Carry C

Here is an example of a carry:

$$
\begin{array}{rl}
(128) & 10000000 \\
+(129) & +10000001 \\
\hline
(257) = (1) & 00000001
\end{array}
$$

where (1) indicates a carry.

The result requires a ninth bit (bit "8", since the right-most bit is "0"). It is the carry bit.

If we assume that the carry is the ninth bit of the result, we recognize the result as being 100000001 = 257.

However, the carry must be recognized and handled with care. Inside the microprocessor, the registers used to hold information are generally only eight-bit wide.When storing the result, only bits 0 to 7 will be preserved.

A carry, therefore, always requires special action: it must be detected by special instructions, then processed. Processing the carry means either storing it somewhere (with a special instruction), or ignoring it, or deciding that it is an error (if the largest authorized result is "11111111").

+	2's complement code	–	2's complement code
+ 127	01111111	– 128	10000000
+ 126	01111110	– 127	10000001
+ 125	01111101	– 126	10000010
. . .		– 125	10000011
		. . .	
+ 65	01000001	– 65	10111111
+ 64	01000000	– 64	11000000
+ 63	00111111	– 63	11000001
. . .		. . .	
+ 33	00100001	– 33	11011111
+ 32	00100000	– 32	11100000
+ 31	00011111	– 31	11100001
. . .		. . .	
+ 17	00010001	– 17	11101111
+ 16	00010000	– 16	11110000
+ 15	00001111	– 15	11110001
+ 14	00001110	– 14	11110010
+ 13	00001101	– 13	11110011
+ 12	00001100	– 12	11110100
+ 11	00001011	– 11	11110101
+ 10	00001010	– 10	11110110
+ 9	00001001	– 9	11110111
+ 8	00001000	– 8	11111000
+ 7	00000111	– 7	11111001
+ 6	00000110	– 6	11111010
+ 5	00000101	– 5	11111011
+ 4	00000100	– 4	11111100
+ 3	00000011	– 3	11111101
+ 2	00000010	– 2	11111110
+ 1	00000001	– 1	11111111
+ 0	00000000		

Fig. 1.3: 2's Complement Table

Overflow V

Here is an example of overflow:

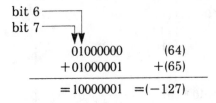

```
    01000000        (64)
  + 01000001       +(65)
  ─────────────────────────
  = 10000001    = (−127)
```

An internal carry has been generated from bit 6 into bit 7. This is called an overflow.

The result is now negative, "by accident." This situation must be detected, so that it can be corrected.

Let us examine another situation:

```
       11111111      (−1)
     + 11111111    +(−1)
  ──────────────────────────
  =(1)  11111110   =(−2)
     ▼
   carry
```

In this case, an internal carry has been generated from bit 6 into bit 7, and also from bit 7 into bit 8 (the formal "Carry" C we have examined in the preceding section). The rules of two's complement arithmetic specify that this carry should be ignored. The result is then correct.

This is because the carry from bit 6 into bit 7 did not change the sign bit.

This is not an *overflow* condition. When operating on negative numbers, the overflow is not simply a carry from bit 6 into bit 7. Let us examine one more example.

```
       11000000     (−64)
     + 10111111     (−65)
  ──────────────────────────
  =(1)  01111111    (+127)
     ▼
   carry
```

This time, there has been no internal carry from bit 6 into bit 7, but there has been an external carry. The result is incorrect, as bit 7 has been changed. An overflow condition should be indicated.

Overflow will occur in four situations:

1—adding large positive numbers
2—adding large negative numbers
3—subtracting a large positive number from a large negative number
4—subtracting a large negative number from a large positive number.

Let us now improve our definition of the overflow:

Technically, the overflow indicator, a special bit reserved for this purpose, and called a "flag," will be set when there is a carry from bit 6 into bit 7 and no external carry, or else when there is no carry from bit 6 into bit 7 but there is an external carry. This indicates that bit 7, i.e., the sign of the result, has been accidentally changed. For the technically-minded reader, the overflow flag is set by Exclusive ORing the carry-in and carry-out of bit 7 (the sign bit). Practically every microprocessor is supplied with a special overflow flag to automatically detect this condition, which requires corrective action.

Overflow indicates that the result of an addition or a subtraction requires more bits than are available in the standard eight-bit register used to contain the result.

The Carry and the Overflow

The carry and the overflow bits are called "flags." They are provided in every microprocessor, and in the next chapter we will learn to use them for effective programming. These two indicators are located in a special register called the flags or "status" register. This register also contains additional indicators whose function will be clarified in Chapter 4.

Examples

Let us now illustrate the operation of the carry and the overflow in actual examples. In each example, the symbol V denotes the overflow, and C the carry.

If there has been no overflow, V = 0. If there has been an overflow, V = 1 (same for the carry C). Remember that the rules of two's complement specify that the carry be ignored. (The mathematical proof is not supplied here.)

Positive-Positive

```
    00000110   (+6)
+   00001000   (+8)
─────────────────────
=   00001110   (+14)   V:0      C:0
```

(CORRECT)

Positive-Positive with Overflow

```
    01111111   (+127)
+   00000001   (+1)
─────────────────────
=   10000000   (−128)  V:1      C:0
```

The above is invalid because an overflow has occurred.

(ERROR)

Positive-Negative (result positive)

```
    00000100   (+4)
+   11111110   (−2)
─────────────────────
=(1)00000010   (+2)    V:0      C:1 (disregard)
```

(CORRECT)

Positive-Negative (result negative)

```
    00000010   (+2)
+   11111100   (−4)
─────────────────────
=   11111110   (−2)    V:0      C:0
```

(CORRECT)

Negative-Negative

```
    11111110   (−2)
+   11111100   (−4)
─────────────────────
=(1)11111010   (−6)    V:0      C:1 (disregard)
```

(CORRECT)

Negative-Negative with Overflow

```
    10000001   (−127)
+   11000010   (−62)
─────────────────────
=(1)01000011   (67)    V:1      C:1
```

(ERROR)

This time an "underflow" has occurred, by adding two large negative numbers. The result would be −189, which is too large to reside in eight bits.

Exercise 1.12: *Complete the following additions. Indicate the result, the carry C, the overflow V, and whether the result is correct or not:*

```
  10111111    (___)              11111010    (___)
+ 11000001    (___)            + 11111001    (___)
_____                    _____
= _____  V:___  C:___        = _____  V:___  C:___
□ CORRECT        □ ERROR        □ CORRECT        □ ERROR


  00010000    (___)              01111110    (___)
+ 01000000    (___)            + 00101010    (___)
_____                    _____
= _____  V:___  C:___        = _____  V:___  C:___
□ CORRECT        □ ERROR        □ CORRECT        □ ERROR
```

Exercise 1.13: *Can you show an example of overflow when adding a positive and a negative number? Why?*

Fixed Format Representation

Now we know how to represent signed integers. However, we have not yet resolved the problem of magnitude. If we want to represent larger integers, we will need several bytes. In order to perform arithmetic operations efficiently, it is necessary to use a fixed number of bytes rather than a variable one. Therefore, once the number of bytes is chosen, the maximum magnitude of the number which can be represented is fixed.

Exercise 1.14: *What are the largest and the smallest numbers which may be represented in two bytes using two's complement?*

The Magnitude Problem

When adding numbers we have restricted ourselves to eight bits because the processor we will use operates internally on eight bits at a time. However, this restricts us to the numbers in the range −128 to +127. Clearly, this is not sufficient for many applications.

Multiple precision will be used to increase the number of digits which can be represented. A two-, three-, or N-byte format may then be used. For example, let us examine a 16-bit, "double-precision" format:

00000000	00000000	is "0"
00000000	00000001	is "1"
. . .		
01111111	11111111	is "32767"
11111111	11111111	is "−1"
11111111	11111110	is "−2"

Exercise 1.15: *What is the largest negative integer which can be represented in a two's complement triple-precision format?*

However, this method will result in disadvantages. When adding two numbers, for example, we will generally have to add them eight bits at a time. This will be explained in Chapter 3 (Basic Programming Techniques). It results in slower processing. Also, this representation uses 16 bits for any number, even if it could be represented with only eight bits. It is, therefore, common to use 16 or perhaps 32 bits, but seldom more.

Let us consider the following important point: whatever the number of bits N chosen for the two's complement representation, it is fixed. If any result or intermediate computation should generate a number requiring more than N bits, some bits will be lost. The program normally retains the N left-most bits (the most significant) and drops the low-order ones. This is called truncating the result.

Here is an example in the decimal system, using a six digit representation:

$$
\begin{array}{r}
123456 \\
\times \quad 1.2 \\
\hline
246912 \\
123456 \\
\hline
= 148147.2
\end{array}
$$

The result requires 7 digits! The "2" after the decimal point will be dropped and the final result will be 148147. It has been truncated. Usually, as long as the position of the decimal point is not lost, this method is used to extend the range of the operations which may be performed, at the expense of precision.

The problem is the same in binary. The details of a binary multiplication will be shown in Chapter 4.

This fixed-format representation may cause a loss of precision, but it may be sufficient for usual computations or mathematical operations.

Unfortunately, in the case of accounting, no loss of precision is tolerable. For example, if a customer rings up a large total on a cash register, it would not be acceptable to have a five figure amount to pay, which would be approximated to the dollar. Another representation must be used wherever precision in the result is essential. The solution normally used is *BCD*, or binary-coded decimal.

BCD Representation

The principle used in representing numbers in BCD is to encode each decimal digit separately, and to use as many bits as necessary to represent the complete number exactly. In order to encode each of the digits from 0 through 9, four bits are necessary. Three bits would only supply eight combinations, and can therefore not encode the ten digits. Four bits allow sixteen combinations and are therefore sufficient to encode the digits "0" through "9". It can also be noted that six of the possible codes will not be used in the BCD representation (see Fig. 1-4). This will result later on in a potential problem during additions and subtractions, which we will have to solve.

CODE	BCD SYMBOL	CODE	BCD SYMBOL
0000	0	1000	8
0001	1	1001	9
0010	2	1010	unused
0011	3	1011	unused
0100	4	1100	unused
0101	5	1101	unused
0110	6	1110	unused
0111	7	1111	unused

Fig. 1.4: BCD Table

Since only four bits are needed to encode a BCD digit, two BCD digits may be encoded in every byte. This is called *"packed BCD."*

As an example, "00000000" will be "00" in BCD. "10011001" will be "99".

A BCD code is read as follows:

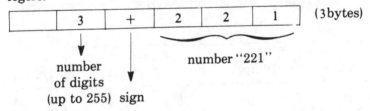

```
            0010    0001
BCD digit "2"  ◄──┘       │
BCD digit "1"  ◄──────────┘
BCD number "21"
```

Exercise 1.16: What is the BCD representation for "29"? "91"?

Exercise 1.17: Is "10100000" a valid BCD representation? Why?

As many bytes as necessary will be used to represent all BCD digits. Typically, one or more nibbles will be used at the beginning of the representation to indicate the total number of nibbles, i.e., the total number of BCD digits used. Another nibble or byte will be used to denote the position of the decimal point. However, conventions may vary.

Here is an example of a representation for multibyte BCD integers:

```
┌─────┬─────┬─────┬─────┬─────┬─────┐
│     │  3  │  +  │  2  │  2  │  1  │   (3 bytes)
└─────┴─────┴─────┴─────┴─────┴─────┘
           │     │       └────┬────┘
           ▼     │       number "221"
      number     │
     of digits   ▼
    (up to 255) sign
```

This represents +221
(The sign may be represented by 0000 for +, and 0001 for −, for example.)

Exercise 1.18: Using the same convention, represent "−23123". Show it in BCD format, as above, then in binary.

Exercise 1.19: Show the BCD for "222" and "111", then for the result of 222 × 111. (Compute the result by hand, then show it in the above representation.)

The BCD representation can easily accommodate decimal numbers.

For example, +2.21 may be represented by:

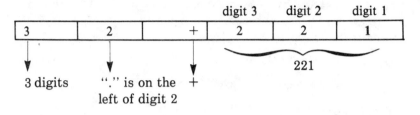

			digit 3	digit 2	digit 1
3	2	+	2	2	1

221

3 digits   "." is on the   +
left of digit 2

The advantage of BCD is that it yields absolutely correct results. Its disadvantage is that it uses a large amount of memory and results in slow arithmetic operations. This is acceptable only in an accounting environment and is normally not used in other cases.

Exercise 1.20:   How many bits are required to encode "9999" in BCD? And in two's complement?

We have now solved the problems associated with the representation of integers, signed integers and even large integers. We have even already presented one possible method of representing decimal numbers, with BCD representation. Let us now examine the problem of representing decimal numbers in a fixed length format.

Floating-Point Representation

The basic principle is that decimal numbers must be represented with a fixed format. In order not to waste bits, the representation will *normalize* all the numbers.

For example, "0.000123" wastes three zeros on the left of the number, which have no meaning except to indicate the position of the decimal point. Normalizing this number results in $.123 \times 10^{-3}$. ".123" is called a *normalized mantissa,* "-3" is called the *exponent.* We have normalized this number by eliminating all the meaningless zeros on the left of it and adjusting the exponent.

Let us consider another example:

22.1 is normalized as $.221 \times 10^{2}$

or $M \times 10^{E}$ where M is the mantissa, and E is the exponent.

It can be readily seen that a normalized number is characterized by a mantissa less than 1 and greater or equal to .1 in all cases where the number is not zero. In other words, this can be represented mathematically by:

$$.1 \leqslant M < 1 \text{ or } 10^{-1} \leqslant M < 10^0$$

Similarly, in the binary representation:

$$2^{-1} \leqslant M < 2^0 \text{ (or } .5 \leqslant M < 1)$$

Where M is the absolute value of the mantissa (disregarding the sign).

For example:

111.01 is normalized as: $.11101 \times 2^3$.

The mantissa is 11101.

The exponent is 3.

Now that we have defined the principle of the representation, let us examine the actual format. A typical floating-point representation appears below.

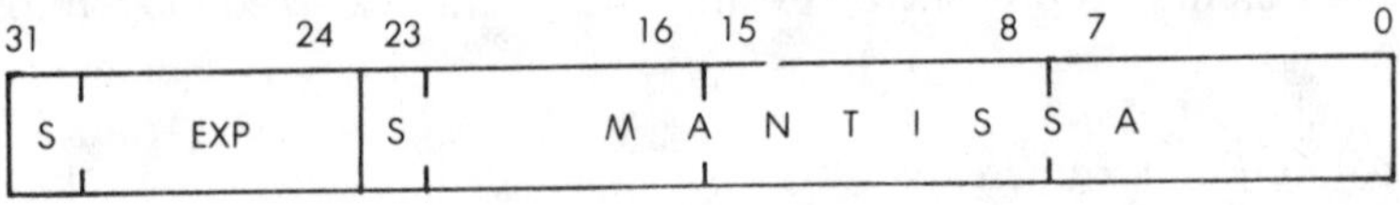

Fig. 1.5: Typical Floating-Point Representation

In the representation used in this example, four bytes are used for a total of 32 bits. The first byte on the left of the illustration is used to represent the exponent. Both the exponent and the mantissa will be represented in two's complement. As a result, the maximum exponent will be −128. "S" in Fig. 1-5 denotes the sign bit.

Three bytes are used to represent the mantissa. Since the first bit in the two's complement representation indicates the sign, this leaves 23 bits for the representation of the magnitude of the mantissa.

Exercise 1.21: How many decimal digits can the mantissa represent with the 23 bits?

This is only one example of a floating point representation. It is possible to use only three bytes, or it is possible to use more. The four-byte representation proposed above is just a common one which represents a reasonable compromise in terms of accuracy, magnitude of numbers, storage utilization, and efficiency in arithmetic operation.

We have now explored the problems associated with the representation of numbers and we know how to represent them in integer form, with a sign, or in decimal form. Let us now examine how to represent alphanumeric data internally.

Representing Alphanumeric Data

The representation of alphanumeric data, i.e. characters, is completely straightforward: all characters are encoded in an eight-bit code. Only two codes are in general use in the computer world, the ASCII Code, and the EBCDIC Code. ASCII stands for "American Standard Code for Information Interchange," and is universally used in the world of microprocessors. EBCDIC is a variation of ASCII used by IBM, and therefore not used in the microcomputer world unless one interfaces to an IBM terminal.

Let us briefly examine the ASCII encoding. We must encode 26 letters of the alphabet for both upper and lower case, plus 10 numeric symbols, plus perhaps 20 additional special symbols. This can be easily accomplished with 7 bits, which allow 128 possible codes. (See Fig.1-6.) All characters are therefore encoded in 7 bits. The eighth bit, when it is used, is the *parity bit*. Parity is a technique for verifying that the contents of a byte have not been accidentally changed. The number of 1's in the byte is counted and the eighth bit is set to one if the count was odd, thus making the total even. This is called even parity. One can also use odd parity, i.e. writing the eighth bit (the left-most) so that the total number of 1's in the byte is odd.

Example: let us compute the parity bit for "0010011" using even parity. The number of 1's is 3. The parity bit must therefore be a 1 so that the total number of bits is 4, i.e. even. The result is 10010011, where the leading 1 is the parity bit and 0010011 identifies the character.

The table of 7-bit ASCII codes is shown in Fig. 1-6. In practice, it is used "as is," i.e. without parity, by adding a 0 in the left-most position, or else with parity, by adding the appropriate extra bit on the left.

Exercise 1.22: Compute the 8-bit representation of the digits "0" through "9", using even parity. (This code will be used in application examples of Chapter 8.)

Exercise 1.23: Same for the letters "A" through "F".

Exercise 1.24: Using a non-parity ASCII code (where the left-most bit is "0"), indicate the binary contents of the 4 characters below:

"A"

"?"

"3"

"b"

HEX	MSD	0	1	2	3	4	5	6	7
LSD	BITS	000	001	010	011	100	101	110	111
0	0000	NUL	DLE	SPACE	0	@	P	—	p
1	0001	SOH	DC1	!	1	A	Q	a	q
2	0010	STX	DC2	"	2	B	R	b	r
3	0011	ETX	DC3	#	3	C	S	c	s
4	0100	EOT	DC4	$	4	D	T	d	t
5	0101	ENQ	NAK	%	5	E	U	e	u
6	0110	ACK	SYN	&	6	F	V	f	v
7	0111	BEL	ETB	'	7	G	W	g	w
8	1000	BS	CAN	(	8	H	X	h	x
9	1001	HT	EM	)	9	I	Y	i	y
A	1010	LF	SUB	*	:	J	Z	j	z
B	1011	VT	ESC	+	;	K	[	k	{
C	1100	FF	FS	,	<	L	\	l	--
D	1101	CR	GS	—	=	M	]	m	}
E	1110	SO	RS	.	>	N	∧	n	~
F	1111	SI	US	/	?	O	←	o	DEL

Fig. 1.6: ASCII Conversion Table
(see Appendix B for abbreviations)

In specialized situations such as telecommunications, other codings may be used such as error-correcting codes. However they are beyond the scope of this book.

We have examined the usual representations for both program and data inside the computer. Let us now examine the possible external representations.

EXTERNAL REPRESENTATION OF INFORMATION

The external representation refers to the way information is presented to the *user*, i.e. generally to the programmer. Information may be presented externally in essentially three formats: binary, octal or hexadecimal and symbolic.

1. Binary

It has been seen that information is stored internally in *bytes*, which are sequences of eight *bits* (0's or 1's). It is sometimes desirable to display this internal information directly in its binary format and this is called *binary representation*. One simple example is provided by Light Emitting Diodes (LEDs) which are essentially miniature lights, on the front panel of the microcomputer. In the case of an eight-bit microprocessor, a front panel will typically be equipped with eight LEDs to display the contents of any internal register. (A register is used to hold eight bits of information and will be described in Chapter 2). A lighted LED indicates a one. A zero is indicated by an LED which is not lighted. Such a binary representation may be used for the fine debugging of a complex program, especially if it involves input/output, but is naturally impractical at the human level. This is because in most cases, one likes to look at information in symbolic form. Thus "9" is much easier to understand or remember than "1001". More convenient representations have been devised, which improve the person-machine interface.

2. Octal and Hexadecimal

"Octal" and "hexadecimal" encode respectively three and four binary bits into a unique symbol. In the octal system, any combination of three binary bits is represented by a number between 0 and 7.

"Octal" is a format using three bits, where each combination of three bits is represented by a symbol between 0 and 7:

binary	octal
000	0
001	1
010	2
011	3
100	4
101	5
110	6
111	7

Fig. 1.7: Octal Symbols

For example, "00 100 100" binary is represented by:

  0   4   4

or "044" in octal.

Another example: 11 111 111 is:

  3   7   7

or "377" in octal.

Conversely, the octal "211" represents:

  010   001   001

or "10001001" binary.

Octal has traditionally been used on older computers which were employing various numbers of bits ranging from 8 to perhaps 64. More recently, with the dominance of eight-bit microprocessors, the eight-bit format has become the standard, and another more practical representation is used. This is *hexadecimal*.

In the hexdecimal representation, a group of four bits is encoded as one hexadecimal digit. Hexadecimal digits are represented by the symbols from 0 to 9, and by the letters A, B, C, D, E, F. For example, "0000" is represented by "0", "0001" is represented by "1" and "1111" is represented by the letter "F" (see Fig. 1-8).

DECIMAL	BINARY	HEX	OCTAL
0	0000	0	0
1	0001	1	1
2	0010	2	2
3	0011	3	3
4	0100	4	4
5	0101	5	5
6	0110	6	6
7	0111	7	7
8	1000	8	10
9	1001	9	11
10	1010	A	12
11	1011	B	13
12	1100	C	14
13	1101	D	15
14	1110	E	16
15	1111	F	17

Fig. 1.8: Hexadecimal Codes

Example: $\underbrace{1010}_{A}$ $\underbrace{0001}_{1}$ in binary is represented by

A   1   in hexadecimal.

Exercise 1.25: What is the hexadecimal representation of "10101010?"

Exercise 1.26: Conversely, what is the binary equivalent of "FA" hexadecimal?

Exercise 1.27: What is the octal of "01000001"?

Hexadecimal offers the advantage of encoding eight bits into only two digits. This is easier to visualize or memorize and faster to type into a computer than its binary equivalent. Therefore, on most new microcomputers, hexadecimal is the preferred method of representation for groups of bits.

Naturally, whenever the information present in the memory has a meaning, such as representing text or numbers, hexadecimal is not convenient for representing the meaning of this information when it is brought out for use by humans.

Symbolic Representation

Symbolic representation refers to the external representation of information in actual symbolic form. For example, decimal numbers are represented as decimal numbers, and not as sequences of hexadecimal symbols or bits. Similarly, text is represented as such. Naturally, symbolic representation is most practical to the user. It is used whenever an appropriate display device is available, such as a CRT display or a printer. (A CRT display is a television-type screen used to display text or graphics.) Unfortunately, in smaller systems such as one-board microcomputers, it is uneconomical to provide such displays, and the user is restricted to hexadecimal communication with the computer.

Summary of External Representations

Symbolic representation of information is the most desirable since it is the most natural for a human user. However, it requires an expensive interface in the form of an alphanumeric keyboard, plus a printer or a CRT display. For this reason, it may not be available on the less expensive systems. An alternative type of representation is then used, and in this case hexadecimal is the dominant representation. Only in rare cases relating to fine de-bugging at the hardware or the software level is the binary representation used. *Binary* directly displays the contents of registers of memory in binary format.

(The utility of a direct binary display on a front panel has always been the subject of a heated emotional controversy, which will not be debated here.)

We have seen how to represent information internally and externally. We will now examine the actual microprocessor which will manipulate this information.

Additional Exercises

Exercise 1.28: *What is the advantage of two's complement over other representations used to represent signed numbers?*

Exercise 1.29: *How would you represent "1024" in direct binary? Signed binary? Two's complement?*

Exercise 1.30: *What is the V-bit? Should the programmer test it after an addition or subtraction?*

Exercise 1.31: *Compute the two's complement of "+16", "+17", "+18", "−16", "−17", "−18".*

Exercise 1.32: *Show the hexadecimal representation of the following text, which has been stored internally in ASCII format, with no parity: = "MESSAGE".*

2

Z80 HARDWARE ORGANIZATION

INTRODUCTION

In order to program at an elementary level, it is not necessary to understand in detail the internal structure of the processor that one is using. However, in order to do efficient programming, such an understanding is required. The purpose of this chapter is to present the basic hardware concepts necessary for understanding the operation of the Z80 system. The complete microcomputer system includes not only the microprocessor unit (here the Z80), but also other components. This chapter presents the Z80 proper, while the other devices (mainly input/output) will be presented in a separate chapter (Chapter 7).

We will review here the basic architecture of the microcomputer system, then study more closely the internal organization of the Z80. We will examine, in particular, the various registers. We will then study the program execution and sequencing mechanism. From a hardware standpoint, this chapter is only a simplified presentation. The reader interested in gaining detailed understanding is referred to our book ref. C201 ("Microprocessors," by the same author).

The Z80 was designed as a replacement for the Intel 8080, and to offer additional capabilities. A number of references will be made in this chapter to the 8080 design.

SYSTEM ARCHITECTURE

The architecture of the microcomputer system appears in Figure 2.1. The microprocessor unit (MPU), which will be a Z80 here, appears on the left of the illustration. It implements the functions of a *central-processing unit* (CPU) within one chip: it includes an *arithmetic-logical unit* (ALU), plus its internal registers, and a *control unit* (CU), in

46

charge of sequencing the system. Its operation will be explained in this chapter.

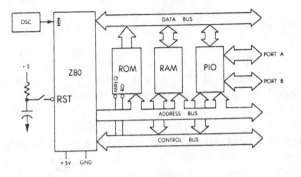

Fig. 2.1: Standard Z80 System

The MPU creates three *buses:* an 8-bit bidirectional *data bus,* which appears at the top of the illustration, a 16-bit unidirectional *address bus,* and a *control bus,* which appears at the bottom of the illustration. Let us describe the function of each of the buses.

The *data bus* carries the data being exchanged by the various elements of the system. Typically, it will carry data from the memory to the MPU or from the MPU to the memory or from the MPU to an input/output chip. (An input/output chip is a component in charge of communicating with an external device.)

The *address bus* carries an address generated by the MPU, which will select one internal register within one of the chips attached to the system. This address specifies the source, or the destination, of the data which will transit along the data bus.

The *control bus* carries the various synchronization signals required by the system.

Having described the purpose of buses, let us now connect the additional components required for a complete system.

Every MPU requires a precise timing reference, which is supplied by a *clock* and a *crystal.* In most "older" microprocessors, the clock-oscillator is external to the MPU and requires an extra chip. In most recent microprocessors, the clock-oscillator is usually incorporated within the MPU. The quartz crystal, however, because of its bulk, is always external to the system. The crystal and the clock appear on the left of the MPU box in Figure 2.1.

Let us now turn our attention to the other elements of the system. Going from left to right on the illustration, we distinguish:

The *ROM* is the *read-only memory* and contains the *program* for the system. The advantage of the ROM memory is that its contents are permanent and do not disappear whenever the system is turned off. The ROM, therefore, always contains a *bootstrap* or a *monitor* program (their function will be explained later) to permit initial system operation. In a process-control environment, nearly all the programs will reside in ROM, as they will probably never be changed. In such a case, the industrial user has to protect the system against power failures; programs must not be volatile. They must be in ROM.

However, in a hobbyist environment, or in a program-development environment (when the programmer tests his program), most of the programs will reside in RAM so that they can be easily changed. Later, they may remain in RAM, or be transferred into ROM, if desired. RAM, however, is volatile. Its contents are lost when power is turned off.

The *RAM (random-access memory)* is the read/write memory for the system. In the case of a control system, the amount of RAM will typically be small (for data only). On the other hand, in a program-development environment, the amount of RAM will be large, as it will contain programs plus development software. All RAM contents must be loaded prior to use from an external device.

Finally the system will contain one or more interface chips so that it may communicate with the external world. The most frequently used interface chip is the PIO or *parallel input/output* chip. It is the one shown on the illustration. This PIO, like all other chips in the system, connects to all three buses and provides at least two 8-bit ports for communication with the outside world. For more details on how an actual PIO works, refer to book C201 or, for specifics of the Z80 system, refer to Chapter 7 (Input/Output Devices).

All the chips are connected to all three buses, including the control bus.

The functional modules which have been described need not necessarily reside on a single LSI chip. In fact, we could use *combination chips,* which may include both PIO and a limited amount of ROM or RAM.

Still more components will be required to build a real system. In particular, the buses usually need to be *buffered*. Also, *decoding logic* may be used for the memory RAM chips, and, finally, some signals may need to be amplified by *drivers*. These auxiliary circuits will not be described here as they are not relevant to programming. The reader interested in specific assembly and interfacing techniques is referred to book C207 "Microprocessor Interfacing Techniques."

INSIDE A MICROPROCESSOR

The large majority of all microprocessor chips on the market today implement the same architecture. This "standard" architecture will be described here. It is shown in Figure 2.2. The modules of this standard microprocessor will now be detailed, from right to left.

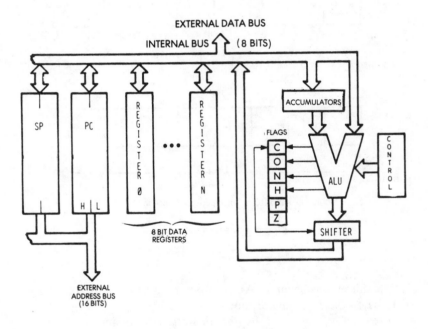

Fig. 2.2: "Standard" Microprocessor Architecture

The *control box* on the right represents the control unit which synchronizes the entire system. Its role will be clarified within the remainder of this chapter.

The *ALU* performs arithmetic and logic operations. A special register equips one of the inputs of the ALU, the left input here. It is called the accumulator. (Several accumulators may be provided.) The accumulator may be referenced both as input and output (source and destination) within the same instruction.

The ALU must also provide *shift* and *rotate* facilities.

A shift operation consists of moving the contents of a byte by one or more positions to the left or to the right. This is illustrated in Figure 2.3. Each bit has been moved to the left by one position. The details of shifts and rotations will be presented in the next chapter.

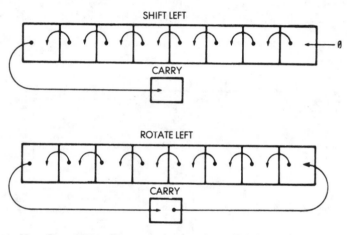

Note: Some Shift and Rotate instructions do not include the Carry.

Fig. 2.3: Shift and Rotate

The shifter may be on the ALU output, as illustrated in Figure 2.2, or may be on the accumulator input.

To the left of the ALU, the *flags* or *status register* appear. Their role is to store exceptional conditions within the microprocessor. The contents of the flags register may be tested by specialized instructions, or may be read on the internal data bus. A *conditional* instruction will cause the execution of a new program, depending on the value of one of these bits.

The role of the status bits in the Z80 will be examined later in this chapter.

Setting Flags

Most of the instructions executed by the processor will modify some or all of the flags. It is important to always refer to the chart provided by the manufacturer listing which bits will be modified by the instructions. This is essential in understanding the way a program is being executed. Such a chart for the Z80 is shown in Figure 4-17.

The Registers

Let us look now at Figure 2.2. On the left of the illustration, the registers of the microprocessor appear. Conceptually, one can distinguish the *general purpose registers* and the *address registers*.

The General-Purpose Registers

General-purpose registers must be provided in order for the ALU to manipulate data at high speed. Because of restrictions on the number of bits which it is reasonable to provide within an instruction, the number of (directly addressable) registers is usually limited to fewer than eight. Each of these registers is a set of eight flip-flops, connected to the bidirectional internal data bus. These eight bits can be transferred simultaneously to or from the data bus. The implementation of these registers in MOS flip-flops provides the fastest level of memory available, and their contents can be accessed within tens of nanoseconds.

Internal registers are usually labelled from 0 to n. The role of these registers is not defined in advance: they are said to be "general purpose." They may contain any data used by the program.

These general-purpose registers will normally be used to store eight-bit data. On some microprocessors, facilities exist to manipulate *two* of these registers at a time. They are then called "register pairs." This arrangement facilitates the storage of 16-bit quantities, whether data or addresses.

The Address Registers

Address registers are 16-bit registers intended for the storage of addresses. They are also often called *data counters* or *pointers*. They are double registers, i.e., two eight-bit registers. Their essential characteristic is to be connected to the address bus. The address registers create the address bus. The address bus appears on the left and the bottom part of the illustration in Figure 2.4.

The only way to load the contents of these 16-bit registers is via the data bus. Two transfers will be necessary along the data bus in order to transfer 16 bits. In order to differentiate between the lower half and the higher half of each register, they are usually labelled as L (low) or H (high), denoting bits 0 through 7, and 8 through 15 respectively. This label is used whenever it is necessary to differentiate the halves of these registers. At least two address registers are present within most microprocessors. "MUX" in Fig. 2.4 stands for multiplexer.

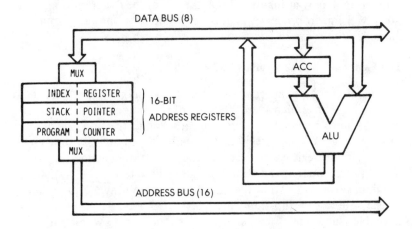

Fig. 2.4: The 16-bit Address Registers Create the Address Bus

Program Counter (PC)

The *program counter* must be present in any processor. It contains the address of the next instruction to be executed. The presence of the program counter is indispensable and fundamental to program execution. The mechanism of program execution and the automatic sequencing implemented with the program counter will be described in the next section. Briefly, execution of a program is normally sequential. In order to access the next instruction, it is necessary to bring it from the memory into the microprocessor. The contents of the PC will be deposited on the address bus, and transmitted towards the memory. The memory will then read the contents specified by this address and send back the corresponding word to the MPU. This is the instruction.

In a few exceptional microprocessors, such as the two-chip F8, there is no PC on the microprocessor. This does not mean that the system does not have a program counter. The PC happens to be implemented directly on the memory chip, for reasons of efficiency.

Stack Pointer (SP)

The *stack* has not been introduced yet and will be described in the next section. In most powerful, general-purpose microprocessors, the stack is implemented in "software," i.e., within the memory. In order to keep track of the top of this stack within the memory, a 16-bit register is dedicated to the *stack pointer* or *SP*. The SP contains the address of the top of the stack within the memory. It will be shown that the stack is indispensable for interrupts and for subroutines.

Index Register (IX)

Indexing is a memory-addressing facility which is not always provided in microprocessors. The various memory-addressing techniques will be described in Chapter 5. Indexing is a facility for accessing blocks of data in the memory with a single instruction. An *index register* will typically contain a displacement which will be automatically added to a base (or it might contain a base which would be added to a displacement). In short, indexing is used to access any word within a block of data.

The Stack

A *stack* is formally called an LIFO structure (last-in, first-out). A stack is a set of registers, or memory locations, allocated to this data structure. The essential characteristic of this structure is that it is a *chronological* structure. The first element introduced into the stack is always at the bottom of the stack. The element most recently deposited in the stack is on the top of the stack. The analogy can be drawn with a stack of plates on a restaurant counter. There is a hole in the counter with a spring in the bottom. Plates are piled up in the hole. With this organization, it is guaranteed that the plate which has been put first in the stack (the oldest) is always at the bottom. The one that has been placed most recently on the stack is the one which is on top of it. This example also illustrates another characteristic of the stack. In normal use, a stack is only accessible via two instructions: "push" and "pop" (or "pull"). The *push* operation results in depositing one element on top of the stack (two in the case of the Z80). The *pull* operation consists of removing one element from the stack. In the case of a microprocessor, it is the *accumulator* that will be deposited on top of the stack. The *pop* will result in a transfer of the top element of the stack into the accumulator. Other specialized instructions may exist to transfer the top of the stack between other specialized registers, such as the status register. The Z80 is more versatile than most in this respect.

The availability of a stack is required to implement three programming facilities within the computer system: subroutines, interrupts, and temporary data storage. The role of the stack during subroutines will be explained in Chapter 3 (Basic Programming Techniques). The role of the stack during interrupts will be explained in Chapter 6 (Input/Output Techniques). Finally, the role of the stack in saving data at high speed will be explained during specific application programs.

We will simply assume at this point that the stack is a required facility in every computer system. A stack may be implemented in two ways:

1. A fixed number of registers may be provided within the microprocessor itself. This is a "hardware stack." It has the advantage of high speed. However, it has the disadvantage of a limited number of registers.

2. Most general-purpose microprocessors choose another approach, the software stack, in order not to restrict the stack to a very small number of registers. This is the approach chosen in the Z80. In the software approach, a dedicated register within the microprocessor, here register SP, stores the stack pointer, i.e., the address of the top element of the stack (or, sometimes, the address of the top element of the stack plus one). The stack is then implemented as an area of memory. The stack pointer will therefore require 16 bits to point anywhere in the memory.

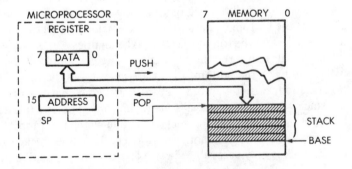

Fig. 2.5: The Two-Stack Manipulation Instructions

The Instruction Execution Cycle

Let us refer now to Figure 2.6. The microprocessor unit appears on the left, and the memory appears on the right. The memory chip may be a ROM or a RAM, or any other chip which happens to contain memory. The memory is used to store instructions and data. Here, we will fetch one instruction from the memory to illustrate the role of the program counter. We assume that the program counter has valid contents. It now holds a 16-bit address which is the address of the next instruction to fetch in the memory. Every processor proceeds in three cycles:

1—fetch the next instruction
2—decode the instruction
3—execute the instruction

Fetch

Let us now follow the sequence. In the first cycle, the contents of the program counter are deposited on the address bus and gated to the memory (on the address bus). Simultaneously, a read signal may be issued on the control bus of the system, if required. The memory will receive the address. This address is used to specify one location within the memory. Upon receiving the read signal, the memory will decode the address it has received, through internal decoders, and will select the location specified by the address. A few hundred nanoseconds later, the memory will deposit the eight-bit data corresponding to the specified address on its data bus. This eight-bit word is the instruction that we want to fetch. In our illustration, this instruction will be deposited the data bus on top of the MPU box.

Let us briefly summarize the sequencing: the contents of the program counter are output on the address bus. A read signal is generated. *The memory cycles,* and perhaps 300 nanoseconds later, the instruction at the specified address is deposited on the data bus (assuming a single byte instruction). The microprocessor then reads the data bus and deposits its contents into a specialized internal register, the IR register. The IR is the *instruction register:* it is eight-bits wide and is used to contain the instruction just fetched from the memory. The fetch cycle is now completed. The 8 bits of the instruction are now physically in the special internal register of the MPU, the IR register. The IR appears on the left of Figure 2.7. It is not accessible to the programmer.

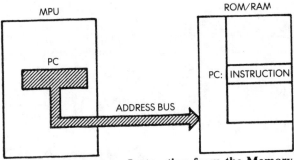

Fig. 2.6: Fetching an Instruction from the Memory

Decoding and Execution

Once the instruction is contained in IR, the control unit of the microprocessor will decode the contents and will be able to generate the correct sequence of internal and external signals for the execution of the specified instruction. There is, therefore, a short decoding delay followed by an execution phase, the length of which depends on the nature of the instruction specified. Some instructions will execute entirely within the MPU. Other instructions will fetch or deposit data from or into the memory. This is why the various instructions of the MPU require various lengths of time to execute. This duration is expressed as a number of (clock) cycles. Refer to Chapter 4 for the number of

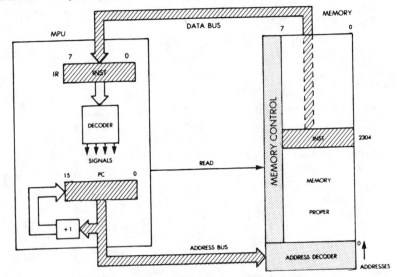

Fig. 2.7: Automatic Sequencing

cycles required by each instruction. Since various clock rates may be used, speed of execution is normally expressed in number of cycles rather than in number of nanoseconds.

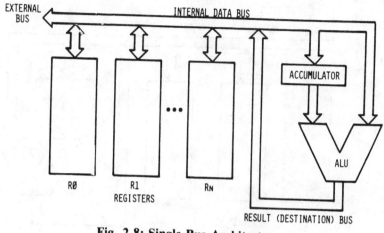

Fig. 2.8: Single-Bus Architecture

Fetching the Next Instruction

We have described how, using the program counter, an instruction can be fetched from the memory. During the execution of a program, instructions are fetched *in sequence* from the memory. An automatic mechanism must therefore be provided to fetch instructions in sequence. This task is performed by a simple incrementer attached to the program counter. This is illustrated in Figure 2.7. Every time that the contents of the program counter (at the bottom of the illustration) are placed on the address bus, its contents will be incremented and written back into the program counter. As an example, if the program counter contained the value "0", the value "0" would be output on the address bus. Then the contents of the program counter would be incremented and the value "1" would be written back into the program counter. In this way, the next time that the program counter is used, it is the instruction at address 1 that will be fetched. We have just implemented an *automatic mechanism for sequencing instructions.*

It must be stressed that the above descriptions are simplified. In reality, some instructions may be two- or even three-bytes long, so that successive bytes will be fetched in this manner from the memory. However, the mechanism is identical. The program counter is used to fetch

57

successive bytes of an instruction as well as to fetch successive instructions themselves. The program counter, together with its incrementer, provides an automatic mechanism for pointing to successive memory locations.

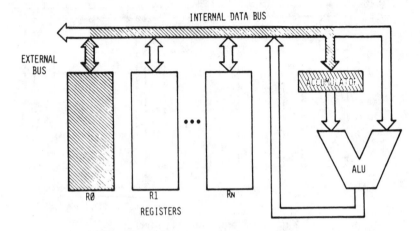

Fig. 2.9: Execution of an Addition—R0 into ACC

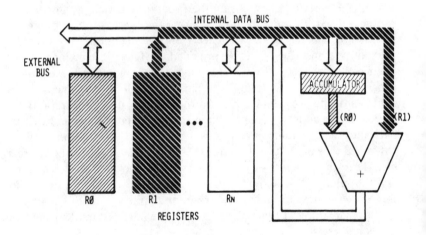

Fig. 2.10: Addition—Second Register R1 into ALU

We will now execute an instruction within the MPU (see Figure 2.8). A typical instruction will be, for example: R0 = R0 + R1. This means: "ADD the contents of R0 and R1, and store the results in R0." To perform this operation, the contents of R0 will be read from register R0, carried via the single bus to the left input of the ALU, and stored in the buffer register there. R1 will then be selected and its contents will be read onto the bus, then transferred to the right input of the ALU. This sequence is illustrated in Figures 2.9 and 2.10. At this point, the right input of the ALU is conditioned by R1, and the left input of the ALU is conditioned by the buffer register, containing the previous value of R0. The operation can be performed. The addition is performed by the ALU, and the results appear on the ALU output, in the lower right-hand corner of Fig. 2.11. The results will be deposited on the single bus, and will be propagated back to R0. This means, in practice, that the input latch of R0 will be enabled, so that data can be written into it. Execution of the instruction is now complete. The results of the addition are in R0. It should be noted that the contents of R1 have not been modified by this operation. This is a general principle: the contents of a register, or of any read/write memory, are not modified by a read operation.

The buffer register on the left input of the ALU was necessary in order to *memorize* the contents of R0, so that the single bus could be used again for another transfer. However, a problem remains.

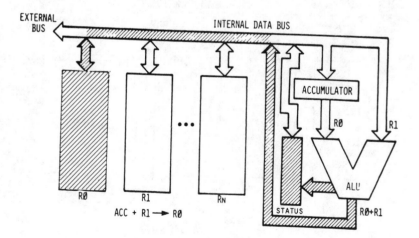

Fig. 2.11: Result Is Generated and Goes into R0

The Critical Race Problem

The simple organization shown in Figure 2.8 will not function correctly.

Question: *What is the timing problem?*

Answer: The problem is that the result which will be propagated out of the ALU will be deposited back on the single bus. It will not propagate just in the direction of R0, but along all of the bus. In particular, it will recondition the right input of the ALU, changing the result coming out of it a few nanoseconds later. This is a *critical race.* The output of the ALU must be isolated from its input (see Figure 2.12).

Several solutions are possible which will isolate the input of the ALU from the output. A buffer register must be used. The buffer register could be placed on the output of the ALU, or on its input. It is usually placed on the input of the ALU. Here it would be placed on its right input. The buffering of the system is now sufficient for a correct operation. It will be shown later in this chapter that if the left register which appears in this illustration is to be used as an accumulator (permitting the use of one-byte long instructions), then the accumulator will require a buffer too, as shown in Figure 2.13.

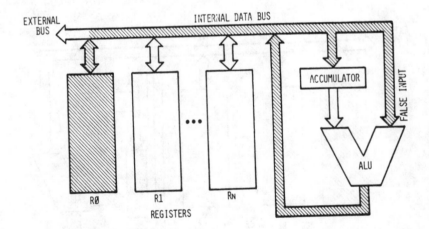

Fig. 2.12: The Critical Race Problem

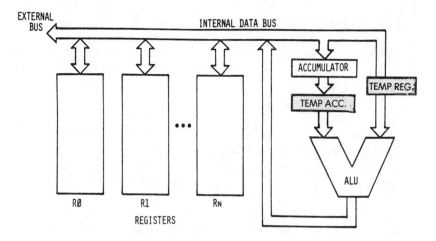

Fig. 2.13: Two Buffers Are Required (Temp Registers)

INTERNAL ORGANIZATION OF THE Z80

The terms necessary in order to understand the internal elements of the microprocessor have been defined. We will now examine in more detail the Z80 itself, and describe its capabilities. The internal organization of the Z80 is shown in Figure 2.14. This diagram presents a logical description of the device. Additional interconnections may exist but are not shown. Let us examine the diagram from right to left.

On the right part of the illustration, the *arithmetic-logical unit* (the ALU) may be recognized by its characteristic "V" shape. The accumulator register, which has been described in the previous section, is identified as A on the right input path of the ALU. It has been shown in the previous section that the accumulator should be equipped with a *buffer register*. This is the register labeled ACT (temporary accumulator). Here, the left input of the ALU is also equipped with a *temporary register,* called TMP. The operation of the ALU will become clear in the next section, where we will describe the execution of actual instructions.

The *flags register* is called "F" in the Z80, and is shown on the right of the accumulator register. The contents of the flags register are essentially conditioned by the ALU, but it will be shown that some of its bits may also be conditioned by other modules or events.

The accumulator and the flags registers are shown as double registers labelled respectively A, A' and F, F'. This is because the Z80 is

61

equipped internally with two sets of registers: A + F, and A' + F'. However, only *one* set of these registers may be used at any one time. A special instruction is provided to exchange the contents of A and F with A' and F'. In order to simplify the explanations, only A and F will be shown on most of the diagrams which follow. The reader should remember that he has the option of switching to the alternate register set A' and F' if desired.

The role of each flag in the flags register will be described in Chapter 3 (Basic Programming Techniques).

A large block of registers is shown at the center of the illustration. On top of the block of registers, two identical groups can be recognized. Each one includes six registers labeled B, C, D, E, H, L. These are the *general-purpose eight-bit registers* of the Z80. There are two peculiarities of the Z80 with respect to the standard microprocessor which has been described at the beginning of this chapter.

First, the Z80 is equipped with *two* banks of registers, i.e., two identical groups of 6 registers. Only six registers may be used at any one time. However, special instructions are provided to switch between the two banks of registers. One bank, therefore, behaves as an internal memory, while the other one behaves as a working set of internal registers. The possible uses of this special facility will be described in the next chapter.

Conceptually, it will be assumed, for the time being, that there are only six working registers, B, C, D, E, H, and L, and the second register bank will temporarily be ignored, in order to avoid confusion.

The MUX symbol which appears above the memory bank is an abbreviation for *multiplexer*. The data coming from the internal data bus will be gated through the multiplexer to the selected register. However, only one of these registers can be connected to the internal data bus at any one time.

A second characteristic of these six registers, in addition to being general-purpose eight-bit registers, is that they are equipped with a connection to the *address bus*. This is why they have been grouped in *pairs*. For example, the contents of B and C can be gated simultaneously onto the 16-bit address bus which appears at the bottom of the illustration. As a result, this group of 6 registers may be used to store either eight-bit data or else 16-bit *pointers* for memory addressing.

The third group of registers, which appears below the two previous ones in the middle of Figure 2.14, contains four "pure" address registers. As in any microprocessor, we find the program counter (PC) and the stack pointer (SP). Recall that the program counter contains the address of the next instruction to be executed.

The stack pointer points to the top of the stack in the memory. In the case of the Z80, the stack pointer points to the *last actual entry* in the stack. (In other microprocessors, the stack pointer points just above the last entry.) Also, the stack grows *"downwards,"* i.e. towards the lower addresses.

This means that the stack pointer must be *decremented* any time a new word is *pushed* on the stack. Conversely, whenever a word is *removed* (popped) from the stack, the stack pointer must be *incremented* by one. In the case of the Z80, the "push" and "pop" always involve *two* words at the same time, so that the contents of the stack pointer will be decremented or incremented by two.

Looking at the remaining two registers of this group of four registers, we find a new type of register which has not been described yet: two *index-registers,* labeled IX (Index Register X) and IY (Index Register Y). These two registers are equipped with a special adder shown as a miniature V-shaped ALU on the right of these registers in Figure 2.14. A byte brought along the internal data bus may be added to the contents of IX or IY. This byte is called the *displacement,* when using an indexed instruction. Special instructions are provided which will automatically add this displacement to the contents of IX or IY and generate an address. This is called *indexing.* It allows convenient access to any sequential block of data. This important facility will be described in Chapter 5 on addressing techniques.

Finally, a special box labeled " ± 1" appears below and to the left of the block of registers. This is an increment/decrement. The contents of any of the register pairs SP, PC, BC, DE, HL (the "pure address" registers) may be automatically incremented or decremented every time they deposit an address on the internal address bus. This is an essential facility for implementing automated *program loops* which will be described in the next section. Using this feature it will be possible to access successive memory locations conveniently.

Let us move now to the left of the illustration. One register pair is shown, isolated on the left: I and R. The I register is called the *interrupt-page address register.* Its role will be described in the section on interrupts of Chapter 6 (Input/Output Techniques). It is used only in a special mode where an indirect call to a memory location is generated in response to an interrupt. The I register is used to store the high-order part of the indirect address. The lower part of the address is supplied by the device which generated the interrupt.

The R register is the *memory-refresh register*. It is provided to refresh dynamic memories automatically. Such a register has traditionally been located outside the microprocessor, since it is associated with the dynamic memory. It is a convenient feature which minimizes the amount of external hardware for some types of dynamic memories. It will not be used here for any programming purposes, as it is essentially a hardware feature (see reference C207 "Microprocessor Interfacing Techniques" for a detailed description of memory refresh techniques). However, it is possible to use it as a software clock, for example.

Let us move now to the far left of the illustration. There the control section of the microprocessor is located. From top to bottom, we find first the *instruction register* IR, which will contain the instruction to be executed. The IR register is totally distinct from the "I, R" register pair described above. The instruction is received from the memory via the data bus, is transmitted along the internal data bus and is finally deposited into the instruction register. Below the instruction register appears the *decoder* which will send signals to the controller-sequencer and cause the execution of the instruction within the microprocessor and outside it. The *control section* generates and manages the control bus which appears at the bottom part of the illustration.

The three buses managed or generated by the system, i.e., the data bus, the address bus, and the control bus, propagate outside the microprocessor through its pins. The external connections are shown on the right-most part of the illustration. The buses are isolated from the outside through buffers shown in Figure 2.14.

All the logical elements of the Z80 have now been described. It is not essential to understand the detailed operation of the Z80 in order to start writing programs. However, for the programmer who wishes to write efficient codes, the speed of a program and its size will depend upon the correct choice of registers as well as the correct choice of techniques. To make a correct choice, it is necessary to understand how instructions are executed within the microprocessor. We will therefore examine here the execution of typical instructions inside the Z80 to demonstrate the role and use of the internal registers and buses.

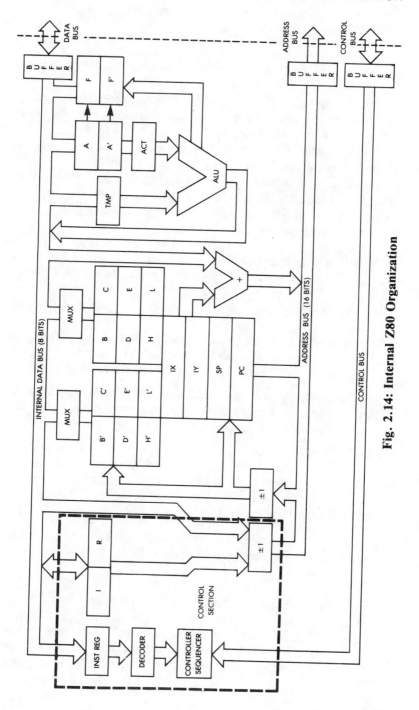

Fig. 2.14: Internal Z80 Organization

INSTRUCTION FORMATS

The Z80 instructions are listed in Chapter 4. Z80 instructions may be formated in one, two, three or four bytes. An instruction specifies the operation to be performed by the microprocessor. From a simplified standpoint, every instruction may be represented as an opcode followed by an optional literal or address field, comprising one or two words. The opcode field specifies the operation to be carried out. In strict computer terminology, the opcode represents only those bits which specify the operation to be performed, exclusive of the register pointers that might be necessary. In the microprocessor world, it is convenient to call opcode the operation code itself, as well as any register pointers which it might incorporate. This "generalized opcode" must reside in an eight-bit word for efficiency (this is the limiting factor on the number of instructions available in a microprocessor).

The 8080 uses instructions which may be one, two, three, bytes long (see Figure 2.15). However, the Z80 is equipped with additional indexed instructions, which require one more byte. In the case of the Z80, opcodes are, in general, one byte long, except for special instructions which require a two-byte opcode.

Some instructions require that one byte of data follow the opcode. In such a case, the instruction will be a two-byte instruction, the second byte of which is data (except for indexing, which adds an extra byte).

In other cases, the instruction might require the specification of an address. An address requires 16 bits and, therefore, two bytes. In that case, the instruction will be a three-byte or a four-byte instruction.

For each byte of the instruction, the control unit will have to perform a memory fetch, which will require four clock cycles. The shorter the instruction, the faster the execution.

A One-Word Instruction

One-word instructions are, in principle, fastest and are favored by the programmer. A typical such instruction for the Z80 is:

LD r, r'

This instruction means: "Transfer the contents of register r' into r." This is a typical "register-to-register" operation. Every microprocessor must be equipped with such instructions, which allow the programmer to transfer information from any of the machine's registers into another one. Instructions referencing special registers of the machine,

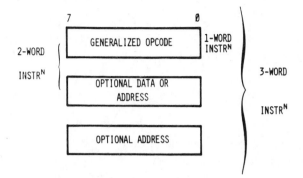

Fig. 2.15 Typical Instruction Formats

such as the accumulator or other special-purpose registers, may have a special opcode.

After execution of the above instruction, the contents of r will be equal to the contents of r'. The contents of r' will *not* have been modified by the read operation.

Every instruction must be represented internally in a binary format. The above representation "LD r,r' " is symbolic or *mnemonic*. It is called the *assembly-language* representation of an instruction. It is simply meant as a convenient symbolic representation of the actual binary encoding for that instruction. The binary code which will represent this instruction inside the memory is: 0 1 D D D S S S (bits 0 to 7).

This representation is still partially symbolic. Each of the letters S and D stands for a binary bit. The three D's, "D D D", represent the three bits pointing to the *destination* register. Three bits allow selection of one out of eight possible registers. The codes for these registers appear in Figure 2.16. For example, the code for register B is "0 0 0", the code for register C is "0 0 1", and so on.

Similarly, "S S S" represents the three bits pointing to the *source* register. The convention here is that register r' is the source, and that register r is the destination. The placement of the bits in the binary representation of an instruction is not meant for the convenience of the programmer, but for the convenience of the control section of the microprocessor, which must decode and execute the instruction. The *assembly-language* representation, however, is meant for the convenience of the programmer. It could be argued that LD r,r' should really mean: "Transfer contents of r into r'." However, the convention has been chosen in order to maintain compatibility with the binary representation in this case. It is naturally arbitrary.

Exercise 2.1: *Write below the binary code which will transfer the contents of register C into register B. Consult Fig. 2.16 for the codes corresponding to C and B.*

Another simple example of a one-word instruction is:

ADD A, r

This instruction will result in adding the contents of a specified register (r) to the accumulator (A). Symbolically, this operation may be represented by: $A = A + r$. It can be verified in Chapter 4 that the binary representation of this instruction is:

1 0 0 0 0 S S S

where S S S specifies the register to be added to the accumulator. Again, the register codes appear in Figure 2.16.

Exercise 2.2: *What is the binary code of the instruction which will add the contents of register D to the accumulator?*

CODE	REGISTER
0 0 0	B
0 0 1	C
0 1 0	D
0 1 1	E
1 0 0	H
1 0 1	L
1 1 0	- (MEMORY)
1 1 1	A

Fig. 2.16: The Register Codes

A Two-Word Instruction

ADD A, n

This simple two-word instruction will add the contents of the second byte of the instruction to the accumulator. The contents of the second word of the instruction are said to be a "literal." They are data and are treated as eight bits without any particular significance. They could happen to be a character or numerical data. This is irrelevant to the operation. The code for this instruction is:

1 1 0 0 0 1 1 0 followed by the 8-bit byte "n"

This is an *immediate* operation. "Immediate," in most programming languages, means that the next word, or words, within the instruction contains a piece of data which should not be *interpreted* (the way an opcode is). It means that the next one or two words are to be treated as a *literal.*

The control unit is programmed to "know" how many words each instruction has. It will, therefore, always fetch and execute the right number of words for each instruction. However, the longer the possible number of words for the instruction, the more complex it is for the control unit to decode.

A Three-Word Instruction

LD A, (nn)

The instruction requires three words. It means: "Load the accumulator from the memory address specified in the next two bytes of the instruction." Since addresses are 16-bits long, they require two words. In binary, this instruction is represented by:

0 0 1 1 1 0 1 0:	8 bits for the opcode
Low address:	8 bits for the lower part of the address
High address:	8 bits for the upper part of the address

EXECUTION OF INSTRUCTIONS WITHIN THE Z80

We have seen that all instructions are executed in three phases: FETCH, DECODE, EXECUTE. We now need to introduce some definitions. Each of these phases will require several clock cycles. The Z80 executes each phase in one or more logical cycles, called a "machine cycle." The shortest machine cycle lasts three clock cycles.

Accessing the memory requires three cycles for any operands, four clock cycles for the initial fetch. Since each instruction must be fetched first from the memory, the fastest instruction will require four clock cycles. Most instructions will require more.

Each machine cycle is labeled as M1, M2, etc., and will require three or more clock cycles, or "states," labeled T1, T2, etc.

The FETCH Phase

The FETCH phase of an instruction is implemented during the first three states of machine cycle M1; they are called T1, T2, and T3. These three states are common to all instructions of the microprocessor, as all instructions must be fetched prior to execution. The FETCH mechanism is the following:

T1 : PC OUT

The first step is to present the address of the next instruction to the memory. This address is contained in the program counter (PC). As the first step of any instruction fetch, the contents of the PC are placed on the address bus (see Figure 2.17). At this point, an address is presented to the memory, and the memory address decoders will decode this address in order to select the appropriate location within the memory. Several hundred ns (a nanosecond is 10^{-9} second) will elapse before the contents of the selected memory location become available on the out-

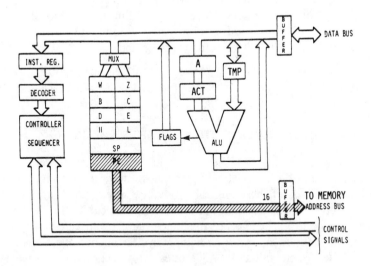

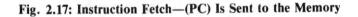

Fig. 2.17: Instruction Fetch—(PC) Is Sent to the Memory

put pins of the memory, which are connected to the data bus. It is standard computer design to use the memory read time to perform an operation within the microprocessor. This operation is the incrementation of the program counter:

$$T2 : PC = PC + 1$$

While the memory is reading, the contents of the PC are incremented by 1 (see Figure 2.18). At the end of state T2, the contents of the memory are available and can be transferred within the microprocessor:

$$T3 : INST \text{ into } IR$$

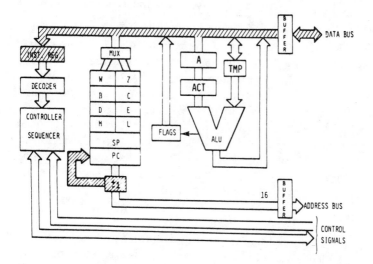

Fig 2.18: PC Is Incremented

The DECODE and EXECUTE Phases

During state T3, the instruction which has been read out of the memory is deposited on the data bus and transferred into the instruction register of the Z80, from which point it is decoded.

71

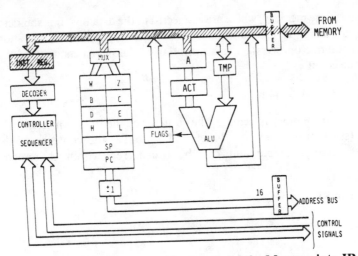

Fig. 2.19: The Instruction Arrives from the Memory into IR

It should be noted that state T4 of M1 will always be required. Once the instruction has been deposited into IR during T3, it is necessary to *decode* and *execute* it. This will require at least one machine state, T4.

A few instructions require an extra state of M1 (state T5). It will be skipped by the processor for most instructions. Whenever the execution of an instruction requires more than M1, i.e., M1, M2 or more cycles, the transition will be directly from state T4 of M1 into state T1 of M2. Let us examine an example. The detailed internal sequencing for each example is shown in the tables of Figure 2.27. As these tables have not been released for the Z80, the 8080 tables are used instead. They provide an in-depth understanding of instruction execution.

LD D, C

This corresponds to MOV rl, r2 for the 8080. Refer to line 1 of Fig. 2.27.

By coincidence, the destination register in this example happens to be named "D". The transfer is illustrated in Figure 2.20.

This instruction has been described in the previous section. It transfers the contents of register C, denoted by "C", into register D.

The first three states of cycle M1 are used to fetch the instruction from the memory. At the end of T3, the instruction is in IR, the Instruction Register, from which point it can be decoded (see Figure 2.19).

During T4: (S S S) ▶ TMP.

The contents of C are deposited into TMP (See Figure 2.21).

During T5: (TMP) ► DDD.

The contents of TMP are deposited into D. This is shown in Figure 2.22.

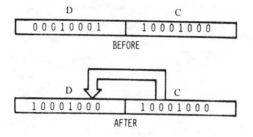

Fig. 2.20: Transferring C into D

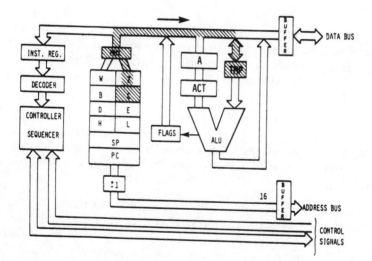

Fig. 2.21: The Contents of C Are Deposited into TMP

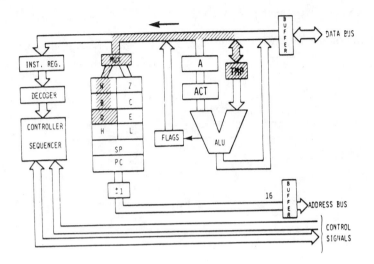

Fig. 2.22: The Contents of TMP are Deposited into D

Execution of the instruction is now complete. The contents of register C have been transferred into the specified destination register D. This terminates execution of the instruction. The other machine cycles M2, M3, M4, and M5 will not be necessary and execution stops with M1.

It is possible to compute the duration of this instruction easily. The duration of every state for the standard Z80 is the duration of the clock: 500 ns. The duration of this instruction is the duration of five states, or 5 × 500 = 2500 ns = 2.5 us. With a 400 ns clock, 5 × 400 = 2000 ns = 2.0 us.

Question: *Why does this instruction require two states, T4 and T5, in order to transfer the contents C into D, rather than just one? It transfers the contents of C into TMP, and then the contents of TMP into D. Wouldn't it be simpler to transfer the contents of C into D directly within a single state?*

Answer: This is not possible because of the implementation chosen for the internal registers. All the internal registers are, in fact, part of a single RAM, a read/write memory internal to the microprocessor chip. Only one word may be addressed or selected at a time within an RAM (single-port). For this reason, it is not possible to both read and write into, or from, an RAM at two different locations. Two RAM cycles are required. It becomes necessary first to read the data out of the register RAM, and store it in a temporary register, TMP, then, to write it back into the final destination register, here D. This is a design inadequacy. However, this limitation is common to virtually all monolithic microprocessors. A dual-port RAM would be required to solve the problem. This limitation is not intrinsic to microprocessors and it normally does not exist in the case of bit-slice devices. It is a result of the constant search for logic density on the chip and may be eliminated in the future.

Important Exercise:

At this point, it is highly recommended that the user review by himself the sequencing of this simple instruction before we proceed to more complex ones. For this purpose, go back to Figure 2.14. Assemble a few small-sized "symbols" such as matches, paperclips, etc. Then move the symbols on Figure 2.14 to simulate the flow of data from the registers into the buses. For example, deposit a symbol into PC. T1 will move the symbol contained in PC out on the address bus towards the memory. Continue simulated execution in this fashion until you feel comfortable with the transfers along the buses and between the registers. At this point, you should be ready to proceed.

Progressively more complex instructions will now be studied:

ADD A, r

This instruction means: "Add the contents of register r (specified by a binary code S S S) to the accumulator (A), and deposit the result in the accumulator." This is an *implicit* instruction. It is called implicit as it does not explicitly reference a second register. The instruction explicitly refers only to register r. It implies that the other register involved in the operation is the accumulator. The accumulator, when used in such an implicit instruction, is referenced both as source and destination. Data will be deposited in the accumulator as a result of this addition. The advantage of such an implicit instruction is that its complete opcode is only eight bits in length. It requires only a three-bit register field for the specification of r. This is a fast way to perform an addition operation.

Other implicit instructions exist in the system which will reference other specialized registers. More complex examples of such implicit instructions are, for example, the PUSH and POP operations, which will transfer information between the top of the stack and the accumulator, and will at the same time update the stack pointer (SP), decrementing it or incrementing it. They implicitly manipulate the SP register.

The execution of the ADD A, r instruction will now be examined in detail. This instruction will require two machine cycles, M1 and M2. As usual, during the first three states of M1, the instruction is fetched from the memory and deposited in the IR register. At the beginning of T4, it is decoded and can be executed. It will be assumed here that register B is added to the accumulator. The code for the instruction will then be: 1 0 0 0 0 0 0 0 (the code for register B is 0 0 0). The 8080 equivalent is ADD r.

$$T4: (S\ S\ S) \blacktriangleright TMP, (A) \blacktriangleright ACT$$

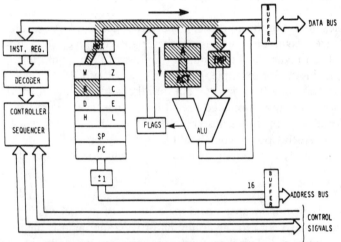

Fig. 2.23: Two Transfers Occur Simultaneously

Two transfers will be executed simultaneously. First, the contents of the specified source register (here B) are transferred into TMP, i.e., to the right input of the ALU (see Fig. 2.23). At the same time, the contents of the accumulator are transferred to the temporary accumulator (ACT). By inspecting Fig. 2.23, you will ascertain that those transfers can occur in parallel. They use different paths within the system. The transfer from B to TMP uses the internal data bus. The transfer from ACT uses a short internal path independent of this data bus. In order to gain time, both transfers are done simultaneously. At this point, both the left and the right input of the ALU are correctly conditioned. The left input of the ALU is now conditioned by the accumulator contents, and the right input of the ALU is conditioned by the contents of register B. We are ready to perform the addition. We would normally expect to see the addition take place during state T5 of M1. However, this state is simply not used. The addition is not performed! We will enter machine cycle M2. During state T1, nothing happens! It is only in state T2 of M2 that the addition takes place (refer to ADD r in Figure 2.27):

T2 of M2: (ACT) + (TMP) ► A

The contents of ACT are added to the contents of TMP, and the result is finally deposited in the accumulator. See Figure 2.24. The operation is now complete.

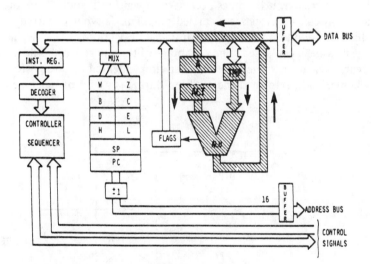

Fig. 2.24: End of ADD r

Question: *Why was the completion of the addition deferred until state T2 of machine cycle M2, rather than taking place during state T5 of M1?* (This is a difficult question, which requires an understanding of CPU design. However, the technique involved is fundamental to clock-synchronous CPU design. Try to see what happens.)

Answer: This is a standard design "trick" used in most CPU's. It is called "fetch/execute overlap." The basic idea is the following: looking back at Figure 2.23 it can be seen that the actual execution of the addition will only require the use of the ALU and of the data bus. In particular, it will not access the register RAM (register block). We (or the control unit) know that the next three states which will be executed after completion of any instruction will be T1, T2, T3 of machine cycle M1 of the next instruction. Looking back at the execution of these three states, it can be seen that their execution will only require access to the program counter (PC) and use of the address bus. Access to the program counter will require access to the register RAM. (This explains why the same trick could not be used in the instruction LD r,r'.) It is therefore possible to use simultaneously the shaded area in Figure 2.17 and the shaded area in Figure 2.24.

The data bus is used during state T1 of M1 to carry status information out. It cannot be used for the addition that we wish to perform. For that reason, it becomes necessary to wait until state T2 before the addition can be effectively carried out. This is what occurred in the chart: the addition is completed during state T2 of M2. The mechanism has now been explained. The advantage of this approach should now be clear. Let us assume that we had implemented a straightforward scheme, and performed the addition during state T5 of machine cycle

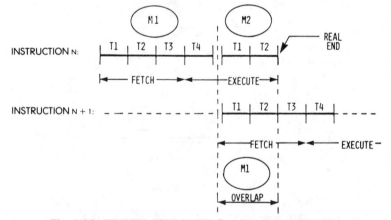

Fig. 2.25: FETCH-EXECUTE Overlap during T1-T2

M1. The duration of the ADD instruction would have been $5 \times 500 = 2500$ ns. With the overlap approach which has been implemented, once state T4 has been executed, the next instruction is initiated. In a manner that is invisible to this next instruction, the "clever" control unit will use state T2 to carry out the end of the addition. On the chart T2 is shown as part of M2. Conceptually, M2 will be the second machine cycle of the addition. In fact, this M2 will be overlapped, i.e., be identical to machine cycle M1 of the next instruction. For the programmer, the delay introduced by ADD will be only four states, i.e., $4 \times 500 = 2000$ ns, instead of 2500 ns using the "straightforward" approach. The speed improvement is 500 ns, or 20%!

The overlap technique is illustrated on Figure 2.25. It is used whenever possible to increase the apparent execution speed of the microprocessor. Naturally, it it not possible to overlap in all cases. Required buses or facilities must be available without conflict. The control unit "knows" whether an overlap is possible.

NOTES:

1. The first memory cycle (M1) is always an instruction fetch; the first (or only) byte, containing the op code, is fetched during this cycle.

2. If the READY input from memory is not high during T2 of each memory cycle, the processor will enter a wait state (TW) until READY is sampled as high.

3. States T4 and T5 are present, as required, for operations which are completely internal to the CPU. The contents of the internal bus during T4 and T5 are available at the data bus; this is designed for testing purposes only. An "X" denotes that the state is present, but is only used for such internal operations as instruction decoding.

4. Only register pairs rp = B (registers B and C) or rp = D (registers D and E) may be specified.

5. These states are skipped.

6. Memory read sub-cycles; an instruction or data word will be read.

7. Memory write sub-cycle.

8. The READY signal is not required during the second and third sub-cycles (M2 and M3). The HOLD signal is accepted during M2 and M3. The SYNC signal is not generated during M2 and M3. During the execution of DAD, M2 and M3 are required for an internal register-pair add; memory is not referenced.

9. The results of these arithmetic, logical or rotate instructions are not moved into the accumulator (A) until state T2 of the next instruction cycle. That is, A is loaded while the next instruction is being fetched; this overlapping of operations allows for faster processing.

10. If the value of the least significant 4-bits of the accumulator is greater than 9 or if the auxiliary carry bit is set, 6 is added to the accumulator. If the value of the most significant 4-bits of the accumulator is now greater than 9, or if the carry bit is set, 6 is added to the most significant 4-bits of the accumulator.

11. This represents the first sub-cycle (the instruction fetch) of the next instruction cycle.

12. If the condition was met, the contents of the register pair WZ are output on the address lines ($A_{0\text{-}15}$) instead of the contents of the program counter (PC).

13. If the condition was not met, sub-cycles M4 and M5 are skipped; the processor instead proceeds immediately to the instruction fetch (M1) of the next instruction cycle.

14. If the condition was not met, sub-cycles M2 and M3 are skipped; the processor instead proceeds immediately to the instruction fetch (M1) of the next instruction cycle.

15. Stack read sub-cycle.

16. Stack write sub-cycle.

17. CONDITION

		CCC
NZ	— not zero (Z = 0)	000
Z	— zero (Z = 1)	001
NC	— no carry (CY = 0)	010
C	— carry (CY = 1)	011
PO	— parity odd (P = 0)	100
PE	— parity even (P = 1)	101
P	— plus (S = 0)	110
M	— minus (S = 1)	111

18. I/O sub-cycle: the I/O port's 8-bit select code is duplicated on address lines 0-7 ($A_{0\text{-}7}$) and 8-15 ($A_{8\text{-}15}$).

19. Output sub-cycle.

20. The processor will remain idle in the halt state until an interrupt, a reset or a hold is accepted. When a hold request is accepted, the CPU enters the hold mode; after the hold mode is terminated, the processor returns to the halt state. After a reset is accepted, the processor begins execution at memory location zero. After an interrupt is accepted, the processor executes the instruction forced onto the data bus (usually a restart instruction).

SSS or DDD	Value	rp	Value
A	111	B	00
B	000	D	01
C	001	H	10
D	010	SP	11
E	011		
H	100		
L	101		

Fig. 2.26: Intel Abbreviations

MNEMONIC	OP CODE		M1[1]					M2		
	D7 D6 D5 D4	D3 D2 D1 D0	T1	T2[2]	T3	T4	T5	T1	T2[2]	T3
MOV r1,r2	0 1 D D	D S S S	PC OUT STATUS	PC = PC +1	INST→TMP/IR	(SSS)→TMP	(TMP)→DDD			
MOV r, M	0 1 D D	D 1 1 0				x[3]		HL OUT STATUS[6]	DATA →DDD	
MOV M, r	0 1 1 1	0 S S S				(SSS)→TMP		HL OUT STATUS[7]	(TMP)→DATA BUS	
SPHL	1 1 1 1	1 0 0 1				(HL) _____ SP				
MVI r, data	0 0 D D	D 1 1 0				x		PC OUT STATUS[6]	B2 →DDDD	
MVI M, data	0 0 1 1	0 1 1 0				x			B2 →TMP	
LXI rp, data	0 0 R P	0 0 0 1				x			PC = PC + 1	B2 →r1
LDA addr	0 0 1 1	1 0 1 0				x			PC = PC + 1	B2 →Z
STA addr	0 0 1 1	0 0 1 0				x			PC = PC + 1	B2 →Z
LHLD addr	0 0 1 0	1 0 1 0				x			PC = PC + 1	B2 →Z
SHLD addr	0 0 1 0	0 0 1 0				x		PC OUT STATUS[6]	PC = PC + 1	B2 →Z
LDAX rp[4]	U 0 R P	1 0 1 0				x		rp OUT STATUS[6]	DATA →A	
STAX rp[4]	0 0 R P	0 0 1 0				x		rp OUT STATUS[7]	(A) →DATA BUS	
XCHG	1 1 1 0	1 0 1 1				(HL)↔(DE)				
ADD r	1 0 0 0	0 S S S				(SSS)→TMP (A)→ACT		[9]	(ACT)+(TMP)→A	
ADD M	1 0 0 0	0 1 1 0				(A)→ACT		HL OUT STATUS[6]	DATA →TMP	
ADI data	1 1 0 0	0 1 1 0				(A)→ACT		PC OUT STATUS[6]	PC = PC + 1	B2 →TMP
ADC r	1 0 0 0	1 S S S				(SSS)→TMP (A)→ACT		[9]	(ACT)+(TMP)+CY→A	
ADC M	1 0 0 0	1 1 1 0				(A)→ACT		HL OUT STATUS[6]	DATA →TMP	
ACI data	1 1 0 0	1 1 1 0				(A)→ACT		PC OUT STATUS[6]	PC = PC + 1	B2 →TMP
SUB r	1 0 0 1	0 S S S				(SSS)→TMP (A)→ACT		[9]	(ACT)-(TMP)→A	
SUB M	1 0 0 1	0 1 1 0				(A)→ACT		HL OUT STATUS[6]	DATA →TMP	
SUI data	1 1 0 1	0 1 1 0				(A)→ACT		PC OUT STATUS[6]	PC = PC + 1	B2 →TMP
SBB r	1 0 0 1	1 S S S				(SSS)→TMP (A)→ACT		[9]	(ACT)-(TMP)-CY→A	
SBB M	1 0 0 1	1 1 1 0				(A)→ACT		HL OUT STATUS[6]	DATA →TMP	
SBI data	1 1 0 1	1 1 1 0				(A)→ACT		PC OUT STATUS[6]	PC = PC + 1	B2 →TMP
INR r	0 0 D D	D 1 0 0				(DDD)→TMP (TMP) + 1→ALU	ALU→DDD			
INR M	0 0 1 1	0 1 0 0				x		HL OUT STATUS[6]	DATA → TMP (TMP)+1 → ALU	
DCR r	0 0 D D	D 1 0 1				(DDD)→TMP (TMP)-1→ALU	ALU→DDD			
DCR M	0 0 1 1	0 1 0 1				x		HL OUT STATUS[6]	DATA → TMP (TMP)-1 → ALU	
INX rp	0 0 R P	0 0 1 1				(RP) + 1 _____ RP				
DCX rp	0 0 R P	1 0 1 1				(RP) - 1 _____ RP				
DAD rp[8]	0 0 R P	1 0 0 1				x		(rl)→ACT	(L)→TMP, (ACT)+(TMP)→ALU	ALU→L, CY
DAA	0 0 1 0	0 1 1 1				DAA→A, FLAGS[10]				
ANA r	1 0 1 0	0 S S S				(SSS)→TMP (A)→ACT		[9]	(ACT)+(TMP)→A	
ANA M	1 0 1 0	0 1 1 0	PC OUT STATUS	PC = PC + 1	INST→TMP/IR	(A)→ACT		HL OUT STATUS[6]	DATA → TMP	

Fig. 2.27: Intel Instruction Formats

	M3			M4			M5			
T1	T2[2]	T3	T1	T2[2]	T3	T1	T2[2]	T3	T4	T5
HL OUT STATUS[7]	(TMP) → DATA BUS									
PC OUT STATUS[6]	PC = PC + 1 B3 → rh									
	PC = PC + 1 B3 → W		WZ OUT STATUS[6]	DATA → A						
	PC = PC + 1 B3 → W		WZ OUT STATUS[7]	(A) → DATA BUS						
	PC = PC + 1 B3 → W		WZ OUT STATUS[6]	DATA → L WZ = WZ + 1		WZ OUT STATUS[6]	DATA → H			
PC OUT STATUS[6]	PC = PC + 1 B3 → W		WZ OUT STATUS[7]	(L) → DATA BUS WZ = WZ + 1		WZ OUT STATUS[7]	(H) → DATA BUS			
[9]	(ACT)+(TMP)→A									
[9]	(ACT)+(TMP)→A									
[9]	(ACT)+(TMP)+CY→A									
[9]	(ACT)+(TMP)+CY→A									
[9]	(ACT)−(TMP)→A									
[9]	(ACT)−(TMP)→A									
[9]	(ACT)−(TMP)−CY→A									
[9]	(ACT)−(TMP)−CY→A									
HL OUT STATUS[7]	ALU → DATA BUS									
HL OUT STATUS[7]	ALU → DATA BUS									
(rh)→ACT	(H)→TMP (ACT)+(TMP)+CY→ALU	ALU→H, CY								
[9]	(ACT)+(TMP)→A									

Fig. 2.27: Intel Instruction Formats (continued)

81

MNEMONIC	OP CODE		M1 [1]					M2		
	D7 D6 D5 D4	D3 D2 D1 D0	T1	T2[2]	T3	T4	T5	T1	T2[2]	T3
ANI data	1 1 1 0	0 1 1 0	PC OUT STATUS	PC = PC + 1	INST→TMP/IR	(A)→ACT		PC OUT STATUS[6]	PC = PC + 1	B2 ——►TMP
XRA r	1 0 1 0	1 S S S				(A)→ACT (SSS)→TMP		[9]	(ACT)+(TPM)→A	
XRA M	1 0 1 0	1 1 1 0				(A)→ACT		HL OUT STATUS[6]		DATA ——►TMP
XRI data	1 1 1 0	1 1 1 0				(A)→ACT		PC OUT STATUS[6]	PC = PC + 1	B2 ——►TMP
ORA r	1 0 1 1	0 S S S				(A)→ACT (SSS)→TMP		[9]	(ACT)+(TMP)→A	
ORA M	1 0 1 1	0 1 1 0				(A)→ACT		HL OUT STATUS[6]		DATA ——►TMP
ORI data	1 1 1 1	0 1 1 0				(A)→ACT		PC OUT STATUS[6]	PC = PC + 1	B2 ——►TMP
CMP r	1 0 1 1	1 S S S				(A)→ACT (SSS)→TMP		[9]	(ACT)-(TMP), FLAGS	
CMP M	1 0 1 1	1 1 1 0				(A)→ACT		HL OUT STATUS[6]		DATA ——►TMP
CPI data	1 1 1 1	1 1 1 0				(A)→ACT		PC OUT STATUS[6]	PC = PC + 1	B2 ——►TMP
RLC	0 0 0 0	0 1 1 1				(A)→ALU ROTATE		[9]	ALU→A, CY	
RRC	0 0 0 0	1 1 1 1				(A)→ALU ROTATE		[9]	ALU→A, CY	
RAL	0 0 0 1	0 1 1 1				(A), CY→ALU ROTATE		[9]	ALU→A, CY	
RAR	0 0 0 1	1 1 1 1				(A), CY→ALU ROTATE		[9]	ALU→A, CY	
CMA	0 0 1 0	1 1 1 1				(Ā)→A				
CMC	0 0 1 1	1 1 1 1				C̄Y→CY				
STC	0 0 1 1	0 1 1 1				1→CY				
JMP addr	1 1 0 0	0 0 1 1				X		PC OUT STATUS[6]	PC = PC + 1	B2 ——►Z
J cond addr[17]	1 1 C C	C 0 1 0				JUDGE CONDITION		PC OUT STATUS[6]	PC = PC + 1	B2 ——►Z
CALL addr	1 1 0 0	1 1 0 1				SP = SP - 1		PC OUT STATUS[6]	PC = PC + 1	B2 ——►Z
C cond addr[17]	1 1 C C	C 1 0 0				JUDGE CONDITION IF TRUE, SP = SP - 1		PC OUT STATUS[6]	PC = PC + 1	B2 ——►Z
RET	1 1 0 0	1 0 0 1				X		SP OUT STATUS[15]	SP = SP + 1	DATA ——►Z
R cond addr[17]	1 1 C C	C 0 0 0				INST→TMP/IR	JUDGE CONDITION[14]	SP OUT STATUS[15]	SP = SP + 1	DATA ——►Z
RST n	1 1 N N	N 1 1 1				ø→W INST→TMP/IR	SP = SP - 1	SP OUT STATUS[16]	SP = SP - 1	(PCH) ——►DATA BUS
PCHL	1 1 1 0	1 0 0 1				INST→TMP/IR	(HL) ——— ——— ——►PC			
PUSH rp	1 1 R P	0 1 0 1					SP = SP - 1	SP OUT STATUS[16]	SP = SP - 1	(rh) ——►DATA BUS
PUSH PSW	1 1 1 1	0 1 0 1					SP = SP - 1	SP OUT STATUS[16]	SP = SP - 1	(A) ——►DATA BUS
POP rp	1 1 R P	0 0 0 1					X	SP OUT STATUS[15]	SP = SP + 1	DATA ——►r1
POP PSW	1 1 1 1	0 0 0 1					X	SP OUT STATUS[15]	SP = SP + 1	DATA ——►FLAGS
XTHL	1 1 1 0	0 0 1 1					X	SP OUT STATUS[15]	SP = SP + 1	DATA ——►Z
IN port	1 1 0 1	1 0 1 1					X	PC OUT STATUS[6]	PC = PC + 1	B2 ——►Z, W
OUT port	1 1 0 1	0 0 1 1					X	PC OUT STATUS[6]	PC = PC + 1	B2 ——►Z, W
EI	1 1 1 1	1 0 1 1				SET INTE F/F				
DI	1 1 1 1	0 0 1 1				RESET INTE F/F				
HLT	0 1 1 1	0 1 1 0				X		PC OUT STATUS	HALT MODE[20]	
NOP	0 0 0 0	0 0 0 0	PC OUT STATUS	PC = PC + 1	INST→TMP/IR	X				

Fig. 2.27[1]: Intel Instruction Formats (continued)

	M3			M4			M5				
T1	T2[2]	T3	T1	T2[2]	T3	T1	T2[2]	T3	T4	T5	
[9]	(ACT)+(TMP)→A										
[9]	(ACT)+(TMP)→A										
[9]	(ACT)+(TMP)→A										
[9]	(ACT)+(TMP)→A										
[9]	(ACT)+(TMP)→A										
[9]	(ACT)−(TMP): FLAGS										
[9]	(ACT)−(TMP): FLAGS										
PC OUT STATUS[6]	PC ← PC + 1 B3 ─►W								WZ OUT STATUS[11]	(WZ) + 1 → PC	
PC OUT STATUS[6]	PC ← PC + 1 B3 ─►W								WZ OUT STATUS[11,12]	(WZ) + 1 → PC	
PC OUT STATUS[6]	PC ← PC + 1 B3 ─►W	SP OUT STATUS[16]	(PCH) ─── ►DATA BUS SP ← SP - 1		SP OUT STATUS[16]	(PCL) ─►DATA BUS			WZ OUT STATUS[11]	(WZ) + 1 → PC	
PC OUT STATUS[6]	PC ← PC + 1 B3 ─►W[13]	SP OUT STATUS[16]	(PCH) ─── ►DATA BUS SP ← SP - 1		SP OUT STATUS[16]	(PCL) ─►DATA BUS			WZ OUT STATUS[11,12]	(WZ) + 1 → PC	
SP OUT STATUS[15]	SP ← SP + 1 DATA ─►W								WZ OUT STATUS[11]	(WZ) + 1 → PC	
SP OUT STATUS[15]	SP ← SP + 1 DATA ─►W								WZ OUT STATUS[11,12]	(WZ) + 1 → PC	
SP OUT STATUS[16]	(TMP = 00NNN000) ─►Z (PCL) ─►DATA BUS								WZ OUT STATUS[11]	(WZ) + 1 → PC	
SP OUT STATUS[16]	(rI) ─►DATA BUS										
SP OUT STATUS[16]	FLAGS ─►DATA BUS										
SP OUT STATUS[15]	SP ← SP + 1 DATA ─►rh										
SP OUT STATUS[15]	SP ← SP + 1 DATA ─►A										
SP OUT STATUS[15]	DATA ─►W	SP OUT STATUS[16]	(H) ─── ►DATA BUS		SP OUT STATUS[16]	(L) ─► DATA BUS	(WZ) ─►HL				
WZ OUT STATUS[18]	DATA ─►A										
WZ OUT STATUS[18]	(A) ─► DATA BUS										

Fig. 2.27[1]: Intel Instruction Formats (continued)

Question: *Would it be possible to go further using this scheme, and to also use state T3 of M2 if we have to execute a longer instruction?*

In order to clarify the internal sequencing mechanism, it is suggested that you examine Figure 2.27, which shows the detailed instruction execution for the 8080. The Z80 includes all 8080 instructions, and more. The information presented in Figure 2.27 is not available for the Z80. It is shown here for its educational value in understanding the internal operation of this microprocessor. The equivalence between Z80 and 8080 instructions is shown in Appendices F and G.

A more complex instruction will now be examined:

ADD A, (HL)

The opcode for this instruction is 10000110. This instruction means "add to the accumulator the contents of memory location (HL)." The memory location is specified through a rather strange system. It is the memory location whose address is contained in registers H and L. This instruction assumes that these two special registers (HL) have been loaded with contents prior to executing the instruction. The 16-bit contents of these registers will now specify the address in the memory where data resides. This data will be added to the accumulator, and the result will be left in the accumulator.

This instruction has a history. It has been supplied in order to provide compatibility between the early 8008, and its successor, the 8080. The early 8008 was not equipped with a direct-memory addressing capability! The procedure used to access the contents of the memory was to load the two registers H and L, and then execute an instruction referencing H and L. ADD A, (HL) is just such an instruction. It must be stressed that the 8080 and the Z80 are not limited in the same way as the 8008 in memory-addressing capability. They do have direct-memory addressing. The facility for using the H and L registers becomes an added advantage, not a drawback, as was the case with the 8008.

Let us now follow the execution of this instruction (it is called ADD M for the 8080 and is the 16th instruction on Figure 2.27). States T1, T2, and T3 of M1 will be used, as usual, to *fetch* the instruction. During state T4, the contents of the accumulator are transferred to its buffer register, ACT, and the left input of the ALU is conditioned.

Memory must be accessed in order to provide the second byte of data which will be added to the accumulator. The address of this byte of data is contained in H and L. The contents of H and L will therefore have to be transferred onto the address bus, where they will be gated to the memory. Let us do it.

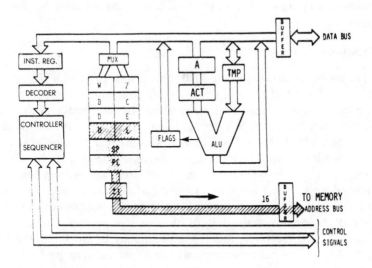

Fig. 2.28: Transfer Contents of HL to Address Bus

During machine cycle M2, we read: HL OUT. H and L are deposited on the address bus, in the same way PC used to be deposited there in previous instructions. As a remark, it has already been indicated that during state T1 *status* is output on the data bus, but no use of this will be made here. From a simplified standpoint, it will require two states: one for the memory to read its data, and one for the data to become available and transferred onto the right input of the ALU, TMP.

Both inputs of the ALU are now conditioned. The situation is analogous to the one we were in with the previous instruction ADDA, r: both inputs of the ALU are conditioned. We simply have to ADD as before. A fetch/execute overlap technique will be used, and, instead of executing the addition within state T4 of M2, final execution is postponed until state T2 of M3. It can be seen in Figure 2.27 that during T2 we indeed have: ACT + TMP→A. The addition is finally performed, the contents of ACT are added to TMP, and the result deposited into the accumulator A.

Question: *What is the apparent execution time (to the programmer) for this instruction? Using a 2.5 Mhz clock, is it 3.6 us? 2.8 us?*

Another more complex instruction will now be examined which is a direct-memory addressing instruction using two invisible W and Z registers:

LD A,(nn)

The opcode is 00111010. The 8080 equivalent is LDA addr. As usual, states T1, T2, T3 of M1 will be used to fetch the instruction from the memory. T4 is used, but no visible result can be described. During state T4, the instruction is in fact decoded. The control unit then finds out that it has to fetch the next two bytes of this instruction in order to obtain the address from which the accumulator will be loaded. The effect of this instruction is to load the accumulator from the memory contents whose address is specified in bytes 2 and 3 of the instruction. Note that state T4 is necessary to *decode* the instruction. It could be considered a waste of time since only part of the state is necessary to do the decoding. It is. However, this is the philosophy of *clock-synchonous logic*. Because *microinstructions* are used internally to perform the decoding and execution, this is the penalty that has to be paid in return for the advantages of microprogramming. The structure of this instruction appears in Figure 2.29.

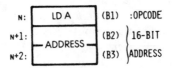

Fig. 2.29: LD A, (ADDRESS) Is a 3-Word Instruction

The next two bytes of instruction will now be fetched. They will specify an address (see Figure 2.30).

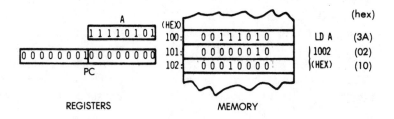

Fig. 2.30: **Before Execution of LD A**

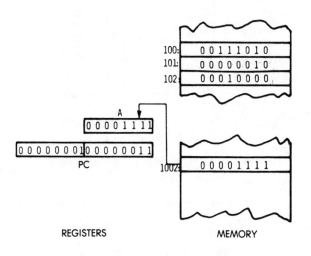

Fig. 2.31: **After Execution of LD A**

The effect of the instruction is shown in Figures 2.30 and 2.31 above.

Two special registers are available to the control unit within the Z80 (but not to the programmer). They are "W" and "Z", and are shown in Figure 2.28.

Second Machine Cycle M2: As usual, the first 2 states, T1 and T2, are used to fetch the contents of memory location PC. During T2, the program counter, PC, is incremented. Sometime by the end of T2, data becomes available from the memory, and appears on the data bus. By the end of T3, the word which has been fetched from memory address PC (B2, second byte of the instruction) is available on the data bus. It must now be stored in a temporary register. It is deposited into Z: B2 ▶ Z (see Figure 2.32).

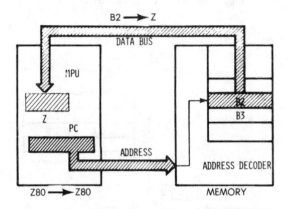

Fig. 2.32: Second Byte of Instruction Goes into Z

Machine Cycle M3: Again, PC is deposited on the address bus, incremented, and finally the third byte, B3, is read from the memory and deposited into register W of the microprocessor. At this point, i.e., by the end of state T3 of M3, registers W and Z inside the microprocessor contain B2 and B3, i.e., the complete 16-bit address which was originally contained in the two words following the instruction in the memory. Execution can now be completed. W and Z contain an address. This address will have to be sent to the memory, in order to extract the data. This is done in the next memory cycle:

Machine Cycle M4: This time, W and Z are output on the address bus. The 16-bit address is sent to the memory, and by the end of state T2, data corresponding to the contents of the specified memory location becomes available. It is finally deposited in A at the end of state T3. This terminates execution of this instruction.

This illustrates the use of an *immediate instruction*. This instruction required three bytes in order to store a two-byte *explicit address*. This instruction also required four memory cycles, as it needed to go to the memory three times in order to extract the three bytes of this three-word instruction, plus one more memory access in order to fetch the data specified by the address. It is a long instruction. However, it is also a basic one for loading the accumulator with specified contents residing at a known memory location. It can be noted that this instruction requires the use of W and Z registers.

Question: *Could this instruction have used other registers than W, Z within the system?*

Answer: No. If this instruction had used other registers, for example the H and L registers, it would have modified their contents. After execution of this instruction, the contents of H and L would have been lost. It is always assumed in a program that an instruction will not modify any registers other than those it is explicitly using. An instruction loading the accumulator should not destroy the contents of any other register. For this reason, it becomes necessary to supply the extra two registers, W and Z, for the internal use of the control unit.

Question: *Would it be possible to use PC instead of W and Z?*

Answer: Positively not. This would be suicidal. The reader should analyze this.

One more type of instruction will be studied now: a *branch* or *jump* instruction, which modifies the sequence in which instructions are executed within the program. So far, we have assumed that instructions were executed sequentially. Instructions exist which allow the programmer to jump out of sequence to another instruction within the program, or in practical terms, to jump to another area of the memory containing the program, or to another address. One such instruction is:

JP nn

This instruction appears on Line 18 of Figure 2.27[1] as "JMP addr." Its execution will be described by following the horizontal line of the Table. This is again a three-word instruction. The first word is the opcode, and contains 11000011. The next two words contain the

16-bit address, to which the jump will be made. Conceptually, the effect of this instruction is to replace the contents of the program counter with the 16 bits following the "JUMP" opcode. In practice, a somewhat different approach will be implemented, for reasons of efficiency.

As before, the first three states of M1 correspond to the instruction-fetch. During state T4 the instruction is decoded and no other event is recorded (X). The next two machine cycles are used to fetch bytes B2 and B3 of the instruction. During M2, B2 is fetched and deposited into internal register Z. The next two steps will be implemented by the processor during the next instruction-fetch, as was the case already with the addition. They will be executed instead of the usual steps for T1 and T2 of the next instruction. Let us look at them.

The next two steps will be: WZ OUT and (WZ) + 1 ► PC. In other words, the contents of WZ will be used instead of the contents of PC during the next instruction-fetch. The control unit will have recorded the fact that a jump was being executed and will execute the beginning of the next instruction differently.

The effect of these two extra states is the following:

The address placed on the address bus of the system will be the address contained in W and Z. In other words, the next instruction will be fetched from the address that was contained in W and Z. This is effectively a *jump*. In addition, the contents of WZ will be incremented by 1 and deposited in the program counter, so that the next instruction will be fetched correctly by using PC as usual. The effect is therefore correct.

Question: *Why have we not loaded the contents of PC directly? Why use the intermediate W and Z registers?*

Answer: It is not possible to use PC. If we had loaded the lower part of PC (PCL) with B2, instead of using Z, we would have destroyed PC! It would then have become impossible to fetch B3.

Question: *Would it be possible to use just Z, instead of W and Z?*

Answer: Yes, but it would be slower. We could have loaded Z with B2, then fetched B3, and deposited it into the high order half of PC (PCH). However, it would then have become necessary to transfer Z into PCL, before using the contents of PC. This would slow down the process. For this reason, both W and Z should be used. Further, and in order to save time, W and Z are not transferred into PC. They are directly gated to the address bus in order to fetch the next instruction.

Understanding this point is crucial to the understanding of efficient execution of instructions within the microprocessor.

Question: *(For the alert and informed reader only). What happens in the case of an interrupt at the end of M3? (If instruction execution is* suspended at this point, the program counter points to the instruction following the jump, and the jump address, contained in W and Z, will be lost.)

The answer is left as an interesting exercise for the alert reader.

The detailed descriptions we have presented for the execution of typical instructions should clarify the role of the registers and of the internal buses. A second reading of the preceding section may help in gaining a detailed understanding of the internal operation of the Z80.

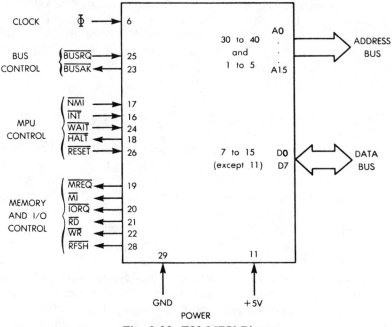

Fig. 2.33: Z80 MPU Pinout

The Z80 Chip

For completeness, the signals of the Z80 microprocessor chip will be examined here. It is not indispensable to understand the functions of the Z80 signals in order to be able to program it. The reader who is not interested in the details of hardware may therefore skip this section. The pinout of the Z80 appears on Fig. 2.33. On the right side of the illustration, the address bus and the data bus perform their usual role, as described at the beginning of this chapter. We will describe here the function of the signals on the control bus. They are shown on the left of Figure 2.33.

The control signals have been partitioned in four groups. They will be described, going from the top of Figure 2.33 towards the bottom.

The clock input is Φ. The Z80 requires an external 330-ohm pull-up resistor. It is connected to the Φ input and to 5 volts. However, at 4 MHz, an external clock driver is required.

The two bus-control signals, BUSRQ and BUSAK, are used to disconnect the Z80 from its busses. They are mainly used by the DMA, but could also be used by another processor in the system. BUSRQ is the bus-request signal. It is issued to the Z80. In response, the Z80 will place its address bus, data bus, and tristate output control signals in the high-impedance state, at the end of the current machine cycle. BUSAK is the acknowledge signal issued by the Z80 once the busses have been placed in the high-impedance state.

Six Z80 control signals are related to its internal status or to its sequencing:

INT and NMI are the two interrupt signals. INT is the usual interrupt request. Interrupts will be described in Chapter 6. A number of input/output devices may be connected to the INT interrupt line. Whenever an interrupt request is present on this line, and when the internal interrupt enable flip-flop (IFF) is enabled, the Z80 will accept the interrupt (provided the BUSRQ is not active). It will then generate an acknowledge signal: IORQ (issued during the M1 state). The rest of the sequence of events is described in Chapter 6.

NMI is the non-maskable interrupt. It is always accepted by the Z80, and it forces the Z80 to jump to location 0066 hexadecimal. It too is described in Chapter 6. (It also assumes that BUSRQ is not active.)

WAIT is a signal used to synchronize the Z80 with slow memory or input/output devices. When active, this signal indicates that the memory or the device is not yet ready for the data transfer. The Z80 CPU will then enter a special wait state until the WAIT signal becomes inactive. It will then resume normal sequencing.

HALT is the acknowledge signal supplied by the Z80 after it has executed the HALT instruction. In this state, the Z80 waits for an external interrupt and keeps executing NOPs to continually refresh memory.

RESET is the signal which usually initializes the MPU. It sets the program counter, register I and R to "0". It disables the interrupt enable flip-flop and sets the interrupt mode to "0". It is normally used after power is applied to the board.

Memory and I/O Control

Six memory and I/O control signals are generated by the Z80. They are: MREQ is the memory request signal. It indicates that the address present on the address bus is valid. A read or write operation can then be performed on the memory.

M1 is machine cycle 1. This cycle corresponds to the fetch cycle of an instruction.

IORQ is the input/output request. It indicates that the I/O address present on bits 0-7 of the address bus is valid. An I/O read or write operation can then be carried out. IORQ is also generated together with M1 when the Z80 acknowledges an interrupt. This information may be used by external chips to place the interrupt response vector on the data bus. (Normal I/O operations never occur during the M1 state. The combination IORQ plus M1 indicates an interrupt-acknowledge situation.)

RD is the read signal.* It indicates the Z80 is ready to read the contents of the data bus into an internal register. It can be used by any external chip, whether memory or I/O, to deposit data onto the data bus.

WR is the write signal.* It indicates that the data bus holds valid data, ready to be written into the specified device.

RFSH is the refresh signal. When RFSH is active, the lower seven bits of the address bus contain a refresh address for dynamic memories. The MREQ signal is then used to perform the refresh by reading the memory.

HARDWARE SUMMARY

This completes our description of the internal organization of the Z80. The exact hardware details of the Z80 are not important here. However, the role of each of the registers is important and should be fully understood before proceeding to the next chapters. The actual instructions available on the Z80 will now be introduced, and basic programming techniques for the Z80 will be presented.

*used in conjunction with MREQ or IOREQ,

3
BASIC PROGRAMMING TECHNIQUES

INTRODUCTION

The purpose of this chapter is to present the basic techniques necessary in order to write a program using the Z80. This chapter will introduce new concepts such as register management, loops, and subroutines. It will focus on programming techniques using only the *internal* Z80 resources, i.e., the registers. Actual programs will be developed, such as arithmetic programs. These programs will serve to illustrate the various concepts presented so far and will use actual instructions. Thus, it will be seen how instructions may be used to manipulate the information between the memory and the MPU, as well as to manipulate information within the MPU itself. The next chapter will then discuss in complete detail the instructions available on the Z80. Chapter 5 will present Addressing Techniques, and Chapter 6 will present the techniques available for manipulating information *outside* the Z80: the Input/Output Techniques.

In this chapter, we will essentially learn by "doing." By examining programs of increasing complexity, we will learn the role of the various instructions, of the registers, and we will apply the concepts developed so far. However, one important concept will not be presented here; it is the concept of addressing techniques. Because of its apparent complexity, it will be presented separately in Chapter 5.

Let us immediately start writing some programs for the Z80. We will start with arithmetic programs. The "programmer's model" of the Z80 registers is shown in Figure 3.0.

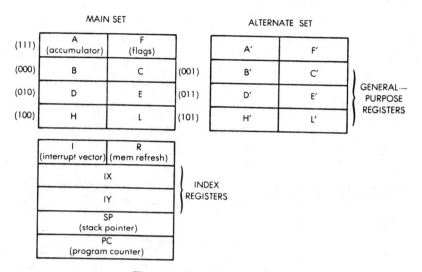

Fig. 3.0: The Z80 Registers

ARITHMETIC PROGRAMS

Arithmetic programs include addition, subtraction, multiplication, and division. The programs presented here will operate on integers. These integers may be positive binary integers or may be expressed in two's complement notation, in which case the left-most bit is the sign bit (see Chapter 1 for a description of the two's complement notation).

8-Bit Addition

We will add two 8-bit operands called OP1 and OP2, respectively stored at memory address ADR1, and ADR2. The sum will be called RES and will be stored at memory address ADR3. This is illustrated in Figure 3.1. The program which will perform this addition is the following:

Instructions	Comments
LD A, (ADR1)	LOAD OP1 INTO A
LD HL, ADR2	LOAD ADDRESS OF OP2 INTO HL
ADD A, (HL)	ADD OP2 TO OP1
LD (ADR 3), A	SAVE RESULT RES AT ADR3

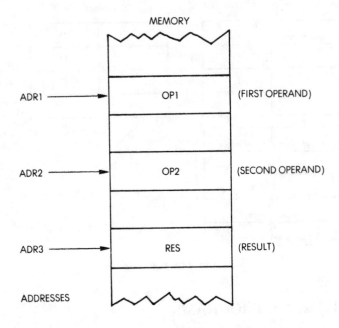

Fig. 3.1: Eight-Bit Addition RES = OP1 + OP2

This is our first program. The instructions are listed on the left and comments appear on the right. Let us now examine the program. It is a four-instruction program. Each line is called an *instruction* and is expressed here in symbolic form. Each such instruction will be translated by the *assembler* program into one, two, three or four binary bytes. We will not concern ourselves here with the translation and will only look at the symbolic representation.

The first line specifies loading the contents of ADR1 into the accumulator A. Referring to Figure 3.1, the contents of ADR1 are the first operand, "OP1". This first instruction therefore results in transferring OP1 from the memory into the accumulator. This is shown in Figure 3.2. "ADR1" is a symbolic representation for the actual 16-bit address in the memory. Somewhere else in the program, the ADR1 symbol will be defined. It could, for example, be defined as being equal to the address "100".

This *load* instruction will result in a *read operation* from address 100 (see Figure 3.2), the contents of which will be transferred along the data

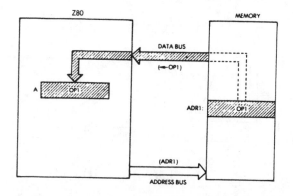

Fig. 3.2: LD A, (ADR1): OPR is Loaded from Memory

bus and deposited inside the accumulator. You will recall from the previous chapter that arithmetic and logical operations operate on the accumulator as one of the source operands. (Refer to the previous chapter for more details.) Since we wish to add the two values OP1 and OP2 together, we must first load OP1 into the accumulator. Then, we will be able to add the contents of the accumulator, i.e., add OP1 to OP2. The right-most field of this instruction is called a *comment* field. It is ignored by the assembler program at translation time, but is provided for program readability. In order to understand what the program does, it is of paramount importance to use good comments. This is called *documenting* a program.

Here the comment is self-explanatory: the value of OP1, which is located at address ADR1, is loaded into the accumulator A.

The result of this first instruction is illustrated by Figure 3.2. The second instruction of our program is:

LD HL, ADR2

It specifies: "Load ADR2 into registers H and L." In order to read the second operand, OP2, from the memory, we must first place its address into a register pair of the Z80, such as H and L. Then, we can add the contents of the memory location whose address is in H and L to the accumulator.

ADD A, (HL)

Referring to Figure 3.1, the contents of memory location ADR2 are OP2, our second operand. The contents of the accumulator are now OP1, our first operand. As a result of the execution of this instruction, OP2 will be fetched from the memory and added to OP1. This is illustrated in Figure 3.3

97

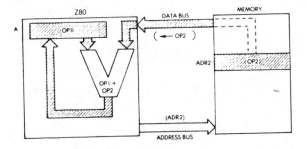

Fig. 3.3: ADD A, (HL)

The sum will be deposited in the accumulator. The reader will remember that, in the case of the Z80, the results of the arithmetic operation are deposited back into the accumulator. In other processors, it may be possible to deposit these results in other registers, or back into the memory.

The sum of OP1 and OP2 is now contained in the accumulator. To complete our program, we simply have to transfer the contents of the accumulator into memory location ADR3, in order to store the results at the specified location. This is performed by the fourth instruction of our program:

LD (ADR3), A

This instruction loads the contents of A into the specified address ADR3. The effect of this final instruction is illustrated by Figure 3.4.

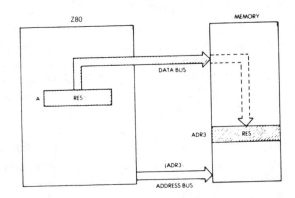

Fig. 3.4: LD (ADR3), A (Save Accumulator in Memory)

Before execution of the ADD operation, the accumulator contained OP1 (see Figure 3.3). After the addition, a new result has been written into the accumulator. It is "OP1 + OP2". Recall that the contents of any register within the microprocessor, as well as any memory location, remain the same after a read operation has been performed on this register. In other words, reading the contents of a register or memory location does not change its contents. It is only, and exclusively, a *write* operation into this register location that will change its contents. In this example, the contents of memory locations ADR1 and ADR2 remain unchanged throughout the program. However, after the ADD instruction, the contents of the accumulator will have been modified, because the output of the ALU has been written into the accumulator. The previous contents of A are then lost.

Actual numerical addresses may be used instead of ADR1, ADR2, and ADR3. In order to keep symbolic addresses, it will be necessary to use so-called "pseudo-instructions" which specify the value of these symbolic addresses, so that the assembly program may, during translation, substitute the actual physical addresses. Such pseudo-instructions could be, for example:

```
ADR1 = 100H
ADR2 = 120H
ADR3 = 200H
```

Exercise 3.1: Now close this book. Refer only to the list of instructions at the end of the book. Write a program which will add two numbers stored at memory locations LOC1 and LOC2. Deposit the results at memory location LOC3. Then, compare your program to the one above.

16-Bit Addition

An 8-bit addition will only allow the addition of 8-bit numbers, i.e., numbers between 0 and 255, if absolute binary is used. For most practical applications it is necessary to add numbers having 16 bits or more, i.e., to use *multiple precision*. We will here present examples of arithmetic on 16-bit numbers. They can be readily extended to 24, 32 bits or more (always multiples of 8 bits). We will assume that the first operand is stored at memory locations ADR1 and ADR1-1. Since OP1 is a 16-bit number this time, it will require two 8-bit memory locations. Similarly,

OP2 will be stored at ADR2 and ADR2-1. The result is to be deposited at memory addresses ADR3 and ADR3-1. This is illustrated in Figure 3.5. H indicates the high half (bits 8 through 15), while L indicates the low half (bits 0 through 7).

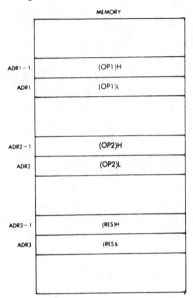

Fig. 3.5: 16-Bit Addition—The Operands

The logic of the program is exactly like the previous one. First, the lower half of the two operands will be added, since the microprocessor can only add on 8 bits at a time. Any carry generated by the addition of these low order bytes will automatically be stored in the internal carry bit ("C"). Then, the high order half of the two operands will be added together along with any carry, and the result will be saved in the memory. The program appears below:

```
LD   A, (ADR1)      LOAD LOW HALF OF OP1
LD   HL, ADR2       ADDRESS OF LOW HALF OF OP2
ADD A, (HL),        ADD OP1 AND OP2 LOW
LD   (ADR3), A      STORE RESULT, LOW
LD   A, (ADR1-1)    LOAD HIGH HALF OF OP1
DEC HL              ADDRESS OF HIGH HALF OF OP2
ADC A, (HL)         (OP1 + OP2) HIGH + CARRY
LD   (ADR3-1), A    STORE RESULT, HIGH
```

The first four instructions of this program are identical to the ones used for the 8-bit addition in the previous section. They result in adding the least significant halves (bits 0-7) of OP1 and OP2. The sum, called "RES" is stored at memory location ADR3 (see Figure 3.5).

Automatically, whenever an addition is performed, any resulting carry (whether "0" or "1") is saved in the carry bit C of the flags register (register F). If the two numbers do generate a carry, then the C bit will be equal to "1" (it will be set). If the two 8-bit numbers do not generate any carry, the value of the carry bit will be "0".

The next four instructions of the program are essentially like those used in the previous 8-bit addition program. This time they add together the most significant half (or high half, i.e., bits 8-15) of OP1 and OP2, plus any carry, and store the result at address ADR3-1.

After execution of this 8-instruction program, the 16-bit result is stored at memory locations ADR3 and ADR3-1, as specified. Note, however, that there is one difference between the second half of this program and the first half. The *"ADD" instruction* which has been used is not the same as in the first half. In the first half of this program (the 3rd instruction), we had used the "ADD" instruction. This instruction adds the two operands, regardless of the carry. In the second half, we use the "ADC" instruction, which adds the two operands together, plus any carry that may have been generated. This is necessary in order to obtain the correct result. The addition initially performed on the low operands may result in a carry. Such a possible carry must be taken into account in the second half of the addition.

The question which comes naturally then is: what if the addition of the high half of the operands also results in a carry? There are two possibilities: the first one is to assume that this is an error. This program is then designed to work for results of only up to 16 bits, but not 17. The other one is to include additional instructions to test explicitly for the possibility of a carry at the end of this program. This is a choice which the programmer must make, the first of many choices.

Note: we have assumed here that the high part of the operand is stored "on top of" the lower part, i.e., at the lower memory address. This need not necessarily be the case. In fact, addresses are stored by the Z80 in the reverse manner: the low part is first saved in the memory, and the high part is saved in the next memory location. In order to use a common convention for both addresses and data, it is recommended that data also be kept with the low part on top of the high part. This is illustrated in Figure 3.6.

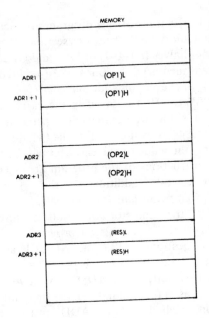

Fig. 3.6: Storing Operands in Reverse Order

When operating on multibyte operand, it is important to keep in mind two essential conventions:
—the order in which data is stored in the memory.
—where data pointers are pointing: low byte or high byte.
Exercises 3.2 and 3.3 are designed to clarify this point.

Exercise 3.2: Rewrite the 16-bit addition program above with the memory layout indicated in Figure 3.6.

Exercise 3.3: Assume now that ADR1 does not point to the lower half of OP1 (as in Figures 3.5 or 3.6), but points to the higher part of OP1. This is illustrated in Figure 3.7. Again, write the corresponding program.

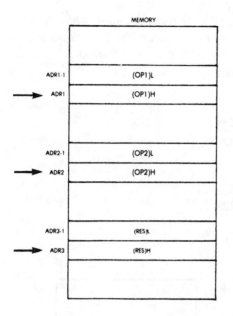

Fig. 3.7: Pointing to the High Byte

It is the programmer, i.e., you, who must decide how to store 16-bit numbers (i.e., low part or high part first) and also whether your address references point to the lower or to the higher half of such numbers. This is another choice which you will learn to make when designing algorithms or data structures.

The programs presented above are traditional programs, using the accumulator. We will now present an alternative program for the 16-bit addition that does not use the accumulator, but instead uses some of the special 16-bit instructions available on the Z80. Operands will be assumed to be stored as indicated in Figure 3.5. The program is:

```
LD    HL, (ADR1)        LOAD HL WITH OP1
LD    BC, (ADR2)        LOAD BC WITH OP2
ADD HL, BC              ADD 16 BITS
LD    (ADR3), HL        STORE RES INTO ADR3
```

Note how much shorter this program is, compared to our previous version. It is more "elegant." *In a limited manner, the Z80 allows registers H and L to be used as a 16-bit accumulator.*

103

Exercise 3.4: Using the 16-bit instructions which have just been introduced, write an addition program for 32-bit operands, assuming that
operands are stored as shown in Figure 3.8. (The answer appears
below.)

Answer:

```
LD  HL, (ADR1)
LD  BC, (ADR2)
ADD HL, BC
LD  (ADR3)
LD  HL, (ADR1 + 2)
LD  BC, (ADR2 + 2)
ADC HL, BC
LD  (ADR3 + 2)
```

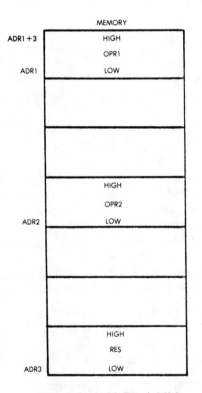

Fig. 3.8: A 32-Bit Addition

Now that we have learned to perform a binary addition, let us turn to subtraction.

Subtracting 16-Bit Numbers

Doing an 8-bit subtract would be too simple. Let us keep it as an exercise and directly perform a 16-bit subtract. As usual, our two numbers, OP1 and OP2, are stored at addresses ADR1 and ADR2. The memory layout will be assumed to be that of Figure 3.6. In order to subtract, we will use a subtract operation (SBC) instead of an add operation (ADD).

Exercise 3.5: Now write a subtraction program.

The program appears below. The data paths are shown in Figure 3.9.

```
LD   HL, (ADR1)      OP1 INTO HL
LD   DE, (ADR2)      OP2 INTO DE
AND A                CLEAR CARRY
SBC  HL, DE          OP1 — OP2
LD   (ADR3), HL      RES INTO ADR3
```

The program is essentially like the one developed for 16-bit addition. However, the Z80 instruction-set has two types of additions on double registers: ADD and ADC, but only one type of subtraction: SBC.

As a result, two changes can be noted.

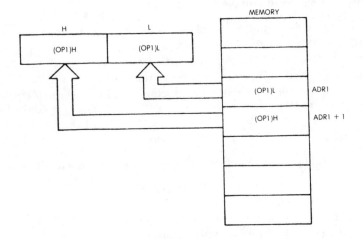

Fig. 3.9: 16-Bit Load — LD HL, (ADR1)

A first change is the use of SBC instead of ADD.

The other change is the "AND A" instruction, used to clear the carry flag prior to the subtraction. This instruction does not modify the value of A.

This precaution is necessary because the Z80 is equipped with two modes of addition, with and without carry on the H and L register, but with only one mode of subtraction, the SBC instruction of "subtract with carry" when operating on the HL register pair. Because SBC automatically takes into account the value of the carry bit, it must be set to 0 prior to starting the subtraction. This is the role of the "AND A" instruction.

Exercise 3.6: Rewrite the subtraction program without using the specialized 16-bit instruction.

Exercise 3.7: Write the subtract program for 8-bit operands.

It must be remembered that in the case of two's complement arithmetic, the final value of the carry flag has no meaning. If an overflow condition has occurred as a result of the subtraction, then the overflow bit (bit V) of the flags register will have been set. It can then be tested.

The examples just presented are simple binary additions or subtractions. However, another type of arithmetic may be necessary; it is BCD arithmetic.

BCD ARITHMETIC

8-Bit BCD Addition

The concept of BCD arithmetic has been presented in Chapter 1. Let us recall its features. It is essentially used for business applications where it is imperative to retain every significant digit in a result. In the BCD notation, a 4-bit nibble is used to store one decimal digit (0 through 9). As a result, every 8-bit byte may store two BCD digits. (This is called *packed BCD)*. Let us now add two bytes each containing two BCD digits.

In order to identify the problems, let us try some numeric examples first.

Let us add "01" and "02":

"01" is represented by: 0000 0001
"02" is represented by: 0000 0010

The result is: 0000 0011

This is the BCD representation for "03". (If you feel unsure of the BCD equivalent, refer to the conversion table at the end of the book.) Everything worked very simply in this case. Let us now try another example.

"08" is represented by 0000 1000
"03" is represented by 0000 0011

Exercise 3.8: Compute the sum of the two numbers above in the BCD representation. What do you obtain? (answer follows)

If you obtain "0000 1011", you have computed the *binary* sum of 8 and 3. You have indeed obtained 11 in *binary*. Unfortunately, "1011" is an *illegal code in BCD.* You should obtain the *BCD* representation of "11", i.e., 0001 0001!

The problem stems from the fact that the BCD representation uses only the first ten combinations of 4 digits in order to encode the decimal symbols 0 through 9. The remaining six possible combinations of 4 digits are unused, and the illegal "1011" is one such combination. In other words, whenever the sum of two BCD digits is greater than 9,

107

then one must add 6 to the result in order to skip over the 6 unused codes.

Add the binary representation of "6" to 1011:

$$1011 \quad \text{(illegal binary result)}$$
$$+ \, 0110 \quad (+6)$$

The result is: 0001 0001

This is, indeed, "11" in the BCD notation! We now have the correct result.

This example illustrates one of the basic difficulties of the BCD mode. One must compensate for the six missing codes. A special instruction, "DAA", called "decimal adjust," must be used to adjust the result of the binary addition. (Add 6 if the result is greater than 9.)

The next problem is illustrated by the same example. In our example, the carry will be generated from the lower BCD digit (the right-most one) into the left-most one. This internal carry must be taken into account and added to the second BCD digit. The addition instruction takes care of this automatically. However, it is often convenient to detect this internal carry from bit 3 to bit 4 (the "half-carry"). The H flag is provided for this purpose.

As an example, here is a program to add the BCD numbers "11" and "22":

```
LD   A, 11H        LOAD LITERAL BCD '11'
ADD A, 22H         ADD LITERAL BCD '22'
DAA                DECIMAL ADJUST RESULT
LD   (ADR), A      STORE RESULT
```

In this program, we are using a new symbol "H". The "H" sign within the operand field of the instruction specifies that the data it follows is expressed in hexadecimal notation. The hexadecimal and the BCD representations for digits "0" through "9" are identical. Here we wish to add the literals (or constants) "11" and "22". The result is stored at the address ADR. When the operand is specified as part of the instruction, as it is in the above example, this is called *immediate addressing*. (The various addressing modes will be discussed in detail in Chapter 5.) Storing the result at a specified address, such as LD (ADR), A is called *absolute addressing* when ADR represents a 16-bit address.

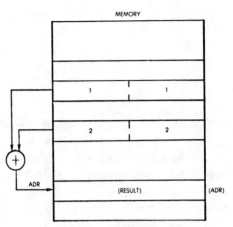

Fig. 3.10: Storing BCD Digits

This program is analogous to the 8-bit binary addition, but uses a new instruction: "DAA". Let us illustrate its role in an example. We will first add "11" and "22" in BCD:

$$
\begin{array}{ll}
\ 00010001 & (11) \\
+\ 00100010 & (22) \\
\hline
=\ 00110011 & (33) \\
\underbrace{}_{3}\underbrace{}_{3}
\end{array}
$$

The result is correct, using the rules of binary addition.

Let us now add "22" and "39", by using the rules of *binary* addition:

$$
\begin{array}{ll}
\ 00100010 & (22) \\
+\ 00111001 & (39) \\
\hline
=\ 01011011 & \\
\underbrace{}_{5}\underbrace{}_{?}
\end{array}
$$

"1011" is an *illegal BCD code*. This is because BCD uses only the first 10 binary codes, and "skips over" the next 6. We must do the same, i.e. add 6 to the result:

$$
\begin{array}{ll}
\ 01011011 & \text{(binary result)} \\
+\ 0110 & (6) \\
\hline
=\ 01100001 & (61) \\
\underbrace{}_{6}\underbrace{}_{1}
\end{array}
$$

This is the correct BCD result.

Exercise 3.9: Could we move the DAA instruction in the program after the instruction LD (ADR), A?

BCD Subtraction

BCD subtraction is, in appearance, complex. In order to perform a BCD subtraction, one must add the *ten's complement* of the number, just as one adds the two's complement of a number to perform a binary subtract. The ten's complement is obtained by computing the complement to 9, then adding "1". This requires typically three to four operations on a standard microprocessor. However, the Z80 is equipped with a powerful DAA instruction which simplifies the program.

The DAA instruction automatically adjusts the value of the result in the accumulator, depending on the value of the C, H and N flags before DAA, to the correct value. (See the next chapter for more details on DAA.)

16-Bit BCD Addition

16-bit addition is performed just as simply as in the binary case. The program for such an addition appears below:

```
LD   A, (ADR1)        LOAD (OP1) L INTO A
LD   HL, (ADR2)       LOAD ADR2 INTO HL
ADD A, (HL)           (OP1 + OP2) LOW
DAA                   DECIMAL ADJUST
LD   (ADR3), A        STORE (RESULT) LOW
LD   A, (ADR1 + 1)    LD (OP1) H INTO A
INC  HL               POINT TO ADR2 + 1
ADC A, (HL)           (OP1 + OP2) HIGH + CARRY
DAA                   DECIMAL ADJUST
LD   (ADR3 + 1), A    STORE (RESULT) HIGH
```

Packed BCD Subtract

Elementary BCD addition and subtraction have been described. However, in actual practice, BCD numbers include any number of bytes. As a simplified example of a packed BCD subtract, we will assume that the two numbers N1 and N2 include the same number of BCD bytes. The number of bytes is called COUNT. The register and memory allocation is shown in Figure 3.11. The program appears below:

```
BCDPAK    LD    B, COUNT
          LD    DE, N2
          LD    HL, N1
          AND   A              CLEAR CARRY
MINUS     LD    A, (DE)        N2 BYTE
          SBC   A, (HL)        N2 - N1
          DAA
          LD    (HL), A        STORE RESULT
          INC   DE
          INC   HL
          DJNZ MINUS           DEC B, LOOP UNTIL B = 0.
```

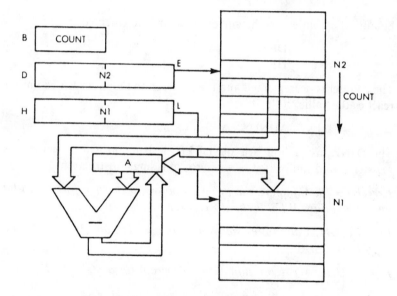

Fig. 3.11: Packed BCD Subtract: N1 ◄— N 2 - N1

N1 and N2 represent the addresses where the BCD numbers are stored. These addresses will be loaded in register pairs DE and HL:

```
BCDPAK LD     B, COUNT
       LD     DE, N2
       LD     HL, N1
```

Then, in anticipation of the first subtraction, the carry bit must be cleared. It has been pointed out that the carry bit can be cleared in a number of equivalent ways. Here, for example, we use:

AND A

The first byte of N2 is loaded into the accumulator, then the first byte of N1 is subtracted from it. The DAA instruction is then used, to obtain the correct BCD value:

```
MINUS   LD      A, (DE)
        SBC     A, (HL)
        DAA
```

The result is then stored into N1:

```
        LD      (HL), A
```

Finally, the pointers to the current byte are incremented:

```
        INC     DE
        INC     HL
```

The counter is decremented and the subtraction loop is executed until it reaches the value "0":

```
        DJNZ    MINUS
```

The DJNZ instruction is a special Z80 instruction which decrements register B and jumps if it is not zero, in a single instruction.

Exercise 3.10: Compare the program above to the one for the 16-bit binary addition. What is the difference?

Exercise 3.11: Can you exchange the roles of DE and HL? (Hint: Be careful with SBC.)

Exercise 3.12: Write the subtraction program for a 16-bit BCD.

BCD Flags

In BCD mode, the carry flag set as the result of an addition indicates the fact that the result is larger than 99. This is not like the two's complement situation, since BCD digits are represented in true binary. Conversely, the presence of the carry flag after a subtraction indicates a borrow.

Instruction Types

We have now used two types of microprocessor instructions. We have used LD, which loads the accumulator from the memory address, or stores its contents at the specified address. This is a *data transfer* instruction.

Next, we have used *arithmetic* instructions, such as ADD, SUB, ADC and SBC. They perform addition and subtraction operations. More ALU instructions will be introduced soon in this chapter.

Still other types of instructions are available within the microprocessor which we have not used yet. They are in particular "jump" instructions, which will modify the order in which the program is being executed. This new type of instruction will be introduced in our next example. Note that jump instructions are often called "branch" for conditional situations, i.e. instances where there is a logical choice in the program. The "branch" derives its name from the analogy to a tree, and implies a fork in the representation of the program.

MULTIPLICATION

Let us now examine a more complex arithmetic problem: the multiplication of binary numbers. In order to introduce the algorithm for a binary multiplication, let us start by examining a usual decimal multiplication: We will multiply 12 by 23.

$$
\begin{array}{r}
12 \quad \text{(Multiplicand)} \\
\times \quad 23 \quad \text{(Multiplier)} \\
\hline
36 \quad \text{(Partial Product)} \\
+\ 24 \quad \\
\hline
=\ 276 \quad \text{(Final Result)}
\end{array}
$$

The multiplication is performed by multiplying the right-most digit of the multiplier by the multiplicand, i.e., "3" × "12". The partial product is "36". Then one multiplies the next digit of the multiplier, i.e., "2", by "12". "24" is then added to the partial product.

But there is one more operation: 24 is *offset to the left* by one position. We will say that 24 is *shifted left* by one position. Equivalently, we could have said that the partial product (36) had been *shifted one position to the right* before adding.

The two numbers, correctly shifted, are then added and the sum is 276. This is simple. The binary multiplication is performed in exactly the same way.

Let us look at an example. We will multiply 5×3:

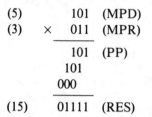

(5)	101	(MPD)
(3)	× 011	(MPR)
	101	(PP)
	101	
	000	
(15)	01111	(RES)

In order to perform the multiplication, we operate exactly as we did above. The formal representation of this algorithm appears in Figure 3-12. It is a flowchart for the algorithm, our first flowchart. Let us examine it more closely.

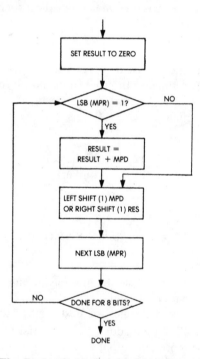

Fig. 3.12: The Basic Multiplication Algorithm—Flowchart

This flowchart is a symbolic representation of the algorithm we have just presented. Every rectangle represents an order to be carried out. It will be translated into one or more program instructions. Every diamond-shaped symbol represents a test being performed. This will be a *branching point* in the program. If the test succeeds, we will branch to a specified location. If the test does not succeed, we will branch to another location. The concept of branching will be explained later, in the program itself. The reader should now examine this flowchart and ascertain that it does indeed exactly represent the algorithm which has been presented. Note that there is an arrow coming out of the last diamond at the bottom of the flowchart, back to the first diamond on top. This is because the same portion of the flowchart will be executed eight times, once for every bit of the multiplier. Such a situation, where execution will restart at the same point, is called a *program loop* for obvious reasons.

Exercise 3.13: Multiply "4" by "7" in binary, using the flowchart, and verify that you obtain "28". If you do not, try again. It is only if you obtain the correct result that you are ready to translate this flowchart into a program.

8-By-8 Multiplication

Let us now translate this flowchart into a program for the Z80. The complete program appears in Figure 3.13. We are going to study it in detail. As you will recall from Chapter 1, programming consists here of translating the flowchart of Figure 3.12 into the program of Figure 3.13. Each of the boxes in the flowchart will be translated by one or more instructions.

It is assumed that MPR and MPD already have a value.

MPY88	LD	BC, (MPRAD)	LOAD MULTIPLIER INTO C
	LD	B, 8	B IS BIT COUNTER
	LD	DE, (MPDAD)	LOAD MULTIPLICAND INTO E
	LD	D, 0	CLEAR D
	LD	HL, 0	SET RESULT TO 0
MULT	SRL	C	SHIFT MULTIPLIER BIT INTO CARRY
	JR	NC, NOADD	TEST CARRY
	ADD	HL, DE	ADD MPD TO RESULT
NOADD	SLA	E	SHIFT MPD LEFT
	RL	D	SAVE BIT IN D
	DEC	B	DECREMENT SHIFT COUNTER
	JP	NZ, MULT	DO IT AGAIN IF COUNTER ≠ 0
	LD	(RESAD), HL	STORE RESULT

Fig. 3.13: 8 × 8 Multiplication Program

The first box of the flowchart is an *initialization box*. It is necessary to set a number of registers or memory locations to "0", as this program will require their use. The registers which will be used by the multiplication program appear in Figure 3.14.

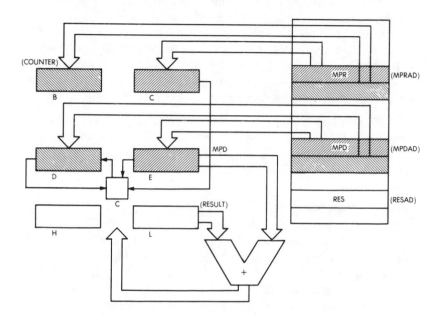

Fig 3.14: 8 × 8 Multiplication—The Registers

Three register pairs of the Z80 are used for the multiplication program. The 8-bit multiplier is assumed to reside at memory address MPRAD. The multiplicand MPD is assumed to reside at memory address MPDAD. The multiplier and the multiplicand respectively will be loaded into registers C and E (see Figure 3.14). Register B will be used as a counter.

Registers D and E will hold the multiplicand as it is shifted left one bit at a time.

Note that, even though only C and E need to be loaded initially, a 16-bit load must be used, so that B and D will also be loaded from memory, and will have to be reset respectively to "8" and to "0".

Finally, the results of an 8-bit by 8-bit multiplication may require up to 16 bits. This is because $2^8 \times 2^8 = 2^{16}$. Two registers must therefore be reserved for the result. They are registers H and L, as indicated on Figure 3.14.

The first step is to load registers B, C, and E with the appropriate contents, and to initialize the result (the partial product) to the value "0" as specified by the flowchart of Figure 3.12. This is accomplished by the following instructions:

```
MPY88   LD    BC, (MPRAD)
        LD    B, 8
        LD    DE, (MPDAD)
        LD    D, 0
        LD    HL, 0
```

The first three instructions respectively load MPR into the register pair BC, the value "8" into register B, and MPD into the register pair DE. Since MPR and MPD are 8-bit words, they are, in fact, loaded into registers C and E respectively, while the next words in the memory after MPR and MPD get loaded into B and D. This is shown in Figure 3.15 and 3.16. The next instruction will zero the contents of D.

In this multiplication program, the multiplicand will be shifted left before being added to the result (remember that, optionally, it is possible to shift the result right instead, as indicated in the fourth box of the flowchart of Figure 3.12). The multiplicand MPD will be shifted into register D at each step. This register D must therefore be initialized to the value "0". This is accomplished by the fourth instruction. Finally, the fifth instruction sets the contents of registers H and L to 0 in a single instruction.

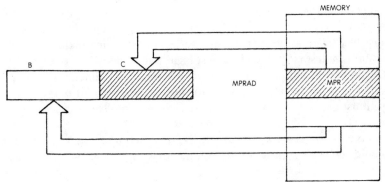

Fig. 3.15: LD BC, (MPRAD)

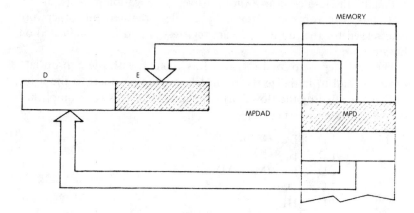

Fig. 3.16: LD DE, (MPDAD)

Referring back to the flowchart of Figure 3.12, the next step is to test the least significant bit (the right-most bit) of the multiplier MPR. If this bit is a "1", then the value of MPD must be added to the partial result, otherwise it will not be added. This is accomplished by the next three instructions:

```
MULT SRL   C
     JR    NC, NOADD
     ADD   HL, DE
```

The first problem we must solve is how to test the least significant bit of the multiplier, contained in register C. We could here use the BIT instruction of the Z80, which allows testing any bit in any register. However, in this case, we would like to construct a program as simple as possible, using a loop. If we were using the BIT instruction here, we would first test bit 0, then later test bit 1, and so on until we reached bit 7. This would require a different instruction every time, and a simple loop could not be used. In order to shorten the length of the program, we must use a different instruction. Here we are using a *shift* instruction.

Note: There is a way to use the BIT instruction and a loop, but this would require the program to modify itself, a practice we will avoid.

SRL is a new type of operation within the arithemetic and logical unit. It stands for "shift right logical." A *logical shift to the right* is characterized by the fact tnat a "0" comes into bit position 7. This can be contrasted to an *arithemtic shift to the right*, where the bit coming into position 7 is identical to the previous value of bit 7. The different types of shift operations will be described in the next chapter. The effect of the SRL C instruction is illustrated in Figure 3.14 by an arrow coming out of register C and into the square used to designate the carry bit (also called "C"). At this point, the right-most bit of the MPR will be in the carry bit C, where it can be tested.

The next instruction, "JR NC, NOADD", is a *jump* operation. It means "jump on no carry" (NC) to the address (the label) NOADD. If the contents of the carry bit are "0" (no carry), then the program will jump to the address NOADD. If the contents of C are "1" (the carry bit is set), then no branch will occur, and the next sequential instruction will be executed, i.e., the instruction "ADD HL, DE" will be executed.

This instruction specifies that the contents of D and E be added to H and L, with the result in H and L. Since E contains the multiplicand MPD (see Figure 3.14), this adds the multiplicand to the partial result.

At this point, regardless of whether MPD has been added to the result or not, the multiplicand must be shifted left (this is the fourth box in the flowchart of Figure 3.12). This is accomplished by:

NOADD SLA E

SLA stands for "shift left arithmetic." It has just been explained above that there are two types of shift operations, a logical shift and an arithmetic shift. This is the arithmetic one. In the case of a left shift, an SLA specifies that the bit coming into the right part of the register (the least significant bit) be a "0" (just as in the case of an SRL before).

As an example, let us assume that the initial contents of register E were 00001001. After the SLA instruction, the contents of E will be 00010010. And the contents of the carry bit will be 0.

However, looking back at Figure 3.14, we really want to shift the most significant bit (called the MSB) of E directly into D (this is illustrated by the arrow on the illustration coming from E into D). However, there is no instruction which will shift a double register such as D and E in one operation. Once the contents of E have been shifted, the left-most bit has "fallen into" the carry bit. We must collect this bit from the carry bit and shift it into register D. This is accomplished by the next instruction:

RL D

119

RL is still another type of shift operation. It stands for "rotate left." In a *rotation* operation, as opposed to a *shift* operation, this bit coming into the register is the contents of the carry bit C (see Figure 3.17). This is exactly what we want. The contents of the carry bit C are loaded into the right-most part of D, and we have effectively transferred the left-most bit of E.

This sequence of two instructions is illustrated in Figure 3.18. It can be seen that the bit marked by an X in the most significant position of E will first be transferred into the carry bit, then into the least significant position of D. Effectively, it will have been shifted from E into D.

At this point, referring back to the flowchart of Figure 3.12, we must point to the next bit of MPR and check for the eighth bit. This is accomplished by decrementing the byte counter, contained in register B (see Figure 3.14). The register is decremented by:

DEC B

This is a *decrement* instruction, which has the obvious effect.

Finally, we must check whether the counter has decremented to the value zero. This is accomplished by checking the value of the Z bit. The reader will recall that the Z (zero) flag indicates whether the previous arithmetic operation (such as a DEC operation) has produced a zero result. However, note that DEC HL, DEC BC, DEC DE, DEC IX, DEC SP do not affect the Z flag. If the counter is not "0", the operation is not finished, and we must execute this program loop again. This is accomplished by the next instruction:

JP NZ MULT

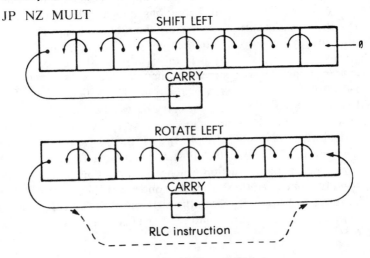

Fig. 3.17: Shift and Rotate

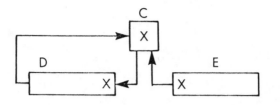

Fig. 3.18: Shifting from E into D

This is a jump instruction which specifies that whenever the Z bit is not set (NZ stands for non-zero), a jump occurs to location MULT. This is the *program loop,* which will be executed repeatedly until B decrements to the value 0. Whenever B decrements to the value 0, the Z bit will be set, and the JP NZ instruction will fail. This will result in the next sequential instruction being executed, namely:

LD (RESAD), HL

This instruction merely saves the contents of H and L, i.e., the result of the multiplication, at address RESAD, the address specified for the result. Note that this instruction will transfer the contents of both registers H and L into two consecutive memory locations, corresponding to addresses RESAD and RESAD + 1. It saves 16 bits at a time.

Exercise 3.14: Could you write the same multiplication program using the BIT instruction (described in the next chapter) instead of the SRL C instruction? What would be the disadvantage?

Let us now improve the program, if possible:

Exercise 3.15: Can JR be substituted for JP at the end of the program? If so, what is the advantage?

Exercise 3.16: Can you use DJNZ to shorten the end of the program?

Exercise 3.17: Examine the two instructions: LD D, 0 and LD HL, 0 at the beginning of the program. Can you substitute:

```
XOR   A
LD    D, A
LD    H, A
LD    L, A
```

If so, what is the impact on size (number of bytes) and speed?

Note that, in most cases, the program that we have just developed will be a subroutine and the final instruction in the subroutine will be RET (return). The subroutine mechanism will be explained later in this chapter.

Important Self-Test

This is the first significant program we have encountered so far. It includes many different types of instructions, including transfer instructions (LD), arithmetic operations (ADD), logical operations (SRL, SLA, RL), and jump operations (JR, JP). It also implements a program loop, in which the lower seven instructions, starting at address MULT, are executed repeatedly. In order to understand programming, it is essential to understand the operation of such a program in complete detail. The program is much longer than the previous simple arithmetic programs we have developed so far, and it should be studied in detail. An important exercise will now be proposed. The reader is strongly urged to do this exercise completely and correctly before proceeding. This will be the only real proof that the concepts presented so far have been understood. If a correct result is obtained, it will mean that you have really understood the mechanism by which instructions manipulate information in the microprocessor, transfer it between the memory and the registers, and process it. If you do not obtain the correct result, or if you do not do this exercse, it is likely that you will experience difficulties later in writing programs yourself. Learning to program requires personal practice. Please pause now, take a piece of paper, or use the illustration of Figure 3.19, and do the following exercise:

Exercise 3.18: Every time that a program is written, it should be verified by hand, in order to ascertain that its results will be correct. We are going to do just that: the goal of this exercise is to fill in the table of Figure 3.19 completely and accurately.

LABEL	INSTRUCTION	B	C	C (CARRY)	D	E	H	L

Fig. 3.19: Form for Multiplication Exercise

You may want to write directly on Figure 3.19 or make a copy of it. You must determine the contents of every relevant register in the Z80 after the execution of each instruction in the program, from beginning to end. All the registers used by the program of Figure 3.13 are shown in Figure 3.19. From left to right, they are registers B and C, the carry C, registers D and E, and, finally, registers H and L. On the left part of this illustration, fill in the label, if applicable, and then the instructions being executed. On the right of the instruction, fill in the contents of each register after execution of the instruction. Whenever the contents of a register are not known (indefinite), you may use dashes to represent its contents. Let us start filling in this table together. You will then have to fill it out by yourself until the end. The first line appears below:

LABEL	INSTRUCTION	B	C	C	D	E	H	L
MPY88	LD BC,(0200)	00	03	-	--	--	--	--

Fig. 3.20: Multiplication: After One Instruction

We will assume here that we are multiplying "3" (MPR) by "5" (MPD).

The first instruction to be executed is "LD BC, (MPRAD)". The contents of memory location MPRAD is loaded into registers B and C. It has been assumed that MPR is equal to 3, i.e., "00000011". After execution of this instruction, the contents of register C have been set to "3". Note that this instruction will also result in loading register B with whatever followed MPR in the memory. However, the next instruction in the program will take care of this by loading register B with "8", as shown in Figure 3.21. Note that, at this point, the contents of D and E and H and L are still undefined, and this is indicated by dashes. The LD instruction does not condition the carry bit, so that the contents of the carry bit C are undefined. This is also indicated by a dash.

LABEL	INSTRUCTION	B	C	C	D	E	H	L
MPY88	LD BC,(0200)	00	03	-	--	--	--	--
	LD B,08	08	03	-	--	--	--	--

Fig. 3.21: Multiplication: After Two Instructions

The situation after the execution of the first five instructions of the program (just before the MULT) is shown in Figure 3.22.

LABEL	INSTRUCTION	B	C	C	D	E	H	L
		--	--	-	--	--	--	--
MPY88	LD BC,(0200)	00	03	-	--	--	--	--
	LD B, 08	08	03	-	--	--	--	--
	LD DE,(0202)	08	03	-	00	05	--	--
	LD D, 00	08	03	-	00	05	--	--
	LD HL,0000	08	03	-	00	05	00	00

Fig. 3.22: Multiplication: After Five Instructions

The SRL instruction will perform a logical shift right, and the right-most bit of MPR will fall into the carry bit. You can see in Figure 3.23 that the contents of MPR after the shift is "0000 0001". The carry bit C is now set to "1". The other registers are unchanged by this operation. Please continue to fill out the chart by yourself.

A second iteration is shown at the end of this chapter in Fig. 3.41.

LABEL	INSTRUCTION	B	C	C	D	E	H	L
		--	--	-	--	--	--	--
MPY88	LD BC,(0200)	00	03	-	--	--	--	--
	LD B, 08	08	03	-	--	--	--	--
	LD DE,(0202)	08	03	-	00	05	--	--
	LD D, 00	08	03	-	00	05	--	--
	LD HL,0000	08	03	-	00	05	00	00
MULT	SRL C	08	01	1	00	05	00	00
	JR NC,0114	08	01	1	00	05	00	00
	ADD HL,DE	08	01	0	00	05	00	05
NOADD	SLA E	08	01	0	00	0A	00	05
	RL D	08	01	0	00	0A	00	05
	DEC B	07	01	0	00	0A	00	05
	JP NZ,010F	07	01	0	00	0A	00	05

Fig. 3.23: One Pass Through The Loop.

A complete listing showing the contents of all the Z80 registers and the flags is shown in Fig. 3.39 at the end of this chapter for the complete multiplication. A hex or decimal listing is shown in Fig. 3.40.

Programming Alternatives

The program that we have just developed could have been written in many other ways. As a general rule, every programmer can usually find ways to modify, and often improve, a program. For example, we have shifted the multiplicand left before adding. It would have been mathematically equivalent to shift the result one position to the right before adding it to the multiplicand. As a matter of fact, this is an interesting exercise!

Exercise 3.19: Write an 8 × 8 multiplication program using the same algorithm, but shifting the result one position to the right instead of shifting the multiplicand by one position to the left. Compare it to the previous program, and determine whether this different approach would be faster or slower than the preceding one. The speeds of the Z80 instructions are given in the next chapter.

Improved Multiplication Program

The program that we have just developed is a straightforward translation of the algorithm to code. However, *effective programming requires close attention to detail,* and the length of the program can often be reduced or its execution speed can be improved. We are now going to study alternatives designed to improve this basic program.

Step 1

A first possible improvement lies in the better utilization of the Z80 instruction set. The second-to-last instruction as well as the preceding one can be replaced by a single instruction:

DJNZ LOOP

This is a special Z80 "automated jump" which decrements the B register and branches to a specified location if it is not "0". To be absolutely correct, the instruction is not completely identical to the previous pair

DEC B
JP NZ, MULT

for it specifies a *displacement,* and one can only jump within the range of − 126 to + 129. However, we must here jump to a location which is only a few bytes away, and this improvement is legitimate. The resulting program is shown in Figure 3.24 below:

```
MPY88B  LD    DE, (MPDAD)
        LD    BC, (MPRAD)
        LD    B, 8            BIT COUNTER
        LD    HL, 0
MULT    SRL   C
        JR    NC, NOADD
        ADD   HL, DE
NOADD   SLA   E
        RL    D
        DJNZ  MULT
        LD    (RESAD), HL
        RET
```

Fig. 3.24: Improved Multiply, Step 1

Step 2

In order to improve this multiplication program further, we will observe that three different shift operations are used in the initial program of Figure 3.13. The multiplier is shifted right, then the multiplicand MPD is shifted left, in two operations, by first shifting register E left, then rotating register D to the left. This is time-consuming. A standard programming "trick" used in the case of multiplication is based on the following observation: every time that the multiplier is shifted by one bit position, another bit position becomes available in the multiplier register. For example, assuming that the multiplier shifts right (in the previous example), a bit position becomes available on the left. Simultaneously, it can be observed that the first partial product (or "result") will use, at most, 9 bits. If a single register had been allocated to the result in the beginning of the program, we could then use the bit position that has been vacated by the multiplier to store the ninth bit of the result.

After the next shift of the MPR, the size of the partial product will be increased by just one bit again. In other words, a single register can be reserved intially for the partial product, and the bit positions which are being freed by the multiplier can then be used as the MPR is being shifted. In order to improve the program, we are therefore going to

127

assign MPR and RES to a register pair. Ideally, they should be shifted together in a single operation. Unfortunately, the Z80 shifts only 8-bit registers at a time. Like most other 8-bit microprocessors, it has no instruction that allows shifting 16 bits at a time.

However, another trick can be used. The Z80 (like the 8080) is equipped with special 16-bit add instructions that we have already used. Provided that the multiplier and the result are stored in the register pair H and L, we can use the instruction:

ADD HL, HL

which adds the contents of H and L to itself. Adding a number to itself is doubling it. Doubling a number in the binary system is equivalent to a left shift. We have just obtained a 16-bit shift in a single instruction. Unfortunately, the shift occurs to the left when we would like it to occur to the right. This is not a problem.

Conceptually, the MPR can be shifted either left or right. We have used a right shift algorithm because this is the one which is used in ordinary addition. However, it does not necessarily need to be so. The addition operation is commutative, and the order can be reversed: shifting the MPR to the left is just as valid.

In order to take advantage of this simulated 16-bit shift, we will have to shift the MPR to the left. Therefore, the MPR will reside in register H and the result in register L. The resulting register configuration is shown in Figure 3.25.

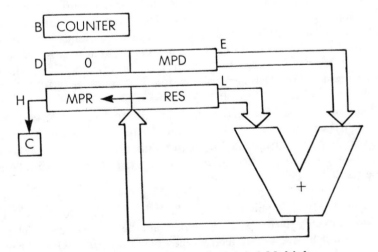

Fig. 3.25: Registers for Improved Multiply

The rest of the program is essentially identical to the previous one. The resulting program appears below:

```
MUL88C  LD    HL, (MPRAD-1)
        LD    L, 0
        LD    DE, (MPDAD)
        LD    D, 0
        LD    B, 8              COUNTER
MULT    ADD   HL, HL            SHIFT LEFT
        JR    NC, NOADD
        ADD   HL, DE
NOADD   DJNZ  MULT
        LD    (RESAD), HL
        RET
```

Fig. 3.26: Improved Multiply, Step 2

When comparing this program to the previous one, it can be seen that the length of the multiplication loop (the number of instructions between MULT and the jump) has been reduced. This program has been written in fewer instructions and this will usually result in faster execution. This shows the advantage of selecting the correct registers to contain the information.

A straightforward design will generally result in a program that works. It will not result in a program that is *optimized*. It is therefore important to understand and use the available registers and instructions in the best possible way. These examples illustrate a rational approach to register selection and instruction selection for maximum efficiency.

Exercise 3.20: Compute the speed of a multiplication operation using this last program. Assume that a branch will occur in 50% of the cases. Look up the number of cycles required by every instruction in the index section. Assume a clock rate of 2 MHz (one cycle = 0.5 us).

Exercise 3.21: Note that here we have used the register pair D and E to contain the multiplicand. How would the above program be changed if we had used the register pair B and C instead? (Hint: this would require a modification at the end.)

Exercise 3.22: Why did we have to bother zeroing register D when loading MPD into E?

Finally, let us address a detail which may look irritating to the programmer who is not yet familiar with the Z80. The reader will have noticed that, in order to load MPD into E from the memory, we had to load both registers D and E at the same time from a memory address. This is because, unless the address is contained in registers H and L, there is no way to fetch a single byte directly and load it into register E. This is a feature carried over from the early 8008, which had no direct addressing mode. The feature was carried forward into the 8080, with some improvements, and improved still further in the Z80, where it is possible to fetch 16 bits directly from a given memory address (but not 8 bits - except toward register A).

Now, having solved this possible mystery, let us execute a more complex multiplication.

A 16 X 16 Multiplication

In order to put our newly acquired skills to a test, we will multiply two 16-bit numbers. However, we will assume that the result requires only 16 bits, so that it can be contained in one of the register pairs.

The result, as in our first multiplication example, is contained in registers H and L (see Figure 3.27). The multiplicand MPD is contained in registers D and E.

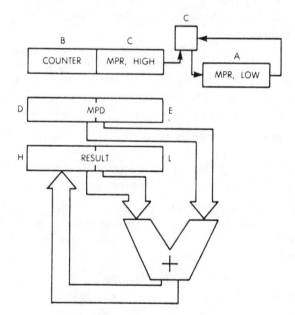

Fig. 3.27: 16 X 16 Multiply—The Registers

It would be tempting to deposit a multiplier into register B and C. However, if we want to take advantage of the DJNZ instruction, register B must be allocated to the counter. As a result, half of the multiplier will be in register C, and the other half in register A (see Figure 3.27). The multiplication program appears below:

```
MUL16   LD      A, (MPRAD + 1)   MPR, HIGH
        LD      C, A
        LD      A, (MPRAD)       MPR, LOW
        LD      B, 16            COUNTER
        LD      DE, (MPDAD)      MPD
        LD      HL, 0
MULT    SRL     C                RIGHT SHIFT MPR,
                                 HIGH
        RRA                      ROTATE RIGHT MPR,
                                 LOW
        JR      NC, NOADD        TEST CARRY
        ADD     HL, DE           ADD MPD TO RESULT
NOADD   EX      DE, HL
        ADD     HL, HL           DOUBLE – SHIFT MPD
                                 LEFT
        EX      DE, HL
        DJNZ    MULT
        RET
```

Fig. 3.28: 16 X 16 Multiplication Program

The program is analogous to those we have developed before. The first six instructions (from label MUL16 to label MULT) perform the initialization of registers with the appropriate contents. One complication is introduced here by the fact that the two halves of MPR must be loaded in separate operations. It is assumed that MPRAD points to the low part of the MPR in the memory, followed in the next sequential memory location by the high part. (Note that the reverse convention can be used.) Once the high part of MPR has been read into A, it must be transferred into C:

```
LD      A, (MPRAD + 1)
LD      C, A
```

Finally, the low part of MPR can be read directly into the accumulator:

```
LD      A, (MPRAD)
```

The rest of the registers, B, D, E, H, and L are initialized as usual:

```
LD    B, 16
LD    DE, (MPDAD)
LD    HL, 0
```

A 16-bit shift must be performed on the multiplier. It requires two separate shift or rotate operations on registers C and A:

```
MULT   SRL   C
       RRA
```

After the 16-bit shift, the right-most bit of the MPR, i.e., the LSB, is contained in the carry bit C where it can be tested:

```
JR    NC, NOADD
```

As usual, the multiplicand is not added to the result if the carry bit is "0", and is added to the result if the carry bit is "1":

```
ADD   HL, DE
```

Next, the multiplicand MPD must be shifted by one position to the left.

However, the Z80 does not have an instruction which will shift the contents of register D and E simultaneously to the left by one bit position, and it can also not add the contents of D and E to itself. The contents of D and E will therefore first be transferred into H and L, then doubled, and transferred back to D and E. This is accomplished by the next three instructions:

```
NOADD  EX    DE, HL
       ADD   HL, HL
       EX    DE, HL
```

Finally, the counter B is decremented and a jump occurs to the beginning of the loop as long as it does not decrement to "0":

```
DJNZ  MULT
```

As usual, it is possible to consider other register allocations which may (or may not) result in shorter codes:

Exercise 3.23: Load the multiplier into registers B and C. Place the counter in A. Write the corresponding multiplication program and discuss the advantages or disadvantages of this register allocation.

Exercise 3.24: Referring to the original 16-bit multiplication program of Figure 3.28, can you propose a way to **shift** the MPD, contained in registers D and E, without transferring it into registers H and L?

Exercise 3.25: Write a 16-by-16 multiplication program which detects the fact that the result has more than 16 bits. This is a simple improvement of our basic program.

Exercise 3.26: Write a 16-by-16 multiplication program with a 32-bit result. The suggested register allocation appears in Figure 3.29. Remember that the initial result after the first addition in the loop will require only 16 bits, and that the multiplier will free one bit for each subsequent iteration.

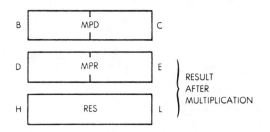

Fig. 3.29: 16 × 16 Multiply with 32-Bit Result

Let us now examine the last usual arithmetic operation, the division.

BINARY DIVISION

The algorithm for binary division is analogous to the one which has been used for the multiplication. The divisor is successively subtracted from the high order bits of the dividend. After each subtraction, the result is used instead of the initial dividend. The value of the quotient is simultaneously increased by 1 every time. Eventually, the result of the subtraction is negative. This is called an *overdraw*. One must then restore the partial result by adding the divisor back to it. Naturally, the quotient must be simultaneously decremented by 1. Quotient and dividend are then shifted by one bit position to the left and the algorithm is repeated. The flow-chart is shown in Figure 3.30.

The method just described is called the *restoring method*. A variation of this method which yields an improved speed of execution is called the *non-restoring* method.

133

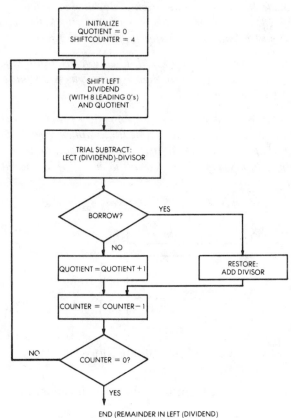

Fig. 3.30: 8-Bit Binary Division Flowchart

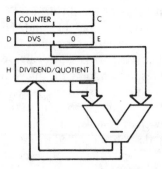

Fig. 3.31: 16/8 Division—The Registers

16-by-8 Division

As an example, let us here examine a 16-by-8 division, which will yield an 8-bit quotient and an 8-bit remainder dividend. The register allocation is shown in Figure 3.31.

The program appears below:

```
DIV168  LD    A, (DVSAD)   LOAD DIVISOR
        LD    D, A         INTO D
        LD    E, 0
        LD    HL, (DVDAD)  LOAD 16-BIT DIVIDEND
        LD    B, 8         INITIALIZE COUNTER
DIV     XOR   A            CLEAR C BIT
        SBC   HL, DE       DIVIDEND – DIVISOR
        INC   HL           QUOTIENT = QUOTIENT + 1
        JP    P, NOADD     TEST IF REMAINDER
                           POSITIVE
        ADD   HL, DE       RESTORE IF NECESSARY
        DEC   HL           QUOTIENT = QUOTIENT – 1
NOADD   ADD   HL, HL       SHIFT DIVIDEND LEFT
        DJNZ  DIV          LOOP UNTIL B = 0
        RET
```

Fig. 3.32: 16/8 Division Program

The first five instructions in the program load the divisor and the dividend respectively into the appropriate registers. They also initialize the counter, in register B, to the value 8. Note again that register B is a preferred location for a counter if the specialized Z80 instruction DJNZ is to be used:

```
DIV168  LD    A, (DVSAD)
        LD    D, A
        LD    E, 0
        LD    HL, (DVDAD)
        LD    B, 8
```

Next, the divisor is subtracted from the dividend. Since an SBC instruction must be used (there is no 16-bit subtract without carry), the carry must be set to the value "0" before subtracting. This can be accomplished in a number of ways. The carry can be cleared by performing instructions such as:

> XOR A
> AND A
> OR A

Here, an XOR is used:

DIV   XOR   A

The subtraction can then be performed:

> SBC   HL, DE

It is anticipated that the subtraction will be successful, i.e., that the remainder will be positive. This is called the "trial subtract" step (refer to the flowchart of Figure 3.30). The quotient is therefore incremented by one. If the subtraction has in fact failed (i.e., if the remainder is negative), the quotient will have to be decremented by one later on:

> INC   HL

The result of the subtraction is then tested:

> JP   P, NOADD

If the remainder is positive or zero, the subtraction has been successful, and it is not necessary to store it. The program jumps to address NOADD. Otherwise, the current dividend must be restored to its previous value, by adding the divisor back to it, and the quotient must be decremented by one. This is performed by the next instructions:

> ADD   HL, DE
> DEC   HL

Finally, the resulting dividend is shifted left, in anticipation of the next trial subtract operation. Finally, the B counter is decremented and tested for the value "0". As long as B is not zero, this loop is executed:

NOADD   ADD   HL, HL
        DJNZ DIV
        RET

Exercise 3.27: Verify the operation of this division program by hand, by filling out the table of Figure 3.33, as in Exercise 3.18 for the multiplication. Note that the contents of D need not be entered on the form of Figure 3.33, since they are never modified.

LABEL	INSTRUCTION	B	H	L

Fig. 3.33: Form for Division Program

8-Bit Division

The following program uses a restoring method, and leaves a complemented quotient in A. It divides 8 bits by 8 bits (unsigned).

```
E IS DIVIDEND
C IS DIVISOR
A IS QUOTIENT
B IS REMAINDER
```

```
DIV88    XOR    A              CLEAR ACCUMULATOR
         LD     B, 8           LOOP COUNTER
LOOP88   RL     E              ROTATE CY INTO ACC-
                               DIVIDEND
         RLA                   CY WILL BE OFF
         SUB    C              TRIAL SUBTRACT DIVISOR
         JR     NC, $ + 3      SUBTRACT OK
         ADD    A, C           RESTORE ACCUM, SET CY
         DJNZ   LOOP88
         LD     B, A           PUT REMAINDER IN B
         LD     A, E           GET QUOTIENT
         RLA                   SHIFT IN LAST RESULT BIT
         CPL                   COMPLEMENT BITS
         RET
```

Note: the "$" symbol in the sixth instruction represents the value of the program counter.

Non Restoring Division

The following program performs a 16-bit by 15-bit integer division, using a non-restoring technique. IX points to the dividend, IY to the divisor (not zero). (see Figure 3.34.).

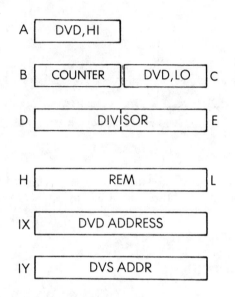

Fig. 3.34: Non-Restoring Division—The Registers

Register B is used as a counter, initially set to 16.
A and C contain the dividend.
D and E contain the divisor.
H and L contain the result.
The 16-bit dividend is shifted left by:

    RL   C
    RLA

The remainder is shifted left by:

    ADC HL, HL.

The final quotient is left in B, C, with the remainder in HL. The program follows.

```
DIV16     LD      B, (IX + 1)
          LD      C, (IX)
          LD      D,(IY + 1)
          LD      E, (IY)
          LD      A, D
          OR      E               (DIVISOR) HIGH OR
                                  (DIVISOR) LOW
          JR      Z, ERROR        CHECK FOR DIVISOR =
                                  ZERO
          LD      A, B            GET (DVD) HI
          LD      HL, 0           CLEAR RESULT
          LD      B, 16           COUNTER
TRIALSB   RL      C               ROTATE RESULT + ACC
                                  LEFT
          RLA
          ADC     HL, HL          LEFT SHIFT. NEVER SETS
                                  CARRY.
          SBC     HL, DE          MINUS DIVISOR
NULL      CCF                     RESULT BIT
          JR      NC, NGV         ACCUMULATOR
                                  NEGATIVE?
PTV       DJNZ    TRIALSB         COUNTER ZERO?
          JP      DONE
RESTOR    RL      C               ROTATE RESULT + ACC
                                  LEFT
          RLA
          ADC     HL, HL          AS ABOVE
          AND     A
          ADC     HL, DE          RESTORE BY ADDING DVSR
          JR      C, PTV          RESULT POSITIVE
          JR      Z, NULL         RESULT ZERO
NGV       DJNZ    RESTOR          COUNTER ZERO?
DONE      RL      C               SHIFT IN RESULT BIT
          RLA
          ADD     HL, DE          CORRECT REMAINDER
          LD      B, A            QUOTIENT IS IN B, C
          RET
```

Exercise 3.28: Compare the previous program to the following one, using a restoring technique:

```
DIVIDEND IN AC
DIVISOR IN DE
QUOTIENT IN AC
REMAINDER IN HL
```

```
DIV16    LD     HL, 0        CLEAR ACCUMULATOR
         LD     B, 16        SET COUNTER
LOOP16   RL     C            ROT ACC-RESULT LEFT
         RLA
         ADC    HL, HL       LEFT SHIFT
         SBC    HL, DE       TRIAL SUBTRACT DIVISOR
         JR     NC, $ + 3    SUB WAS OK
         ADD    HL, DE       RESTORE ACCUM
         CCF                 CALC RESULT BIT
         DJNZ   LOOP16       COUNTER NOT ZERO
         RL     C            SHIFT IN LAST RESULT BIT
         RLA
         RET
```

Note: The symbol "$" means "current location" (eighth instruction).

LOGICAL OPERATIONS

The other class of instructions which can be executed by the ALU inside the microprocessor is the set of *logical instructions*. They include: AND, OR and exclusive OR (XOR). In addition, one can also include here the shift and rotate operations which have already been utilized, and the comparison instruction, called CP for the Z80. The individual use of AND, OR, XOR, will be described in Chapter 4 on the instruction set.

Let us now develop a brief program which will check whether a given memory location called LOC contains the value "0", the value "1", or something else.

The program will introduce the comparison instruction, and perform a series of logical tests. Depending on the result of the comparison, one program segment or another will be executed.

The program appears below:

```
           LD    A, (LOC)      READ CHARACTER IN
                               LOC
           CP    00H           COMPARE TO ZERO
           JP    Z, ZERO       IS IT A 0?
           CP    01H           COMPARE TO ONE
           JP    Z, ONE
NONEFOUND  ...
           ...
ZERO       ...
           ...
ONE        ...
```

The first instruction: "LD A, (LOC)" reads the contents of memory location LOC, and loads it into the accumulator. This is the character we want to test. It is compared to the value 0 by the following instruction:

                    CP   00H

This instruction compares the contents of the accumulator to the hexadecimal value "00", i.e., the bit pattern "0000 0000". This comparison instruction will set the Z bit in the flags register to the value "1", if it succeeds. This bit can then be tested by the next instruction:

          JP   Z, ZERO

The jump instruction tests the value of the Z bit. If the comparison succeeds, the Z bit has been set to one, and the jump will succeed. The program will then jump to the address ZERO. If the test fails, then the next sequential instruction will be executed:

          CP   01H

Similarly, the following jump instruction will branch to location ONE if the comparison succeeds. If none of the comparisons succeed, then the instruction at location NONEFOUND will be executed.

```
          JP    Z, ONE
NONEFOUND ...
```

This program was introduced to demonstrate the value of the comparison instruction followed by a jump. This combination will be used in many of the following programs.

Exercise 3.29: Refer to the definition of the LD A, (LOC) instruction in the next chapter. Examine the effect of this instruction on the flags, if any. Is the second instruction of this program necessary (CP 00H)?

Exercise 3.30: Write the program which will read the contents of memory location "24" and branch to an address called"STAR"if there was a "" in memory location 24. The bit pattern for a "*" in binary notation will be assumed to be represented by "00101010".*

INSTRUCTION SUMMARY

We have now studied most of the important instructions of the Z80 by using them. We have transferred values between the memory and the registers. We have performed arithmetic and logical operations on such data. We have tested it, and depending on the results of these tests, have executed various portions of the program. In particular, special "automated" Z80 instructions such as DJNZ have been used to shorten programs. Other automated instructions: LDDR, CPIR, INIR will be introduced throughout the remainder of this book.

Full use has been made of special Z80 features, such as 16-bit register instructions to simplify the programs, and the reader should be careful not to use these programs on an 8080: they have been optimized for the Z80.

We have also introduced a structure called a loop. Another important programming structure will be introduced now: the subroutine.

SUBROUTINES

In concept, a subroutine is simply a block of instructions which has been given a name by the programmer. From a practical standpoint, a subroutine must start with a special instruction called a *subroutine declaration*, which identifies it as such for the assembler. It is also terminated by another special instruction called a *return*. Let us first illustrate the use of a subroutine in a program in order to demonstrate its value. Then, we will examine how it is actually implemented.

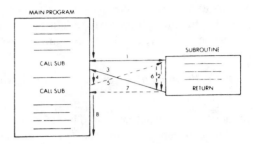

Fig. 3.35: Subroutine Calls

The use of a subroutine is illustrated in Figure 3.35. The main program appears on the left of the illustration. The subroutine is shown symbolically on the right. Let us examine the subroutine mechanism. The lines of the main program are executed successively until a new instruction "CALL SUB" is met. This special instruction is the *subroutine call* and results in a transfer to the subroutine. This means that the next instruction to be executed after the CALL SUB is the first instruction within the subroutine. This is illustrated by arrow 1 on the illustration.

Then, the subprogram within the subroutine executes just like any other program. We will assume that the subroutine does not contain any other calls. The last instruction of this subroutine is a RETURN. This is a special instruction which will cause a return to the main program. The next instruction to be executed after the RETURN is the one following the CALL SUB in the main program. This is illustrated by arrow 3 on the illustration. Program execution continues then, as illustrated by arrow 4.

In the body of the main program a second CALL SUB appears. A new transfer occurs, shown by arrow 5. This means that the body of the subroutine is again executed following the CALL SUB instruction.

Whenever the RETURN within the subroutine is encountered, a return occurs to the instruction following the CALL SUB in question. This is illustrated by arrow 7. Following the return to the main program, program execution proceeds normally, as illustrated by arrow 8.

The effect of the two special instructions CALL SUB and RETURN should now be clear. What is the value of the subroutine mechanism?

The essential value of the subroutine is that it can be called from any number of points in the main program, and used repeatedly *without rewriting it.* A first advantage is that this approach saves memory space, since there is no need to rewrite the subroutine every time. A second advantage is that the programmer can design a specific subroutine only once and then use it repeatedly. This is a significant simplification in program design.

Exercise 3.31: What is the main disadvantage of a subroutine? (Answer follows.)

The disadvantage of the subroutine should be clear just by examining the flow of execution between the main program and the subroutine. A subroutine results in a *slower execution,* since extra instructions must be executed: the CALL SUB and the RETURN.

Implementation of the Subroutine Mechanism

We will examine here how the two special instructions, CALL SUB and RETURN, are implemented internally within the processor. The effect of the CALL SUB instruction is to cause the next instruction to be fetched at a new address. You will remember (or else read Chapter 1 again) that the address of the next instruction to be executed in a computer is contained in the program counter (PC). This means that the effect of the CALL SUB is to substitute new contents in register PC. Its effect is to load the start address of the subroutine in the program counter. *Is that really sufficient?*

To answer this question, let us consider the other instruction which has to be implemented: the RETURN. The RETURN must cause, as its name indicates, a return to the instruction that follows the CALL SUB. This is possible only if the address of this instruction has been preserved somewhere. This address happens to be the value of the program counter at the time that the CALL SUB was encountered. This is because the program counter is automatically incremented every time it is used (read Chapter 1 again). This is precisely the address that we want to preserve, so that we can later perform the RETURN.

The next problem is: where can we save this return address? This address must be saved in a location where it is guaranteed that it will not be erased.

However, let us now consider the following situation, illustrated by Figure 3.36. In this example, subroutine 1 contains a call to SUB2. Our mechanism should work in this case as well. Naturally, there might even be more than two subroutines, say N "nested" calls. Whenever a new

CALL is encountered, the mechanism must therefore again store the program counter. This implies that we need at least 2N memory locations for this mechanism. Additionally, we will need to return from SUB2 first and SUB1 next. In other words, we need a structure which can preserve the chronological ordering in which addresses have been saved.

The structure has a name and has already been introduced. It is *the stack*. Figure 3.38 shows the actual contents of the stack during successive subroutine calls. Let us look at the main program first. At address 100, the first call is encountered: CALL SUB1. We will assume that, in this microprocessor, the subroutine call uses 3 bytes (RST is an exception). The next sequential address is therefore not "101", but "103". The CALL instruction uses addresses "100", "101", "102". Because the control unit of the Z80 "knows" that it is a 3-byte instruction, the value of the program counter, when the call has been completely decoded, will be "103". The effect of the call will be to load the value "280" in the program counter. "280" is the starting address of SUB1.

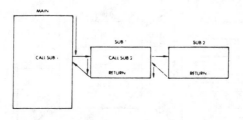

Fig. 3.36: Nested Calls

We are now ready to demonstrate the effect of the RETURN instruction and the correct operation of our stack mechanism. Execution proceeds within SUB2 until the RETURN instruction is encountered at time 3. The effect of the RETURN instruction is simply to pop the top of the stack into the program counter. In other words, the program counter is restored to its value prior to the entry into the subroutine. The top of the stack in our example is "303". Figure 3.38 shows that, at time 3, value "303" has been removed from the stack and has been put back into the program counter. As a result, instruction execution proceeds from address "303". At time 4, the RETURN of SUB1 is encountered. The value on top of the stack is "103". It is popped and is installed in the program counter. As a result, program execution will proceed from location "103" on within the main program. This is, indeed, the effect that we wanted. Figure 3.38 shows that at time 4 the stack is again empty. The mechanism works.

The subroutine call mechanism works up to the maximum dimension of the stack. This is why early microprocessors which had a 4- or 8-register stack were essentially limited to 4 or 8 levels of subroutine calls.

Note that, on Figures 3.36 and 3.37, the subroutines have been shown to the right of the main program. This is only for the clarity of the diagram. In reality, the subroutines are typed by the user as regular instructions of the program. On a sheet of paper, when producing the listing of the complete program, the subroutines may be at the beginning of the text, in its middle, or at the end. This is why they are preceded by a subroutine declaration: they must be identified. The special instructions tell the assembler that what follows should be treated as a subroutine. Such assembler *directives* will be discussed in Chapter 10.

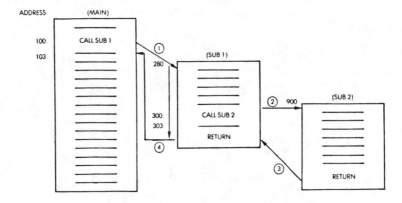

Fig. 3.37: The Subroutine Calls

STACK:	TIME ①	TIME ②	TIME ③	TIME ④
	103	103	103	
		303		

Fig. 3.38: Stack vs. Time

Z80 Subroutines

The basic concepts relating to subroutines have now been presented. It has been shown that the stack is required in order to implement this mechanism. The Z80 is equipped with a 16-bit stack-pointer register. The stack can therefore reside anywhere within the memory and may have up to 64K (1K = 1024) bytes, assuming they are available for that purpose. In practice, the start address for the stack, as well as its maximum dimension, will be defined by the programmer before writing his program. A memory area will then be reserved for the stack.

The subroutine-call instruction, in the case of the Z80, is called CALL, and comes in two versions; the direct or unconditional call, such as CALL ADDRESS, is the one we have already described. In addition, the Z80 is equipped with a conditional call instruction which will call a subroutine if a condition is met. For example: CALL NZ, SUB1 will result in a call to subroutine 1 if the Z flag is zero at the time of the test. This is a powerful facility, since many subroutine calls are conditional, i.e., occur only if some specific condition is met.

CALL CC, NN is executed only if the condition specified by "CC" is true. CC is a set of three bits (bits 3, 4, and 5 of the opcode) which may specify up to eight conditions. They correspond respectively to the four flags "Z", "C", "P/V", "S" being either zero or non-zero.

Similarly, two types of return instructions are provided: RET and RET CC.

RET is the basic return instruction. It occupies one byte, and causes the top two bytes of the stack to be re-installed in the program counter. It is unconditional.

RET CC has the same effect except that it is executed only if the conditions specified by CC are true. The condition bits are the same as for the CALL instruction just described.

Additionally, two specialized types of return are available which are used to terminate interrupt routines: RETI, RETN. They are described in the section on the Z80 instructions as well as in the section on interrupts.

Finally, one more specialized instruction is provided which is analogous to a subroutine call, but allows the program to branch to only one of eight starting locations located in page zero. This is the RST P instruction. This is a one-byte instruction which automatically preserves the program counter in the stack, and causes a branch to the address specified by the three-bit P field. The P field corresponds to bits 3, 4 and 5 of the insrtuction, multiplied by eight.

In other words, if bits 3, 4, 5 are "000", the jump will occur to location 00H. If these bits are "001", the branch will occur to 08H, etc. up to 111, which will cause a branch to location 38H. The RST instruction is very efficient in terms of speed since it is a single-byte instruction. However, it can jump to only eight locations, in page 0. Additionally, these addresses in page 0 are only eight bytes apart. This instruction is a carry-over from the 8080 and was extensively used for interrupts. This will be described in the interrupt section. However, this instruction may be used for any other purpose by the programmer, and should be considered as a possible specialized subroutine call.

Subroutine Examples

Most of the programs that we have developed and are going to develop would usually be written as subroutines. For example, the multiplication program is likely to be used by many areas of the program. In order to facilitate and clarify program development, it is therefore convenient to define a subroutine whose name would be, for example, MULT. At the end of this subroutine we would simply add the instruction RET.

Exercise 3.32: If MULT is used as a subroutine, would it "damage" any internal flags or registers?

Recursion

Recursion is a word used to indicate that a subroutine is calling itself. If you have understood the implementation mechanism, you should now be able to answer the following question:

Exercise 3.33: Is it legal to let a subroutine call itself? (In other words, will everything work even if a subroutine calls itself?) If you are not sure, draw the stack and fill it with the successive addresses. Then, look at the registers and memory (see Exercise 3.18) and determine if a problem exists.

Interrupts will be discussed in the input/output chapter (Chapter 6). All returns except returns from interrupts are one-byte instructions; all calls are 3-byte instructions (except RST).

Exercise 3.34: Look at the execution times of the CALL and the RET instructions in the next chapter. Why is the return from a subroutine so much faster than the CALL? (Hint: if the answer is not obvious, look again at the stack implementation of the subroutine mechanism, and analyze the internal operations that must be performed.)

Subroutine Parameters

When calling a subroutine, one normally expects the subroutine to work on some data. For example, in the case of multiplication, one wants to transmit two numbers to the subroutine which will perform the multiplication. We saw in the case of the multiplication routine that this subroutine expected to find the multiplier and the multiplicand in given memory locations. This illustrates one method of passing parameters: through memory. Two other techniques are used, so that we have three ways of passing parameters.

1—through registers
2—through memory
3—through the stack

Registers can be used to pass parameters. This is an advantageous solution, provided that registers are available, since one does not need to use a fixed memory location: the subroutine remains memory-independent. If a fixed memory location is used, any other user of the subroutine must be very careful that he uses the same convention and that the memory location is indeed available (look at Exercise 3.19 above). This is why, in many cases, a block of memory locations is reserved simply to pass parameters among various subroutines.

Using memory has the advantage of greater flexibility (more data), but results in poorer performance and also in tying the subroutine to a given memory area.

Depositing parameters in *the stack* has the same advantage as using registers: it is memory-independent. The subroutine simply knows that it is supposed to receive, say, two parameters which are stored on top of the stack. Naturally, it has disadvantages: it clutters the stack with data and, therefore, reduces the number of possible levels of subroutine calls. It also significantly complicates the use of the stack, and may require multiple stacks.

The choice is up to the programmer. In general, one wishes to remain independent from actual memory locations as long as possible.

If registers are not available, a possible solution is the stack. However, if a large quantity of information should be passed to a subroutine, this information may have to reside directly in the memory. An elegant way around the problem of passing a block of data is simply to transmit a pointer to the information. A *pointer* is the address of the beginning of the block. A pointer can be transmitted in a register, or in the stack (two-stack locations can be used to store a 16-bit address), or in a given memory location(s).

Finally, if neither of the two solutions is applicable, then an agreement may be made with the subroutine that the data will be at some fixed memory location (the "mail-box").

Exercise 3.35: Which of the three methods above is best for recursion?

Subroutine Library

There is a strong advantage to structuring portions of a program into identifiable subroutines: they can be debugged independently and can have a mnemonic name. Provided that they will be used in other areas of the program, they become shareable, and one can thus build a library of useful subroutines. However, there is no general panacea in computer programming. Using subroutines systematically for any group of instructions that can be grouped by function may also result in poor efficiency. The alert programmer will have to weigh the advantages against the disadvantages.

SUMMARY

This chapter has presented the way information is manipulated inside the Z80 by instructions. Increasingly complex algorithms have been introduced and translated into programs. The main types of instructions have been used and explained.

Important structures such as loops, stacks and subroutines, have been defined.

You should now have acquired a basic understanding of programming, and of the major techniques used in standard applications. Let us study the instructions available.

```
        A=00  BC=0000  DE=0000  HL=0000  S=0300  P=0100  0100'  LD    BC,(0200)
        A'=00 B'=0000  D'=0000  H'=0000  X=0000  Y=0000  I=00          (0200')
        A=00  BC=0003  DE=0000  HL=0000  S=0300  P=0104  0104'  LD    B,08
        A'=00 B'=0000  D'=0000  H'=0000  X=0000  Y=0000  I=00
        A=00  BC=0803  DE=0000  HL=0000  S=0300  P=0106  0106'  LD    DE,(0202)
        A'=00 B'=0000  D'=0000  H'=0000  X=0000  Y=0000  I=00          (0202')
        A=00  BC=0803  DE=0005  HL=0000  S=0300  P=010A  010A'  LD    D,00
        A'=00 B'=0000  D'=0000  H'=0000  X=0000  Y=0000  I=00
        A=00· BC=0803  DE=0005  HL=0000  S=0300  P=010C  010C'  LD    HL,0000
        A'=00 B'=0000  D'=0000  H'=0000  X=0000  Y=0000  I=00          (0000')
        A=00  BC=0803  DE=0005  HL=0000  S=0300  P=010F  010F'  SRL   C
        A'=00 B'=0000  D'=0000  H'=0000  X=0000  Y=0000  I=00
    C   A=00  BC=0801  DE=0005  HL=0000  S=0300  P=0111  0111'  JR    NC,0114
        A'=00 B'=0000  D'=0000  H'=0000  X=0000  Y=0000  I=00          (0114')
    C   A=00  BC=0801  DE=0005  HL=0000  S=0300  P=0113  0113'  ADD   HL,DE
        A'=00 B'=0000  D'=0000  H'=0000  X=0000  Y=0000  I=00
        A=00  BC=0801  DE=0005  HL=0005  S=0300  P=0114  0114'  SLA   E
        A'=00 B'=0000  D'=0000  H'=0000  X=0000  Y=0000  I=00
  V     A=00  BC=0801  DE=000A  HL=0005  S=0300  P=0116  0116'  RL    D
        A'=00 B'=0000  D'=0000  H'=0000  X=0000  Y=0000  I=00
Z V     A=00  BC=0801  DE=000A  HL=0005  S=0300  P=0118  0118'  DEC   B
        A'=00 B'=0000  D'=0000  H'=0000  X=0000  Y=0000  I=00
    N   A=00  BC=0701  DE=000A  HL=0005  S=0300  P=0119  0119'  JP    NZ,010F
        A'=00 B'=0000  D'=0000  H'=0000  X=0000  Y=0000  I=00          (010F')
    N   A=00  BC=0701  DE=000A  HL=0005  S=0300  P=010F  010F'  SRL   C
        A'=00 B'=0000  D'=0000  H'=0000  X=0000  Y=0000  I=00
Z V C   A=00  BC=0700  DE=000A  HL=0005  S=0300  P=0111  0111'  JR    NC,0114
        A'=00 B'=0000  D'=0000  H'=0000  X=0000  Y=0000  I=00          (0114')
Z V C   A=00  BC=0700  DE=000A  HL=0005  S=0300  P=0113  0113'  ADD   HL,DE
        A'=00 B'=0000  D'=0000  H'=0000  X=0000  Y=0000  I=00
Z V     A=00  BC=0700  DE=000A  HL=000F  S=0300  P=0114  0114'  SLA   E
        A'=00 B'=0000  D'=0000  H'=0000  X=0000  Y=0000  I=00
  V     A=00  BC=0700  DE=0014  HL=000F  S=0300  P=0116  0116'  RL    D
        A'=00 B'=0000  D'=0000  H'=0000  X=0000  Y=0000  I=00
Z V     A=00  BC=0700  DE=0014  HL=000F  S=0300  P=0118  0118'  DEC   B
        A'=00 B'=0000  D'=0000  H'=0000  X=0000  Y=0000  I=00
    N   A=00  BC=0600  DE=0014  HL=000F  S=0300  P=0119  0119'  JP    NZ,010F
        A'=00 B'=0000  D'=0000  H'=0000  X=0000  Y=0000  I=00          (010F')
    N   A=00  BC=0600  DE=0014  HL=000F  S=0300  P=010F  010F'  SRL   C
        A'=00 B'=0000  D'=0000  H'=0000  X=0000  Y=0000  I=00
Z V     A=00  BC=0600  DE=0014  HL=000F  S=0300  P=0111  0111'  JR    NC,0114
        A'=00 B'=0000  D'=0000  H'=0000  X=0000  Y=0000  I=00          (0114')
Z V     A=00  BC=0600  DE=0014  HL=000F  S=0300  P=0114  0114'  SLA   E
        A'=00 B'=0000  D'=0000  H'=0000  X=0000  Y=0000  I=00
  V     A=00  BC=0600  DE=0028  HL=000F  S=0300  P=0116  0116'  RL    D
        A'=00 B'=0000  D'=0000  H'=0000  X=0000  Y=0000  I=00
Z V     A=00  BC=0600  DE=0028  HL=000F  S=0300  P=0118  0118'  DEC   B
        A'=00 B'=0000  D'=0000  H'=0000  X=0000  Y=0000  I=00
    N   A=00  BC=0500  DE=0028  HL=000F  S=0300  P=0119  0119'  JP    NZ,010F
        A'=00 B'=0000  D'=0000  H'=0000  X=0000  Y=0000  I=00          (010F')
    N   A=00  BC=0500  DE=0028  HL=000F  S=0300  P=010F  010F'  SRL   C
        A'=00 B'=0000  D'=0000  H'=0000  X=0000  Y=0000  I=00
Z V     A=00  BC=0500  DE=0028  HL=000F  S=0300  P=0111  0111'  JR    NC,0114
        A'=00 B'=0000  D'=0000  H'=0000  X=0000  Y=0000  I=00          (0114')
Z V     A=00  BC=0500  DE=0028  HL=000F  S=0300  P=0114  0114'  SLA   E
        A'=00 B'=0000  D'=0000  H'=0000  X=0000  Y=0000  I=00
  V     A=00  BC=0500  DE=0050  HL=000F  S=0300  P=0116  0116'  RL    D
        A'=00 B'=0000  D'=0000  H'=0000  X=0000  Y=0000  I=00
Z V     A=00  BC=0500  DE=0050  HL=000F  S=0300  P=0118  0118'  DEC   B
        A'=00 B'=0000  D'=0000  H'=0000  X=0000  Y=0000  I=00
    N   A=00  BC=0400  DE=0050  HL=000F  S=0300  P=0119  0119'  JP    NZ,010F
        A'=00 B'=0000  D'=0000  H'=0000  X=0000  Y=0000  I=00          (010F')
    N   A=00  BC=0400  DE=0050  HL=000F  S=0300  P=010F  010F'  SRL   C
        A'=00 B'=0000  D'=0000  H'=0000  X=0000  Y=0000  I=00
```

Fig. 3.39: Multiplication: A Complete Trace

```
Z  V      A=00 BC=0400 DE=0050 HL=000F S=0300 P=0111 0111' JR   NC,0114
          A'=00 B'=0000 D'=0000 H'=0000 X=0000 Y=0000 I=00        (0114')
Z  V      A=00 BC=0400 DE=0050 HL=000F S=0300 P=0114 0114' SLA  E
          A'=00 B'=0000 D'=0000 H'=0000 X=0000 Y=0000 I=00
S  V      A=00 BC=0400 DE=00A0 HL=000F S=0300 P=0116 0116' RL   D
          A'=00 B'=0000 D'=0000 H'=0000 X=0000 Y=0000 I=00
Z  V      A=00 BC=0400 DE=00A0 HL=000F S=0300 P=0118 0118' DEC  B
          A'=00 B'=0000 D'=0000 H'=0000 X=0000 Y=0000 I=00
      N   A=00 BC=0300 DE=00A0 HL=000F S=0300 P=0119 0119' JP   NZ,010F
          A'=00 B'=0000 D'=0000 H'=0000 X=0000 Y=0000 I=00        (010F')
      N   A=00 BC=0300 DE=00A0 HL=000F S=0300 P=010F 010F' SRL  C
          A'=00 B'=0000 D'=0000 H'=0000 X=0000 Y=0000 I=00
Z  V      A=00 BC=0300 DE=00A0 HL=000F S=0300 P=0111 0111' JR   NC,0114
          A'=00 B'=0000 D'=0000 H'=0000 X=0000 Y=0000 I=00        (0114')
Z  V      A=00 BC=0300 DE=00A0 HL=000F S=0300 P=0114 0114' SLA  E
          A'=00 B'=0000 D'=0000 H'=0000 X=0000 Y=0000 I=00
   C      A=00 BC=0300 DE=0040 HL=000F S=0300 P=0116 0116' RL   D
          A'=00 B'=0000 D'=0000 H'=0000 X=0000 Y=0000 I=00
          A=00 BC=0300 DE=0140 HL=000F S=0300 P=0118 0118' DEC  B
          A'=00 B'=0000 D'=0000 H'=0000 X=0000 Y=0000 I=00
      N   A=00 BC=0200 DE=0140 HL=000F S=0300 P=0119 0119' JP   NZ,010F
          A'=00 B'=0000 D'=0000 H'=0000 X=0000 Y=0000 I=00        (010F')
      N   A=00 BC=0200 DE=0140 HL=000F S=0300 P=010F 010F' SRL  C
          A'=00 B'=0000 D'=0000 H'=0000 X=0000 Y=0000 I=00
Z  V      A=00 BC=0200 DE=0140 HL=000F S=0300 P=0111 0111' JR   NC,0114
          A'=00 B'=0000 D'=0000 H'=0000 X=0000 Y=0000 I=00        (0114')
Z  V      A=00 BC=0200 DE=0140 HL=000F S=0300 P=0114 0114' SLA  E
          A'=00 B'=0000 D'=0000 H'=0000 X=0000 Y=0000 I=00
S         A=00 BC=0200 DE=0180 HL=000F S=0300 P=0116 0116' RL   D
          A'=00 B'=0000 D'=0000 H'=0000 X=0000 Y=0000 I=00
          A=00 BC=0200 DE=0280 HL=000F S=0300 P=0118 0118' DEC  B
          A'=00 B'=0000 D'=0000 H'=0000 X=0000 Y=0000 I=00
      N   A=00 BC=0100 DE=0280 HL=000F S=0300 P=0119 0119' JP   NZ,010F
          A'=00 B'=0000 D'=0000 H'=0000 X=0000 Y=0000 I=00        (010F')
      N   A=00 BC=0100 DE=0280 HL=000F S=0300 P=010F 010F' SRL  C
          A'=00 B'=0000 D'=0000 H'=0000 X=0000 Y=0000 I=00
Z  V      A=00 BC=0100 DE=0280 HL=000F S=0300 P=0111 0111' JR   NC,0114
          A'=00 B'=0000 D'=0000 H'=0000 X=0000 Y=0000 I=00        (0114')
Z  V      A=00 BC=0100 DE=0280 HL=000F S=0300 P=0114 0114' SLA  E
          A'=00 B'=0000 D'=0000 H'=0000 X=0000 Y=0000 I=00
Z  V C    A=00 BC=0100 DE=0200 HL=000F S=0300 P=0116 0116' RL   D
          A'=00 B'=0000 D'=0000 H'=0000 X=0000 Y=0000 I=00
   V      A=00 BC=0100 DE=0500 HL=000F S=0300 P=0118 0118' DEC  B
          A'=00 B'=0000 D'=0000 H'=0000 X=0000 Y=0000 I=00
Z  N      A=00 BC=0000 DE=0500 HL=000F S=0300 P=0119 0119' JP   NZ,010F
          A'=00 B'=0000 D'=0000 H'=0000 X=0000 Y=0000 I=00        (010F')
Z  N      A=00 BC=0000 DE=0500 HL=000F S=0300 P=011C 011C' LD   (0204),HL
          A'=00 B'=0000 D'=0000 H'=0000 X=0000 Y=0000 I=00        (0204')
Z  N      A=00 BC=0000 DE=0500 HL=000F S=0300 P=011F 011F' NOP
          A'=00 B'=0000 D'=0000 H'=0000 X=0000 Y=0000 I=00
```

Fig. 3.39: Multiplication: A Complete Trace (continued)

ANSWERS TO EXERCISE 3.18 (MULTIPLICATION):

```
CROMEMCO CDOS Z80 ASSEMBLER version 02.15                    PAGE 0001

0000'              0001         ORG    0100H
      (0200)       0002 MPRAD   DL     0200H
      (0202)       0003 MPDAD   DL     0202H
      (0204)       0004 RESAD   DL     0204H
                   0005 ;
0100  ED4B0002     0006 MP488   LD     BC,(MPRAD)    ;LOAD MULTIPLIER INTO C
0104  0608         0007         LD     B,8           ;B IS BIT COUNTER
0106  ED5B0202     0008         LD     DE,(MPDAD)    ;LOAD MUTIFLICAND INTO E
010A  1600         0009         LD     D,0           ;CLEAR D
010C  210000       0010         LD     HL,0          ;SET RESULT TO 0
010F  CB39         0011 MULT    SRL    C             ;SHIFT MULTIPLIER BIT INTO CARRY
0111  3001         0012         JR     NC,NOADD      ;TEST CARRY
0113  19           0013         ADD    HL,DE         ;ADD MPD TO RESULT
0114  CB23         0014 NOADD   SLA    E             ;SHIFT MPD LEFT
0116  CB12         0015         RL     D             ;SAVE BIT IN D
0118  05           0016         DEC    B             ;DECREMENT SHIFT COUNTER
0119  C20F01       0017         JP     NZ,MULT       ;DO IT AGAIN IF COUNTER <> 0
011C  220402       0018         LD     (RESAD),HL    ;STORE RESULT
011F  (0000)       0019         END

Errors       0
```

Fig. 3.40: The Multiplication Program (Hex)

LABEL	INSTRUCTION	B	C	C (CARRY)	D	E	H	L
		00	00	0	00	00	00	00
MP488	LD BC,(0200)	00	03	0	00	00	00	00
	LD B,08	08	03	0	00	00	00	00
	LD DE,(0202)	08	03	0	00	05	00	00
	LD D,00	08	03	0	00	05	00	00
	LD HL,0000	08	03	0	00	05	00	00
MULT	SRL C	08	01	1	00	05	00	00
	JR NC,0114	08	01	1	00	05	00	00
	ADD HL,DE	08	01	0	00	05	00	05
NOADD	SLA E	08	01	0	00	0A	00	05
	RL D	08	01	0	00	0A	00	05
	DEC B	07	01	0	00	0A	00	05
	JP NZ,010F	07	01	0	00	0A	00	05
MULT	SRL C	07	00	1	00	0A	00	05
	JR NC,0114	07	00	1	00	0A	00	05
	ADD HL,DE	07	00	0	00	0A	00	0F
NOADD	SLA E	07	00	0	00	14	00	0F
	RL D	07	00	0	00	14	00	0F
	DEC B	06	00	0	00	14	00	0F
	JP NZ,010F	06	00	0	00	14	00	0F

Fig. 3.41: Two Iterations Through the Loop

153

4

THE Z80 INSTRUCTION SET

INTRODUCTION

This chapter will first analyze the various classes of instructions which should be available in a general-purpose computer. It will then analyze one by one all of the instructions available for the Z80, and explain in detail their purpose and the manner in which they affect flags or can be used in conjunction with various addressing modes. A detailed discussion of addressing techniques will be presented in Chapter 5.

CLASSES OF INSTRUCTIONS

Instructions may be classified in many ways, and there is no standard. We will here distinguish five main categories of instructions:

1—data transfers
2—data processing
3—test and branch
4—input/output
5—control

Let us now examine each of these classes of instructions in turn.

Data Transfers

Data transfer instructions will transfer data between registers, or between a register and memory, or between a register and an input/output device. Specialized transfer instructions may exist for registers which play a specific role. For example, push and pop operations are provided for efficient stack operation. They will move a word of data between the top of the stack and the accumulator in a single instruction, while automatically updating the stack-pointer register.

Data Processing

Data processing instructions fall into five general categories:

1—arithmetic operations (such as plus/minus)
2—bit manipulation (set and reset)
3—increment and decrement
4—logical operations (such as AND, OR, exclusive OR)
5—skew and shift operations (such as shift, rotate)

It should be noted that, for efficient data processing, it is desirable to have powerful arithmetic instructions, such as multiply and divide. Unfortunately, they are not available on most microprocessors. It is also desirable to have powerful shift and skew instructions, such as shift n bits, or a nibble exchange, where the right half and the left half of the byte are exchanged. These are also usually unavailable on most microprocessors.

Before examining the actual Z80 instructions, let us recall the difference between a *shift* and a *rotation*. The shift will move the contents of a register or a memory location by one bit location to the left or to the right. The bit falling out of the register will go into the carry bit. The bit coming in on the other side will be a "0" except in the case of an "arithmetic shift right," where the MSB will be duplicated.

In the case of a rotation, the bit coming out still goes in the carry. However, the bit coming in is the previous value which was in the carry bit. This corresponds to a 9-bit rotation. It is often desirable to have a true 8-bit rotation where the bit coming in on one side is the one falling from the other side. This is not provided on most microprocessors but is available on the Z80 (see Figure 4.1).

Finally, when shifting a word to the right, it is convenient to have one more type of shift, called a sign extension or an "arithmetic shift right." When doing operations on two's complement numbers, particularly when implementing floating-point routines, it is often necessary to shift a negative number to the right. When shifting a two's complement number to the right, the bit which must come in on the left side should be a "1" (the sign should get repeated as many times as needed by the successive shifts). This is the arithmetic shift right.

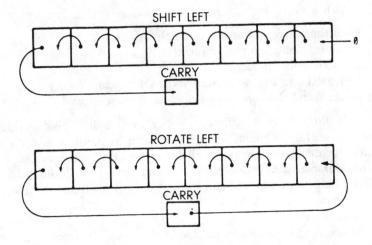

Fig. 4.1: Shift and Rotate

Test and Jump

The test instructions will test bits in the specified register for "0" or "1", or combinations. At a minimum, it must be possible to test the flags register. It is, therefore, desirable to have as many flags as possible in this register. In addition, it is convenient to be able to test for combinations of such bits with a single instruction. Finally, it is desirable to be able to test *any bit position in any register,* and to test the value of a register compared to the value of any other register (greater than, less than, equal). Microprocessor test instructions are usually limited to testing single bits of the flags register. The Z80, however, offers better facilities than most.

The jump instructions that may be available generally fall into three categories:

1—the jump, which specifies a full 16-bit address
2—the relative jump, which often is restricted to an 8-bit displacement field
3—the call, which is used with subroutines

It is convenient to have two- or even three-way jumps, depending, for example, on whether the result of a comparison is "greater than," "less than," or "equal." It is also convenient to have skip operations, which will jump forward or backwards by a few instructions. However, a "skip" is equivalent to a "jump." Finally, in most loops, there is usually a decrement or increment operation at the end, followed by a test-and-branch. The availability of a single-instruction increment/decrement plus test-and-branch is, therefore, a significant advantage for efficient loop implementation. This is not available in most microprocessors. Only simple branches, combined with simple tests, are available. This, naturally, complicates programming and reduces efficiency. In the case of the Z80, a "decrement and jump" instruction is available. However, it only tests a specific register (B) for zero.

Input/Output

Input/output instructions are specialized instructions for the handling of input/output devices. In practice, a majority of the 8-bit microprocessors use *memory-mapped I/O:* input/output devices are connected to the address bus just like memory chips, and addressed as such. They appear to the programmer as memory locations. All memory-type operations normally require 3 bytes and are, therefore, slow. For efficient input/output handling in such an environment, it is desirable to have a short addressing mechanism available so that I/O devices whose handling speed is crucial may reside in page 0. However, if page 0 addressing is available, it is usually used for RAM memory, which prevents its effective use for input/output devices. The Z80, like the 8080, is equipped with specialized I/O instructions. As a result, in the case of the Z80, the designer may use either method: input/output devices may be addressed as memory devices, or else as input/output devices, using the I/O instructions.

They will be described later in this chapter.

Control Instructions

Control instructions supply synchronization signals and may suspend or interrupt a program. They can also function as a break or a simulated interrupt. (Interrupts will be described in Chapter 6 on Input/Output Techniques.)

157

THE Z80 INSTRUCTION SET

Introduction

The Z80 microprocessor was designed to be a replacement for the 8080, and to offer additional capabilities. As a result of this design philosophy, the Z80 offers all the instructions of the 8080, plus additional instructions. In view of the limited number of bits available in an 8-bit opcode, one may wonder how the designers of the Z80 succeeded in implementing many additional ones. They did so by using a few unused 8080 opcodes and by adding an additional byte to the opcode for indexed operations. This is why some of the Z80 instructions occupy up to five bytes in the memory.

It is important to remember that any program can be written in many different ways. A thorough knowledge and understanding of the instruction set is indispensable for achieving efficient programming. However, when learning how to program, it is not essential to write optimized programs. During a first reading of this chapter, it is therefore unimportant to remember all the various instructions. It is important to remember the categories of instructions and to study typical examples. Then, when writing programs, the reader should consult the Z80 instruction-set description, and select the instructions best suited to his needs. The various instructions of the Z80 will therefore be reviewed in this section with the intent of simplifying them and grouping them in logical categories. The reader interested in exploring the capabilities of the various instructions is referred to the individual descriptions of the instructions.

We will now examine the capabilities provided by the Z80 in terms of the five classes of instructions which have been defined at the beginning of this chapter.

Data Transfer Instructions

Data transfer instructions on the Z80 may be classified in four categories: 8-bit transfers, 16-bit transfers, stack operations, and block transfers. Let us examine them.

Eight-Bit Data Transfers

All eight-bit data transfers are accomplished by load instructions. The format is:

LD   destination, source

For example, the accumulator A may be loaded from register B by using the instructions:

LD   A,B

Direct transfers may be accomplished between any two of the working registers (ABCDEHL).

In order to load any of the working registers, except for the accumulator, from a memory location, the address of this memory location must first be loaded into the H-L register pair.

For example, in order to load register C from memory location 1234, register H and L will first have to be loaded with the value "1234". (A load instruction operating on 16 bits will be used. This is described in the following section.)

Then, the instruction LD C, (HL) will be used and will accomplish the desired result.

The accumulator is an exception. It can be loaded directly from any specified memory location. This is called the extended addressing mode. For example, in order to load the accumulator with the contents of memory location 1234, the following instruction will be used:

LD A, (1234H)   (Note the use of "( )" to denote "contents of.")

The instruction will be stored in the memory as follows:

```
address   PC    :3A      (opcode)
          PC + 1:34      (low order half of the address)
          PC + 2:12      (high order half of the address)
```

Note that the address is stored in "reverse order" in the instruction itself:

3A	low addr	high addr

All the working registers may also be loaded with any specified eight-bit value, or "literal," contained in the second byte of the instruction (this is called *immediate addressing).* An example is:

LD E, 12H

which loads register E with the value 12 hexadecimal.

In the memory, the instruction appears as:

```
          PC: 1E      (opcode)
          PC + 1: 12  (literal operand)
```

159

As a result of this instruction, the immediate operand, or literal value will be contained in register E.

The *indexed addressing* mode is also available for loading register contents, and will be fully described in the next chapter on addressing techniques. Other miscellaneous possibilities exist for loading specific registers, and a table listing all the possibilities is shown in Figure 4.2 (tables supplied by Zilog, Inc.). The grey areas show instructions common with the 8080A.

		IMPLIED		REGISTER							REG INDIRECT			INDEXED		EXT. ADDR.	IMME.
		I	R	A	B	C	D	E	H	L	(HL)	(BC)	(DE)	(IX+d)	(IY+d)	(nn)	n
REGISTER	A	ED 57	ED 5F	7F	78	79	7A	7B	7C	7D	7E	0A	1A	DD 7E d	FD 7E d	3A n n	3E n
	B			47	40	41	42	43	44	45	46			DD 46 d	FD 46 d		06 n
	C			4F	48	49	4A	4B	4C	4D	4E			DD 4E d	FD 4E d		0E n
	D			57	50	51	52	53	54	55	56			DD 56 d	FD 56 d		16 n
	E			5F	58	59	5A	5B	5C	5D	5E			DD 5E d	FD 5E d		1E n
	H			67	60	61	62	63	64	65	66			DD 66 d	FD 66 d		26 n
	L			6F	68	69	6A	6B	6C	6D	6E			DD 6E d	FD 6E d		2E n
REG INDIRECT	(HL)			77	70	71	72	73	74	75							36 n
	(BC)			02													
	(DE)			12													
INDEXED	(IX+d)			DD 77 d	DD 70 d	DD 71 d	DD 72 d	DD 73 d	DD 74 d	DD 75 d							DD 36 d n
	(IY+d)			FD 77 d	FD 70 d	FD 71 d	FD 72 d	FD 73 d	FD 74 d	FD 75 d							FD 36 d n
EXT. ADDR.	(nn)			32 n n													
IMPLIED	I			ED 47													
	R			ED 4F													

Fig. 4.2: Eight-Bit Load Group—'LD'

16-Bit Data Transfers

Basically, any of the 16-bit register pairs, BC, DE, HL, SP, IX, IY, may be loaded with a literal 16-bit operand, or from a specified memory address *(extended addressing)*, or from the top of the stack, i.e., from the address contained in SP. Conversely, the contents of these register pairs may be stored in the same manner at a specified memory address or on top of the stack. Additionally, the SP register may be loaded from HL, IX, and IY. This facilitates creating multiple stacks. The register pair AF may also be pushed on top of the stack.

The table listing all the possibilities is shown in Figure 4.3. The stack push and pop operations are included as parts of the 16-bit data transfers. All stack operations transfer the contents of a register pair to or from the stack. Note that there are no single push and pop instructions for saving individual eight-bit registers.

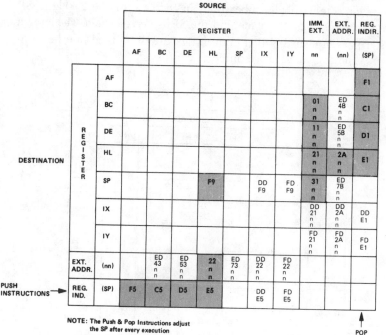

DESTINATION		AF	BC	DE	HL	SP	IX	IY	IMM. EXT. nn	EXT. ADDR. (nn)	REG. INDIR. (SP)
REGISTER	AF										F1
	BC								01 n n	ED 4B n n	C1
	DE								11 n n	ED 5B n n	D1
	HL								21 n n	2A n n	E1
	SP				F9		DD F9	FD F9	31 n n	ED 7B n n	
	IX								DD 21 n n	DD 2A n n	DD E1
	IY								FD 21 n n	FD 2A n n	FD E1
EXT. ADDR.	(nn)		ED 43 n n	ED 53 n n	22 n n	ED 73 n n	DD 22 n n	FD 22 n n			
REG. IND.	(SP)	F5	C5	D5	E5		DD E5	FD E5			

NOTE: The Push & Pop Instructions adjust the SP after every execution

← PUSH INSTRUCTIONS

POP INSTRUCTIONS →

Fig. 4.3: 16-Bit Load Group—'LD', 'PUSH' and 'POP'

A double-byte push or pop is always executed on a register pair: AF, BC, DE, HL, IX, IY (see the bottom row and right-most column in Figure: 4.3).

When operating on AF, BC, DE, HL, a single-byte is required for the instruction, resulting in good efficiency. For example, assume that the stack pointer SP contains the value "0100". The following instruction is executed:

PUSH AF

When pushing the contents of the register pair on the stack, the stack pointer SP is first decremented, then the contents of register A are deposited on top of the stack. Then the SP is decremented again, and the contents of F are deposited on the stack. At the end of the stack transfer, SP points to the top element of the stack, which in our example is the value of F.

It is important to remember that, in the case of the Z80, the SP points to the *top* of the stack and the SP is *decremented* whenever a register pair is pushed. Other conventions are often used in other processors, and this may be a source of confusion.

		IMPLIED ADDRESSING				
		AF'	BC', DE' & HL'	HL	IX	IY
IMPLIED	AF	08				
	BC, DE & HL		D9			
	DE			EB		
REG. INDIR.	(SP)			E3	DD E3	FD E3

Fig. 4.4: Exchanges 'EX' and 'EXX'

Exchange Instructions

Additionally, a specialized mnemonic EX has been reserved for exchange operations. EX is not a simple data transfer, but a dual data transfer. It actually changes the contents of *two* specified locations. EX may be used to exchange the top of the stack with HL, IX, IY and also to swap the contents of DE and HL and AF and AF' (remember that AF' stands for the other AF register pair available in the Z80).

Finally, a special EXX instruction is available to exchange the contents of BC, DE, HL with the contents of the corresponding registers in the second register bank of the Z80.

The possible exchanges are summarized in Figure 4.4.

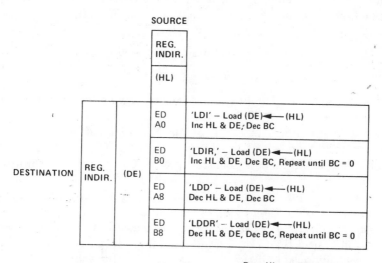

			SOURCE

			REG. INDIR.
			(HL)

			ED A0	'LDI' – Load (DE)◄——(HL) Inc HL & DE, Dec BC
			ED B0	'LDIR,' – Load (DE)◄——(HL) Inc HL & DE, Dec BC, Repeat until BC = 0
DESTINATION	REG. INDIR.	(DE)	ED A8	'LDD' – Load (DE)◄——(HL) Dec HL & DE, Dec BC
			ED B8	'LDDR' – Load (DE)◄——(HL) Dec HL & DE, Dec BC, Repeat until BC = 0

Reg HL   points to source
Reg DE   points to destination
Reg BC   is byte counter

Fig. 4.5: Block Transfer Group

Block Transfer Instructions

Block transfer instructions are instructions which will result in the transfer of a block of data rather than a single or double byte. Block transfer instructions are more complex for the manufacturer to implement than most instructions and are usually not provided on microprocessors. They are convenient for programming, and may improve the performance of a program, especially during input/output operation. Their use and advantages will be demonstrated throughout this book. Some automatic block transfer instructions are available in the case of the Z80. They use specific conventions.

All block transfer instructions require the use of three pairs of registers: BC, DE, HL:

BC is used as a 16-bit counter. This means that up to 2^{16} = 64K bytes may be moved automatically. HL is used as the source pointer. It may point anywhere in the memory. DE is used as the destination pointer and may point anywhere in the memory.

Four block transfer instructions are provided:

LDD, LDDR, LDI, LDIR

All of them decrement the counter register BC with each transfer. Two of them decrement the pointer registers DE and HL, LDD and LDDR, while the two others increment DE and HL, LDI and LDIR. For each of these two groups of instructions, the letter R at the end of the mnemonic indicates an automatic repeat. Let us examine these instructions.

LDI stands for "load and increment." It transfers one byte from the memory location pointed to by H and L to the destination in the memory pointed to by D and E. It also decrements BC. It will automatically increment H and L and D and E so that all register pairs are properly conditioned to perform the next byte transfer whenever required.

LDIR stands for "load increment and repeat," i.e., execute LDI repeatedly until the counter registers BC reach the value "0". It is used to move a continuous block of data automatically from one memory area to another.

LDD and LDDR operate in the same way except that the address pointer is *decremented* rather than incremented. The transfer therefore starts at the *highest* address in the block instead of the lowest. The effect of the four instructions is summarized in Figure 4.5.

Similar automated instructions are available for CP (compare) and are summarized in Figure 4.6.

Data Processing Instructions

Arithmetic

Two main arithmetic operations are provided: addition and subtraction. They have been used extensively in the previous chapter. There are two types of addition, with and without carry, ADC and ADD respec-

SEARCH
LOCATION

REG. INDIR. (HL)	
ED A1	'CPI' Inc HL, Dec BC
ED B1	'CPIR', Inc HL, Dec BC repeat until BC = 0 or find match
ED A9	'CPD' Dec HL & BC
ED' B9	'CPDR' Dec HL & BC Repeat until BC = 0 or find match

HL points to location in memory
to be compared with accumulator
contents
BC is byte counter

Fig. 4.6: Block Search Group

tively. Similarly, two types of subtraction are provided with and without carry. They are SBC and SUB.

Additionally, three special instructions are provided: DAA, CPL, and NEG. The Decimal Adjust Accumulator instruction DAA has been used to implement BCD operations. It is normally used for each BCD add or subtract. Two complementation instructions also are available. CPL will compute the one's complement of the accumulator, and NEG will negate the accumulator into its complement format (two's complement).

All the previous instructions operate on eight-bit data. 16-bit operations are more restricted. ADD, ADC, and SBC are available on specific registers, as described in Figure 4.8.

Finally, increment and decrement instructions are available which operate on all the registers, both in an eight-bit and a 16-bit format. They are listed in Figure 4.7 (eight-bit operations) and 4.8 (16-bit operations).

SOURCE

	REGISTER ADDRESSING							REG. INDIR.	INDEXED		IMMED.
	A	B	C	D	E	H	L	(HL)	(IX+d)	(IY+d)	n
'ADD'	87	80	81	82	83	84	85	86	DD 86 d	FD 86 d	C6 n
ADD w CARRY 'ADC'	8F	88	89	8A	8B	8C	8D	8E	DD 8E d	FD 8E d	CE n
SUBTRACT 'SUB'	97	90	91	92	93	94	95	96	DD 96 d	FD 96 d	D6 n .
SUB w CARRY 'SBC'	9F	98	99	9A	9B	9C	9D	9E	DD 9E d	FD 9E d	DE n
'AND'	A7	A6	A1	A2	A3	A4	A5	A6	DD A6 d	FD A6 d	E6 n
'XOR'	AF	A8	A9	AA	AB	AC	AD	AE	DD AE d	FD AE d	EE n
'OR'	B7	B0	B1	B2	B3	B4	B5	B6	DD B6 d	FD B6 d	F6 n
COMPARE 'CP'	BF	B8	B9	BA	BB	BC	BD	BE	DD BE d	FD BE d	FE n
INCREMENT 'INC'	3C	04	0C	14	1C	24	2C	34	DD 34 d	FD 34 d	
DECREMENT 'DEC'	3D	05	0D	15	1D	25	2D	35	DD 35 d	FD 35 d	

Fig. 4.7: Eight-Bit Arithmetic and Logic

Note that, in general, all arithmetic operations modify some of the flags. Their effect is fully described in the instruction descriptions later in this chapter. However, it is important to note that the INC and DEC instructions which operate on register pairs do not modify any of the flags. This detail is important to keep in mind. This means that if you increment or decrement one of the register pairs to the value "0", the Z-bit in the flags register F will not be set. The value of the register must be explicitly tested for the value "0" in the program.

Also, it is important to remember that the instructions ADC and SBC always affect all the flags. This does not mean that all the flags will necessarily be different after their execution. However, they might.

SOURCE

DESTINATION			BC	DE	HL	SP	IX	IY
'ADD'		HL	09	19	29	39		
		IX	DD 09	DD 19		DD 39	DD 29	
		IY	FD 09	FD 19		FD 39		FD 29
ADD WITH CARRY AND SET FLAGS 'ADC'		HL	ED 4A	ED 5A	ED 6A	ED 7A		
SUB WITH CARRY AND SET FLAGS 'SBC'		HL	ED 42	ED 52	ED 62	ED 72		
INCREMENT 'INC'			03	13	23	33	DD 23	FD 23
DECREMENT 'DEC'			0B	1B	2B	3B	DD 2B	FD 2B

Fig. 4.8: Sixteen-Bit Arithmetic and Logic

Logical

Three logical operations are provided: AND, OR (inclusive) and XOR (exclusive), plus a comparison instruction CP. They all operate exclusively on eight-bit data. Let us examine them in turn. (A table listing all the possibilities and operation codes for these instructions is part of Figure 4.7.)

AND

Each logical operation is characterized by a *truth table,* which expresses the logical value of the result in function of the inputs. The truth table for AND appears below:

AND	0	1
0	0	0
1	0	1

0 AND 0 = 0
0 AND 1 = 0 or
1 AND 0 = 0
1 AND 1 = 1

The AND operation is characterized by the fact that the output is "1" only if both inputs are "1". In other words, if one of the inputs is "0", it is guaranteed that the result is "0". This feature is used to zero a bit position in a word. This is called "masking."

One of the important uses of the AND instruction is to clear or "mask out" one or more specified bit positions in a word. Assume for example that we want to zero the right-most four-bit positions in a word. This will be performed by the following program:

```
LD    A,  WORD       WORD CONTAINS '10101010'
AND   11110000B      '11110000' IS MASK
```

Let us assume that WORD is equal to '10101010'. The result of this program is to leave the value '10100000' in the accumulator. "B" is used to indicate a binary value.

Exercise 4.1: Write a three-line program which will zero bits 1 and 6 of WORD.

Exercise 4.2: What happens with a MASK = '11111111'?

OR

This instruction is the inclusive OR operation. It is characterized by the following truth table:

OR	0	1
0	0	1
1	1	1

0 OR 0 = 0
0 OR 1 = 1 or
1 OR 0 = 1
1 OR 1 = 1

The logical OR is characterized by the fact that if one of the operands is "1", then the result is always "1". The obvious use of OR is to set any bit in a word to "1".

Let us set the right-most four bits of WORD to 1's. The program is:

```
LD A, WORD
OR 00001111B
```

Let us assume that WORD did contain '10101010'. The final value of the accumulator will be '10101111'.

Exercise 4.3: What would happen if we were to use the instruction OR 10101111 B?

Exercise 4.4: What is the effect of ORing with "FF" hexadecimal?

XOR

XOR stands for "exclusive OR." The exclusive OR differs from the inclusive OR that we have just described in one respect: the result is "1" only if one, and only one, of the operands is equal to "1". If both operands are equal to "1", the normal OR would give a "1" result. The exclusive OR gives a "0" result. The truth table is:

	XOR	0	1
0 XOR 0 = 0	0	0	1
0 XOR 1 = 1 or	1	1	0
1 XOR 0 = 1			
1 XOR 1 = 0			

The exclusive OR is used for comparisons. If any bit is different, the exclusive OR of two words will be non-zero. In addition, in the case of the Z80, the exclusive OR may be used to *complement* a word, since there is no complement instruction on anything but the accumulator. This is done by performing the XOR of a word with all ones. The program appears below:

LD A, WORD
XOR, 11111111 B

Let us assume that WORD contained "10101010". The final value of the register will be "01010101". You can verify that this is the complement of the original value.

XOR can be used to advantage as a "bit toggle."

Exercise 4.5: What is the effect of XOR using a register with "00" hexadecimal?

Skew Operations (Shift and Rotate)

Let us first differentiate between the shift and the rotate operations, which are illustrated in Figure 4.9. In a shift operation, the contents of the register are shifted to the left or to the right by one bit position. The bit which falls out of the register goes into the carry bit C, and the bit which comes in is zero. This was explained in the previous section.

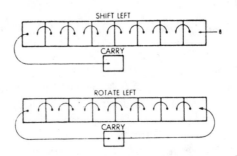

Fig. 4.9: Shift and Rotate

One exception exists: it is the *shift-right-arithmetic*. When performing operations on negative numbers in the two's complement format, the left-most bit is the sign bit. In the case of negative numbers it is "1". When dividing a negative number by "2" by shifting it to the right, it should remain negative, i.e., the left-most bit should remain a "1". This is performed automatically by the SRA instruction or Shift Right Arithmetic. In this arithmetic shift right, the bit which comes in on the left is identical to the sign bit. It is "0" if the left-most bit was a "0", and "1" if the left-most bit was a "1". This is illustrated on the right of Figure 4.10, which shows all the possible shift and rotate operations.

Rotations

A rotation differs from a shift by the fact that the bit coming into the register is the one which will fall from either the other end of the register or the carry bit. Two types of rotations are supplied in the case of the Z80: an eight-bit rotation and a nine-bit rotation.

The nine-bit rotation is illustrated in Figure 4.11. For example, in the case of a right rotation, the eight bits of the register are shifted right by one bit position. The bit which falls off the right part of the register goes, as usual, into the carry bit. At this time the bit which comes in on the left end of the register is the previous value of the carry bit (before it is overwritten with the bit falling out.) In mathematics this is called a nine-bit rotation since the eight bits of the register plus the ninth bit (the carry bit) are rotated to the right by one bit position. Conversely, the left rotation accomplishes the same result in the opposite direction.

Source and Destination

TYPE OF ROTATE OR SHIFT		A	B	C	D	E	H	L	(HL)	(IX + d)	(IY + d)
	'RLC'	CB 07	CB 00	CB 01	CB 02	CB 03	CB 04	CB 05	CB 06	DD CB d 06	FD CB d 06
	'RRC'	CB 0F	CB 08	CB 09	CB 0A	CB 0B	CB 0C	CB 0D	CB 0E	DD CB d 0E	FD CB d 0E
	'RL'	CB 17	CB 10	CB 11	CB 12	CB 13	CB 14	CB 15	CB 16	DD CB d 16	FD CB d 16
	'RR'	CB 1F	CB 18	CB 19	CB 1A	CB 1B	CB 1C	CB 1D	CB 1E	DD CB d 1E	FD CB d 1E
	'SLA'	CB 27	CB 20	CB 21	CB 22	CB 23	CB 24	CB 25	CB 26	DD CB d 26	FD CB d 26
	'SRA'	CB 2F	CB 28	CB 29	CB 2A	CB 2B	CB 2C	CB 2D	CB 2E	DD CB d 2E	FD CB d 2E
	'SRL'	CB 3F	CB 38	CB 39	CB 3A	CB 3B	CB 3C	CB 3D	CB 3E	DD CB d 3E	FD CB d 3E
	'RLD'								ED 6F		
	'RRD'								ED 67		

	A
RLCA	07
RRCA	0F
RLA	17
RRA	1F

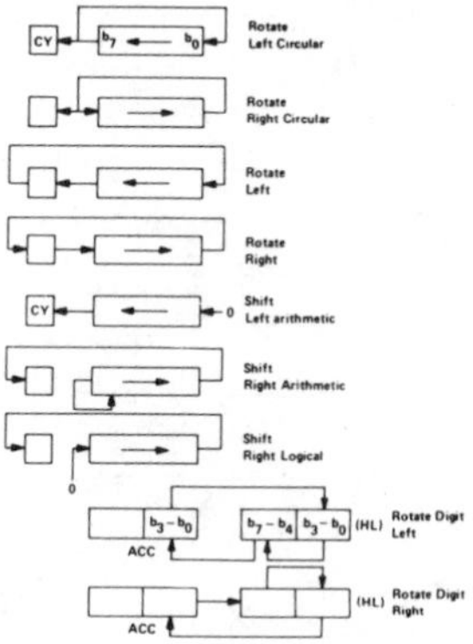

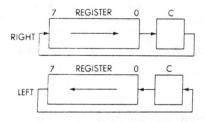

Fig. 4.10: Rotates and Shifts

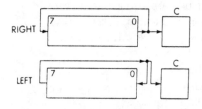

Fig. 4.11: Nine-Bit Rotation

The eight-bit rotation operates in a similar way. Bit 0 is copied into bit seven, or else bit seven is copied into bit 0, depending on the direction of the rotation. In addition, the bit coming out of the register is also copied in the carry bit. This is illustrated by Figure 4.12.

Fig. 4.12: Eight-Bit Rotation

Special Digit Instructions

Two special digit-rotate instructions are provided to facilitate BCD arithmetic. The result is a four-bit rotation between two digits contained in the memory location pointed to by the HL registers and one digit in the lower half of the accumulator. This is illustrated by Figure 4.13.

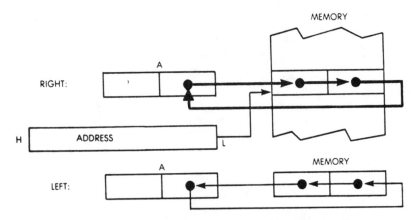

Fig. 4.13: Digit Rotate Instructions (Rotate Decimal)

Bit Manipulation

It has been shown above how the logical operations may be used to set or reset bits or groups of bits in the accumulator. However, it is convenient to set or reset any bit in any register or memory location with a single instruction. This facility requires a considerable number of opcodes and is therefore usually not provided on most microprocessors. However, the Z80 is equipped with extensive bit-manipulation facilities. They are shown in Figure 4.14. This table also includes the test instructions which will be described only in the next section.

Two special instructions are also available for operating on the carry flag. They are CCF (Complement Carry Flag) and SCF (Set Carry Flag). They are shown in Figure 4.15.

Test and Jump

Since testing operations rely heavily on the use of the flags register, we will here describe in detail the role of each of the flags. The contents of the flags register appear in Figure 4.16.

	BIT	REGISTER ADDRESSING							REG. INDIR.	INDEXED	
		A	B	C	D	E	H	L	(HL)	(IX+d)	(IY+d)
TEST 'BIT'	0	CB 47	CB 40	CB 41	CB 42	CB 43	CB 44	CB 45	CB 46	DD CB d 46	FD CB d 46
	1	CB 4F	CB 48	CB 49	CB 4A	CB 4B	CB 4C	CB 4D	CB 4E	DD CB d 4E	FD CB d 4E
	2	CB 57	CB 50	CB 51	CB 52	CB 53	CB 54	CB 55	CB 56	DD CB d 56	FD CB d 56
	3	CB 5F	CB 58	CB 59	CB 5A	CB 5B	CB 5C	CB 5D	CB 5E	DD CB d 5E	FD CB d 5E
	4	CB 67	CB 60	CB 61	CB 62	CB 63	CB 64	CB 65	CB 66	DD CB d 66	FD CB d 66
	5	CB 6F	CB 68	CB 69	CB 6A	CB 6B	CB 6C	CB 6D	CB 6E	DD CB d 6E	FD CB d 6E
	6	CB 77	CB 70	CB 71	CB 72	CB 73	CB 74	GB 75	CB 76	DD CB d 76	FD CB d 76
	7	CB 7F	CB 78	CB 79	CB 7A	CB 7B	CB 7C	CB 7D	CB 7E	DD CB d 7E	FD CB d 7E
RESET BIT 'RES'	0	CB 87	CB 80	CB 81	CB 82	CB 83	CB 84	CB 85	CB 86	DD CB d 86	FD CB d 86
	1	CB 8F	CB 88	CB 89	CB 8A	CB 8B	CB 8C	CB 8D	CB 8E	DD CB d 8E	FD CB d 8E
	2	CB 97	CB 90	CB 91	CB 92	CB 93	CB 94	CB 95	CB 96	DD CB d 96	FD CB d 96
	3	CB 9F	CB 98	CB 99	CB 9A	CB 9B	CB 9C	CB 9D	CB 9E	DD CB d 9E	FD CB d 9E
	4	CB A7	CB A0	CB A1	CB A2	CB A3	CB A4	CB A5	CB A6	DD CB d A6	FD CB d A6
	5	CB AF	CB A8	CB A9	CB AA	CB AB	CB AC	CB AD	CB AE	DD CB d AE	FD CB d AE
	6	CB B7	CB B0	CB B1	CB B2	CB B3	CB B4	CB B5	CB B6	DD CB d B6	FD CB d B6
	7	CB BF	CB B8	CB B9	CB BA	CB BB	CB BC	CB BD	CB BE	DD CB d BE	FD CB d BE
SET BIT 'SET'	0	CB C7	CB C0	CB C1	CB C2	CB C3	CB C4	CB C5	CB C6	DD CB d C6	FD CB d C6
	1	CB CF	CB C8	CB C9	CB CA	CB CB	CB CC	CB CD	CB CE	DD CB d CE	FD CB d CE
	2	CB D7	CB D0	CB D1	CB D2	CB D3	CB D4	CB D5	CB D6	DD CB d D6	FD CB d D6
	3	CB DF	CB D8	CB D9	CB DA	CB DB	CB DC	CB DD	CB DE	DD CB d DE	FD CB d DE
	4	CB E7	CB E0	CB E1	CB E2	CB E3	CB E4	CB E5	CB E6	DD CB d E6	FD CB d E6
	5	CB EF	CB E8	CB E9	CB EA	CB EB	CB EC	CB ED	CB EE	DD CB d EE	FD CB d EE
	6	CB F7	CB F0	CB F1	CB F2	CB F3	CB F4	CB F5	CB F6	DD CB d F6	FD CB d F6
	7	CB FF	CB F8	CB F9	CB FA	CB FB	CB FC	CB FD	CB FE	DD CB d FE	FD CB d FE

Fig. 4.14: Bit Manipulation Group

Decimal Adjust Acc, 'DAA'	27
Complement Acc, 'CPL'	2F
Negate Acc, 'NEG' (2's complement)	ED 44
Complement Carry Flag, 'CCF'	3F
Set Carry Flag, 'SCF'	37

Fig. 4.15: General-Purpose AF Operations

7	6	5	4	3	2	1	0
S	Z	—	H	—	P/V	N	C
(T)	(T)				(T)		(T)

Fig. 4.16: The Flags Register

C is the carry, N is add or subtract, P/V is parity or overflow, H is half carry, Z is zero, S is sign. Bits 3 and 5 of the flags register are not used (" – "). The two flags H and N are used for BCD arithmetic and cannot be tested. The other four flags (C, P/V, Z, S) can be tested in conjunction with conditional jump or call instructions.

The role of each flag will now be described.

Carry (C)

In the case of nearly all microprocessors, and of the Z80 in particular, the carry bit assumes a dual role. First, it is used to indicate whether an addition or subtraction operation has resulted in a carry (or borrow). Secondly, it is used as a ninth bit in the case of shift and rotate operations. Using a single bit to perform both roles facilitates some operations, such as a multiplication operation. This should be clear from the explanation of the multiplication which has been presented in the previous chapter.

When learning to use the carry bit, it is important to remember that all arithmetic operations will either set it or reset it, depending on the result of the instructions. Similarly, all shift and rotation operations use the carry bit and will either set it or reset it, depending on the value of the bit which comes out of the register.

In the case of logical instructions (AND, OR, XOR), the carry bit will always be reset. They may be used to zero the carry explicitly.

Instructions which affect the carry bit are: ADD A,s; ADC A,s; SUB s; SBC A,s; CP s; NEG; AND s; OR s; XOR s; ADD DD,ss; ADC HL,ss; SBC HL,ss; RLA; RLCA; RRA; RRCA; RL m; RLC m; RR m; RRC m; SLA m; SRA m; SRL m; DAA; SCF; CCF.

Subtract (N)

This flag is normally not used by the programmer, and is used by the Z80 itself during BCD operations. The reader will remember from the previous chapter that, following a BCD add or subtract, a DAA (Decimal Adjust Accumulator) instruction is executed to obtain the valid BCD results. However, the "adjustment" operation is different after an addition and after a subtraction. The DAA therefore executes differently depending on the value of the N flag. The N flag is set to "0" after an addition and is set to a "1" after a subtraction.

The symbol used for this flag, "N", may be confusing to programmers who have used other processors, since it may be mistaken for the sign bit. It is an internal operation sign bit.

N is set to "0" by: ADD A,s; ADC A,s; AND s; OR s; XOR s; INC s; ADD DD,ss; ADC HL,ss; RLA; RLCA; RRA; RRCA; RL m; RLC m; RR m; RRC m; SLA m; SRA m; SRL m; RLD; RRD; SCF; CCF; IN r, (C); LDI; LDD; LDIR; LDDR; LD A, I; LD A, R; BIT b, s.

N is set to "1" by: SUB s; SBC A,s; CP s; NEG; DEC m; SBC HL, ss; CPL; INI; IND; OUTI; OUTD; INIR; INDR; OTIR; OTDR; CPI; CPIR; CPD; CPDR.

Parity/Overflow (P/V)

The parity/overflow flag performs two different functions. Specific instructions will set or reset this flag depending on the parity of the result; parity is determined by counting the total number of ones in the result. If this number is odd, the parity bit will be set to "0" (odd parity). If it is even, the parity bit will be set to "1" (even parity). Parity is most frequently used on blocks of characters (usually in the ASCII format). The parity bit is an additional bit which is added to the seven-bit code representing the character, in order to verify the integrity of data which has been stored in a memory device. For example, if one bit in the code representing the character has been changed by accident, due to a malfunction in the memory device (such as a disk or RAM memory), or during transmission, then the total number of ones in the seven-bit code will have been changed. By checking the parity bit, the discrepancy will be detected, and an error will be flagged. In particular, the flag is used with logical and rotate instructions. Also, naturally, during an input operation from an I/O device, the parity flag will indicate the parity of the data being read.

For the reader familiar with the Intel 8080, note that the parity flag in the 8080 is used exclusively as such. In the case of the Z80, it is used for several additional functions. This flag should therefore be handled with care when going from one of the microprocessors to the other.

In the case of the Z80, the second essential use of this flag is as an overflow flag (not available in the 8080). The overflow flag has been described in Chapter 1, when the two's complement notation was introduced. It detects the fact that, during an addition or subtraction, the sign of the result is "accidentally" changed due to the overflow of the result into the sign bit. (Recall that, using an eight-bit representation, the largest positive number is +127, and the smallest negative number is −128 in two's complement.)

Finally, this bit is also used, in the case of the Z80, for two unrelated functions.

During the block transfer instructions (LDD, LDDR, LDI, LDIR), and during the search instructions (CPD, CPDR, CPI, CPIR), this flag is used to detect whether the counter register B has attained the value "0". With decrementing instructions, this flag is reset to "0" if the byte counter register pair is "0". When incrementing, it is reset if BC − 1 = 0 at the beginning of the instruction, i.e., if BC will be decremented to "0" by the instruction.

Finally, when executing the two special instructions LD A,I and LD A,R, the P/V flag reflects the value of the interrupt enable flip-flop (IFF2). This feature can be used to preserve or test this value.

The P flag is affected by: AND s; OR s; XOR s; RL m; RLC m; RR m; RRC m; SLA m; SRA m; SRL m; RLD; RRD; DAA; IN r,(C).

The V flag is affected by: ADD A,s; ADC A,s; SUB s; SBC A,s; CP s; NEG; INC s; DEC m; ADC HL,ss; SBC HL,ss.

It is also used by: LDIR; LDDR (set to "0"); LDI; LDD; CPI; CPIR; CPD; CPDR.

The Half-Carry Flag (H)

The half-carry flag indicates a possible carry from bit 3 into bit 4 during an arithmetic operation. In other words, it represents the carry from the low-order nibble (group of 4 bits) into the high order one. Clearly, it is primarily used for BCD operations. In particular, it is used internally within the microprocessor by the Decimal Adjust Accumulator (DAA) instruction in order to adjust the result to its correct value.

This flag will be set during an addition when there is a carry from bit 3 to bit 4 and reset when there is no carry. Conversely, during a subtract operation, it will be set if there is a borrow from bit 4 to bit 3, and reset if there is no borrow.

The flag will be conditioned by addition, subtraction, increment, decrement, comparisons, and logical operations.

Instructions which affect the H bit are: ADD A,r ; ADC A,s; SUB s; SBC A,s; CP s; NEG; AND s; OR s; XOR s; INC s; DEC m; RLA; RLCA; RRA; RRCA; RL m; RLC m; RR m; RRC m; SLA m; SR m; SRL m; RLD; RRD; DAA; CPL; SCF; IN r,(C) ; LDI; LLD; LDIR; LDDR; LD A; LD A,R; BIT b,r; CPI; CPIR; CPD; CPDR.

Note that the H bit is randomly affected by the 16-bit add and subtract instructions, and by block input and output instructions.

Zero (Z)

The Z flag is used to indicate whether the value of a byte which has been computed, or is being transferred, is zero. It is also used with comparison instructions to indicate a match, and for other miscellaneous functions.

In the case of an operation resulting in a zero result, or of a data transfer, the Z bit is set to "1" whenever the byte is zero. Z is reset to "0" otherwise.

In the case of comparison instructions, the Z bit is set to "1" whenever the comparison succeeds and to "0" otherwise.

Additionally, in the case of the Z80, it is used for three more functions: it is used with the BIT instruction to indicate the value of a bit being tested. It is set to "1" if the specified bit is "0" and reset otherwise.

With the special "block input-output instructions" (INI, IND, OUTI, OUTD), the Z flag is set if $D - 1 = 0$, and reset otherwise; it is set if the byte counter will decrement to "0" (INIR, INDR, OTIR, OTDR).

Finally, with the special instructions IN r,(C), the Z flag is set to "1" to indicate that the input byte has the value "0".

In summary, the following instructions condition the value of the Z bit: ADD A,s; ADC A,s; SUB s; SBC A,s; CP s; NEG; AND s; OR s; XOR s; INC s; DEC m; ADC HL, ss; SBC HL,ss; RL m; RLC m;

RR m; RRC m; SLA m; SRA m; SRL m; RLD; RRD; DAA; IN r,(C); INI; IND; OUTI; OUTD; INIR; INDR; OTIR; OTDR; CPI; CPIR; CPD; CPDR; LD A, I; LD A, R; BIT b,s; NEG s.

Usual instructions which do not affect the Z bit are: ADD DD,ss; RLA; RLCA; RRA; RRCA; CPL; SCF; CCF; LDI; LDD; LDIR; LDDR; INC DD; DEC DD.

Sign (S)

This flag reflects the value of the most significant bit of a result or of a byte being transferred (bit seven). In two's complement notation, the most significant bit is used to represent the sign. "0" indicates a positive number and a "1" indicates a negative number. As a result, bit seven is called the sign bit.

In the case of most microprocessors, the sign bit plays an important role when communicating with input/output devices. Most microprocessors are not equipped with a BIT instruction for testing the contents of any bits in a register or the memory. As a result, the sign bit is usually the most convenient bit to test. When examining the status of an input/output device, reading the status register will automatically condition the sign bit, which will be set to the value of bit seven of the status register. It can then be tested conveniently by the program. This is why the status register of most input/output chips connected to microprocessor systems have their most important indicator (usually ready/not ready) in bit position seven.

A special BIT instruction is provided in the case of the Z80. However, in order to test a memory location (which may be the address of an I/O status register), the address must first be loaded into registers IX, IY or HL. There is no bit instruction provided to test a specified memory address directly (i.e., no direct addressing mode for this instruction). The value of positioning an input/output ready flag in bit position seven, therefore, remains intact, even in the case of the Z80.

Finally, the sign flag is used by the special instruction IN, (C) to indicate the sign of the data being read.

Instructions which affect the sign bit are: ADD A,s; SUB s; SBC A,s; CP s; NEG; AND s; OR s; XOR s; INC s; DEC m; ADC HL, ss; SBC HL, ss; RL m; RLC m; RR m; RRC m; SLA m; SRA m; SRL m; RLD ; RRD; DAA; IN r,(C); CPI; CPIR; CPD; CPDR; LD A,I;LD A,r; NEG, ADC A,s.

Summary of the Flags

The flag bits are used to automatically detect special conditions within the ALU of the microprocessor. They can be conveniently tested by specialized instructions, so that specific action can be taken in response to the condition detected. It is important to understand the role of the various indicators available, since most decisions taken within the program will be taken in function of these flag bits. All jumps executed within a program will jump to specified locations depending on the status of these flags. The only exception involves the interrupt mechanism, which will be described in the chapter on input/output and may cause jumping to specific locations whenever a hardware signal is received on specialized pins of the Z80.

At this point, it is only necessary to remember the main function of each of these bits. When programming, the reader can refer to the description of the instruction later in this chapter to verify the effect of every instruction of the various flags. Most flags can be ignored most of the time, and the reader who is not yet familiar with them should not feel intimidated by their apparent complexity. Their use will become clearer as we examine more application programs.

A summary of the six flags and the way they are set or reset by the various instructions is shown in Figure 4.17.

The Jump Instructions

A branch instruction is an instruction which causes a forced branching to a specified program address. It changes the normal flow of execution of the program from a sequential mode into one where a different segment of the program is suddenly executed. Jumps may be conditional or unconditional. An unconditional jump is one in which the branching occurs to a specific address, regardless of any other condition.

A conditional jump is one which occurs to a specific address only if one or more conditions are met. This is the type of jump instruction used to make decisions based upon data or computed results.

In order to explain the conditional jump instructions, it is necessary to understand the role of the flags register, since all branching decisions are based upon these flags. This was the purpose of the preceding section. We can now examine in more detail the jump instructions provided by the Z80.

Two main types of jump instructions are provided: jump instructions within the main program (they are called "jumps"), and the special

INSTRUCTION	C	Z	P/V	S	N	H	COMMENTS
ADD A, s; ADC A, s	‡	‡	V	‡	0	‡	8-bit add or add with carry
SUB s; SBC A, s, CP s, NEG	‡	‡	V	‡	1	‡	8-bit subtract, subtract with carry, compare and negate accumulator
AND s	0	‡	P	‡	0	1	Logical operations
OR s; XOR s	0	‡	P	‡	0	0	And sets different flags
INC s	•	‡	V	‡	0	‡	8-bit increment
DEC m	•	‡	V	‡	1	‡	8-bit decrement
ADD DD, ss	‡	•	•	•	0	X	16-bit add
ADC HL, ss	‡	‡	V	‡	0	X	16-bit add with carry
SBC HL, ss	‡	‡	V	‡	1	X	16-bit subtract with carry
RLA; RLCA, RRA, RRCA	‡	•	•	•	0	0	Rotate accumulator
RL m; RLC m; RR m; RRC m SLA m; SRA m; SRL m	‡	‡	P	‡	0	0	Rotate and shift location m
RLD, RRD	•	‡	P	‡	0	0	Rotate digit left and right
DAA	‡	‡	P	‡	•	‡	Decimal adjust accumulator
CPL	•	•	•	•	1	1	Complement accumulator
SCF	1	•	•	•	0	0	Set carry
CCF	‡	•	•	•	0	X	Complement carry
IN r, (C)	•	‡	P	‡	0	0	Input register indirect
INI; IND; OUTI; OUTD	•	‡	X	X	1	X	Block input and output
INIR; INDR; OTIR; OTDR	•	1	X	X	1	X	Z = 0 if B ≠ 0 otherwise Z = 1
LDI, LDD	•	X	‡	X	0	0	Block transfer instructions
LDIR, LDDR	•	X	0	X	0	0	P/V = 1 if BC ≠ 0, otherwise P/V = 0
CPI, CPIR, CPD, CPDR	•	‡	‡	‡	1	X	Block search instructions Z = 1 if A = (HL), otherwise Z = 0 P/V = 1 if BC ≠ 0, otherwise P/V = 0
LD A, I; LD A, R	•	‡	IFF	‡	0	0	The content of the interrupt enable flip-flop (IFF) is copied into the P/V flag
BIT b, s	•	‡	X	X	0	1	The complement of bit b of location is copied into the Z flag
NEG	‡	‡	V	‡	1	‡	Negate accumulator

The following notation is used in this table:

SYMBOL	OPERATION
C	Carry/link flag. C=1 if the operation produced a carry from the MSB of the operand or result.
Z	Zero flag. Z=1 if the result of the operation is zero.
S	Sign flag. S=1 if the MSB of the result is one.
P/V	Parity or overflow flag. Parity (P) and overflow (V) share the same flag. Logical operations affect this flag with the parity of the result while arithmetic operations affect this flag with the overflow of the result. If P/V holds parity, P/V=1 if the result of the operation is even, P/V=0 if result is odd. If P/V holds overflow, P/V=1 if the result of the operation produced an overflow.
H	Half-carry flag. H=1 if the add or subtract operation produced a carry into or borrow from bit 4 of the accumulator.
N	Add/Subtract flag. N=1 if the previous operation was a subtract.
	H and N flags are used in conjunction with the decimal adjust instruction (DAA) to properly correct the result into packed BCD format following addition or subtraction using operands with packed BCD format.
‡	The flag is affected according to the result of the operation.
•	The flag is unchanged by the operation.
0	The flag is reset by the operation.
1	The flag is set by the operation.
X	The flag is a "don't care."
V	P/V flag affected according to the overflow result of the operation.
P	P/V flag affected according to the parity result of the operation.
r	Any one of the CPU registers A, B, C, D, E, H, L.
s	Any 8-bit location for all the addressing modes allowed for the particular instruction.
ss	Any 16-bit location for all the addressing modes allowed for that instruction.
ii	Any one of the two index registers IX or IY.
R	Refresh counter.
n	8-bit value in range <0, 255>.
nn	16-bit value in range <0, 65535>.
m	Any 8-bit location for all the addressing modes allowed for the particular instruction.

Fig. 4.17: Summary of Flag Operation

type of branch instructions used to jump to a subroutine and to return from it ("call" and "return"). As a result of any jump instruction, the program counter PC will be reloaded with a new address, and the usual program execution will resume from this point on. The full power of the various jump instructions can be understood only in the context of the various addressing modes provided by the microprocessor. This part of the discussion will be deferred until the next chapter, where the addressing modes are discussed. We will only consider here the other aspects of these instructions.

Jumps may be unconditional (branching to a specified memory address) or else conditional. In the case of a conditional jump, one of four flag bits may be tested. They are the Z, C, P/V, and S flags. Each of them may be tested for the value "0" or "1".

The corresponding abbreviations are:

Z = zero (Z = 1)
NZ = non zero (Z = 0)
C = carry (C = 1)
NC = no carry (C = 0)
PO = odd parity
PE = even parity
P = positive (S = 0)
M = minus (S = 1)

In addition, a special combination instruction is available in the Z80 which will decrement the B register and jump to a specified memory address as long as it is not zero. This is a powerful instruction used to terminate a loop, and it has already been used several times in the previous chapter: it is the DJNZ instruction.

Similarly, the CALL and the RET (return) instructions may be conditional or unconditional. They test the same flags as the branch instruction which we have already described.

The availability of conditional branches is a powerful resource in a computer and is generally not provided on other eight-bit microprocessors. It improves the efficiency of programs by implementing in a single instruction what requires two instructions otherwise.

Finally, two special return instructions have been provided in the case of interrupt routines. They are RETI and RETN. They will be described in the section of Chapter 6 on interrupts.

The addressing modes and the opcodes for the various branches available are shown in Figure 4.18.

CONDITION

			UN-COND.	CARRY	NON CARRY	ZERO	NON ZERO	PARITY EVEN	PARITY ODD	SIGN NEG	SIGN POS	REG B≠0
JUMP 'JP'	IMMED. EXT.	nn	C3 n n	DA n n	D2 n n	CA n n	C2 n n	EA n n	E2 n n	FA n n	F2 n n	
JUMP 'JR'	RELATIVE	PC+e	18 e-2	38 e-2	30 e-2	28 e-2	20 e-2					
JUMP 'JP'		(HL)	E9									
JUMP 'JP'	REG. INDIR.	(IX)	DD E9									
JUMP 'JP'		(IY)	FD E9									
'CALL'	IMMED. EXT.	nn	CD n n	DC n n	D4 n n	CC n n	C4 n n	EC n n	E4 n n	FC n n	F4 n n	
DECREMENT B, JUMP IF NON ZERO 'DJNZ'	RELATIVE	PC+e										10 e-2
RETURN 'RET'	REGISTER INDIR.	(SP) (SP+1)	C9	D8	D0	C8	C0	E8	E0	F8	F0	
RETURN FROM INT 'RETI'	REG. INDIR.	(SP) (SP+1)	ED 4D									
RETURN FROM NON MASKABLE INT 'RETN'	REG. INDIR.	(SP) (SP+1)	ED 45									

Fig. 4.18: Jump Instructions

A detailed discussion of the various addressing modes is presented in Chapter 5.

By examining Figure 4.18, it becomes apparent that many addressing modes are restricted. For example, the absolute jump JP nn can test four flags, while JR can only test two flags.

Note an important observation: JR tends to be used whenever possible as it is shorter than JP (one less byte) and facilitates program relocation. However, JR and JP are not interchangeable: JR cannot test the parity or the sign flags.

One more type of specialized branch is available; this is the *restart* or RST instruction. It is a one-byte instruction which allows jumping to any one of eight starting addresses at the low end of the memory. Its starting addresses are, in decimal, 0, 8, 16, 24, 32, 40, 48 and 56. It is a powerful instruction because it is implemented in a single byte. It provides a fast branch, and for this reason is used essentially to respond to interrupts. However, it is also available to the programmer for other uses. A summary of the opcodes for this instruction is shown in Figure 4.19.

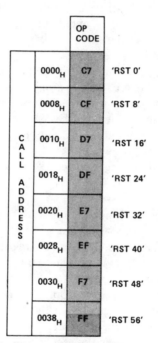

H indicates a hexidecimal number.

Fig. 4.19: Restart Group

Input/Output Instructions

Input/output techniques will be described in detail in Chapter 6. Simply, input/output devices may be addressed in two ways: as memory locations, using any one of the instructions that have already been described, or using specific input/output instructions. Usual memory addressing instructions use three bytes: one byte for the opcode and two bytes for the address. As a result, they are slow to execute, since they require three memory accesses. The main purpose of specialized input/output instructions is to provide shorter and, therefore faster, instructions. However, input/output instructions have two disadvantages.

First, they "waste" several of the precious few opcodes available (since usually only 8 bits are used to supply all opcodes necessary for a microprocessor). Secondly, they require the generation of one or more specialized input/output signals, and therefore "waste" one or more of the few pins available in the microprocessor. The number of pins is usually limited to 40. Because of these possible disadvantages, specific input/output instructions are not provided on most microprocessors. They are, however, provided on the original 8080 (the first powerful eight-bit general-purpose microprocessor introduced) and on the Z80, which we know is compatible with the 8080.

The advantage of input/output instructions is to execute faster by requiring only two bytes. However, a similar result can be obtained by supplying a special addressing mode called "page 0" addressing, where the address is limited to a field of eight bits. This solution is often chosen in other microprocessors.

The two basic input/output instructions are IN and OUT. They transfer either the contents of the specified I/O locations into any of the working registers or the contents of the register into the I/O device. They are naturally two bytes long. The first byte is reserved for the opcode, the second byte of the instruction forms the low part of the address. The accumulator is used to supply the upper part of the address. It is therefore possible to select one of the 64K devices. However, this requires that the accumulator be loaded with the appropriate contents every time, and this may slow the execution.

Additionally, the Z80 provides a register-indirect mode, plus four specialized block-transfer instructions for input and output.

In the *register-input* mode, whose format is IN r, (C), the register pair B and C is used as a pointer to the I/O device. The contents of B are placed on the high-order part of the address bus. The contents of the specified I/O device are then loaded into the register designated by r.

The same applies to the OUT instruction.

The four block-transfer instructions on input are: INI, INIR (repeated INI), IND and INDR (repeated IND). Similarly, on output, they are: OUTI, OTIR, OUTD, and OTDR.

In this automated block transfer, the register pair H and L is used as a destination pointer. Register C is used as the I/O device selector (one out of 256 devices). In the case of the output instruction, H and L point to the source. Register B is used as a counter and can be incremented or decremented. The corresponding instructions on input are INI when incrementing and IND when decrementing.

INI is an automated single-byte transfer. Register C selects the input device. A byte is read from the device and is transferred to the memory address pointed to by H and L. H and L are then incremented by 1, and the counter B is decremented by 1.

INIR is the same instruction, automated. It is executed repeatedly until the counter decrements to "0". Thus, up to 256 bytes may be transferred automatically. Note that to achieve a total transfer of exactly 256, register B should be set to the value "0" prior to executing this instruction.

The opcodes for the input and output instructions are summarized in Figures 4.20 and 4.21.

Control Instructions

Control instructions are instructions which modify the operating mode of the CPU or manipulate its internal status information. Seven such instructions are provided.

The NOP instruction is a no-operation instruction which does nothing for one cycle. It is typically used either to introduce a deliberate delay (4 states = 2 microseconds with a 2MHz clock), or to fill the gaps created in a program during the debugging phase. In order to facilitate program debugging, the opcode for the NOP is traditionally all 0's. This is because, at execution time, the memory is often cleared, i.e., all 0's. Executing NOP's is guaranteed to cause no damage and will not stop the program execution.

The HALT instruction is used in conjunction with interrupts or a reset. It actually suspends the operation of the CPU. The CPU will then resume operation whenever either an interrupt or a reset signal is received. In this mode, the CPU keeps executing NOP's. A halt is often placed at the end of programs during the debugging phase, as there is usually nothing else to be done by the main program. The program must then be explicitly restarted.

Two specialized instructions are used to disable and enable the internal interrupt flag. They are EI and DI. Interrupts will be described in

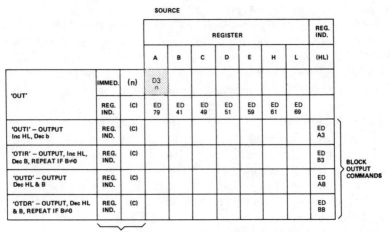

SOURCE

			REGISTER							REG. IND.
			A	B	C	D	E	H	L	(HL)
'OUT'	IMMED.	(n)	D3 n							
	REG. IND.	(C)	ED 79	ED 41	ED 49	ED 51	ED 59	ED 61	ED 69	
'OUTI' – OUTPUT Inc HL, Dec b	REG. IND.	(C)								ED A3
'OTIR' – OUTPUT, Inc HL, Dec B, REPEAT IF B≠0	REG. IND.	(C)								ED B3
'OUTD' – OUTPUT Dec HL & B	REG. IND.	(C)								ED AB
'OTDR' – OUTPUT, Dec HL & B, REPEAT IF B≠0	REG. IND.	(C)								ED BB

BLOCK OUTPUT COMMANDS

PORT DESTINATION ADDRESS

Fig. 4.20: Output Group

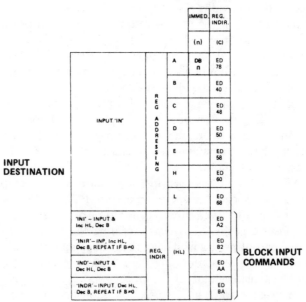

SOURCE PORT ADDRESS

			IMMED.	REG. INDIR.
			(n)	(C)
INPUT 'IN'	REG. ADDRESSING	A	D8 n	ED 78
		B		ED 40
		C		ED 48
		D		ED 50
		E		ED 58
		H		ED 60
		L		ED 68
'INI' – INPUT & Inc HL, Dec B	REG. INDIR	(HL)		ED A2
'INIR' – INP, Inc HL, Dec B, REPEAT IF B≠0				ED B2
'IND' – INPUT & Dec HL, Dec B				ED AA
'INDR' – INPUT Dec HL, Dec B, REPEAT IF B≠0				ED BA

INPUT DESTINATION

BLOCK INPUT COMMANDS

Fig. 4.21: Input Group

186

Chapter 6. The interrupt flag is used to authorize or not authorize the interruption of a program. To prevent interrupts from occurring during any specific portion of a program, the interrupt flip-flop (flag) may be disabled by this instruction. It will be used in Chapter 6. These instructions are shown in Figure 4.22.

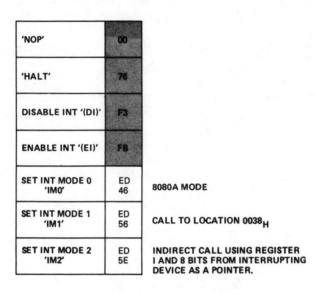

'NOP'	00	
'HALT'	76	
DISABLE INT '(DI)'	F3	
ENABLE INT '(EI)'	FB	
SET INT MODE 0 'IM0'	ED 46	8080A MODE
SET INT MODE 1 'IM1'	ED 56	CALL TO LOCATION 0038$_H$
SET INT MODE 2 'IM2'	ED 5E	INDIRECT CALL USING REGISTER I AND 8 BITS FROM INTERRUPTING DEVICE AS A POINTER.

Fig. 4.22: Miscellaneous CPU Control

Finally, three interrupt modes are provided in the Z80. (Only one is available on the 8080). Interrupt mode 0 is the 8080 mode, interrupt 1 is a call to location 038H, and interrupt mode 2 is an indirect call which uses the contents of the special register I, plus 8 bits provided by the interrupting device as a pointer to the memory location whose contents are the address of the interrupt routine. These modes will be explained in Chapter 6.
which will also be explained in Chapter 6. They are the IRQ and the NMI pins.

SUMMARY

The five categories of instructions available on the Z80 have now been described. The details on individual instructions are supplied in the following section of the book. It is not necessary to understand the role of each instruction in order to start to program. The knowledge of a few essential instructions of each type is sufficient at the beginning. However, as you begin to write programs by yourself, you should learn about all the instructions of the Z80 if you want to write good programs. Naturally, at the beginning, efficiency is not important, and this is why most instructions can be ignored.

One important aspect has not yet been described. This is the set of addressing techniques implemented on the Z80 to facilitate the retrieval of data within the memory space. These addressing techniques will be studied in the next chapter.

THE Z80 INSTRUCTIONS: INDIVIDUAL DESCRIPTION

ABBREVIATIONS

FLAG	ON	OFF
Carry	C (carry)	NC (no carry)
Sign	M (minus)	P (plus)
Zero	Z (zero)	NZ (non zero)
Parity	PE (even)	PO (odd)

●   changed functionally according to operation
O   flag is set to zero
1   flag is set to one
?   flag is set randomly by operation
X   special case, see accompanying note on that page

bit positions 3 and 5 are always random

ADC A, s

Add accumulator and specified operand with carry.

Function: $A \leftarrow A + s + C$

Format: s: may be r, n, (HL), (IX + d), or (IY + d)

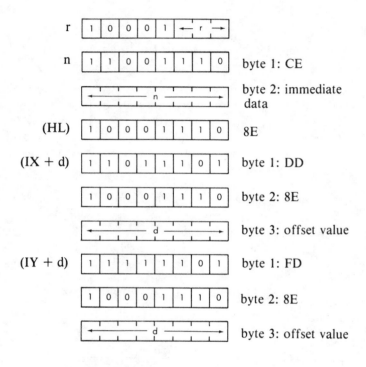

r may be any one of:

A	– 111	E	– 011
B	– 000	H	– 100
C	– 001	L	– 101
D	– 010		

Description: The operand s and the carry flag C from the status register are added to the accumulator, and the result is stored in the accumulator. s is defined in the description of the similar ADD instructions.

Data Flow:

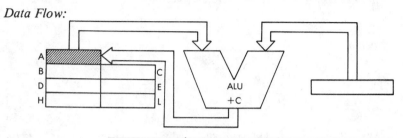

Timing:

s:	M cycles:	T states:	usec @ 2 MHz:
r	1	4	2
n	2	7	3.5
(HL)	2	7	3.5
(IX + d)	5	19	9.5
(IY + d)	5	19	9.5

Addressing Mode: r: implicit; n: immediate; (HL): indirect; (IX + d), (IY + d): indexed.

Byte Codes: ADC A,r

r:	A	B	C	D	E	H	L
	8F	88	89	8A	8B	8C	8D

Flags:

S	Z		H		P/V	N	C
●	●		●		●	○	●

Example: ADC A, 1A

Before:

A | 06 | 13 | F

After:

A | 21 | 10 | F

CE
1A

OBJECT CODE

191

ADC HL, ss   Add with carry HL and register pair ss.

Function: $HL \leftarrow HL + ss + C$

Format:

1	1	1	0	1	1	0	1

byte 1: ED

0	1	s	s	1	0	1	0

byte 2

Description: The contents of the HL register pair are added to
the contents of the specified register pair, and then
the contents of the carry flag are added. The final
result is stored back in HL. ss may be any one of:

BC − 00	HL − 10
DE − 01	SP − 11

Data Flow:

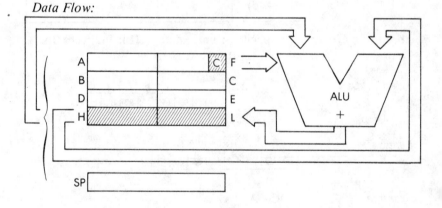

Timing: 4 M cycles; 15 T states: 75 usec @ 2 MHz

Addressing Mode: Implicit.

Byte Codes: ss:

	BC	DE	HL	SP
ED−	4A	5A	6A	7A

Flags:

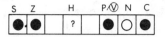

H is set if there is a carry from bit 11.

Example:

ADC   HL, DE

Before: After:

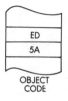

OBJECT
CODE

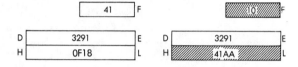

ADD A, (HL)   Add accumulator with indirectly addressed memory location (HL).

Function: A ← A + (HL)

Format:

| 1 | 0 | 0 | 0 | 0 | 1 | 1 | 0 | 86

Description: The contents of the accumulator are added to the contents of the memory location addressed by the HL register pair. The result is stored in the accumulator.

Data Flow:

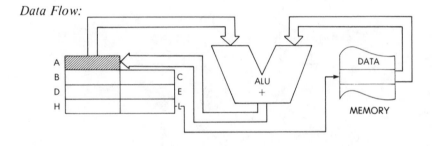

Timing: 2 M cycles; 7 T states: 3.5 usec @ 2 MHz

Addressing Mode: Indirect.

Flags:

S Z   H   P/V N C

194

Example: ADD   A, (HL)

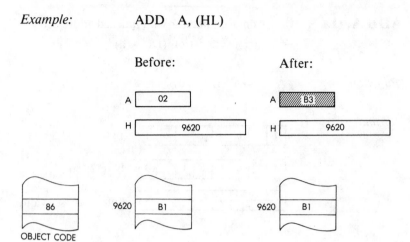

Before: After:

A [02]   A [//// B3 ////]

H [9620]   H [9620]

86
OBJECT CODE

9620 [B1]   9620 [B1]

ADD A, (IX + d)   Add accumulator with indexed addressed memory location (IX + d)

Function: A ← A + (IX + d)

Format:

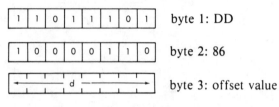

| 1 | 1 | 0 | 1 | 1 | 1 | 0 | 1 | byte 1: DD

| 1 | 0 | 0 | 0 | 0 | 1 | 1 | 0 | byte 2: 86

← d →   byte 3: offset value

Description: The contents of the accumulator are added to the contents of the memory location addressed by the contents of the IX register plus the immediate off-set value. The result is stored in the accumulator.

Data Flow:

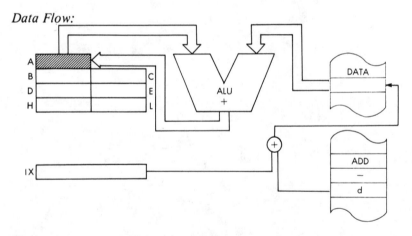

Timing: 5 M cycles; 19 T states: 9.5 usec @ 2 MHz

Addressing Mode: Indexed.

Flags:

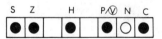

Example: ADD   A, (IX + 3)

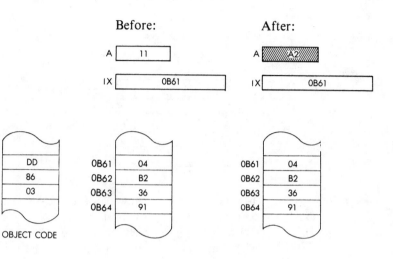

Before:

A [11]

IX [0B61   ]

After:

A [////A2////]

IX [0B61   ]

DD	
86	
03	

OBJECT CODE

0B61	04
0B62	B2
0B63	36
0B64	91

0B61	04
0B62	B2
0B63	36
0B64	91

ADD A, (IY + d)
Add accumulator with indexed addressed memory location (IY + d)

Function: $A \leftarrow A + (IY + d)$

Format:

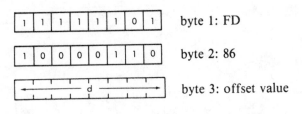

| 1 | 1 | 1 | 1 | 1 | 1 | 0 | 1 | byte 1: FD

| 1 | 0 | 0 | 0 | 0 | 1 | 1 | 0 | byte 2: 86

| ← d → | byte 3: offset value

Description: The contents of the accumulator are added to the contents of the memory location addressed by the contents of the IY register plus the given offset value. The result is stored in the accumulator.

Data Flow:

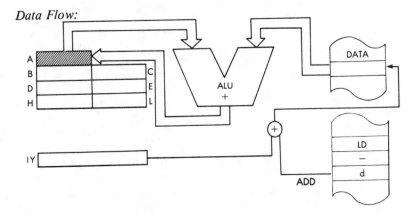

Timing: 5 M cycles; 19 T states; 9.5 usec @ 2 MHz

Addressing Mode: Indexed.

Flags:

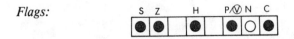

S Z H P/V N C

198

Example: ADD   A, (IY + 1)

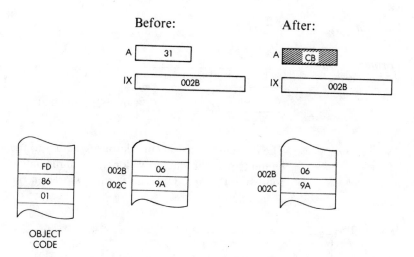

Before:

A [31]

IX [002B]

FD	
86	
01	

OBJECT
CODE

002B	06
002C	9A

After:

A [CB]

IX [002B]

002B	06
002C	9A

ADD A, n

Add accumulator with immediate data n.

Function: $A \leftarrow A + n$

Format:

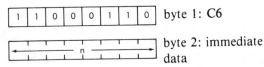

| 1 | 1 | 0 | 0 | 0 | 1 | 1 | 0 |

byte 1: C6

byte 2: immediate data

Description: The contents of the accumulator are added to the contents of the memory location immediately following the op code. The result is stored in the accumulator.

Data Flow:

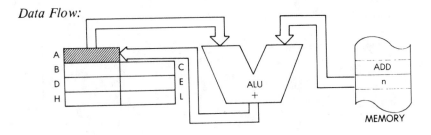

Timing: 2 M cycles; 7 T states: 3.5 usec @ 2 MHz

Addressing Mode: Immediate.

Flags:

S Z   H   P/Ⓥ N C
● ●   ●   ● ○ ●

Example: ADD   A, E2

Before: After:

A [43]   A [25]

C6
E2

OBJECT CODE

200

ADD A, r

Add accumulator with register r.

Function: $A \leftarrow A + r$

Format:

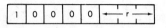

Description: The contents of the accumulator are added with the contents of the specified register. The result is placed in the accumulator. r may be any one of:

A – 111		E – 011	
B – 000		H – 100	
C – 001		L – 101	
D – 010			

Data Flow:

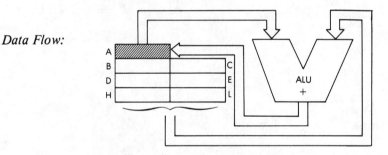

Timing: 1 M cycle; 4 T states: 2 usec @ 2 MHz.

Addressing Mode: Implicit.

Byte Codes: r:

A	B	C	D	E	H	L
87	80	81	82	83	84	85

Flags:

S	Z		H		P/Ⓥ	N	C
●	●		●		●	○	●

201

Example: ADD   A, B

Before: After:

A [3D]   A [3F]

B [02]   B [02]

OBJECT CODE

ADD HL, ss   Add HL and register pair ss.

Function: HL ← HL + ss

Format:

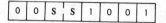

Description: The contents of the specified register pair are added to the contents of the HL register pair and the result is stored in HL. ss may be any one of:

BC – 00	HL – 10
DE – 01	SP – 11

Data Flow:

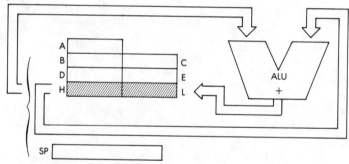

Timing: 3 M cycles; 11 T states: 5.5 usec @ 2 MHz

Addressing Mode: Implicit.

Byte Codes: ss:

BC	DE	HL	SP
09	19	29	39

Flags:

S	Z		H		P/V	N	C
			?			○	●

C is set by carry from bit 15, reset otherwise.

H is set by a carry from bit 11

203

Example: ADD   HL, HL

Before: After:

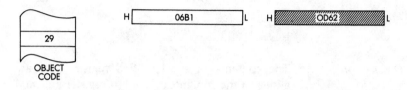

OBJECT
CODE

ADD IX, rr   Add IX with register pair rr.

Function: IX ← IX + rr

Format:

| 1 | 1 | 0 | 1 | 1 | 1 | 0 | 1 | byte 1: DD

| 0 | 0 | r | r | 1 | 0 | 0 | 1 | byte 2

Description: The contents of the IX register are added to the contents of the specified register pair and the result is stored back in IX. rr may be anyone of:

BC – 00	IX – 10
DE – 01	SP – 11

Data Flow:

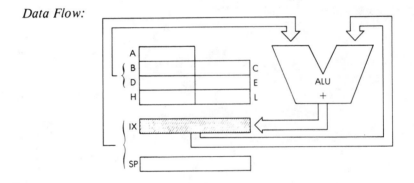

Timing: 4 M cycles; 15 T states: 7.5 usec @ 2 MHz

Addressing Mode: Implicit.

Byte Codes: rr:

	BC	DE	IX	SP
DD–	09	19	29	39

Flags:

S	Z		H	P/V	N	C
			?		○	●

H is set by carry out of bit 11.
C is set by carry from bit 15.

Example: ADD   IX, SP

DD
39

OBJECT
CODE

Before: After:

IX | 0000 | IX | 3021 |

SP | 3021 | SP | 3021 |

ADD IY, rr

Add IY and register pair rr.

Function:

IY ← IY + rr

Format:

| 1 | 1 | 1 | 1 | 1 | 1 | 0 | 1 | byte 1: FD

| 0 | 0 | r | r | 1 | 0 | 0 | 1 | byte 2

Description:

The contents of the IY register are added to the contents of the specified register pair and the result is stored back in IY. rr may be any one of:

BC – 00   IY – 10
DE – 01   SP – 11

Data Flow:

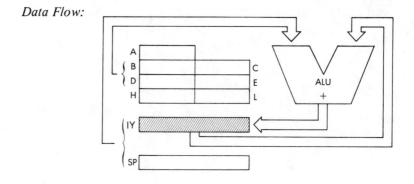

Timing:

4 M cycles; 15 T states: 7.5 usec @ 2 MHz

Addressing Mode: Implicit.

Byte Codes:

rr:

	BC	DE	IY	SP
FD–	09	19	29	39

Flags:

S	Z	H	P/V	N	C
		?		○	●

H is set by carry out of bit 11.
C is set by carry out of bit 15.

Example: ADD   IY, DE

Before: After:

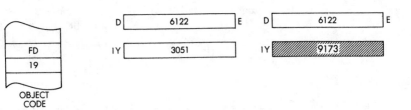

OBJECT
CODE

FD
19

AND s   Logical AND accumulator with operand s.

Function: A ← A ∧ s

Format: s: may be r, n, (HL), (IX + d), or (IY + d)

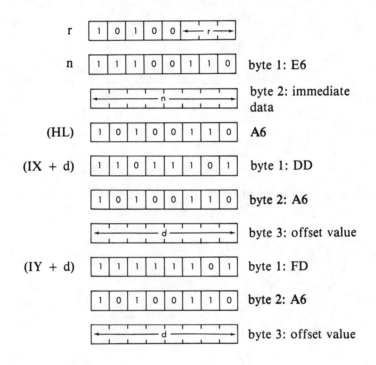

r may be any one of:

A – 111		E – 011	
B – 000		H – 100	
C – 001		L – 101	
D – 010			

Description: The accumulator and the specified operand are logically 'and'ed and the result is stored in the accumulator. s is defined in the description of the similar ADD instructions.

Data Flow:

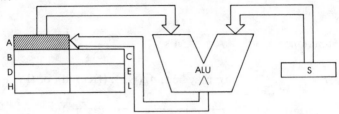

Timing:

s:	M cycles:	T states:	usec @ 2 MHz:
r	1	4	2
n	2	7	3.5
(HL)	2	7	3.5
(IX + d)	5	19	9.5
(IY + d)	5	19	9.5

Addressing Mode: r: implicit; n: immediate; (HL): indirect; (IX + d), (IY + d): indexed.

Byte Codes: AND r

r: | A | B | C | D | E | H | L |
|---|---|---|---|---|---|---|
| A7 | A0 | A1 | A2 | A3 | A4 | A5 |

Flags:

S	Z		H		P/V	N	C
●	●		1		●	○	○

Example: AND 4B

Before: After:

A [36]   A [02]

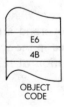

E6
4B

OBJECT
CODE

0011 0010

1000 1011

0000 0010

210

BIT b, (HL)   Test bit b of indirectly addressed memory location (HL)

Function: $Z \leftarrow \overline{(HL)}_b$

Format:

byte 1: CB

| 0 | 1 | ←—b—→ | | 1 | 1 | 0 |

byte 2

Description: The specified bit of the memory location address-ed by the contents of the HL register pair is tested and the Z flag is set according to the result. b may be any one of:

0	– 000	4	– 100
1	– 001	5	– 101
2	– 010	6	– 110
3	– 011	7	111

Data Flow:

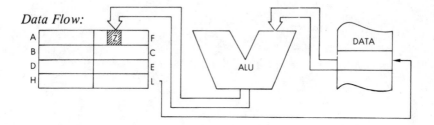

Timing: 3 M cycles; 12 T states; 6 usec @ 2 MHz

Addressing Mode: Indirect.

Flags:

S	Z		H		P/V	N	C
?	●		1		?	0	

211

Byte Codes:

b:	0	1	2	3	4	5	6	7
CB-	46	4E	56	5E	66	6E	76	7E

Example:

BIT   3, (HL)

Before: After:

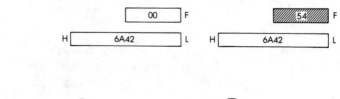

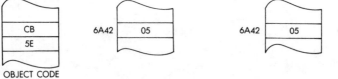

OBJECT CODE

BIT b, (IX + d) Test bit b of indexed addressed memory location
(IX + d)

Function: $Z \leftarrow \overline{(IX + d)_b}$

Format:

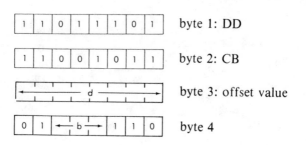

1	1	0	1	1	1	0	1	byte 1: DD

1	1	0	0	1	0	1	1	byte 2: CB

byte 3: offset value (← d →)

| 0 | 1 | ← b → | 1 | 1 | 0 | byte 4 |

Description: The specified bit of the memory location addressed by the contents of the IX register plus the given
offset value is tested and the Z flag is set according
to the result. b may be any one of:

0	–	000	
1	–	001	
2	–	010	
3	–	011	
4	–	100	

5	–	101
6	–	110
7	–	111

Data Flow:

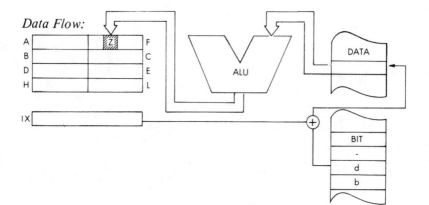

Timing: 5 M cycles; 20 T states: 10 usec @ 2 MHz

Addressing Mode: Indexed.

Byte Codes:

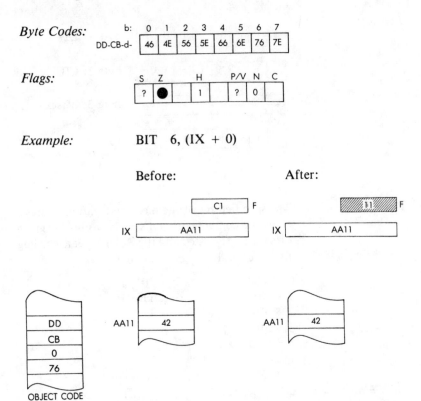

Flags:

Example: BIT   6, (IX + 0)

OBJECT CODE

BIT b, (IY + d) Test bit b of the indexed addressed memory location (IY + d)

Function: $Z \leftarrow \overline{(IY + d)_b}$

Format:

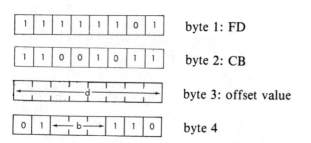

byte 1: FD

byte 2: CB

byte 3: offset value

byte 4

Description: The specified bit of the memory location addressed by the contents of the IY register plus the given offset value is tested and the Z flag is set according to the result. b may be any one of:

0 − 000	4 − 100
1 − 001	5 − 101
2 − 010	6 − 110
3 − 011	7 − 111

Data Flow:

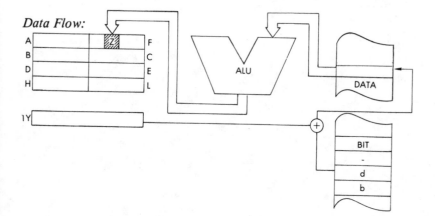

Timing: 5 M cycles; 20 T states; 10 usec @ 2 MHz

Addressing Mode: Indexed.

Byte Codes: b :

	0	1	2	3	4	5	6	7
FD-CB-d-	46	4E	56	5E	66	6E	76	7E

Flags:

S	Z		H		P/V	N	C
?	●		1		?	0	

Example: BIT   0, (IY + 1)

Before: After:

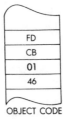

FD	
CB	
01	
46	

OBJECT CODE

FF12	61
FF13	B2

FF12	61
FF13	B2

BIT b, r

Test bit b of register r.

Function:

$$Z \leftarrow \overline{r_b}$$

Format:

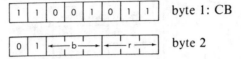

byte 1: CB

byte 2

Description:

The specified bit of the given register is tested and the zero flag is set according to the results. b and r may be any one of:

b:
0 – 000	4 – 100
1 – 001	5 – 101
2 – 010	6 – 110
3 – 011	7 – 111

r:
A – 111	E – 011
B – 000	H – 100
C – 001	L – 101
D – 010	

Data Flow:

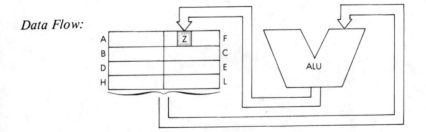

Timing:

2 M cycles; 8 T states; 4 usec @ 2 MHz

Addressing Mode: Implicit.

217

Byte Codes:

	b:	r: A	B	C	D	E	H	L
CB-	0	47	40	41	42	43	44	45
	1	4F	48	49	4A	4B	4C	4D
	2	57	50	51	52	53	54	55
	3	5F	58	59	5A	5B	5C	5D
	4	67	60	61	62	63	64	65
	5	6F	68	69	6A	6B	6C	6D
	6	77	70	71	72	73	74	75
	7	7F	78	79	7A	7B	7C	7D

Flags:

S	Z		H		P/V	N	C
?	●		1		?	0	

Example: **BIT   4, B**

Before: After:

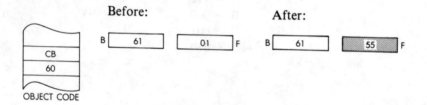

CB
60

OBJECT CODE

B [61]   [01] F   B [61]   [55] F

CALL cc, pq   Call subroutine on condition.

Function:

if cc true: $(SP - 1) \leftarrow PC_{high}$; $(SP - 2) \leftarrow PC_{low}$; $SP \leftarrow SP - 2$; $PC \leftarrow pq$
If cc false: $PC \leftarrow PC + 3$

Format:

byte 1
byte 2: address, low order
byte 3: address, high order

Description:

If the condition is met, the contents of the program counter are pushed onto the stack as described for the PUSH instructions. Then, the contents of the memory location immediately following the opcode are loaded into the low order of the PC and the contents of the second memory location after the the opcode are loaded into the high order half of the PC. The next instruction fetched will be from this new address. If the condition is not met, the address pq is ignored and the following instruction is executed. cc may be any one of:

NZ – 000   PO – 100
 Z – 001   PE – 101
NC – 010   P – 100
 C – 011   M – 111

An RET instruction can be used at the end of the subroutine being called to restore the PC.

Data Flow:

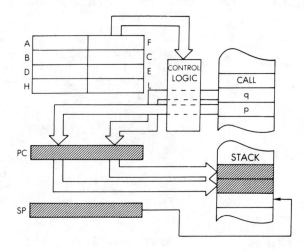

Timing:

	M cycles:	T states:	usec @ 2 MHz
condition true:	5	17	8.5
condition not true:	3	10	5

Addressing Mode: Immediate.

Byte Codes:

CC: NZ . Z   NC   C   PO   PE   P   M

C4	CC	D4	DC	E4	EC	F4	FC	-q-p

Flags:

S   Z   H   P/V   N   C

(no effect)

Example: CALL   Z, **B042**

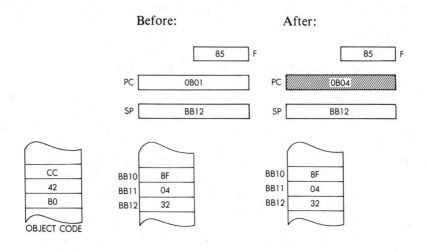

OBJECT CODE

CALL pq Call subroutine at location pq.

Function: $(SP - 1) \leftarrow PC_{high}$; $(SP - 2) \leftarrow PC_{low}$; $SP \leftarrow SP - 2$; $PC \leftarrow pq$

Format:

| 1 | 1 | 0 | 0 | 1 | 1 | 0 | 1 | byte 1: CD

←————q————→ byte 2: address, low order

←————p————→ byte 3: address, high order

Description: The contents of the program counter are pushed onto the stack as described for the PUSH instructions. The contents of the memory location immediately following the opcode are then loaded into the low order half of the PC and the contents of the second memory location after the opcode are loaded in the high order half of the PC. The next instruction will be fetched from this new address.

Data Flow:

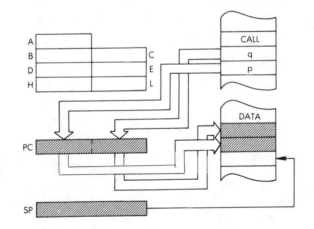

Timing: 5 M cycles; 17 T states: 8.5 usec @ 2 MHz

Addressing Mode: Immediate.

Flags:

S	Z		H		P/V	N	C

(no effect)

Example: CALL   40B1

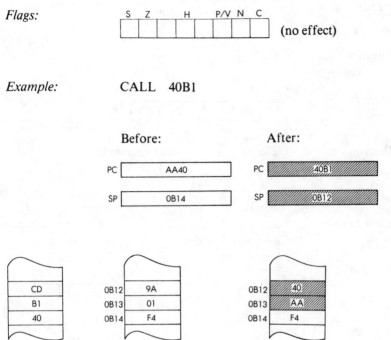

Before:

PC AA40

SP 0B14

After:

PC 40B1

SP 0B12

CD
B1
40

OBJECT CODE

0B12	9A
0B13	01
0B14	F4

0B12	40
0B13	AA
0B14	F4

223

CCF

Complement carry flag.

Function: $C \leftarrow \overline{C}$

Format:

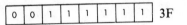

0	0	1	1	1	1	1	1

3F

Description: The carry flag is complemented.

Data Flow:

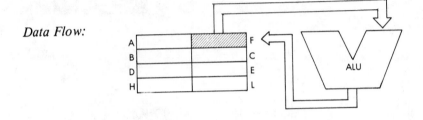

Timing: 1 M cycle; 4 T states: 2 usec @ 2 MHz

Addressing Mode: Implicit.

Flags:

S	Z		H		P/V	N	C
			?			○	●

CP s

Compare operand s to accumulator.

Function: A − s

Format: s: may be r, n, (HL), (IX + d), or (IY + d).

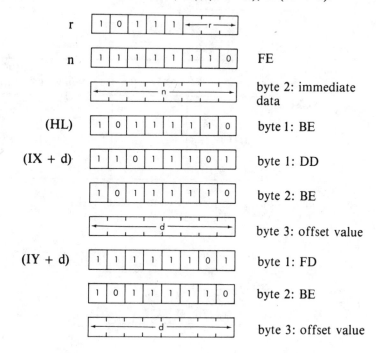

r

n   FE

byte 2: immediate
data

(HL)   byte 1: BE

(IX + d)   byte 1: DD

byte 2: BE

byte 3: offset value

(IY + d)   byte 1: FD

byte 2: BE

byte 3: offset value

r may be any one of:

A − 111		E − 011	
B − 000		H − 100	
C − 001		L − 101	
D − 010			

Description: The specified operand is subtracted from the accumulator, and the result is discarded. s is defined in the description of the similar ADD instructions.

225

Data Flow:

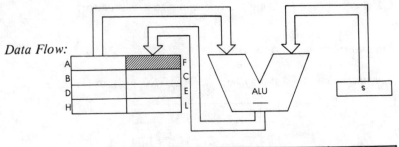

Timing:

s:	M cycles:	T states:	usec @ 2 MHz:
r	1	4	2
n	2	7	3.5
(HL)	2	7	3.5
(IX + d)	5	19	9.5
(IY + d)	5	19	9.5

Addressing Modes: r: implicit; n: immediate; (HL): indirect; (IX + d), (IY + d): indexed

Byte Codes: CP r:

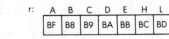

r:

A	B	C	D	E	H	L
BF	B8	B9	BA	BB	BC	BD

Flags:

S Z   H   P/V N C

| ● | ● | | ● | | ● | 1 | ● |

Example: CP (HL)

Before:

After:

A [96 | 36] F   A [96 | 06] F

H [B203] L   H [B203] L

BE

OBJECT
CODE

B203 | 42

B203 | 42

CPD   Compare with decrement.

Function: $A - [HL]; HL \leftarrow HL - 1; BC \leftarrow BC - 1$

Format:

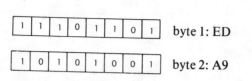

byte 1: ED

byte 2: A9

Description: The contents of the memory location addressed by the HL register pair are subtracted from the contents of the accumulator and the result is discarded. Then both the HL register pair and the BC register pair are decremented.

Data Flow:

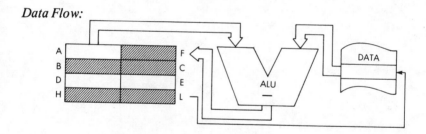

Timing: 4 M cycles; 16 T states: 8 usec @ 2 MHz

Addressing Mode: indirect.

Flags:

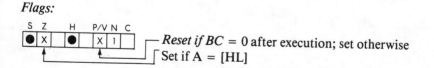

— *Reset if BC* = 0 after execution; set otherwise
Set if A = [HL]

227

Example: CPD

Before: After:

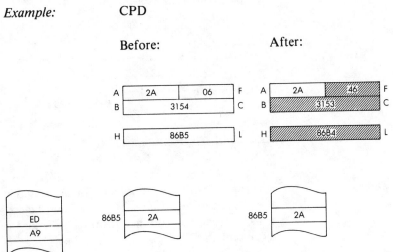

OBJECT CODE

CPDR

Block compare with decrement.

Function:

A — [HL]; HL ← HL — 1; BC ← BC — 1;
Repeat until BC = 0 or A = [HL]

Format:

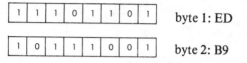

| 1 | 1 | 1 | 0 | 1 | 1 | 0 | 1 | byte 1: ED

| 1 | 0 | 1 | 1 | 1 | 0 | 0 | 1 | byte 2: B9

Description:

The contents of the memory location addressed by the HL register pair are subtracted from the contents of the accumulator and the result is discarded. Then both the BC register pair and the HL register pair are decremented. If BC ≠ 0 and A ≠ [HL], the program counter is decremented by two and the instruction is re-executed.

Data Flow:

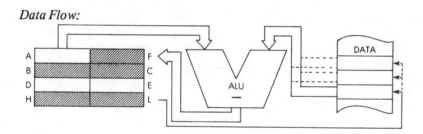

Timing:

BC = 0 or A = [HL]: 4 M cycles; 16 T states:
8 usec @ 2 MHz
BC ≠ 0 and A ≠ [HL]: 5 M cycles; 21 T states:
10.5 usec @ 2 MHz

Flags:

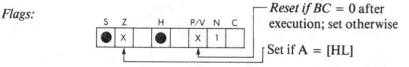

Reset if BC = 0 after execution; set otherwise

Set if A = [HL]

229

Example: CPDR

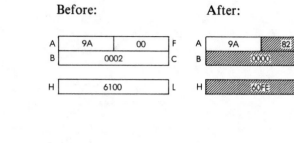

Before: After:

A	9A	00	F
B	0002		C
H	6100		L

A	9A	82	F
B	0000		C
H	60FE		L

ED
B9

OBJECT CODE

60FE	08
60FF	00
6100	2A

60FE	08
60FF	00
6100	2A

CPI

Compare with increment.

Function: $A - [HL]; HL \leftarrow HL + 1; BC \leftarrow BC - 1$

Format:

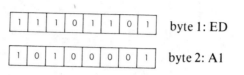

| 1 | 1 | 1 | 0 | 1 | 1 | 0 | 1 | byte 1: ED

| 1 | 0 | 1 | 0 | 0 | 0 | 0 | 1 | byte 2: A1

Description: The contents of the memory location addressed by the HL register pair are subtracted from the contents of the accumulator and the result is discarded. The HL register pair is incremented and the BC register pair is decremented.

Data Flow:

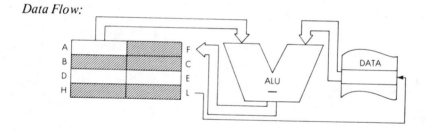

Timing: 4 M cycles; 16 T states: 8 usec @ 2 MHz

Addressing Mode: indirect.

Flags:

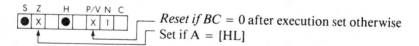

Reset if BC = 0 after execution set otherwise
Set if A = [HL]

Example: CPI

Before: After:

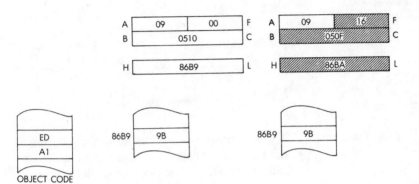

OBJECT CODE

CPIR   Block compare with increment.

Function: A — [HL]; HL ← HL + 1; BC ← BC — 1;
                     Repeat until BC = 0 or A = [HL]

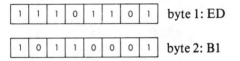

| 1 | 1 | 1 | 0 | 1 | 1 | 0 | 1 | byte 1: ED

| 1 | 0 | 1 | 1 | 0 | 0 | 0 | 1 | byte 2: B1

Description: The contents of the memory location addressed by
                     the HL register pair are subtracted from the con-
                     tents of the accumulator and the result is discarded.
                     Then the HL register pair is incremented and the
                     BC register pair is decremented. If BC ≠ 0 and A
                     ≠ [HL], then the program counter is decremented
                     by 2 and the instruction is re-executed.

Data Flow:

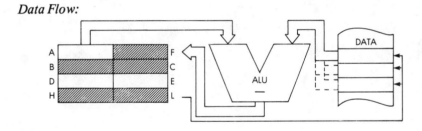

Timing: BC = 0 or A = [HL] : 4 M cycles; 16 T states:
                     8 usec @ 2 MHz
                     BC ≠ 0 and A ≠ [HL] : 5 M cycles; 21 T states:
                     10.5 usec @ 2 MHz

Addressing Mode: indirect.

233

Flags:

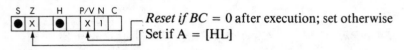

Reset if BC = 0 after execution; set otherwise
Set if A = [HL]

Example: CPIR

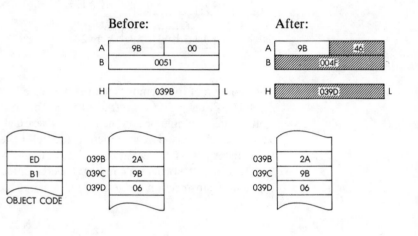

CPL

Complement accumulator.

Function:

$A \leftarrow \bar{A}$

Format:

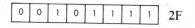

0	0	1	0	1	1	1	1

2F

Description:

The contents of the accumulator are complemented, or inverted, and the result is stored back in the accumulator (one's complement).

Data Flow:

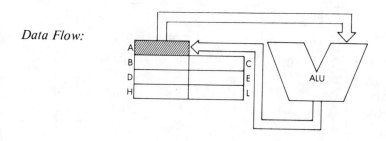

Timing:

1 M cycle; 4 T states; 2 usec @ 2 MHz

Addressing Mode:

Implicit.

Flags:

S	Z		H		P/V	N	C
			1			1	

Example:

CPL

Before: After:

A [3D]   A [C2]

2F

OBJECT
CODE

235

DAA

Decimal adjust accumulator.

Function: See below.

Format:

| 0 | 0 | 1 | 0 | 0 | 1 | 1 | 1 | 27

Description: The instruction conditionally adds "6" to the right and/or left nibble of the accumulator, based on the status register, for BCD conversion after arithmetic operations.

N	C	value of high nibble	H	value of low nibble	# added to A	C after execution
0	0	0-9	0	0-9	00	0
(ADD,	0	0-8	0	A-F	06	0
ADC,	0	0-9	1	0-3	06	0
INC)	0	A-F	0	0-9	60	1
	0	9-F	0	A-F	66	1
	0	A-F	1	0-3	66	1
	1	0-2	0	0-9	60	1
	1	0-2	0	A-F	66	1
	1	0-3	1	0-3	66	1
1	0	0-9	0	0-9	00	0
(SUB,	0	0-8	1	6-F	FA	0
SBC,	1	7-F	0	0-9	AO	1
DEC,	1	6-F	1	6-F	9A	1
NEG)						

Data Flow:

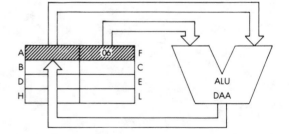

236

Timing: 1 M cycle; 4 T states; 2 usec @ 2 MHz

Addressing Mode: Implicit.

Flags:

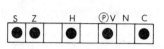

Example: DAA

Before: After:

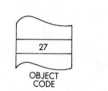

OBJECT
CODE

A B2 94 F   A 18 05 F

DEC m

Decrement operand m.

Function:　　　　$m \leftarrow m - 1$

Format:　　　　m: may be r, (HL), (IX+d), (IY+d)

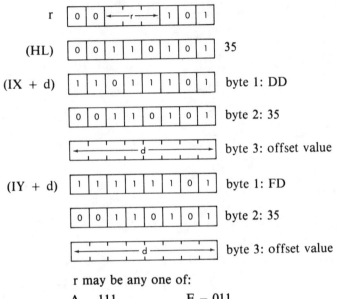

r

(HL) | 0 0 1 1 0 1 0 1 | 35

(IX + d) | 1 1 0 1 1 1 0 1 | byte 1: DD

| 0 0 1 1 0 1 0 1 | byte 2: 35

| ◄─── d ───► | byte 3: offset value

(IY + d) | 1 1 1 1 1 1 0 1 | byte 1: FD

| 0 0 1 1 0 1 0 1 | byte 2: 35

| ◄─── d ───► | byte 3: offset value

r may be any one of:

A − 111	E − 011
B − 000	H − 100
C − 001	L − 101
D − 010	

Description:　The contents of the location addressed by the specific operand are decremented and stored back at that location. m is defined in the description of the similar INC instructions.

Data Flow:

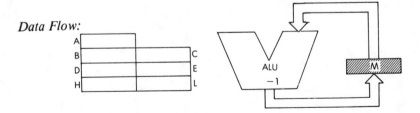

Timing:

m:	M cycles:	T states:	usec @ 2 MHz:
r	1	4	2
(HL)	3	11	5.5
(IX + d)	6	23	11.5
(IY + d)	6	23	11.5

Addressing Mode: r: implicit; (HL): indirect; (IX + d), (IY + d): indexed.

Byte Codes: DEC r

r:

A	B	C	D	E	H	L
3D	05	0D	15	1D	25	2D

Flags:

S	Z		H		P/V	N	C
●	●		●		●	1	

Example: DEC   C

Before:

| 0F | C

After:

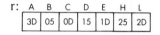 C

OD

OBJECT
CODE

DEC rr

Decrement register pair rr.

Function: rr ← rr − 1

Format:

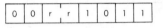

| 0 | 0 | r | r | 1 | 0 | 1 | 1 |

Description: The contents of the specified register pair are decremented and the result is stored back in the register pair. rr may be any one of:

BC	− 00	HL	− 10
DE	− 01	SP	− 11

Data Flow:

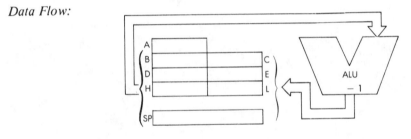

Timing: 1 M cycle; 6 T states; 3 usec @ 2 MHz

Addressing Mode: Implicit.

Byte Codes: rr:

	BC	DE	HL	SP
	0B	1B	2B	3B

Flags:

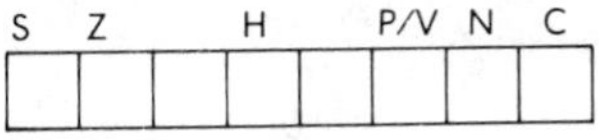

S	Z		H		P/V	N	C

(no effect).

Example: DEC BC

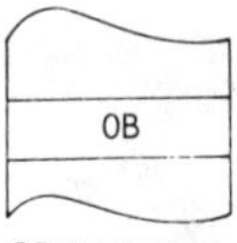

Before: 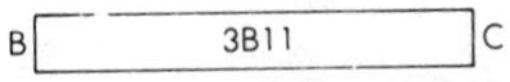 After:

OBJECT CODE

0B

B | 3B11 | C   B | 3B10 | C

DEC IX

Decrement IX.

Function: IX ← IX − 1

Format:

byte 1: DD

byte 2: 2B

Description: The contents of the IX register are decremented and the result is stored back in IX.

Data Flow:

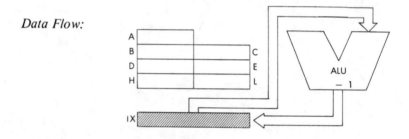

Timing: 2 M cycles; 10 T states; 5 usec @ 2 MHz

Addressing Modes: Implicit.

Flags:

S Z   H   P/V N C

(no effect).

Example: DEC IX

Before: After:

IX 6114   IX 6113

DD
2B

OBJECT CODE

DEC IY
Decrement IY.

Function: IY ← IY − 1

Format:

byte 1: FD

byte 2: 2B

Description: The contents of the IY register are decremented and the result is stored back in IY.

Data Flow:

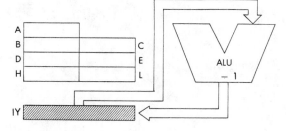

Timing: 2 M cycles; 10 T states; 5 usec @ 2 MHz

Addressing Mode: Implicit.

Flags:

S   Z   H   P/V N   C

(no effect).

Example: DEC   IY

Before: After:

IY [900F   ]   IY [900E   ]

FD
2B

OBJECT CODE

DI   Disable interrupts.

Function: IFF ← 0

Format:

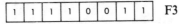   F3

Description: The interrupt flip-flops are reset, thereby disabling all maskable interrupts. It is reenabled by an EI instruction.

Timing: 1 M cycle; 4 T states; 2 usec @ 2 MHz

Addressing Mode: Implicit.

Flags:

S   Z   H   P/V   N   C

(no effect).

DJNZ e

Decrement B and jump e relative on no zero.

Function:

$B \leftarrow B - 1$; if $B \neq 0$: $PC \leftarrow PC + e$

Format:

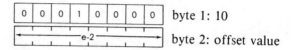

| 0 | 0 | 0 | 1 | 0 | 0 | 0 | 0 | byte 1: 10 |

e-2 byte 2: offset value

Description:

The B register is decremented. If the result is not zero, the immediate offset value is added to the program counter using two's complement arithmetic so as to enable both forward and backward jumps. The offset value is added to the value of PC + 2 (after the jump). As a result, the effective offset is -126 to +129 bytes. The assembler automatically subtracts from the source offset value to generate the hex code.

Data Flow:

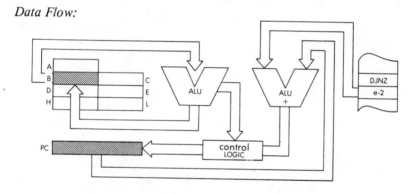

Timing:

$B \neq 0$: 3 M cycles; 13 T states; 6.5 usec @ 2 MHz.
$B = 0$: 2 M cycles; 8 T states; 4 usec @ 2 MHz

Addressing Modes: Immediate.

Flags:

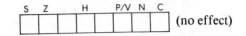

S   Z   H   P/V N   C

(no effect)

Example: DJNZ $ – 5   ($ = current PC)

Before: After:

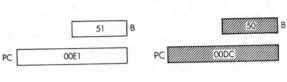

51 | B

PC | 00E1

50 | B

PC | 00DC

10
F9

OBJECT CODE

EI

Enable interrupts.

Function: IFF ← 1

Format:

| 1 | 1 | 1 | 1 | 1 | 0 | 1 | 1 | FB

Description: The interrupt flip-flops are set, thereby enabling maskable interrupts after the execution of the instruction following the EI instruction. In the meantime maskable interrupts are disabled.

Timing: 1 M cycle; 4 T states; 2 usec @ 2 MHz

Addressing Mode: Implicit.

Flags:

S   Z   H   P/V N C

(no effect).

Example: A usual sequence at the end of an interrupt routine is:
EI
RETI
The maskable interrupt is re-enabled following completion of RETI.

EX AF, AF'

Exchange accumulator and flags with alternate registers.

Function: **AF⟷AF'**

Format:

| 0 | 0 | 0 | 0 | 1 | 0 | 0 | 0 | 08 |

Description: The contents of the accumulator and status register are exchanged with the contents of the alternate accumulator and status register.

Data Flow:

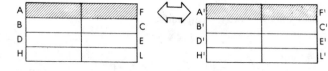

Timing: 1 M cycle; 4 T states; 2 usec @ 2 MHz

Addressing Mode: Implicit.

Flags:

Example: EX AF, AF'

Before: After:

OBJECT CODE

| A | 04 | 81 | F |

| A' | 90 | 3A | F' |

| A | 90 | 3A | F |

| A' | 04 | 81 | F' |

EX DE, HL   Exchange the HL and DE registers.

Function: DE ←→ HL

Format:

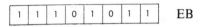

| 1 | 1 | 1 | 0 | 1 | 0 | 1 | 1 |

EB

Description: The contents of the register pairs DE and HL are exchanged.

Data Flow:

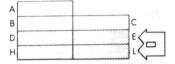

Timing: 1 M cycle; 4 T states; 2 usec @ 2 MHz

Addressing Mode: Implicit.

Flags:

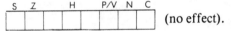

(no effect).

Example: EX   DE, HL

Before: After:

| D | A4E6 | E |
| H | 9604 | L |

| D | 9604 | E |
| H | A4E6 | L |

EB

OBJECT CODE

249

EX (SP), HL   Exchange HL with top of stack.

Function: (SP) ←→L; (SP + 1) ← H

Format:

1 1 1 0 0 0 1 1   E3

Description: The contents of the L register are exchanged with the contents of the memory location addressed by the stack pointer. The contents of the H register are exchanged with the contents of the memory location immediately following the one addressed by the stack pointer.

Data Flow:

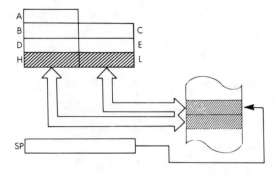

Timing: 5 M cycles; 19 T states; 9.5 usec @ 2 MHz

Addressing Mode: Indirect.

Flags:

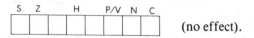

(no effect).

250

Example: EX (SP), HL

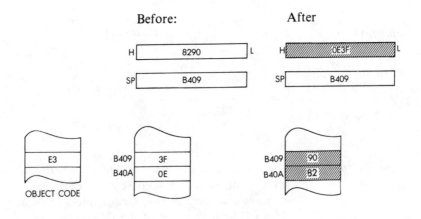

Before:

H | 8290 | L

SP | B409

After

H | 0E3F | L

SP | B409

E3

OBJECT CODE

B409 | 3F
B40A | 0E

B409 | 90
B40A | 82

Used for properly passing data to a subroutine (+ from)
(Ref: Miller, p 37/38) (also 39/40)

EX (SP), IX

Exchange IX with top of stack.

Function:

$(SP) \leftrightarrow IX_{low}; (SP + 1) \leftrightarrow IX_{high}$

Format:

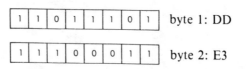

| 1 | 1 | 0 | 1 | 1 | 1 | 0 | 1 | byte 1: DD

| 1 | 1 | 1 | 0 | 0 | 0 | 1 | 1 | byte 2: E3

Description:

The contents of the low order of the IX register are exchanged with the contents of the memory location addressed by the stack pointer. The contents of the high order of the IX register are exchanged with the contents of the memory location immediately following the one addressed by the stack pointer.

Data Flow:

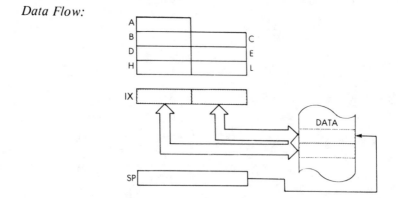

Timing:

6 M cycles; 23 T states; 11.5 usec @ 2 MHz

Addressing Mode: Indirect.

Flags:

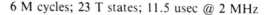

(no effect).

Example: EX   (SP), IX

Before: After:

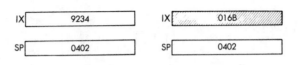

OBJECT CODE

EX (SP), IY   Exchange IY with top of stack.

Function: $(SP) \leftrightarrow IY_{low}; (SP + 1) \leftrightarrow IY_{high}$

Format:

| 1 | 1 | 1 | 1 | 1 | 1 | 0 | 1 |

byte 1: FD

| 1 | 1 | 1 | 0 | 0 | 0 | 1 | 1 |

byte 2: E3

Description: The contents of the low order of the IY register are exchanged with the contents of the memory location addressed by the stack pointer. The contents of the high order of the IY register are exchanged with the contents of the memory location immediately following the one addressed by the stack pointer.

Data Flow:

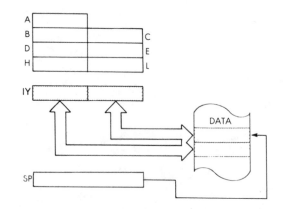

Timing: 6 M cycles; 23 T states; 11.5 usec @ 2 MHz

Addressing Mode: Indirect.

Flags:

(no effect).

Example: EX   (SP), IY

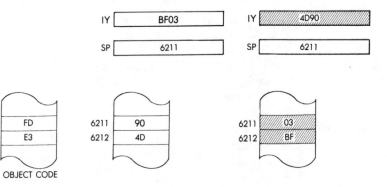

Before: After:

IY [BF03]   IY [4D90]

SP [6211]   SP [6211]

| FD |
| E3 |

OBJECT CODE

| 6211 | 90 |
| 6212 | 4D |

| 6211 | 03 |
| 6212 | BF |

255

EXX

Exchange alternate registers.

Function:

BC ↔ BC'; DE ↔ DE'; HL ↔ HL'

Format:

1	1	0	1	1	0	0	1	D9

Description:

The contents of the general purpose registers are exchanged with the contents of the corresponding alternate registers.

Data Flow:

Timing:

1 M cycle; 4 T states; 2 usec @ 2 MHz

Addressing Mode: Implicit.

Flags:

S	Z		H		P/V	N	C

(no effect).

Example:

EXX

Before:

A	04	2B	F
B	39	26	C
D	54	02	E
H	F1	D0	L

After:

A	04	2B	F
B	8C	00	C
D	93	D0	E
H	4F	E3	L

OBJECT CODE

D9

A'	3F	2A	F'
B'	8C	00	C'
D'	93	D0	E'
H'	4F	E3	L'

A'	3F	2A	F'
B'	39	26	C'
D'	54	02	E'
H'	F1	D0	L'

HALT

Halt CPU.

Function: CPU suspended.

Format:

0	1	1	1	0	1	1	0

76

Description: CPU suspends operation and executes NOP's so as to continue memory refresh cycles, until interrupt or reset is received.

Timing: 1 M cycle; 4 T states; 2 usec @ 2 MHz + indefinite Nop's.

Addressing Mode: Implicit.

Flags:

S	Z		H		P/V	N	C

(no effect).

IM 0

Set interrupt mode 0 condition.

Function: Internal interrupt control.

Format:

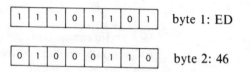

| 1 | 1 | 1 | 0 | 1 | 1 | 0 | 1 | byte 1: ED |

| 0 | 1 | 0 | 0 | 0 | 1 | 1 | 0 | byte 2: 46 |

Description: Sets interrupt mode 0. In this condition, the interrupting device may insert one instruction onto the data bus for execution, the first byte of which must occur during the interrupt acknowledge cycle.

Timing: 2 M cycle; 8 T states; 4 usec @ 2 MHz

Addressing Mode: Implicit.

Flags:

S	Z		H		P/V	N	C

(no effect).

IM 1

Set interrupt mode 1 condition.

Function: Internal interrupt control.

Format:

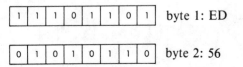

| 1 | 1 | 1 | 0 | 1 | 1 | 0 | 1 | byte 1: ED

| 0 | 1 | 0 | 1 | 0 | 1 | 1 | 0 | byte 2: 56

Description: Sets interrupt mode 1. A RST 0038H instruction will be executed when an interrupt occurs.

Data Flow:

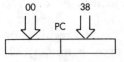

(at time of interrupt)

Timing: 2 M cycles; 8 T states; 4 usec @ 2 MHz

Addressing Mode: Implicit.

Flags:

S	Z		H		P/V	N	C

(no effect).

259

IM 2

Set interrupt mode 2 condition.

Function: Internal interrupt control.

Format:

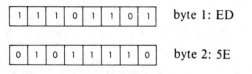

byte 1: ED

byte 2: 5E

Description: Set interrupt mode 2. When an interrupt occurs, one byte of data must be provided by the peripheral which is used as the low order of an address. The high order of this vector address is taken from the contents of the I register. This points to a second address stored in memory, which is loaded into the program counter and begins execution.

Timing: 2 M cycles; 8 T states; 4 usec @ 2 MHz

Addressing Mode: Implicit.

Flags:

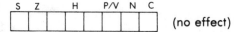

(no effect)

IN r, (C)

Load register r from port(C)

Function: r ← (C)

Format:

byte 1: ED
byte 2

Description: The peripheral device addressed by the contents of the C register is read and the result is loaded into the specified register.
C provides bits A0 to A7 of the address bus.
B provides bits A8 to A15.

Data Flow:

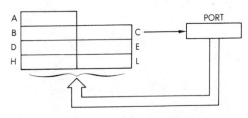

r may be any one of:

A – 111		E – 011	
B – 000		H – 100	
C – 001		L – 101	
D – 010			

Timing: 3 M cycles; 12 T states; 6 usec @ 2 MHz

Addressing Mode: External.

Byte Codes:

r:	A	B	C	D	E	H	L
ED	78	40	48	50	58	60	68

261

Flags:

S	Z		H		P/V	N	C
●	●		●		●	O	

It is important to note that INA,(N) does not have any effect on the flags, while IN r, (C) does.

Example: IN   D, (C)

Before: After:

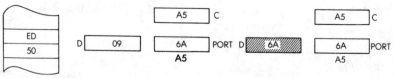

OBJECT CODE

IN A, (N)   Load accumulator from input port N.

Function: $A \leftarrow (N)$

Format:

| 1 | 1 | 0 | 1 | 1 | 0 | 1 | 1 | byte 1: DB |

| ← N → | byte 2: port address |

Description: The peripheral device N is read and the result is loaded into the accumulator.
The literal N is placed on lines A0 to A7 of the address bus. A supplies bits A8 to A15.

Data Flow:

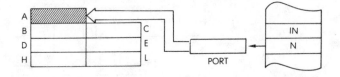

Timing: 3 M cycles; 11 T states; 5.5 usec @ 2 MHz

Addressing Mode: External.

Flags:

S	Z		H		P/V	N	C

(no effect).

Example: IN A, (B2)

Before: After:

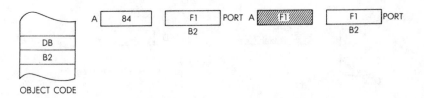

OBJECT CODE

263

INC r

Increment register r.

Function: r ← r + 1

Format:

| 0 | 0 | ← r → | 1 | 0 | 0 |

Description: The contents of the specified register are incremented. r may be any one of:

A – 111 E – 011
B – 000 H – 100
C – 001 L – 101
D – 010

Data Flow:

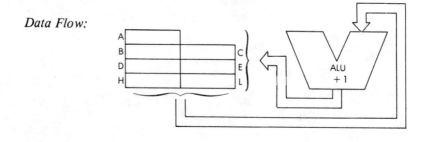

Timing: 1 M cycle; 4 T states; 2 usec @ 2 MHz

Addressing Mode: Implicit.

Byte Codes:

r: | A | B | C | D | E | H | L |
|---|---|---|---|---|---|---|
| 3C | 04 | 0C | 14 | 1C | 24 | 2C |

Flags:

Example: INC   D

OBJECT CODE

Before:

D | 06 |

After:

D | 07 |

264

INC rr

Increment register pair rr.

Function:

$$rr \leftarrow rr + 1$$

Format:

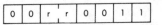

Description:

The contents of the specified register pair are incremented and the result is stored back in the register pair. rr may be any one of:

BC – 00	HL – 10
DE – 01	SP – 11

Data Flow:

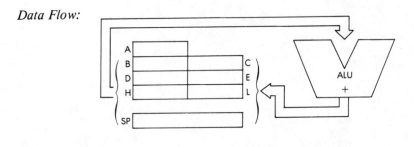

Timing:

1 M cycle; 6 T states; 3 usec @ 2 MHz

Addressing Mode: Implicit.

Byte Codes:

rr:
BC	DE	HL	SP
03	13	23	33

Flags:

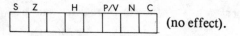

(no effect).

Example: INC HL

Before: After:

OBJECT
CODE

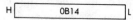

H [0B14   ] L   H [//////// 0B15 ////////] L

INC (HL)

Increment indirectly addressed memory location (HL).

Function: (HL) ← (HL) + 1

Format:

| 0 | 0 | 1 | 1 | 0 | 1 | 0 | 0 | 34

Description: The contents of the memory location addressed by the HL register pair are incremented and stored back at that location.

Data Flow:

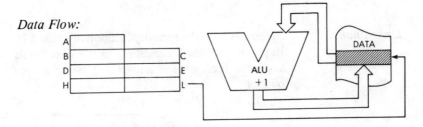

Timing: 3 M cycles; 11 T states; 5.5 usec @ 2 MHz

Addressing Mode: Indirect.

Flags:

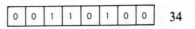

Example: INC   (HL)

Before: After:

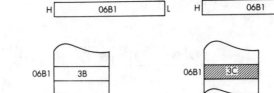

267

INC (IX + d)

Increment indexed addressed memory location (IX + d).

Function: $(IX + d) \leftarrow (IX + d) + 1$

Format:

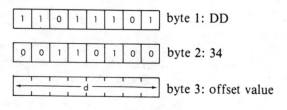

| 1 | 1 | 0 | 1 | 1 | 1 | 0 | 1 | byte 1: DD

| 0 | 0 | 1 | 1 | 0 | 1 | 0 | 0 | byte 2: 34

| ← d → | byte 3: offset value

Description: The contents of the memory location addressed by the contents of the IX register plus the given offset value are incremented and stored back at that location.

Data Flow:

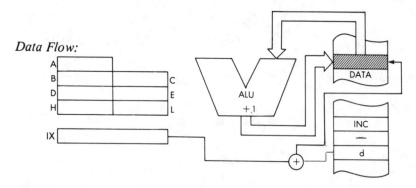

Timing: 6 M cycles; 23 T states; 11.5 usec @ 2 MHz

Addressing Mode: Indexed.

Flags:

```
  S  Z     H    P/V  N  C
 [●][●][ ][●][ ][●][○][ ]
```

Example:　　　INC　(IX + 2)

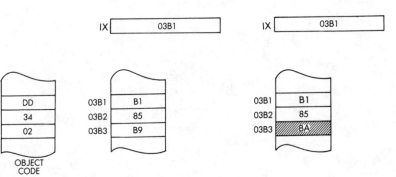

Before:

After:

IX [　　03B1　　]　　IX [　　　03B1　　　]

| DD |
| 34 |
| 02 |

OBJECT
CODE

03B1	B1
03B2	85
03B3	B9

03B1	B1
03B2	85
03B3	BA

INC (IY + d)

Increment indexed addressed memory location (IY + d).

Function: $(IY + d) \leftarrow (IY + d) + 1$

Format:

| 1 | 1 | 1 | 1 | 1 | 1 | 0 | 1 | byte 1: FD

| 0 | 0 | 1 | 1 | 0 | 1 | 0 | 0 | byte 2: 34

← d →   byte 3: offset value

Description: The contents of the memory location addressed by the contents of the IY register plus the given offset value are incremented and stored back at that location.

Data Flow:

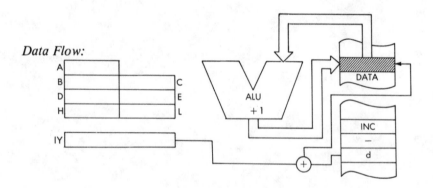

Timing: 6 M cycles; 23 T states; 11.5 usec @ 2 MHz

Addressing Mode: Indexed.

Flags:

| S | Z | | H | | P/V | N | C |
| ● | ● | | ● | | ● | ○ | |

270

Example: INC   (IY + 0)

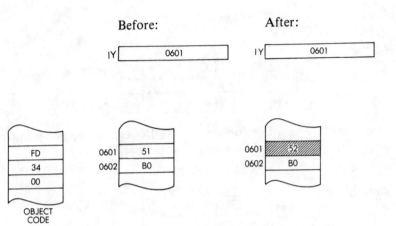

Before:

After:

IY [0601]   IY [0601]

FD
34
00

OBJECT
CODE

0601	51
0602	B0

0601	52
0602	B0

INC IX

Increment IX.

Function: $IX \leftarrow IX + 1$

Format:

| 1 | 1 | 0 | 1 | 1 | 1 | 0 | 1 | byte 1: DD

| 0 | 0 | 1 | 0 | 0 | 0 | 1 | 1 | byte 2: 23

Description: The contents of the IX register are incremented and the result is stored back in IX.

Data Flow:

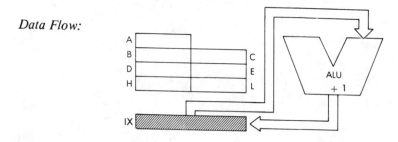

Timing: 2 M cycles; 10 T states; 5 usec @ 2 MHz

Addressing Mode: Implicit.

Flags:

S	Z		H		P/V	N	C

(no effect).

Example: INC IX

Before: After:

IX [B1B0]   IX [B1B1]

DD
23

OBJECT CODE

INC IY

Increment IY

Function: IY ← IY + 1

Format:

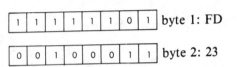

| 1 | 1 | 1 | 1 | 1 | 1 | 0 | 1 | byte 1: FD

| 0 | 0 | 1 | 0 | 0 | 0 | 1 | 1 | byte 2: 23

Description: The contents of the IY register are incremented and the result is stored back in IY.

Data Flow:

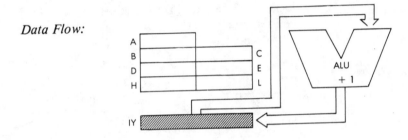

Timing: 2 M cycles; 10 T states; 5 usec @ 2 MHz

Addressing Mode: Implicit.

Flags:

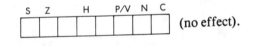

(no effect).

Example: INC IY

Before: After:

FD
23

OBJECT CODE

273

IND

Input with decrement.

Function:

$(HL) \leftarrow (C); B \leftarrow B - 1; HL \leftarrow HL - 1$

Format:

| 1 | 1 | 1 | 0 | 1 | 1 | 0 | 1 | byte 1: ED

| 1 | 0 | 1 | 0 | 1 | 0 | 1 | 0 | byte 2: AA

Description:

The peripheral device addressed by the C register is read and the result is loaded into the memory location addressed by the HL register pair. The B register and the HL register pair are then each decremented.

Data Flow:

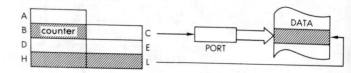

Timing:

4 M cycles; 16 T states; 8 usec @ 2 MHz

Addressing Mode: External.

Flags:

S	Z		H		P/V	N	C
?	X		?		?	1	

— Set if B = 0 after execution
Reset otherwise

Example: IND

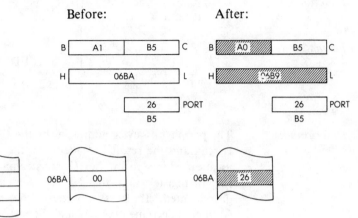

INDR

Block input with decrement.

Function: (HL) ← (C); B ← B − 1; HL ← HL − 1
Repeat until B = 0

Format:

| 1 | 1 | 1 | 0 | 1 | 1 | 0 | 1 | byte 1: ED |

| 1 | 0 | 1 | 1 | 1 | 0 | 1 | 0 | byte 2: BA |

Description: The peripheral device addressed by the C register is read and the result is loaded into the memory location addressed by the HL register pair. Then the B register and the HL register pair are decremented. If B is not zero, the program counter is decremented by 2 and the instruction is re-executed.

Data Flow:

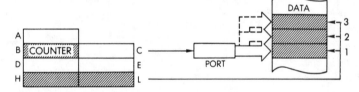

Timing: B = 0:4 M cycles; 16 T states; 8 usec @ 2 MHz.
B ≠ 0:5 M cycles; 21 T states; 10.5 usec @ 2 MHz.

Addressing Mode: External

Flags:

S	Z		H		P/V	N	C
?	1		?		?	1	

Example: INDR

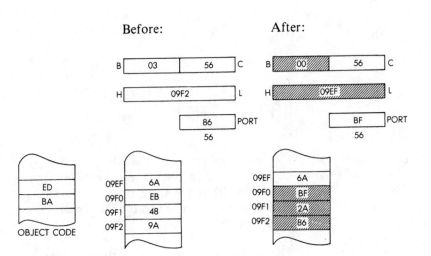

Before:

After:

INI   Input with increment.

Function: $(HL) \leftarrow (C); B \leftarrow B - 1; HL \leftarrow HL + 1$

Format:

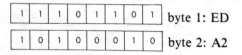

| 1 | 1 | 1 | 0 | 1 | 1 | 0 | 1 | byte 1: ED

| 1 | 0 | 1 | 0 | 0 | 0 | 1 | 0 | byte 2: A2

Description: The peripheral device addressed by the C register is read and the result is loaded into the memory location addressed by the HL register pair. The B register is decremented and the HL register pair is incremented.

The contents of C are placed on the low half of the address bus. The contents of B are placed on the high half. I/O selection is generally made by C, i.e., by A0 to A7. B is a byte counter.

Data Flow:

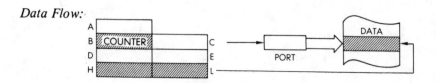

Timing: 4 M cycles; 16 T states; 8 usec @ 2 MHz

Addressing Mode: External.

Flags:

S	Z		H		P/V	N	C
?	X		?		?	1	

Z is set if B = 0 after execution, Reset otherwise

278

Example: INI

Before: After:

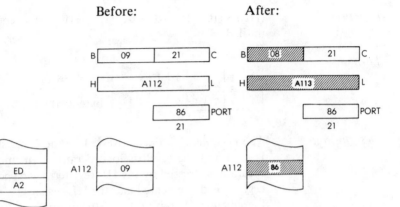

ED
A2

OBJECT CODE

INIR

Block input with increment.

Function:

(HL) ← (C); B ← B − 1; HL ← HL + 1; Repeat until B = 0

Format:

| 1 | 1 | 1 | 0 | 1 | 1 | 0 | 1 | byte 1: ED

| 1 | 0 | 1 | 1 | 0 | 0 | 1 | 0 | byte 2: B2

Description:

The peripheral device addressed by the C register is read and the result is loaded into the memory location addressed by the HL register pair. The B register is decremented and the HL register pair is incremented. If B is not zero, the program counter is decremented by 2 and the instruction is re-executed.

Data Flow:

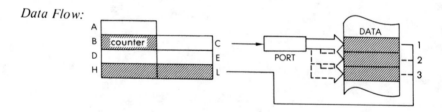

Timing:

B = 0: 4 M cycles; 16 T states; 8 used @ 2 MHz.
B ≠ 0: 5 M cycles; 21 T states; 10.5 usec @ 2 MHz.

Addressing Mode: External.

Flags:

S	Z		H		P/V	N	C
?	1		?		?	1	

Example: INIR

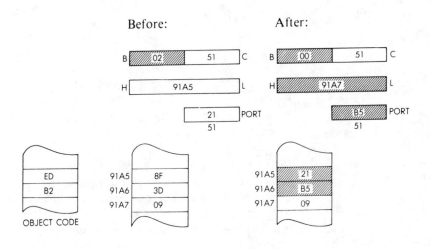

Before:

After:

OBJECT CODE

JP cc, pq

Jump on condition to location pq.

Function: if cc true: PC ← pq

Format:

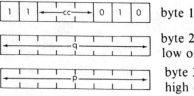

byte 1

byte 2: address, low order

byte 3: address, high order

Description: If the specified condition is true, the two-byte address immediately following the opcode will be loaded into the program counter with the first byte following the opcode being loaded into the low order of the PC. If the condition is not met, the address is ignored. cc may be any one of:

NZ	–	000	no zero
Z	–	001	zero
NC	–	010	no carry
C	–	011	carry
PO	–	100	parity odd
PE	–	101	parity even
P	–	110	plus
M	–	111	minus

Data Flow:

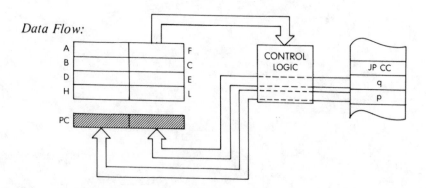

282

Timing: 3 M cycles; 10 T states; 5 usec @ 2 MHz

Addressing Mode: Immediate.

Byte Codes:

C C

	NZ	Z	NC	C	PO	PE	P	M
	C2	CA	D2	DA	E2	EA	F2	FA

Flags:

S	Z		H		P/V	N	C

(no effect)

Example: JP   C, 3B24

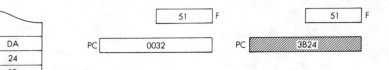

Before: After:

| 51 | F | 51 | F

PC | 0032 | PC | 3B24 |

DA
24
3B

OBJECT CODE

JP pq

Jump to location pq.

Function: $PC \leftarrow pq$

Format:

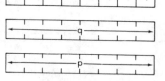

byte 1: C3

byte 2: address, low order

byte 3: address, high order

Description: The contents of the memory location immediately following the opcode are loaded into the low order half of the program counter and the contents of the second memory location immediately following the opcode are loaded into the high order of the program counter. The next instruction will be fetched from this new address.

Data Flow:

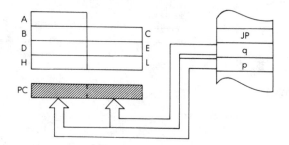

Timing: 3 M cycles; 10 T states; 5 usec @ 2 MHz

Addressing Mode: Immediate.

Flags:

S Z   H   P/V N C

(No effect)

Example: JP   3025

Before: After:

PC 5520   PC 3025

C3
25
30

OBJECT CODE

JP (HL)

Jump to HL.

Function: PC ← HL

Format:

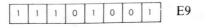 E9

Description: The contents of the HL register pair are loaded into the program counter. The next instruction is fetched from this new address.

Data Flow:

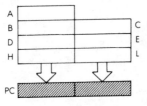

Timing: 1 M cycle; 4 T states; 2 usec @ 2 MHz

Addressing Mode: Implicit.

Flags:

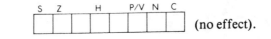 (no effect).

Example: JP (HL)

Before: After:

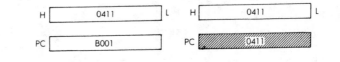

E9

OBJECT CODE

285

JP (IX)

Jump to IX.

Function: PC ← IX

Format:

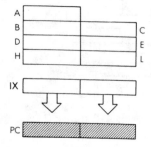

byte 1: DD

byte 2: E9

Description: The contents of the IX register are loaded into the program counter. The next instruction is fetched from this new address.

Data Flow:

Timing: 2 M cycles; 8 T states; 4 usec @ 2 MHz

Addressing Mode: Implicit.

Flags:

S Z   H   P/V N C

(no effect).

Example: JP (IX)

Before: After:

IX [80F1]   IX [80F1]

PC [3B4A]   PC [80F1]

DD

E9

OBJECT CODE

JP (IY)

Jump to IY.

Function: PC ← IY

Format:

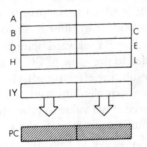

byte 1: FD

byte 2: E9

Description: The contents of the IY register are moved into the program counter. The next instruction will be fetched from this new address.

Data Flow:

Timing: 2 M cycles; 8 T states; 4 usec @ 2 MHz

Addressing Mode: Implicit.

Flags:

(no effect).

Example: JP (IY)

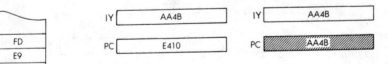

Before:

After:

IY AA4B   IY AA4B

PC E410   PC AA4B

FD
E9

OBJECT CODE

287

JR cc, e Jump e relative on condition.

Function: if cc true, PC ← PC + e

Format:

| 0 | 0 | 1 | c | c | 0 | 0 | 0 | byte 1

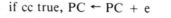 byte 2: offset value

Description: If the specified condition is met, the given offset value is added to the program counter using two's complement arithmetic so as to enable both forward and backward jumps. The offset value is added to the value of PC + 2 (after the jump). As a result, the effective offset is -126 to +129 bytes. The assembler automatically subtracts 2 from the source offset value to generate the hex code. If the condition is not met, the offset value is ignored and instruction execution continues in sequence. cc may any one of:

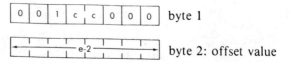

NZ – 00   NC – 10
Z – 01   C – 11

Data Flow:

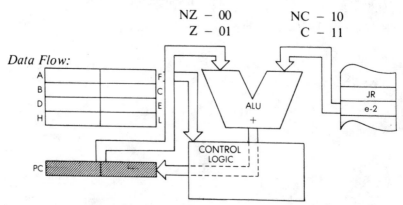

Timing:

	M cycles:	T states:	usec @ 2 MHz:
condition met:	3	12	6
condition not met:	2	7	3.5

Addressing Mode: Relative.

Byte Codes:

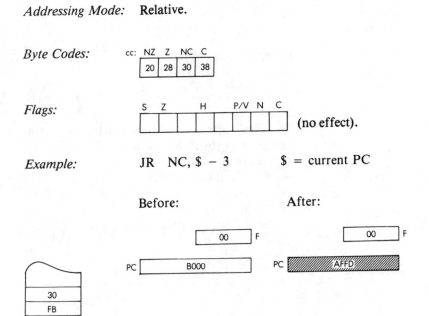

Flags:

Example: JR   NC, $ – 3 $ = current PC

Before: After:

OBJECT CODE

JR e

Jump e relative.

Function: PC ← PC + e

Format:

| 0 | 0 | 0 | 1 | 1 | 0 | 0 | 0 | byte 1: 18

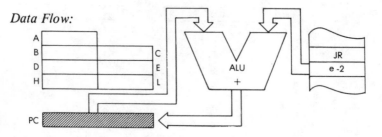 byte 2: offset value

Description: The given offset value is added to the program counter using two's complement arithmetic so as to enable both forward and backward jumps. The offset value is added to the value of PC + 2 (after the jump). As a result, the effective offset is -126 to + 129 bytes. The assembler automatically subtracts 2 from the source offset value to generate the hex code.

Data Flow:

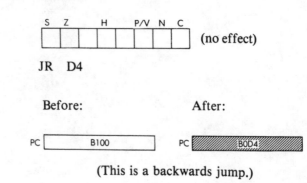

Timing: 3 M cycles; 12 T states; 6 usec @ 2 MHz

Addressing Mode: Relative.

Flags:

S	Z		H		P/V	N	C
								(no effect)

Example: JR D4

Before: After:

PC | B100 | PC | B0D4 |

(This is a backwards jump.)

| 18 |
| D2 |

OBJECT CODE

290

LD dd, (nn)   Load register pair dd from memory locations addressed by **nn**.

Function: $dd_{low} \leftarrow (nn); dd_{high} \leftarrow (nn+1)$

Format:

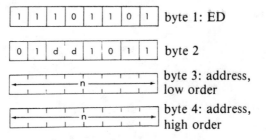

| 1 | 1 | 1 | 0 | 1 | 1 | 0 | 1 | byte 1: ED

| 0 | 1 | d | d | 1 | 0 | 1 | 1 | byte 2

n — byte 3: address, low order

n — byte 4: address, high order

Description: The contents of the memory location addressed by the memory locations immediately following the opcode are loaded into the low order of the specified register pair. The contents of the memory location immediately following the one previously loaded are then loaded into the high order of the register pair. The low order byte of the nn address immediately follows the opcode. dd may be any one of:

BC – 00   HL – 10
DE – 01   SP – 11

Data Flow:

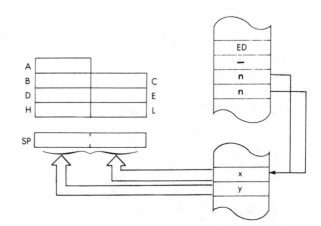

Timing: 6 M cycles; 20 T states; 10 usec @ 2 MHz

Addressing Mode: Direct.

Byte Codes: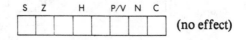

Flags:

S Z   H   P/V N C

(no effect)

Example: LD   DE, (5021)

Before: After:

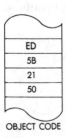

OBJECT CODE

LD dd, nn

Load register pair dd with immediate data nn.

Function: dd ← nn

Format:

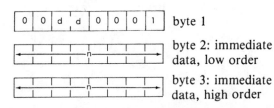

byte 1

byte 2: immediate data, low order

byte 3: immediate data, high order

Description: The contents of the two memory locations immediately following the opcode are loaded into the specified register pair. The lower order byte of the data occurs immediately after the opcode. dd may be any one of:

BC – 00   HL – 10
DE – 01   SP – 11

Data Flow:

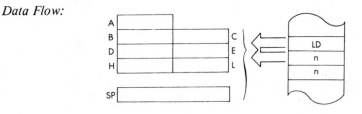

Timing: 3 M cycles; 10 T states; 5 usec @ 2 MHz

Addressing Mode: Immediate.

Byte Codes:

dd: BC DE HL SP

BC	DE	HL	SP
01	11	21	31

Flags:

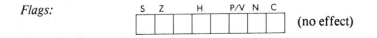

(no effect)

Example: LD   DE, 4131

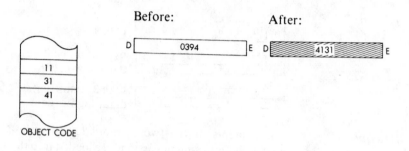

Before: After:

D [0394   ] E   D [4131   ] E

11
31
41

OBJECT CODE

LD r, n   Load register r with immediate data n.

Function: r ← n

Format:

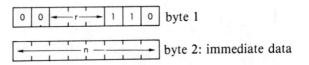

| 0 | 0 | ←——r——→ | 1 | 1 | 0 | byte 1

| ←———— n ————→ | byte 2: immediate data

Description: The contents of the memory location immediately following the opcode location are loaded into the specified register. r may be any one of:

A – 111	E – 011
B – 000	H – 100
C – 001	L – 101
D – 010	

Data Flow:

```
A
B        C        LD
D        E         n
H        L
```

Timing: 2 M cycles; 7 T states; 3.5 usec @ 2 MHz

Addressing Mode: Immediate.

Byte Codes: r:

A	B	C	D	E	H	L
3E	06	0E	16	1E	26	2E

Flags:

S	Z		H		P/V	N	C

(no effect).

295

Example: LD   C, 3B

Before: After:

C [01   ]   C [//// 3B ////]

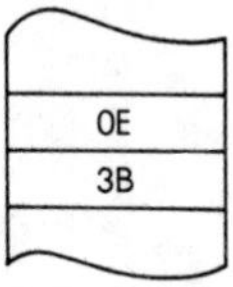

| OE |
| 3B |

OBJECT CODE

LD r, r'

Load register r from register r'.

Function: r ← r¹

Format:

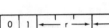

```
0  1  ←— r —→  ←—r'—→
```

Description: The contents of the specified source register are loaded into the specified destination register. r and r' may be any one of:

A – 111		E – 011	
B – 000		H – 100	
C – 001		L – 101	
D – 010			

Data Flow:

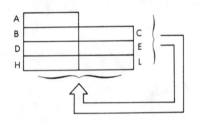

Timing: 1 M cycle; 4 T states; 2 usec @ 2 MHz

Addressing Mode: Implicit.

Byte Codes:

A B C D E H L (source)

(dest.)	A	B	C	D	E	H	L
A	7F	78	79	7A	7B	7C	7D
B	47	40	41	42	43	44	45
C	4F	48	49	4A	4B	4C	4D
D	57	50	51	52	53	54	55
E	5F	58	59	5A	5B	5C	5D
H	67	60	61	62	63	64	65
L	6F	68	69	6A	6B	6C	6D

Flags:

S	Z		H		P/V	N	C

(no effect).

Example: LD   H, A

Before: After:

OBJECT CODE

LD (BC), A   Load indirectly addressed memory location (BC) from the accumulator.

Function: (BC) ← A

Format:

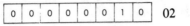 02

Description: The contents of the accumulator are loaded into the memory location addressed by the contents of the BC register pair.

Data Flow:

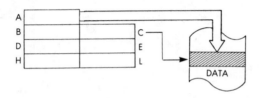

Timing: 2 M cycles; 7 T states; 3.5 usec @ 2 MHz

Addressing Mode: Indirect.

Flags:

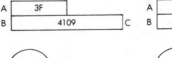 (no effect).

Example: LD   (BC), A

Before: After:

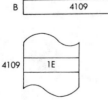

OBJECT CODE

299

LD (DE), A

Load indirectly addressed memory location (DE) from the accumulator.

Function: (DE) ← A

Format:

| 0 | 0 | 0 | 1 | 0 | 0 | 1 | 0 | 12 |

Description: The contents of the accumulator are loaded into the memory location addressed by the contents of the DE register pair.

Data Flow:

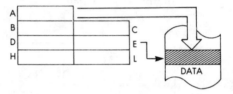

Timing: 2 M cycles; 7 T states; 3.5 usec @ 2 MHz

Addressing Mode: Indirect.

Flags:

S Z   H   P/V N C

(no effect)

Example: LD (DE), A

Before: After:

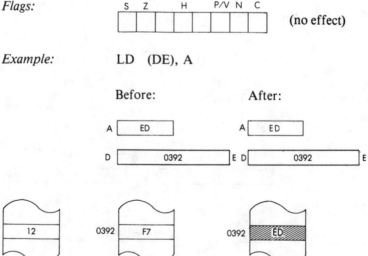

300

LD (HL), n   Load immediate data n into the indirectly addressed memory location (HL).

Function: (HL) ← n

Format:

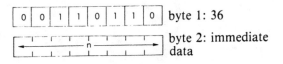

byte 1: 36

byte 2: immediate data

Description: The contents of the memory location immediately following the opcode are loaded into the memory location indirectly addressed by the HL data pointer

Data Flow:

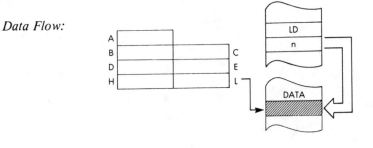

Timing: 3 M cycles; 10 T states; 5 usec @ 2 MHz

Addressing Mode: Immediate/indirect.

Flags:

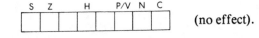

(no effect).

Example: LD   (HL), 5A

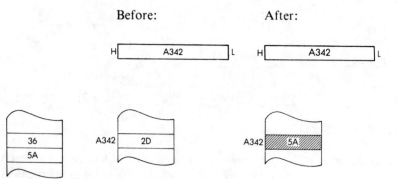

Before: After:

OBJECT CODE

LD (HL), r

Load indirectly addressed memory location (HL) from register r.

Function: (HL) ← r

Format:

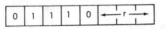

Description: The contents of the specified register are loaded into the memory location addressed by the HL register pair. r may be any one of:

A – 111	E – 011
B – 000	H – 100
C – 001	L – 101
D – 010	

Data Flow:

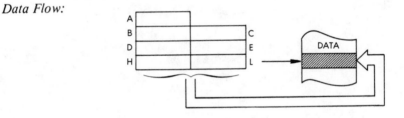

Timing: 2 M cycles; 7 T states; 3.5 usec @ 2 MHz

Addressing Mode: Indirect.

Byte Codes:

r:

A	B	C	D	E	H	L
77	70	71	72	73	74	75

Flags:

(no effect).

Example: LD   (HL), B

Before: After:

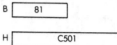

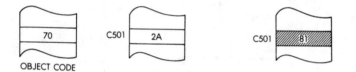

OBJECT CODE

LD r, (IX + d)   Load register r indirect from indexed memory location (IX + d)

Function: r ← (IX + d)

Format:

| 1 | 1 | 0 | 1 | 1 | 1 | 0 | 1 | byte 1: DD

| 0 | 1 | ←— r —→ | 1 | 1 | 0 | byte 2

| ←——— d ———→ | byte 3: offset value

Description: The contents of the memory location addressed by the IX index register plus the given offset value, are loaded into the specified register. r may be any one of:

A – 111	E – 011
B – 000	H – 100
C – 001	L – 101
D – 010	

Data Flow:

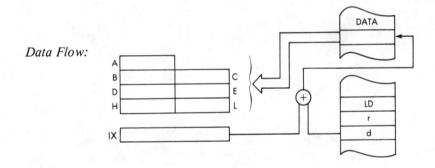

Timing: 5 M cycles; 19 T states; 9.5 usec @ 2 MHz

Addressing Mode: Indexed.

Byte Codes:

r:	A	B	C	D	E	H	L
DD-	7E	46	4E	56	5E	66	6E	-d

305

Flags:

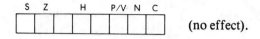

(no effect).

Example: LD   E, (IX + 5)

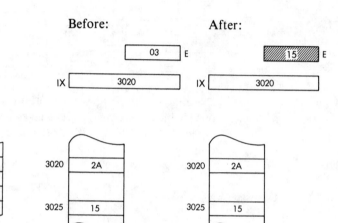

LD r, (IY + d)   Load register r indirect from indexed memory
location (IY + d)

Function: r ← (IY + d)

Format:

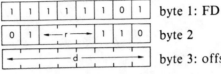

byte 1: FD

byte 2

byte 3: offset value

Description: The contents of the memory location addressed by
the IY index register plus the given offset value,
are loaded into the specified register. r may be any
one of:

A – 111		E – 011
B – 000		H – 100
C – 001		L – 101
D – 010		

Data Flow:

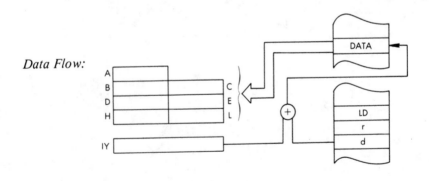

Timing: 5 M cycles, 19 T states; 9.5 usec @ 2 MHz

Addressing Mode: Indexed.

307

Byte Codes:

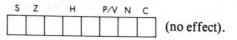

Flags:

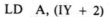

(no effect).

Example:

LD   A, (IY + 2)

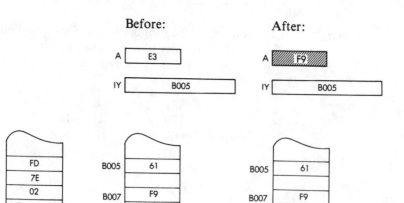

Before: After:

A [E3]   A [F9]

IY [B005   ]   IY [B005   ]

| FD |
| 7E |
| 02 |

OBJECT CODE

| B005 | 61 |
| B007 | F9 |

| B005 | 61 |
| B007 | F9 |

LD (IX + d), n   Load indexed addressed memory location (IX + d) with immediate data n.

Function: (IX + d) ← n

Format:

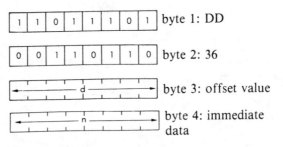

| 1 | 1 | 0 | 1 | 1 | 1 | 0 | 1 | byte 1: DD

| 0 | 0 | 1 | 1 | 0 | 1 | 1 | 0 | byte 2: 36

d — byte 3: offset value

n — byte 4: immediate data

Description: The contents of the memory location immediately following the offset are transferred into the memory location addressed by the contents of the index register plus the given offset value.

Data Flow:

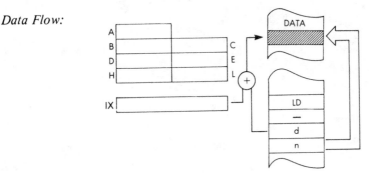

Timing: 5 M cycles; 19 T states; 9.5 usec @ 2 MHz

Addressing Mode: Indexed/immediate.

Flags:

S Z   H   P/V N C

(no effect).

309

Example: LD   (IX + 4), FF

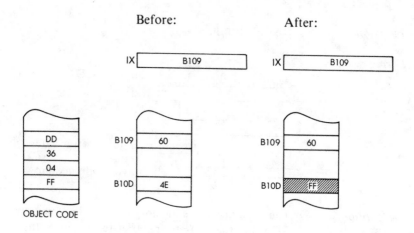

Before: After:

OBJECT CODE

LD (IY + d), n   Load indexed addressed memory location (IY + d) with immediate data n.

Function: (IY + d) ← n

Format:

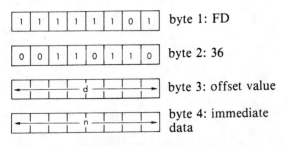

| 1 | 1 | 1 | 1 | 1 | 1 | 0 | 1 | byte 1: FD |

| 0 | 0 | 1 | 1 | 0 | 1 | 1 | 0 | byte 2: 36 |

d — byte 3: offset value

n — byte 4: immediate data

Description: The contents of the memory location immediately following the offset are transferred into the memory location addressed by the contents of the index register plus the given offset value.

Data Flow:

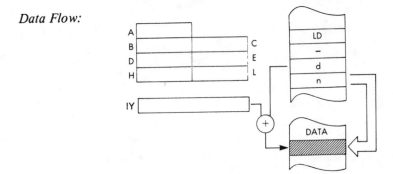

Timing: 5 M cycles; 19 T states; 9.5 usec @ 2 MHz

Addressing Mode: Indexed/immediate.

Flags:

S Z   H   P/V N C

(no effect).

Example: LD   (IY + 3), BA

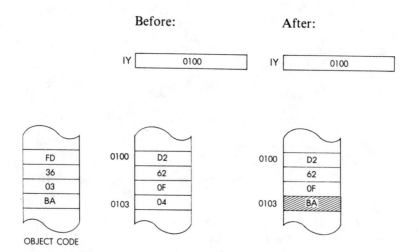

Before: After:

IY [0100]   IY [0100]

FD
36
03
BA

OBJECT CODE

LD (IX + d),r

Load indexed addressed memory location (IX + d) from register r.

Function: (IX + d)◀━r

Format:

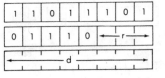

byte 1:DD

byte 2

byte 3: offset value

Description:

The contents of specified register are loaded into the memory location addressed by the contents of the index register plus the given offset value. r may be any one of:

A − 111		E − 011	
B − 000		H − 100	
C − 001		L − 101	
D − 010			

Data Flow:

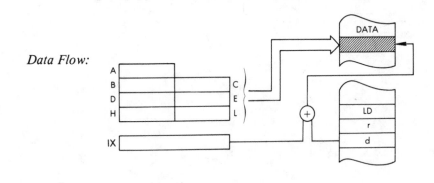

Timing: 5 M cycles; 19 T states; 9.5 usec @ 2 MHz

313

Addressing Mode: Indexed.

Byte Codes:

r: A B C D E H L
DD- | 77 | 70 | 71 | 72 | 73 | 74 | 75 | - d

Flags:

S Z   H   P/V N C

(no effect).

Example: LD   (IX + 1), C

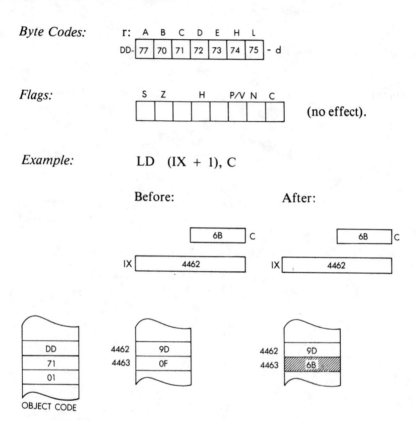

Before: After:

6B   C   6B   C

IX   4462   IX   4462

DD   4462   9D   4462   9D
71   4463   0F   4463   6B
01

OBJECT CODE

314

LD (IY + d), r Load indexed addressed memory location (IY + d) from register r.

Function: (IY + d) ← r

Format:

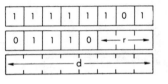

byte 1: FD

byte 2

byte 3: offset value

Description: The contents of the specified register are loaded into the memory location addressed by the contents of the index register plus the given offset value. r may be any one of:

A – 111   E – 011
B – 000   H – 100
C – 001   L – 101
D – 010

Data Flow:

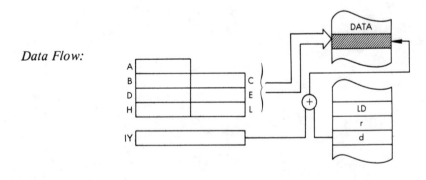

Timing: 5 M cycles; 19 T states; 9.5 usec @ 2 MHz

Addressing Mode: Indexed.

Byte Codes:

r:	A	B	C	D	E	H	L	
FD-	77	70	71	72	73	74	75	-d

Flags:

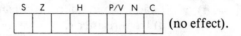 (no effect).

Example: LD   (1Y + 3), A

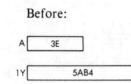

Before: After:

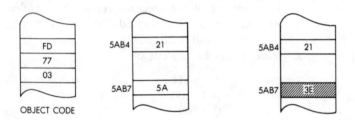

OBJECT CODE

LD A, (nn)

Load accumulator from the memory location (nn).

Function:

A ← (nn)

Format:

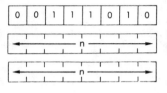

byte 1: 3A

byte 2: address, low order byte

byte 3: address, high order byte

Description:

The contents of the memory location addressed by the contents of the 2 memory locations immediately following the opcode are loaded into the accumulator. The low byte of the address occurs immediately after the opcode.

Data Flow:

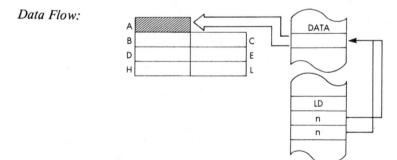

Timing:

4 M cycles; 13 T states; 6.5 usec @ 2 MHz

Addressing Mode: Direct.

Flags:

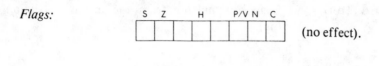

(no effect).

Example: LD   A, (3301)

Before: After:

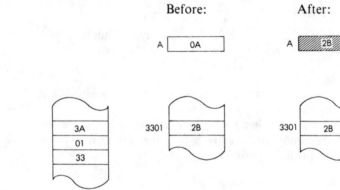

OBJECT CODE

LD (nn), A

Load directly addressed memory location (nn) from accumulator.

Function: (nn) ← A

Format:

0	0	1	1	0	0	1	0

byte 1: 32

					n					

byte 2: address, low order

					n					

byte 3: address, high order

Description: The contents of the accumulator are loaded into the memory location addressed by the contents of the memory locations immediately following the opcode. The low byte of the address immediately follows the opcode.

Data Flow:

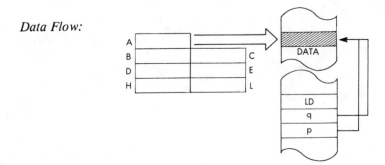

Timing: 4 M cycles; 13 T states; 6.5 usec @ 2 MHz

Addressing Mode: Direct.

Flags:

S   Z   H   P/V N   C

(no effect)

Example: LD   (0321), A

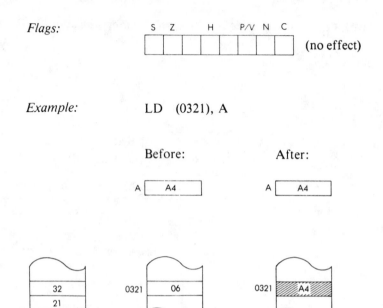

Before: After:

A [A4]   A [A4]

32
21
03

OBJECT CODE

0321 [06]   0321 [A4]

LD (nn), dd   Load memory locations addressed by nn from register pair rr.

Function: $(nn) \leftarrow dd_{low}; (nn + 1) \leftarrow dd_{high}$

Format:

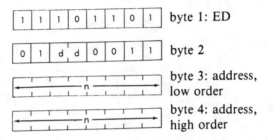

| 1 | 1 | 1 | 0 | 1 | 1 | 0 | 1 | byte 1: ED |

| 0 | 1 | d | d | 0 | 0 | 1 | 1 | byte 2 |

byte 3: address, low order

byte 4: address, high order

Descriptions: The contents of the low order of the specified register pair are loaded into the memory location addressed by the memory locations immediately following the opcode. The contents of the high order of the register pair are loaded into the memory location immediately following the one loaded from the low order. The low order of the nn address occurs immediately after the opcode. dd may be anyone of:

BC – 00   HL – 10
DE – 01   SP – 11

Data Flow:

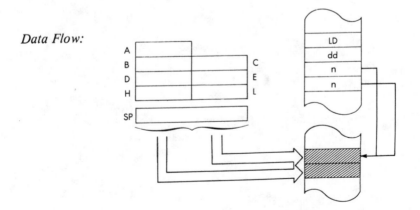

Timing:　　　　　　6 M cycles; 20 T states; 10 usec @ 2 MHz

Addressing Mode:　Direct.

Byte Codes:

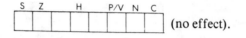

dd: BC DE HL SP

ED- 43 53 63 73

Flags:

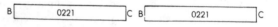

S	Z		H		P/V	N	C

(no effect).

Example:　　　　　LD　(040B), BC

Before:　　　　　　　　After:

B[　　　0221　　　]C　B[　　　0221　　　]C

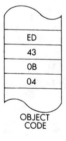

ED	
43	
0B	
04	

OBJECT
CODE

040B	06
040C	AB

040B	21
040C	02

LD (nn), HL

Load the memory locations addressed by nn from HL.

Function:

$(nn) \leftarrow L; (nn + 1) \leftarrow H$

Format:

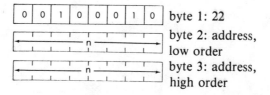

byte 1: 22

byte 2: address, low order

byte 3: address, high order

Description:

The contents of the L register are loaded into the memory location addressed by the memory locations immediately following the opcode. The contents of the H register are loaded into the memory location immediately following the location loaded from the L register. The low order of the nn address occurs immediately after the opcode.

Data Flow:

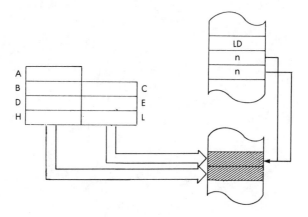

Timing:

5 M cycles; 16 T states; 8 usec @ 2 MHz

Addressing Mode: Direct.

Flags:

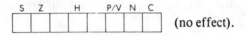

(no effect).

Example: LD   (40B9), HL

Before: After:

H [304A   ] L   H [304A   ] L

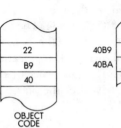

OBJECT
CODE

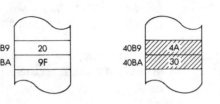

LD (nn), IX

Load memory locations addressed by nn from IX.

Function:

$(nn) \leftarrow IX_{low}; (nn + 1) \leftarrow IX_{high}$

Format:

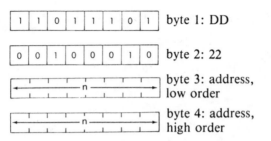

| 1 | 1 | 0 | 1 | 1 | 1 | 0 | 1 | byte 1: DD

| 0 | 0 | 1 | 0 | 0 | 0 | 1 | 0 | byte 2: 22

n — byte 3: address, low order

n — byte 4: address, high order

Description:

The contents of the low order of the IX register are loaded into the memory location addressed by the contents of the memory location immediately following the opcode. The contents of the high order of the IX register are loaded into the memory location immediately following the one loaded from the low order. The low order of the nn address occurs immediately after the op code.

Data Flow:

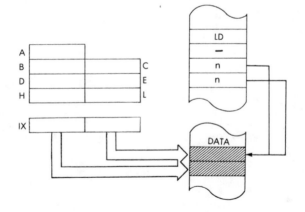

Timing:

6 M cycles; 20 T states; 10 usec @ 2 MHz

Addressing Mode: Direct.

325

Flags:

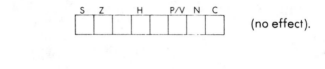

(no effect).

Example: LD   (012B), IX

Before: After:

IX [0406   ]   IX [0406   ]

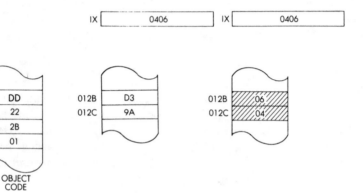

OBJECT
CODE

LD (nn), IY

Load memory locations addressed by nn from IY.

Function: $(nn) \leftarrow IY_{low}; (nn + 1) \leftarrow IY_{high}$

Format:

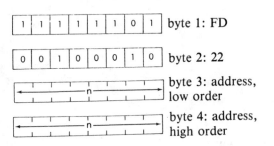

| 1 | 1 | 1 | 1 | 1 | 1 | 0 | 1 | byte 1: FD

| 0 | 0 | 1 | 0 | 0 | 0 | 1 | 0 | byte 2: 22

n — byte 3: address, low order

n — byte 4: address, high order

Description: The contents of the low order of the IY register are loaded into the memory location addressed by the contents of the memory locations immediately following the opcode. The contents of the high order of the IY register are loaded into the memory location immediately following the one loaded from the low order. The low order of the nn address occurs immediately after the opcode.

Data Flow:

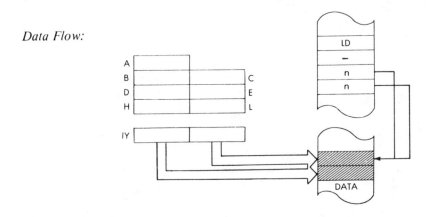

Timing: 6 M cycles; 20 T states; 10 usec @ 2 MHz

Addressing Mode: Direct.

Flags:

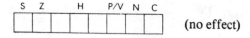

S   Z   H   P/V   N   C

(no effect)

Example: LD (BD04), IY

Before: After:

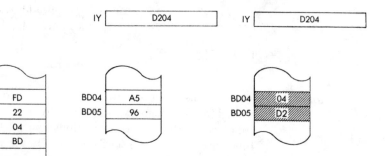

IY [D204]   IY [D204]

| FD |
| 22 |
| 04 |
| BD |

OBJECT CODE

| BD04 | A5 |
| BD05 | 96 · |

| BD04 | 04 |
| BD05 | D2 |

LD A, (BC)

Load accumulator from the memory location indirectly addressed by the BC register pair.

Function: A ← (BC)

Format:

| 0 | 0 | 0 | 0 | 1 | 0 | 1 | 0 | 0A |

Description: The contents of the memory location addressed by the contents of the BC register pair are loaded into the accumulator.

Data Flow:

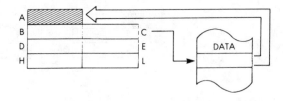

Timing: 2 M cycles; 7 T states; 3.5 usec @ 2 MHz

Addressing Mode: Indirect.

Flags:

S   Z   H   P/V   N   C

(no effect).

Example: LD   A, (BC)

Before:

After:

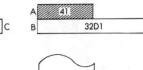

OBJECT CODE

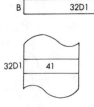

329

LD A, (DE)

Load the accumulator from the memory location indirectly addressed by the DE register pair.

Function: $A \leftarrow (DE)$

Format:

0	0	0	1	1	0	1	0	1A

Description: The contents of the memory location addressed by the contents of the DE register pair are loaded into the accumulator.

Data Flow:

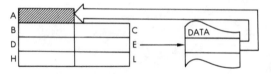

Timing: 2 M cycles; 7 T states; 3.5 usec @ 2 MHz

Addressing Mode: Indirect.

Flags:

S Z H P/V N C

(No effect).

Example: LD A, (DE)

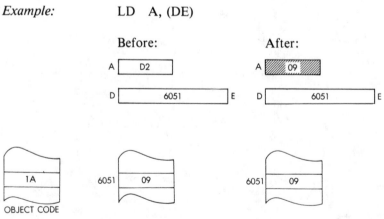

Before:

A D2

D 6051 E

After:

A 09

D 6051 E

1A
OBJECT CODE

6051 09

6051 09

330

LD A, I

Load accumulator from interrupt vector register I.

Function: $A \leftarrow I$

Format:

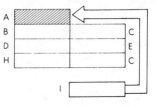

byte 1: ED

byte 2: 57

Description: The contents of the interrupt vector register are loaded into the accumulator.

Data Flow:

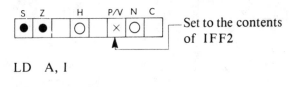

Timing: 2 M cycles; 9 T states; 4.5 usec @ 2 MHz

Addressing Mode: Implicit.

Flags:

Set to the contents of IFF2

Example: LD   A, I

Before: After:

A [30]   I [4B]   A [////4B////]   I [4B]

| ED |
| 57 |

OBJECT CODE

331

LD I, A

Load Interrupt Vector register I from the accumulator.

Function: I ← A

Format:

byte 1: ED

byte 2: 47

Description: The contents of the accumulator are loaded into the Interrupt Vector register.

Data Flow:

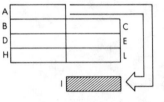

Timing: 2 M cycles; 9 T states; 4.5 usec @ 2 MHz

Addressing Mode: Implicit.

Flags:

S	Z		H		P/V	N	C

(no effect)

Example: LD I, A

Before: After:

A | 06 | I | D2 | A | 06 | I | 06 |

ED

47

OBJECT CODE

LD A, R

Load accumulator from Memory Refresh register R.

Function: A ← R

Format:

| 1 | 1 | 1 | 0 | 1 | 1 | 0 | 1 | byte 1: ED

| 0 | 1 | 0 | 1 | 1 | 1 | 1 | 1 | byte 2: 5F

Description: The contents of the Memory Refresh register are loaded into the accumulator.

Data Flow:

Timing: 2 M cycles; 9 T states; 4.5 usec @ 2 MHz

Addressing Mode: Implicit.

Flags:

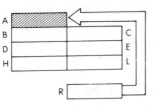

set to contents of IFF2

Example: LD   A, R

Before: After:

| ED |
| 5F |

OBJECT CODE

333

LD HL, (nn)

Load HL register from memory locations addressed by nn.

Function:

$L \leftarrow (nn); H \leftarrow (nn + 1)$

Format:

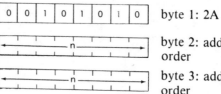

| 0 | 0 | 1 | 0 | 1 | 0 | 1 | 0 |

byte 1: 2A

byte 2: address, low order

byte 3: address, high order

Description:

The contents of the memory location addressed by the memory locations immediately after the opcode are loaded into the L register. The contents of the memory location after the one loaded into the L register are loaded into the H register. The low byte of the nn address occurs immediately after the opcode.

Data Flow:

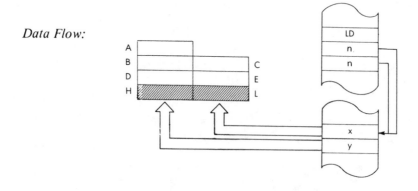

Timing:

5 M cycles, 16 T states; 8 usec @ 2 MHz

Addressing Mode: Direct.

Flags:

S Z   H   P/V N C

(no effect)

334

Example: LD   HL, (0024)

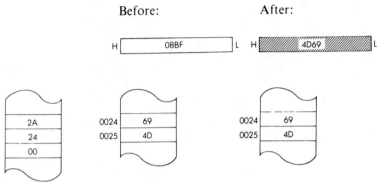

Before: After:

H [08BF   ] L   H [//// 4D69 ////] L

```
          2A        0024 | 69        0024 | 69
          24        0025 | 4D        0025 | 4D
          00
```

OBJECT CODE

LD IX, nn

Load IX register with immediate data nn.

Function: IX ← nn

Format:

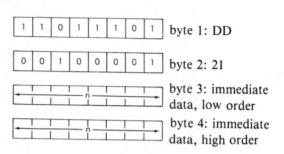

| 1 | 1 | 0 | 1 | 1 | 1 | 0 | 1 | byte 1: DD

| 0 | 0 | 1 | 0 | 0 | 0 | 0 | 1 | byte 2: 21

byte 3: immediate data, low order

byte 4: immediate data, high order

Description: The contents of the memory locations immediately following the opcode are loaded into the IX register. The low order byte occurs immediately after the opcode.

Data Flow:

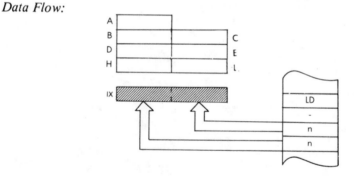

Timing: 4 M cycles; 14 T states; 7 usec @ 2 MHz

Addressing Mode: Immediate.

Flags:

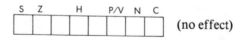

S Z H P/V N C (no effect)

Example: LD   IX, B0B 1

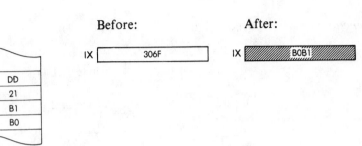

Before: After:

IX [306F   ]   IX [/////// B0B1 ///////]

DD
21
B1
B0

OBJECT CODE

LD IX, (nn)

Load IX register from memory locations addressed by nn.

Function:

$IX_{low} \leftarrow (nn); IX_{high} \leftarrow (nn + 1)$

Format:

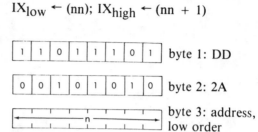

| 1 | 1 | 0 | 1 | 1 | 1 | 0 | 1 | byte 1: DD

| 0 | 0 | 1 | 0 | 1 | 0 | 1 | 0 | byte 2: 2A

byte 3: address, low order

byte 4: address, high order

Descriptions:

The contents of the memory location addressed by the memory locations immediately following the opcode are loaded into the low order of the IX register. The contents of the memory location immediately following the one loaded into the low order are loaded into the high order of the IX register. The low order of the nn address immediately follows the opcode.

Data Flow:

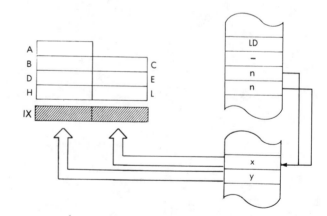

Timing:

6 M cycles; 20 T states; 10 usec @ 2 MHz

Addressing Mode: Direct.

338

Flags:

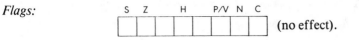

(no effect).

Example: LD   IX, (010B)

Before: After:

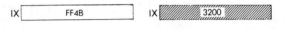

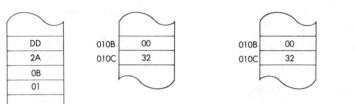

DD	
2A	
0B	
01	

OBJECT CODE

010B	00
010C	32

010B	00
010C	32

LD IY, nn

Load IY register with immediate data nn.

Function: IY ← nn

Format:

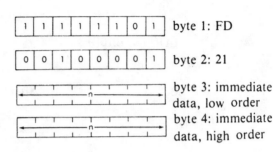

byte 1: FD

byte 2: 21

byte 3: immediate data, low order

byte 4: immediate data, high order

Description: The contents of the memory locations immediately following the opcode are loaded into the IY register. The low order byte occurs immediately after the opcode.

Data Flow:

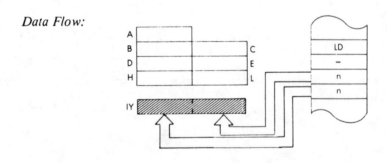

Timing: 4 M cycles; 14 T states; 7 usec @ 2 MHz

Addressing Mode: Immediate.

Flags:

S	Z		H		P/V	N	C

(no effect)

Example: LD IY, 21

Before: After:

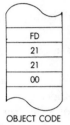

OBJECT CODE

FD
21
21
00

IY [069B]   IY [0021]

LD IY, (nn)

Load register IY from memory locations addressed by nn.

Function:

$IY_{low} \leftarrow (nn); IY_{high} \leftarrow (nn + 1)$

Format:

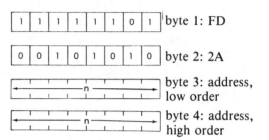

| 1 | 1 | 1 | 1 | 1 | 1 | 0 | 1 | byte 1: FD

| 0 | 0 | 1 | 0 | 1 | 0 | 1 | 0 | byte 2: 2A

n — byte 3: address, low order

n — byte 4: address, high order

Description:

The contents of the memory location addressed by the memory locations immediately following the opcode are loaded into the low order of the IY register. The contents of the memory location immediately following the one loaded into the low order are loaded into the high order of the IY register. The low order of the nn address immediately follows the opcode.

Data Flow:

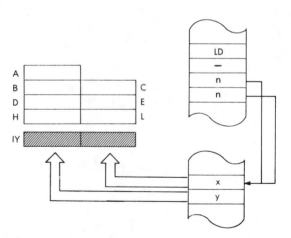

Timing: 6 M cycles; 20 T states; 10 usec @ 2 MHz

Addressing Mode: Direct.

Flags:

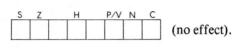 (no effect).

Example: LD IY, (500D)

Before: After:

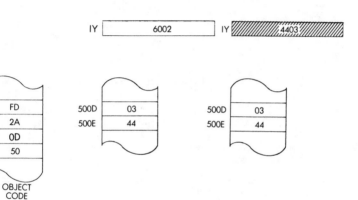

LD R,A

Load Memory Refresh register R from the accumulator.

Function: R ← A

Format:

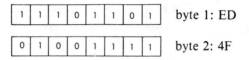

| 1 | 1 | 1 | 0 | 1 | 1 | 0 | 1 |

byte 1: ED

| 0 | 1 | 0 | 0 | 1 | 1 | 1 | 1 |

byte 2: 4F

Description: The contents of the accumulator are loaded into the Memory Refresh register.

Data Flow:

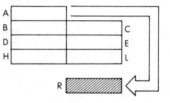

Timing: 2 M cycles; 9 T states; 4.5 usec @ 2 MHz

Addressing Mode: Implicit.

Flags:

S Z   H   P/V N C

(no effect)

Example: LD R, A

Before: After:

A [0F   ] R [40   ]   A [0F   ] R [///0F///]

| ED |
| 4F |

OBJECT CODE

LD SP, HL   Load stack pointer from HL.

Function: SP ← HL

Format:

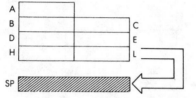

| 1 | 1 | 1 | 1 | 1 | 0 | 0 | 1 |

F9

Description: The contents of the HL register pair are loaded into the stack pointer.

Data Flow:

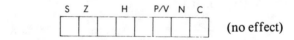

Timing: 1 M cycles; 6 T states; 3 usec @ 2 MHz

Addressing Mode: Implicit.

Flags:

S   Z   H   P/V   N   C

(no effect)

Example: LD   SP, HL

Before: After:

OBJECT
CODE

LD SP, IX

Load stack pointer from IX register.

Function: SP ← IX

Format:

byte 1: DD

byte 2: F9

Description: The contents of the IX register are loaded into the stack pointer.

Data Flow:

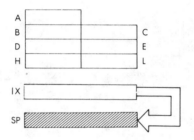

Timing: 2 M cycles; 10 T states; 5 usec @ 2 MHz

Addressing Mode: Implicit.

Flags:

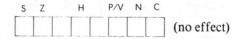

(no effect)

Example: LD SP, IX

Before: After:

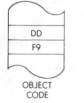

OBJECT
CODE

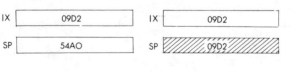

LD SP, IY

Load stack pointer from IY register.

Function: SP ← IY

Format:

| 1 | 1 | 1 | 1 | 1 | 1 | 0 | 1 | byte 1: FD

| 1 | 1 | 1 | 1 | 1 | 0 | 0 | 1 | byte 2: F9

Description: The contents of the IY register are loaded into the stack pointer.

Data Flow:

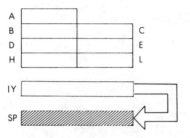

Timing: 2 M cycles; 10 T states; 5 usec @ 2 MHz

Addressing Mode: Implicit.

Flags:

S Z   H   P/V N C

(no effect)

Example: LD SP, IY

Before: After:

FD
F9

OBJECT CODE

IY | 09AB   IY | 09AB

SP | 6004   SP | 09AB

347

LDD

Block load with decrement.

Function: (DE) ← (HL); DE ← DE − 1; HL ← HL − 1;
BC ← BC − 1

Format:

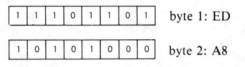

| 1 | 1 | 1 | 0 | 1 | 1 | 0 | 1 | byte 1: ED

| 1 | 0 | 1 | 0 | 1 | 0 | 0 | 0 | byte 2: A8

Description: The contents of the memory location addressed by HL are loaded into the memory location addressed by DE. Then BC, DE, and HL are all decremented.

Data Flow:

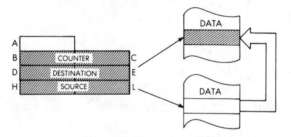

Timing: 4 M cycles; 16 T states; 8 usec @ 2 MHz

Addressing Modes: Indirect.

Flags:

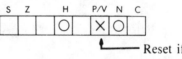

Reset if BC = 0 after execution, set otherwise.

Example: LDD

Before: After:

OBJECT CODE

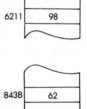

LDDR

Repeating block load with decrement.

Function: (DE) ← (HL); DE ← DE − 1; HL ← HL − 1;
BC ← BC − 1; Repeat until BC = 0

Format:

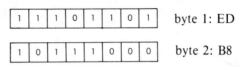

| 1 | 1 | 1 | 0 | 1 | 1 | 0 | 1 |

byte 1: ED

| 1 | 0 | 1 | 1 | 1 | 0 | 0 | 0 |

byte 2: B8

Description: The contents of the memory location addressed by HL are loaded into the memory location addressed by DE. Then DE, HL, and BC are all decremented. If BC ≠ 0, then the program counter is decremented by 2 and the instruction re-executed.

Data Flow:

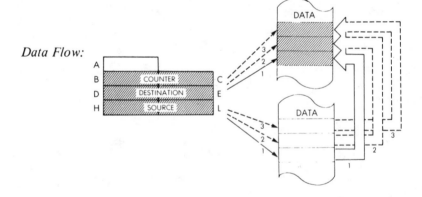

Timing: BC ≠ 0: 5 M cycles; 21 T states; 10.5 usec @ 2 MHz.
BC = 0: 4 M cycles; 16 T states; 8 usec @ 2 MHz

Addressing Mode: Indirect.

Flags:

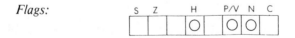

S Z   H   P/V N C

Example: LDDR

Before: After:

B	0003	C		B	0000	C
D	06B2	E		D	06AF	E
H	9035	L		H	9032	L

| ED |
| B8 |

OBJECT CODE

06AF	B1
06B0	04
06B1	DF
06B2	36

06AF	B1
06B0	DE
06B1	E1
06B2	BF

9032	92
9033	DE
9034	E1
9035	BF

9032	92
9033	DE
9034	E1
9035	BF

LDI

Block load with increment.

Function: (DE) ← (HL); DE ← DE + 1; HL ← HL + 1;
BC ← BC − 1

Format:

| 1 | 1 | 1 | 0 | 1 | 1 | 0 | 1 |

byte 1: ED

| 1 | 0 | 1 | 0 | 0 | 0 | 0 | 0 |

byte 2: A0

Description: The contents of the memory location addressed by HL are loaded into the memory location addressed by DE. Then both DE and HL are incremented, and the register pair BC is decremented.

Data Flow:

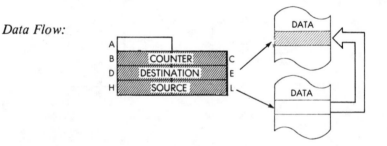

Timing: 4 M cycles; 16 T states; 8 usec @ 2 MHz

Addressing Mode: Indirect.

Flags:

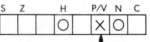

Reset if BC = 0 after execution, set otherwise.

Example: LDI

Before: After:

OBJECT CODE

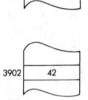

LDIR

Repeating block load with increment.

Function:

(DE) ← (HL); DE ← DE + 1; HL ← HL + 1;
BC ← BC − 1; Repeat until BC = 0

Format:

| 1 | 1 | 1 | 0 | 1 | 1 | 0 | 1 | byte 1: ED

| 1 | 0 | 1 | 1 | 0 | 0 | 0 | 0 | byte 2: B0

Description:

The contents of the memory location addressed by HL are loaded into the memory location addressed by DE. Then both DE and HL are incremented. BC is decremented. If BC ≠ 0 then the program counter is decremented by 2 and the instruction is re-executed.

Data Flow:

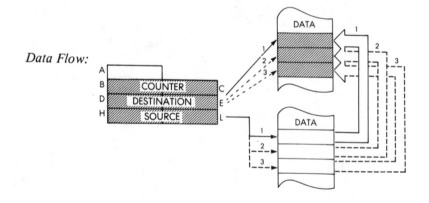

Timing:

For BC ≠ 0: 5M cycles; 21 T states; 10.5 usec @ 2 MHz.
For BC = 0: 4 M cycles; 16 T states; 8 usec @ 2 MHz

Addressing Mode: Indirect.

Flags:

S	Z		H		P/V	N	C
			○		○	○	

Example: **LDIR**

Before: After:

B	0002	C
D	4A03	E
H	962A	L

B	0000	C
D	4A05	E
H	962C	L

ED	
BO	

OBJECT CODE

4A03	12
4A04	F4
4A05	AA

4A03	3B
4A04	90
4A05	AA

962A	3B
962B	90
962C	6E

962A	3B
962B	90
962C	6E

LD r, (HL)

Load register r indirect from memory location (HL).

Function: r ← (HL)

Format:

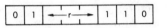

Description: The contents of the memory location addressed by HL are loaded into the specified register. r may be any one of:

A − 111		E − 011	
B − 000		H − 100	
C − 001		L − 101	
D − 010			

Data Flow:

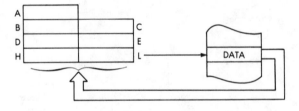

Timing: 2 M cycles; 7 T states; 3.5 usec @ 2 MHz

Addressing Mode: Indirect.

Byte Codes:

r:	A	B	C	D	E	H	L
	7E	46	4E	56	5E	66	6E

356

Flags:

S	Z		H		P/V	N	C

(no effect).

Example: LD   D, (HL)

Before: After:

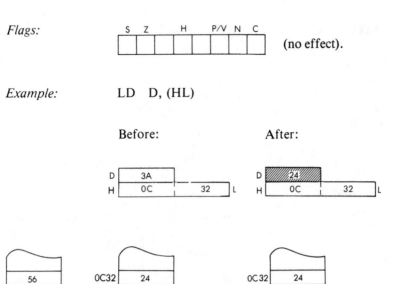

OBJECT CODE

NEG Negate accumulator.

Function: $A \leftarrow 0 - A$

Format:

| 1 | 1 | 1 | 0 | 1 | 1 | 0 | 1 | byte 1: ED

| 0 | 1 | 0 | 0 | 0 | 1 | 0 | 0 | byte 2: 44

Description: The contents of the accumulator are subtracted from zero (two's complement) and the result is stored back in the accumulator.

Data Flow:

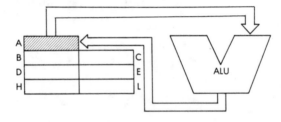

Timing: 2 M cycles; 8 T states; 4 usec @ 2 MHz

Addressing Mode: Implicit.

Flags:

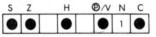

C will be set if A was 0 before the instruction.
P will be set if A was 80H.

Example: NEG

Before: After:

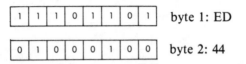

A [32] A [CE]

ED
44
OBJECT
CODE

NOP

No operation.

Function: Delay.

Format:

 00

Description: Nothing is done for 1 M cycle.

Data Flow:

```
A [        ]  No action
B [        ]        C
D [        ]        E
H [        ]        L
```

Timing: 1 M cycle; 4 T states; 2 usec @ 2 MHz

Addressing Mode: Implicit

Flags:

```
S  Z    H   P/V N  C
[ ][ ][ ][ ][ ][ ][ ][ ]   (no effect).
```

359

OR s

Logical or accumulator and operand s.

Function: $A \leftarrow A \vee s$

Format: <u>s</u>: may be r, n, (HL), (IX+ d), or (IY + d)

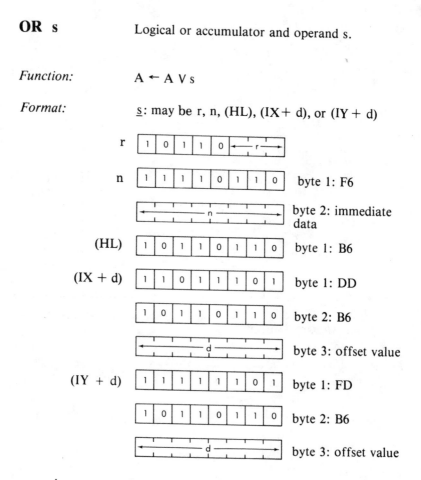

r | 1 | 0 | 1 | 1 | 0 | ←—— r ——→ |

n | 1 | 1 | 1 | 1 | 0 | 1 | 1 | 0 | byte 1: F6

| ←——————— n ———————→ | byte 2: immediate data

(HL) | 1 | 0 | 1 | 1 | 0 | 1 | 1 | 0 | byte 1: B6

(IX + d) | 1 | 1 | 0 | 1 | 1 | 1 | 0 | 1 | byte 1: DD

| 1 | 0 | 1 | 1 | 0 | 1 | 1 | 0 | byte 2: B6

| ←——————— d ———————→ | byte 3: offset value

(IY + d) | 1 | 1 | 1 | 1 | 1 | 1 | 0 | 1 | byte 1: FD

| 1 | 0 | 1 | 1 | 0 | 1 | 1 | 0 | byte 2: B6

| ←——————— d ———————→ | byte 3: offset value

r may be any one of:

A	– 111	E	– 011
B	– 000	H	– 100
C	– 001	L	– 101
D	– 010		

Description: The accumulator and the specified operand are logically 'or'ed, and the result is stored in the accumulator. s is defined in the description of the similar ADD instructions.

Data Flow:

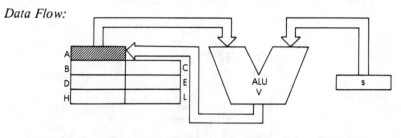

Timing:

s:	M cycles:	T states:	usec @ 2 MHz:
r	1	4	4
n	2	7	3.5
(HL)	2	7	3.5
(IX + d)	5	19	9.5
(IY + d)	5	19	9.5

Addressing Mode: r: implicit; n: immediate; (HL): indirect; (IX + d), (IY + d): indexed.

Byte Codes: OR r

r:

A	B	C	D	E	H	L
B7	B0	B1	B2	B3	B4	B5

Flags:

S	Z		H		℗/V	N	C
●	●		○		●	○	○

Example: OR B

Before:

A | 06
B | B9

After:

A | BF
B | B9

B0

OBJECT
CODE

OTDR

Block output with decrement

Function:

$(C) \leftarrow (HL); B \leftarrow B - 1; HL \leftarrow HL - 1;$
Repeat until $B = 0$.

Format:

| 1 | 1 | 1 | 0 | 1 | 1 | 0 | 1 | byte 1: ED

| 1 | 0 | 1 | 1 | 1 | 0 | 1 | 1 | byte 2: BB

Description:

The contents of the memory location addressed by the HL register pair are output to the peripheral device addressed by the contents of the C register. Both the B register and the HL register pair are then decremented. If $B \neq 0$, the program counter is decremented by 2 and the instruction is re-executed. C supplies bits A0 to A7 of the address bus. B supplies (after decrementation) bits A8 to A15.

Data Flow:

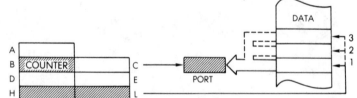

Timing:

$B = 0$: 4 M cycles; 16 T states; 8 usec @ 2 MHz.
$B \neq 0$: 5 M cycles; 21 T states; 10.5 usec @ 2 MHz

Addressing Mode: External.

Flags:

S	Z		H		P/V	N	C
?	1		?		?	1	

Example: OTDR

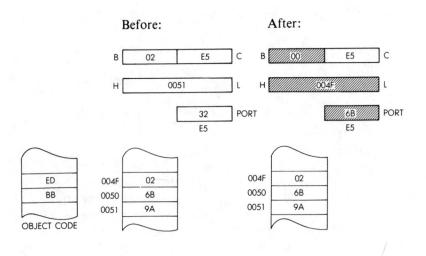

OTIR

Block output with increment.

Function: (C) ← (HL); B ← B − 1; HL ← HL + 1; Repeat until B = 0

Format:

| 1 | 1 | 1 | 0 | 1 | 1 | 0 | 1 | byte 1: ED

| 1 | 0 | 1 | 1 | 0 | 0 | 1 | 1 | byte 2: B3

Description: The contents of the memory location addressed by the HL register pair are output to the peripheral device addressed by the contents of the C register. The B register is decremented and the HL register pair is incremented. If B ≠ 0, the program counter is decremented by 2 and the instruction is re-executed. C supplies bits A0 to A7 of the address bus. B supplies (after decrementation) bits A8 to A15.

Data Flow:

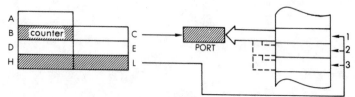

Timing: B = 0: 4 M cycles; 16 T states; 8 usec @ 2 MHz.
B ≠ 0: 5 M cycles; 21 T states; 10.5 usec @ 2 MHz

Addressing Mode: External.

Flags:

S	Z		H		P/V	N	C
?	1		?		?	1	

Example: OTIR

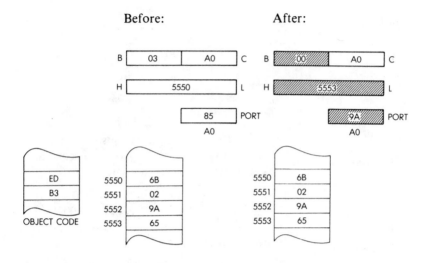

Before: After:

B	03	A0	C
H	5550	L
	85	PORT
	A0	

B	00	A0	C
H	5553	L
	9A	PORT
	A0	

| ED |
| B3 |
| OBJECT CODE |

5550	6B
5551	02
5552	9A
5553	65

5550	6B
5551	02
5552	9A
5553	65

OUT (C), r

Output register r to port C.

Function: (C) ← r

Format:

| 1 | 1 | 1 | 0 | 1 | 1 | 0 | 1 | byte 1: ED |

| 0 | 1 | ← r → | 0 | 0 | 1 | byte 2 |

Description: The contents of the specified register are output to the peripheral device addressed by the contents of the C register. r may be any one of:

A − 111		E − 011	
B − 000		H − 100	
C − 001		L − 101	
D − 010			

Register C supplies bits A0 to A7 of the address bus. Register B supplies bits A8 to A15.

Data Flow:

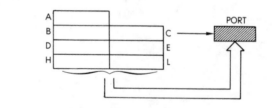

Timing: 3 M cycles; 12 T states; 6 usec @ 2 MHz

Addressing Mode: External.

Flags:

S	Z		H		P/V	N	C

(no effect).

Byte Codes:

r:	A	B	C	D	E	H	L
ED-	79	41	49	51	59	61	69

Example: OUT (C), B

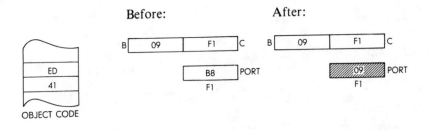

Before: After:

OBJECT CODE

OUT (N), A   Output accumulator to peripheral port N.

Function: (N) ← A

Format:

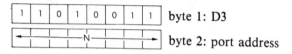

byte 1: D3
byte 2: port address

Description: The contents of the accumulator are output to the peripheral device addressed by the contents of the memory location immediately following the opcode.

Data Flow:

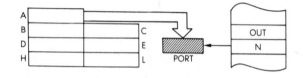

Timing: 3 M cycles, 11 T states; 5.5 usec @ 2 MHz

Addressing Mode: External.

Flags:

S Z   H   P/V N C

(no effect).

Example: OUT (0A), A

Before: After:

OUTD   Output with decrement.

Function: (C) ← (HL); BC ← B − 1; HL ← HL − 1

Format:

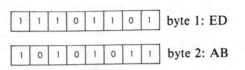

| 1 | 1 | 1 | 0 | 1 | 1 | 0 | 1 | byte 1: ED

| 1 | 0 | 1 | 0 | 1 | 0 | 1 | 1 | byte 2: AB

Description: The contents of the memory location addressed by
                          the HL register pair are output to the peripheral
                          device addressed by the contents of the C register.
                          Then both the B register and the HL register pair
                          are decremented. C supplies bits A0 to A7 of the
                          address bus. B supplies (after decrementation) A8
                          to A15.

Data Flow:

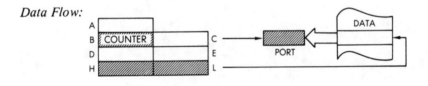

Timing: 4 M cycles; 16 T states; 8 usec @ 2 MHz

Addressing Mode: External.

Flags:

Set *if B* = 0 after execution,
reset otherwise.

Example: OUTD

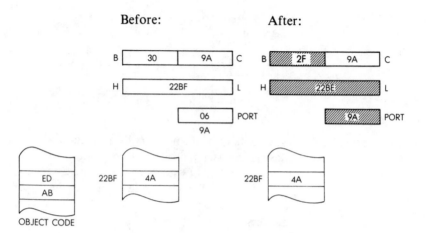

Before: After:

B [30 | 9A] C   B [2F | 9A] C

H [22BF] L   H [22BE] L

[06] PORT   [9A] PORT
    9A

ED
AB
OBJECT CODE

22BF [4A]   22BF [4A]

OUTI

Output with increment.

Function: (C) ← (HL); B ← B − 1; HL ← HL + 1

Format:

| 1 | 1 | 1 | 0 | 1 | 1 | 0 | 1 | byte 1: ED

| 1 | 0 | 1 | 0 | 0 | 0 | 1 | 1 | byte 2: A3

Description: The contents of the memory location addressed by the HL register pair are output to the peripheral device addressed by the C register. The B register is decremented and the HL register pair is incremented.

C supplies bits A0 to A7 of the address bus.
B (after decrementation) supplies bits A8 to A15.

Data Flow:

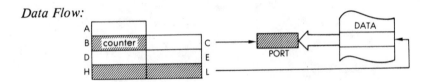

Timing: 4 M cycles; 16 T states; 8 usec @ 2 MHz

Addressing Mode: External.

Flags:

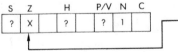

Set if B = 0 after execution, reset otherwise.

Example: OUTI

Before: After:

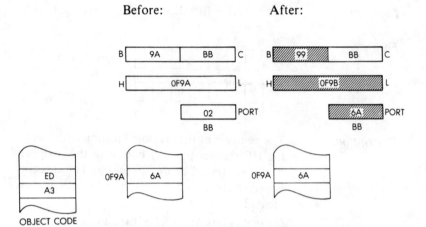

ED
A3

OBJECT CODE

POP qq

Pop register pair qq from stack.

Function:

$$qq_{low} \leftarrow (SP); \; qq_{high} \leftarrow (SP + 1); \; SP \leftarrow SP + 2$$

Format:

1	1	q	q	0	0	0	1

Description:

The contents of the memory location addressed by the stack pointer are loaded into the low order of the specified register pair and then the stack pointer is incremented. The contents of the memory location now addressed by the stack pointer are loaded into the high order of the register pair, and the stack pointer is again incremented. qq may be any one of:

BC – 00   HL – 10
DE – 01   AF – 11

Data Flow:

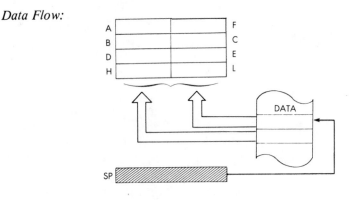

Timing: 3 M cycles; 10 T states; 5 usec @ 2 MHz

Addressing Mode: Indirect.

Byte Codes: qq:

	BC	DE	HL	AF
	C1	D1	E1	F1

373

Flags:

S	Z		H		P/V	N	C

(no effect).

Example: POP   BC

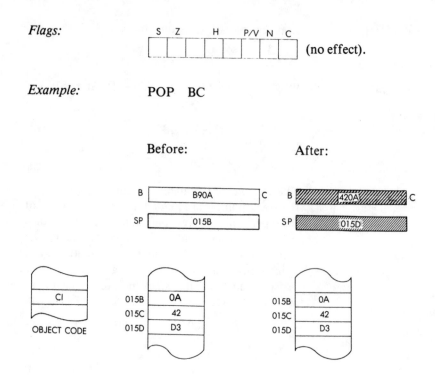

Before: After:

B [B90A] C   B [420A] C

SP [015B]   SP [015D]

CI

OBJECT CODE

015B	0A
015C	42
015D	D3

015B	0A
015C	42
015D	D3

POP IX

POP IX register from stack.

Function:

$$IX_{low} \leftarrow (SP); IX_{high} \leftarrow (SP + 1); SP \leftarrow SP + 2$$

Format:

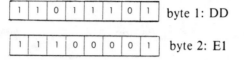

| 1 | 1 | 0 | 1 | 1 | 1 | 0 | 1 | byte 1: DD

| 1 | 1 | 1 | 0 | 0 | 0 | 0 | 1 | byte 2: E1

Description:

The contents of the memory location addressed by the stack pointer are loaded into the low order of the IX register, and the stack pointer is incremented. The contents of the memory location now addressed by the stack pointer are loaded into the high order of the IX register, and the stack pointer is again incremented.

Data Flow:

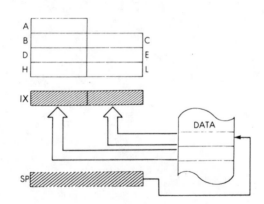
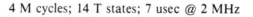

Timing:

4 M cycles; 14 T states; 7 usec @ 2 MHz

Addressing Mode: Indirect.

375

Flags:

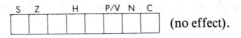

(no effect).

Example: POP   IX

Before: After:

IX [0001   ]   IX 0436

SP [090B   ]   SP 090D

OBJECT CODE

090B	36
090C	04
090D	B2

090B	36
090C	04
090D	B2

POP IY

POP IY register from stack.

Function: $IY_{low} \leftarrow (SP); IY_{high} \leftarrow (SP + 1); SP \leftarrow SP + 2$

Format:

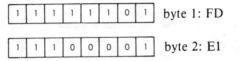

| 1 | 1 | 1 | 1 | 1 | 1 | 0 | 1 | byte 1: FD

| 1 | 1 | 1 | 0 | 0 | 0 | 0 | 1 | byte 2: E1

Description: The contents of the memory location addressed by the stack pointer are loaded into the low order of the IY register, and then the stack pointer is incremented. The contents of the memory location now addressed by the stack pointer are loaded into the high order of the IY register, and the stack pointer is again incremented.

Data Flow:

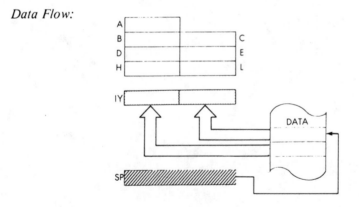

Timing: 4 M cycles; 14 T states; 2 usec @ 2 MHz

Addressing Mode: Indirect.

Flags:

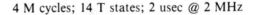

S Z H P/V N C

(no effect).

Example: POP   IY

Before: After:

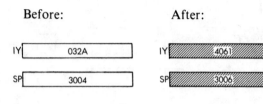

IY	032A

SP	3004

IY [4061]

SP [3006]

FD
E1

OBJECT CODE

3004	61
3005	40
3006	39

3004	61
3005	40
3006	39

PUSH qq

Push register pair onto stack.

Function:

$(SP - 1) \leftarrow qq\text{high}; (SP - 2) \leftarrow qq\text{low};$
$SP \leftarrow SP - 2$

Format:

1	1	q	q	0	1	0	1

Description:

The stack pointer is decremented and the contents of the high order of the specified register pair are then loaded into the memory location addressed by the stack pointer. The stack pointer is again decremented and the contents of the low order of the register pair are loaded into the memory location currently addressed by the stack pointer. qq may be any one of:

BC – 00	HL – 10
DE – 01	AF – 11

Data Flow:

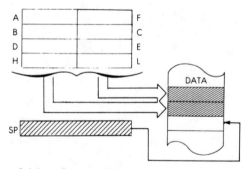

Timing:

3 M cycles; 11 T states; 6.5 usec @ 2 MHz

Addressing Mode: Indirect.

Byte Codes:

qq:
	BC	DE	HL	AF
	C5	D5	E5	F5

Flags:

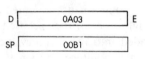

(no effect).

Example: PUSH DE

Before: After:

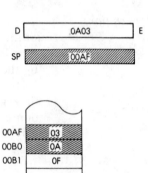

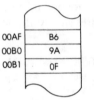

D5

OBJECT CODE

PUSH IX

Push IX onto stack.

Function:

$(SP - 1) \leftarrow IX_{high}; (SP - 2) \leftarrow IX_{low};$
$SP \leftarrow SP - 2$

Format:

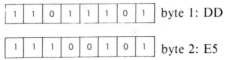

| 1 | 1 | 0 | 1 | 1 | 1 | 0 | 1 | byte 1: DD

| 1 | 1 | 1 | 0 | 0 | 1 | 0 | 1 | byte 2: E5

Description:

The stack pointer is decremented, and the contents of the high order of the IX register are loaded into the memory location addressed by the stack pointer. The stack pointer is again decremented and then the contents of the low order of the IX register are loaded into the memory location addressed by the stack pointer.

Data Flow:

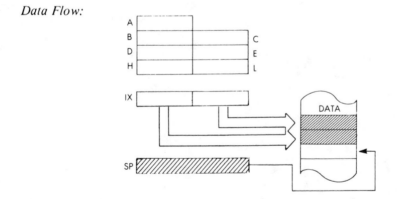

Timing:

4 M cycles; 15 T states; 7.5 usec @ 2 MHz

Addressing Mode: Indirect.

Flags:

| S | Z | | H | | P/V | N | C |

(no effect)

381

Example: PUSH   IX

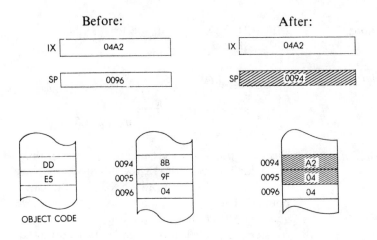

Before:

After:

IX   04A2

IX   04A2

SP   0096

SP   0094

DD	
E5	

OBJECT CODE

0094	8B
0095	9F
0096	04

0094	A2
0095	04
0096	04

PUSH IY

Push IY onto stack.

Function:

$(SP - 1) \leftarrow IY_{high}; (SP - 2) \leftarrow IY_{low};$
$SP \leftarrow SP - 2$

Format:

| 1 | 1 | 1 | 1 | 1 | 1 | 0 | 1 | byte 1: FD

| 1 | 1 | 1 | 0 | 0 | 1 | 0 | 1 | byte 2: E5

Description:

The stack pointer is decremented and the contents of the high order of the IY register are loaded into the memory location addressed by the stack pointer. The stack pointer is again decremented and the contents of the low order of the IY register are loaded into the memory location addressed by the stack pointer.

Data Flow:

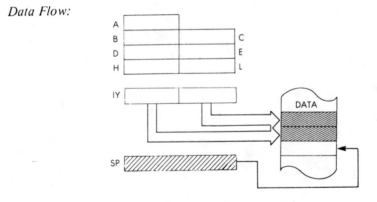

Timing:

3 M cycles; 15 T states; 7.5 usec @ 2 MHz

Addressing Mode: Indirect.

Flags:

S Z   H   P/V N C

(no effect)

Example: PUSH   IY

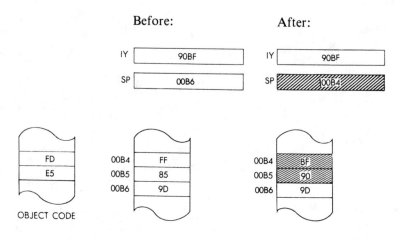

Before: After:

OBJECT CODE

RES b, s

Reset bit b of operand s.

Function: $s_b \leftarrow 0$

Format: s:

r

1	1	0	0	1	0	1	1

byte 1: CB

1	0	←—b—→	←—r—→

byte 2

(HL)

1	1	0	0	1	0	1	1

byte 1: CB

1	0	←—b—→	1	1	0

byte 2

(IX + d)

1	1	0	1	1	1	0	1

byte 1: DD

1	1	0	0	1	0	1	1

byte 2: CB

←————d————→

byte 3: offset value

1	0	←—b—→	1	1	0

byte 4

(IY + d)

1	1	1	1	1	1	0	1

byte 1: FD

1	1	0	0	1	0	1	1

byte 2: CB

←————d————→

byte 3: offset value

1	0	←—b—→	1	1	0

byte 4

b may be any one of:

0 – 000		4 – 100
1 – 001		5 – 101
2 – 010		6 – 110
3 – 011		7 – 111

r may be any one of:

A – 111		E – 011
B – 000		H – 100
C – 001		L – 101
D – 010		

385

Description: The specified bit of the location determined by s is reset. s is defined in the description of the similar BIT instructions.

Data Flow:

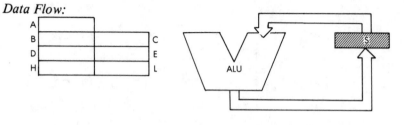

Timing:

s:	M cycles:	T states:	usec @ 2 MHz:
r	2	8	4
(HL)	4	15	7.5
(IX + d)	6	23	11.5
(IY + d)	6	23	11.5

Addressing Mode: r: implicit; (HL): indirect; (IX + d), (IY + d): indexed.

Byte Codes: RES   b, r

b: r: A   B   C   D   E   H   L

CB— 0	87	80	81	82	83	84	85
1	8F	88	89	8A	8B	8C	8D
2	97	90	91	92	93	94	95
3	9F	98	99	9A	9B	9C	9D
4	A7	A0	A1	A2	A3	A4	A5
5	AF	A8	A9	AA	AB	AC	AD
6	B7	B0	B1	B2	B3	B4	B5
7	BF	B8	B9	BA	BB	BC	BD

RES   b, (HL)

b: 0   1   2   3   4   5   6   7

CB—	86	8E	96	9E	A6	AE	B6	BE

386

			b:	0	1	2	3	4	5	6	7
RES	b, (IX + d)	DDCB —									
RES	r/ (HL)	CB —		86	8E	96	9E	A6	AE	B6	BE
RES	b, (IY + d)	FDCB —									

Flags:

S	Z		H		P/V	N	C	
								(No effect)

Examples: RES   1, H

Before: After:

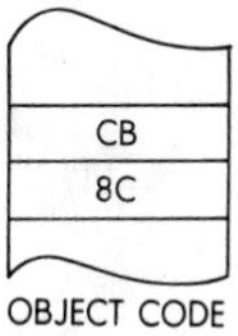

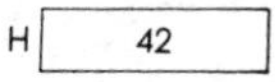

H [42]   H [40]

```
CB
8C
```
OBJECT CODE

387

RET   Return from subroutine

Function: $PC_{low} \leftarrow (SP); PC_{high} \leftarrow (SP + 1); SP \leftarrow SP + 2$

Format:

1	1	0	0	1	0	0	1	C9

Description: The program counter is popped off the stack as described for the POP instructions. The next instruction fetched is from the location pointed to by PC.

Data Flow:

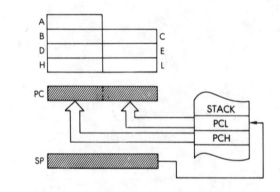

Timing: 3 M cycles; 10 T states; 5 usec @ 2 MHz

Addressing Mode: Indirect.

Flags:

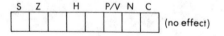

(no effect)

Example: RET

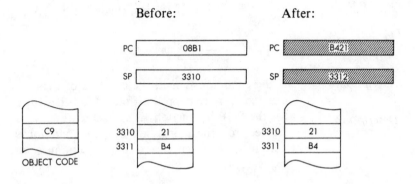

Before: After:

PC   08B1   PC   B421

SP   3310   SP   3312

C9   3310   21   3310   21
           3311   B4   3311   B4
OBJECT CODE

RET cc

Return from subroutine on condition.

Function: If cc true: $PC_{low} \leftarrow (SP)$; $PC_{high} \leftarrow (SP + 1)$; $SP \leftarrow SP + 2$

Format:

| 1 | 1 | ←—cc—→ | 0 | 0 | 0 |

Description: If the condition is met, the contents of the program counter are popped off the stack as described for the POP instructions. The next instruction is fetched from the address in PC. If the condition is not met, instruction execution continues in sequence.

Data Flow:

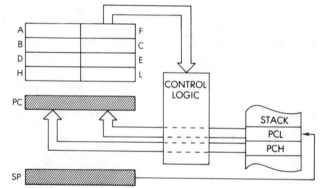

cc may be any one of:

NZ	– 000	PO	– 100
Z	– 001	PE	– 101
NC	– 010	P	– 110
C	– 011	M	– 111

Timing: Condition met: 3 M cycles; 11 T states; 6.5 usec @ 2 MHz.
Condition not met: 1 M cycle; 5 T states; 2.5 usec @ 2 MHz

Addressing Mode: Indirect.

Byte Codes:

CC:	NZ	Z	NC	C	PO	PE	P	M
	C0	C8	D0	D8	E0	E8	F0	F8

Flags:

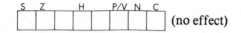

(no effect)

Example: RET NC

Before: After:

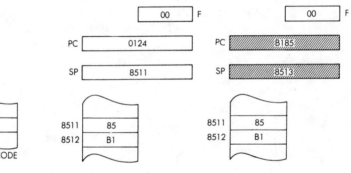

OBJECT CODE

RETI

Return from interrupt.

Function: $PC_{low} \leftarrow (SP); PC_{high} \leftarrow (SP + 1); SP \leftarrow SP + 2$

Format:

| 1 | 1 | 1 | 0 | 1 | 1 | 0 | 1 | byte 1: ED |

| 0 | 1 | 0 | 0 | 1 | 1 | 0 | 1 | byte 2: 4D |

Description: The program counter is popped off the stack as described for the POP instructions. This instruction is recognized by Zilog peripheral devices as the end of a peripheral service routine so as to allow proper control of nested priority interrupts. An EI instruction must be executed prior to RETI in order to re-enable interrupts.

Data Flow:

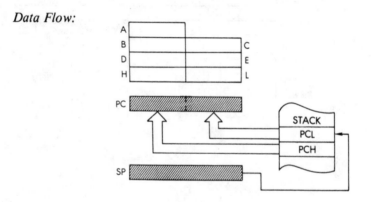

Timing: 4 M cycles; 14 T states; 7 usec @ 2 MHz

Addressing Modes: Indirect.

Flags:

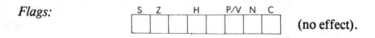

(no effect).

Example: RETI

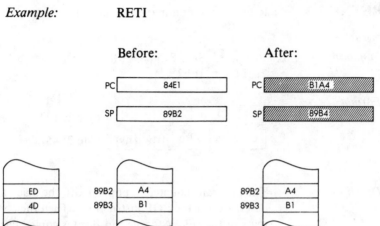

Before: After:

PC [84E1]   PC [B1A4]

SP [89B2]   SP [89B4]

| ED |
| 4D |

OBJECT CODE

| 89B2 | A4 |
| 89B3 | B1 |

| 89B2 | A4 |
| 89B3 | B1 |

393

RETN Return from non-maskable interrupt.

Function: $PC_{low} \leftarrow (SP); PC_{high} \leftarrow (SP + 1); SP \leftarrow SP + 2; IFF'1 \leftarrow IFF2$

Format:

| 1 | 1 | 1 | 0 | 1 | 1 | 0 | 1 | byte 1: ED |

| 0 | 1 | 0 | 0 | 0 | 1 | 0 | 1 | byte 2: 45 |

Description: The program counter is popped off the stack as described for the POP instructions. Then the contents of the IFF2 (storage flip-flop) is copied back into the IFF1 to restore the state of the interrupt flag before the non-maskable interrupt.

Data Flow:

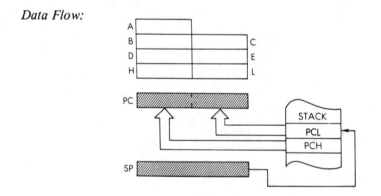

Timing: 4 M cycles; 14 T states; 7 usec @ 2 MHz

Addressing Mode: Indirect.

Flags:

S	Z		H		P/V	N	C

(no effect).

Example: RETN

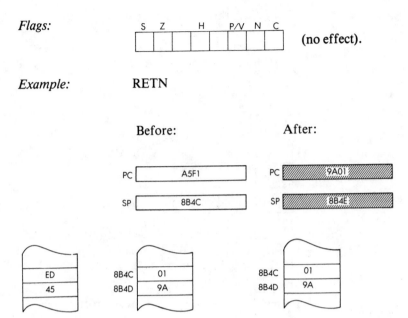

Before:

After:

PC | A5F1 |

PC | 9A01 |

SP | 8B4C |

SP | 8B4E |

ED
45

OBJECT CODE

| 8B4C | 01 |
| 8B4D | 9A |

| 8B4C | 01 |
| 8B4D | 9A |

RL s

Rotate left through carry operand s.

Function:

Format: s:

r

| 1 | 1 | 0 | 0 | 1 | 0 | 1 | 1 | byte 1: CB |

| 0 | 0 | 0 | 1 | 0 | ← r → | byte 2 |

(HL)

| 1 | 1 | 0 | 0 | 1 | 0 | 1 | 1 | byte 1: CB |

| 0 | 0 | 0 | 1 | 0 | 1 | 1 | 0 | byte 2: 16 |

(IX + d)

| 1 | 1 | 0 | 1 | 1 | 1 | 0 | 1 | byte 1: DD |

| 1 | 1 | 0 | 0 | 1 | 0 | 1 | 1 | byte 2: CB |

| ← d → | byte 3: offset value |

| 0 | 0 | 0 | 1 | 0 | 1 | 1 | 0 | byte 4: 16 |

(IY + d)

| 1 | 1 | 1 | 1 | 1 | 1 | 0 | 1 | byte 1: FD |

| 1 | 1 | 0 | 0 | 1 | 0 | 1 | 1 | byte 2: CB |

| ← d → | byte 3: offset value |

| 0 | 0 | 0 | 1 | 0 | 1 | 1 | 0 | byte 4: 16 |

r may be any one of:

A	– 111	E	– 011
B	– 000	H	– 100
C	– 001	L	– 101
D	– 010		

Description:

The contents of the location of the specific operand are shifted left one bit place. The contents of the carry flag are moved to bit 0 and the contents of bit 7 are moved to the carry flag. The final result is stored back in the original location. s is defined in the description of the similar RLC instructions.

Data Flow:

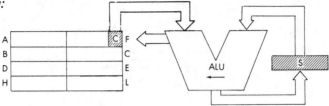

Timing:

s:	M cycles:	T states:	usec @ 2 MHz:
r	2	8	4
(HL)	4	15	7.5
(IX + d)	6	23	11.5
(IY + d)	6	23	11.5

Addressing Mode: r: implicit; (HL): indirect; (IX + d), (IY + d): indexed.

Byte Codes: RL r

r:	A	B	C	D	E	H	L
CB-	17	10	11	12	13	14	15

Flags:

S	Z		H		P/V	N	C
●	●		○		●	○	●

C is set by bit 7 of source.

Example: RL E

OBJECT CODE

CB
13

Before:

| 41 | F |
| 6E | E |

After:

| 84 | F |
| DD | E |

RLA

Rotate accumulator left through carry flag.

Function:

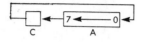

Format:

0	0	0	1	0	1	1	1

17

Description: The contents of the accumulator are shifted left one bit position. The contents of the carry flag are moved into bit 0 and the original contents of bit 7 are moved into the carry flag. (9 bit rotation.)

Data Flow:

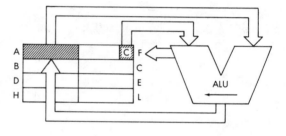

Timing: 1 M cycle; 4 T states; 2 usec @ 2 MHz

Addressing Mode: Implicit.

Flags:

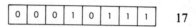

C is set by bit 7 of A.

Example: RLA

Before:

After:

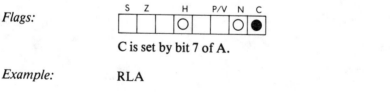

17

OBJECT CODE

RLCA

Rotate accumulator left with branch carry.

Function:

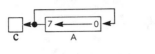

Format:

07

Description:

The contents of the accumulator are rotated left one bit position. The original contents of bit 7 is moved to the carry flag as well as to bit 0.

Data Flow:

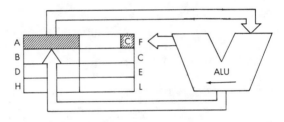

Timing:

1 M cycle; 4 T states; 2 usec @ 2 MHz

Addressing Mode:

Implicit.

Flags:

C is set by bit 7 of A.

Example:

RLCA

Before:

After:

Note: This instruction is identical to RLC A, except for the flags. It is provided for compatibility with the 8080.

RLC r

Rotate register r left with branch carry.

Function:

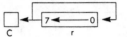

Format:

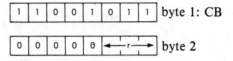

| 1 | 1 | 0 | 0 | 1 | 0 | 1 | 1 | byte 1: CB |

| 0 | 0 | 0 | 0 | 0 | ←—r—→ | byte 2 |

Description:

The contents of the specified register are rotated left. The original contents of bit 7 are moved to the carry flag as well as bit 0. r may be any one of:

A – 111	E – 011
B – 000	H – 100
C – 001	L – 101
D – 010	

Data Flow:

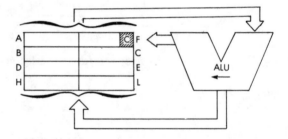

Timing: 2 M cycles; 8 T states; 4 usec @ 2 MHz

Addressing Mode: Implicit.

Byte Codes: r:

	A	B	C	D	E	H	L
CB-	07	00	01	02	03	04	05

Timing: 6 M cycles; 23 T states; 11.5 usec @ 2 MHz

Addressing Mode: Indexed.

Flags:

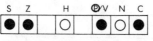

C is set by bit 7 of memory location.

Example: RLC   (IX + 1)

Before: After:

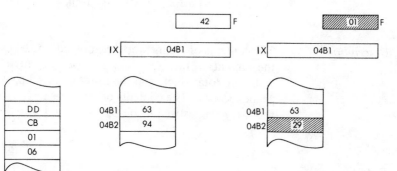

RLC (IY + d)   Rotate left with carry memory location (IY + d).

Function:

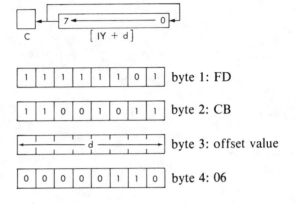

C   [IY + d]

Format:

| 1 | 1 | 1 | 1 | 1 | 1 | 0 | 1 | byte 1: FD

| 1 | 1 | 0 | 0 | 1 | 0 | 1 | 1 | byte 2: CB

| d | byte 3: offset value

| 0 | 0 | 0 | 0 | 0 | 1 | 1 | 0 | byte 4: 06

Description: The contents of the memory location addressed by the contents of the IY register plus the given offset value are rotated left and the result is stored back at the location. The contents of bit 7 are moved to the carry flag as well as bit 0.

Data Flow:

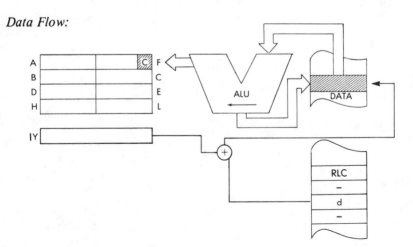

Timing: 6 M cycles; 23 T states; 11.5 usec @ 2 MHz

Addressing Mode: Indexed.

Flags:

S   Z   H   (P)/V N   C

● ●   ○   ● ○ ●

C is set by bit 7 of memory location.

Example: RLC   (IY + 2)

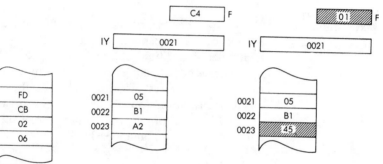

Before: After:

C4 F   01 F

IY 0021   IY 0021

FD
CB   0021 05   0021 05
02   0022 B1   0022 B1
06   0023 A2   0023 45

OBJECT CODE

RLD   Rotate left decimal.

Function:

A $\boxed{7 \quad 4 | 3 \quad 0}$ $\boxed{7 \quad 4 | 3 \quad 0}$ [HL]

Format:

1	1	1	0	1	1	0	1

byte 1: ED

0	1	1	0	1	1	1	1

byte 2: 6F

Description: The 4 low order bits of the memory location addressed by the contents of HL are moved to the high order bit positions of that same location. The 4 high order bits are moved to the 4 low order bits of the accumulator. The low order of the accumulator is moved to the 4 low order bits of the memory location originally specified. All of these operations occur simultaneously.

Data Flow:

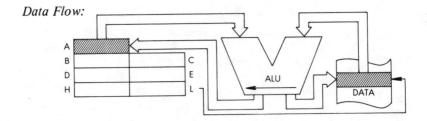

Timing: 5 M cycles; 18 T states; 9 usec @ 2 MHz

Addressing Mode: Indirect.

Flags:

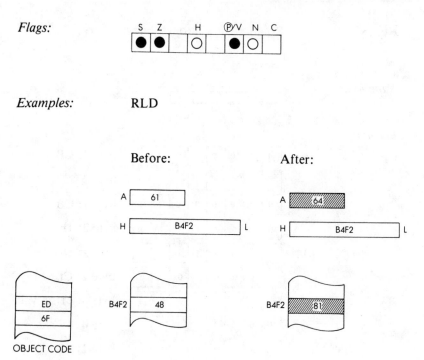

Examples: RLD

Before: **After:**

OBJECT CODE

RR s

Rotate right s through carry.

Function:

Format:

r

| 1 | 1 | 0 | 0 | 1 | 0 | 1 | 1 | byte 1: CB

| 0 | 0 | 0 | 1 | 1 | ← r → | byte 2

(HL)

| 1 | 1 | 0 | 0 | 1 | 0 | 1 | 1 | byte 1: CB

| 0 | 0 | 0 | 1 | 1 | 1 | 1 | 0 | byte 2: 1E

(IX + d)

| 1 | 1 | 0 | 1 | 1 | 1 | 0 | 1 | byte 1: DD

| 1 | 1 | 0 | 0 | 1 | 0 | 1 | 1 | byte 2: CB

| ← d → | byte 3: offset value

| 0 | 0 | 0 | 1 | 1 | 1 | 1 | 0 | byte 4: 1E

(IY + d)

| 1 | 1 | 1 | 1 | 1 | 1 | 0 | 1 | byte 1: FD

| 1 | 1 | 0 | 0 | 1 | 0 | 1 | 1 | byte 2: CB

| ← d → | byte 3: offset value

| 0 | 0 | 0 | 1 | 1 | 1 | 1 | 0 | byte 4: 1E

r may be any one of:

A	– 111	E	– 011
B	– 000	H	– 100
C	– 001	L	– 101
D	– 010		

Description:

The contents of the location determined by the specific operand are shifted right. The contents of the carry flag are moved to bit 7 and the contents of bit 0 are moved to the carry flag. The final result is stored back in the original location. s is defined in the description of the similar RLC instructions.

Data Flow:

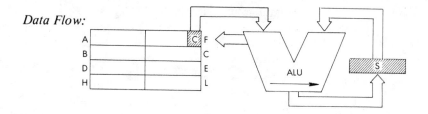

Timing:

s:	M cycles:	T states:	usec @ 2 MHz:
r	2	8	4
(HL)	4	15	7.5
(IX + d)	6	23	11.5
(IY + d)	6	23	11.5

Addressing Mode: r: implicit; (HL): indirect; (IX + d), (IY + d): indexed.

Byte Codes: RR r:

r:	A	B	C	D	E	H	L
CB-	1F	18	19	1A	1B	1C	1D

Flags:

S	Z		H		P/V	N	C
●	●		○		●	○	●

C is set by bit 0 of source data.

Example: RR H

Before: After:

H [6B] [41] F   H [B5] [81] F

CB
1C
OBJECT CODE

RRA

Rotate accumulator right through carry.

Function:

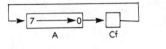

Format:

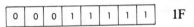 1F

Description:

The contents of the accumulator are shifted right-one bit position. The contents of the carry flag are moved to bit 7 and the contents of bit 0 are moved to the carry flag (9-bit rotation).

Data Flow:

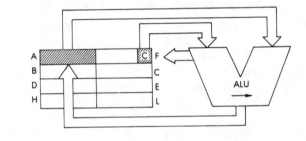

Timing: 1 M cycle; 4 T states; 2 usec @ MHz

Addressing Mode: Implicit.

Flags:

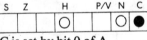

C is set by bit 0 of A.

Example: RRA

Before: After:

1F

OBJECT CODE

Note: This instruction is almost identical to RR A. It is provided for 8080 compatibility.

RRC s   Rotate right with branch carry s.

Function:

Format: s: s is any of r, (HL), (IX + d), (IY + d).

r

| 1 | 1 | 0 | 0 | 1 | 0 | 1 | 1 | byte 1: CB

| 0 | 0 | 0 | 0 | 1 | ←—r—→ | byte 2

(HL)

| 1 | 1 | 0 | 0 | 1 | 0 | 1 | 1 | byte 1: CB

| 0 | 0 | 0 | 0 | 1 | 1 | 1 | 0 | byte 2: 0E

(IX + d)

| 1 | 1 | 0 | 1 | 1 | 1 | 0 | 1 | byte 1: DD

| 1 | 1 | 0 | 0 | 1 | 0 | 1 | 1 | byte 2: CB

| ←————— d —————→ | byte 3: offset value

| 0 | 0 | 0 | 0 | 1 | 1 | 1 | 0 | byte 4: 0E

(IY + d)

| 1 | 1 | 1 | 1 | 1 | 1 | 0 | 1 | byte 1: FD

| 1 | 1 | 0 | 0 | 1 | 0 | 1 | 1 | byte 2: CB

| ←————— d —————→ | byte 3: offset value

| 0 | 0 | 0 | 0 | 1 | 1 | 1 | 0 | byte 4: 0E

r may be any one of:

A – 111	E – 011
B – 000	H – 100
C – 001	L – 101
D – 010	

Description: The contents of the location determined by the specified operand are rotated right and the result is stored back in the original location. The contents of bit 0 are moved to the carry flag as well as to bit 7. s is defined in the description of the similar RLC instructions.

Data Flow:

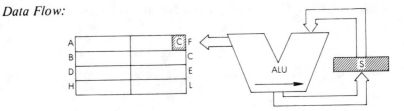

Timing:

s:	M cycles:	T states:	usec @ 2 MHz:
r	2	8	4
(HL)	4	15	7.5
(IX + d)	6	23	11.5
(IY + d)	6	23	11.5

Addressing Mode: r: implicit; (HL): indirect; (IX + d), (IY + d): in-dexed.

Byte codes:

RRC r   r:

	A	B	C	D	E	H	L
CB-	0F	08	09	0A	0B	0C	0D

Flags:

S	Z		H		(P)/V	N	C
●	●		○		●	○	●

C is set by bit 0 of source data.

Example: RRC   (HL)

Before: After:

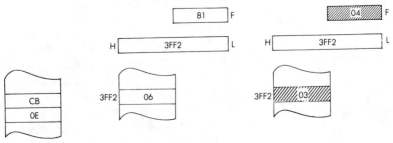

OBJECT CODE

RRCA

Rotate accumulator right with branch carry.

Function:

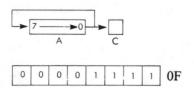

Format:

| 0 | 0 | 0 | 0 | 1 | 1 | 1 | 1 | 0F |

Description: The contents of the accumulator are rotated right one bit position. The contents of bit 0 are moved to the carry flag as well as to bit 7.

Data Flow:

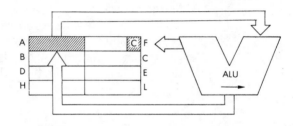

Timing: 1 M cycle; 4 T states; 2 usec @ 2 MHz

Addressing Mode: Implicit.

Flags:

| S | Z | | H | | P/V | N | C |

C is set by bit 0 of A.

Example: RRCA

Before: After:

A | D4 | 51 | F   A | 6A | 40 | F

OF

OBJECT CODE

415

RRD   Rotate right decimal.

Function:

Format:

| 1 | 1 | 1 | 0 | 1 | 1 | 0 | 1 | byte 1: ED
|---|---|---|---|---|---|---|---|

| 0 | 1 | 1 | 0 | 0 | 1 | 1 | 1 | byte 2: 67
|---|---|---|---|---|---|---|---|

Description: The 4 high order bits of the memory location addressed by the contents of the HL register pair are moved to the low order 4 bits of that location. The 4 low order bits are moved to the 4 low order bits of the accumulator. The low order bits of the accumulator are moved to the 4 high order bit positions of the memory location originally specified. All of the above operations occur simultaneously.

Data Flow:

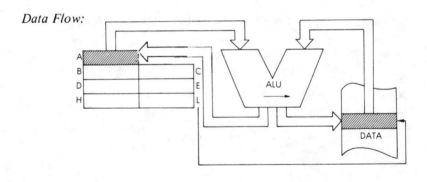

Timing: 5 M cycles; 18 T states; 9 usec @ 2 MHz

Addressing Mode: Indirect.

416

Flags:

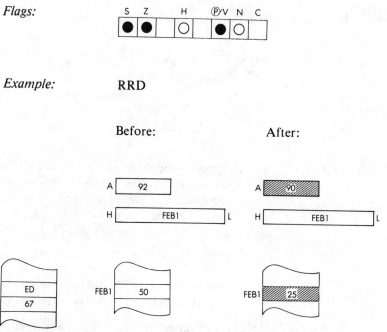

Example: RRD

Before: After:

OBJECT CODE

RST p

Restart at p.

Function:

$(SP - 1) \leftarrow PC_{high}; (SP - 2) \leftarrow PC_{low}; SP \leftarrow SP - 2; PC_{high} \leftarrow 0; PC_{low} \leftarrow p$

Format:

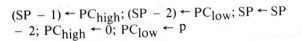

| 1 | 1 | ←—— p ——→ | 1 | 1 | 1 |

Description:

The contents of the program counter are pushed onto the stack as described for the PUSH instructions. The specified value for p is then loaded into the PC and the next instruction is fetched from this new address. p may be any one of:

00H – 000	20H – 100
08H – 001	28H – 101
10H – 010	30H – 110
18H – 011	38H – 111

This instruction performs a jump to any of eight starting addresses in low memory and requires only a single byte. It may be used as a fast response to an interrupt.

Data Flow:

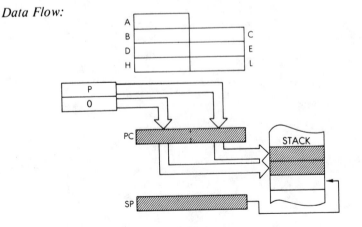

Timing: 3 M cycles; 11 T states; 5.5 usec @ 2 MHz

Addressing Mode: Indirect.

Byte Codes: p:

00	08	10	18	20	28	30	38
C7	CF	D7	DF	E7	EF	F7	FF

Flags:

S	Z		H		P/V	N	C

(no effect).

Example: RST   38H

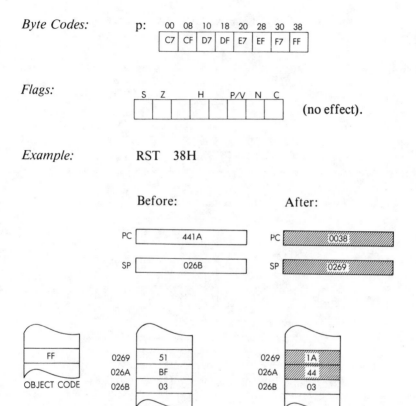

419

SBC A, s

Subtract with borrow accumulator and specified operand.

Function: $A \leftarrow A - s - C$

Format: *s:* may be r, n, (HL), (IX + d), or (IY + d)

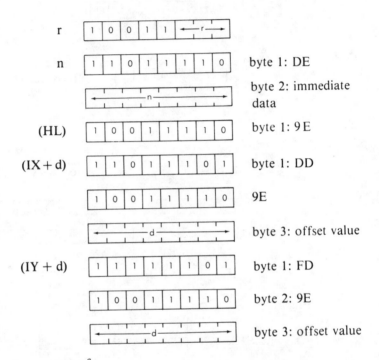

r

n — byte 1: DE

byte 2: immediate data

(HL) — byte 1: 9E

(IX + d) — byte 1: DD

9E

byte 3: offset value

(IY + d) — byte 1: FD

byte 2: 9E

byte 3: offset value

r may be any one of:

A – 111		E – 011	
B – 000		H – 100	
C – 001		L – 101	
D – 010			

Description: The specified operand s, summed with the contents of the carry flag, is subtracted from the contents of the accumulator, and the result is placed in the accumulator. s is defined in the description of the similar ADD instructions.

Data Flow:

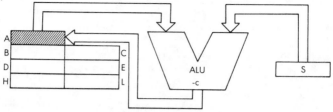

Timing:

s:	M cycles:	T states:	usec @ 2 MHz:
r	1	4	2
n	2	7	3.5
(HL)	2	7	3.5
(IX + d)	5	19	9.5
(IY + d)	5	19	9.5

Addressing Mode: r: implicit; n: immediate; (HL): indirect; (IX + d), (IY + d): indexed.

Byte Codes: SBC A, r

r: A	B	C	D	E	H	L
9F	98	99	9A	9B	9C	9D

Flags:

S	Z		H		P/V	N	C
●	●		●		●	1	●

Example: SBC A, (HL)

Before: After:

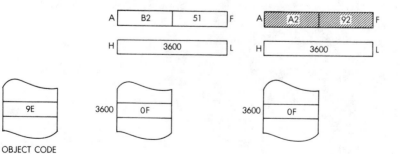

9E

OBJECT CODE

SBC   HL, ss   Subtract with borrow HL and register pair ss.

Function: HL ← HL – ss – C

Format:

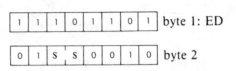

| 1 | 1 | 1 | 0 | 1 | 1 | 0 | 1 | byte 1: ED

| 0 | 1 | S | S | 0 | 0 | 1 | 0 | byte 2

Description: The contents of the specified register pair plus the contents of the carry flag are subtracted from the contents of the HL register pair and the result is stored back in HL. ss may be any one of:

BC – 00	HL – 10
DE – 01	SP – 11

Data Flow:

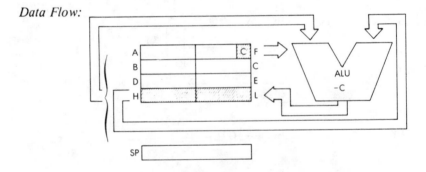

Timing: 4 M cycles; 15 T states; 7.5 usec @ 2 MHz

Addressing Mode: Implicit.

Byte Codes:

ss:

	BC	DE	HL	SP
ED–	42	52	62	72

Flags:

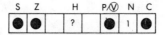

H is set if borrow from bit 12.
C is set if borrow.

Example: SBC   HL, DE

OBJECT
CODE

Before: After:

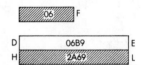

SCF

Set carry flag.

Function: C ← 1

Format:

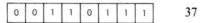

| 0 | 0 | 1 | 1 | 0 | 1 | 1 | 1 | 37 |

Description: The carry flag is set.

Timing: 1 M cycle; 4 T states; 2 usec @ 2 MHz

Addressing Mode: Implicit.

Flags:

S	Z		H		P/V	N	C
			○			○	1

SET b, s

Set bit b of operand s

Function: $s_b \leftarrow 1$

Format: s:

r	`1 1 0 0 1 0 1 1`	byte 1: CB
	`1 1 ←—b—→ ←—r—→`	byte 2
(HL)	`1 1 0 0 1 0 1 1`	byte 1: CB
	`1 1 ←—b—→ 1 1 0`	byte 2
(IX + d)	`1 1 0 1 1 1 0 1`	byte 1: DD
	`1 1 0 0 1 0 1 1`	byte 2: CB
	`←———d———→`	byte 3: offset value
	`1 1 ←—b—→ 1 1 0`	byte 4
(IY + d)	`1 1 1 1 1 1 0 1`	byte 1: FD
	`1 1 0 0 1 0 1 1`	byte 2: CB
	`←———d———→`	byte 3: offset value
	`1 1 ←—b—→ 1 1 0`	byte 4

r may be any one of:

A – 111	E – 011
B – 000	H – 100
C – 001	L – 101
D – 010	

b may be any one of:

0 – 000	4 – 100
1 – 001	5 – 101
2 – 010	6 – 110
3 – 011	7 – 111

Description: The specified bit of the location determined by s is set. s is defined in the description of the similar BIT instructions.

425

Data Flow:

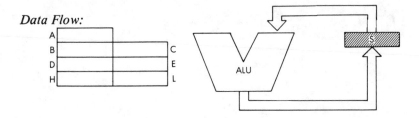

Timing:

s:	M cycles:	T states:	usec @ 2 MHz:
r	2	8	4
(HL)	4	15	7.5
(IX + d)	6	23	11.5
(IY + d)	6	23	11.5

Addressing Mode: r: implicit; (HL): indirect; (IX + d), (IY + d): indexed.

Byte Codes: SET b, r

b: r: A   B   C   D   E   H   L

CB-

b: \ r:	A	B	C	D	E	H	L
0	C7	C0	C1	C2	C3	C4	C5
1	CF	C8	C9	CA	CB	CC	CD
2	D7	D0	D1	D2	D3	D4	D5
3	DF	D8	D9	DA	DB	DC	DD
4	E7	E0	E1	E2	E3	E4	E5
5	EF	E8	E9	EA	EB	EC	ED
6	F7	F0	F1	F2	F3	F4	F5
7	FF	F8	F9	FA	FB	FC	FD

SET   b, (HL)

SET   b, (IX + d)

SET   b, (IY + d)

b:	0	1	2	3	4	5	6	7
	C6	CE	D6	DE	E6	EE	F6	FE

Flags:

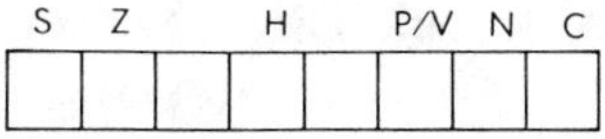

S	Z		H		P/V	N	C

(no effect)

Example: SET   7, A

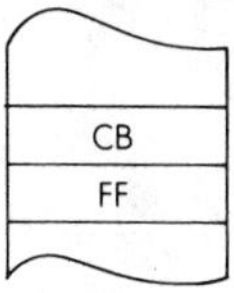

Before: After:

```
      CB
      FF
OBJECT CODE
```

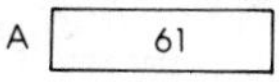

A [61   ]   A [//// E1 ////]

SLA s   Arithmetic shift left operand s.

Function:

```
┌───┐    ┌─7◄────0┐◄─ 0
│   │◄───│        │
└───┘    └────────┘
  C          S
```

Format: s:

r

1	1	0	0	1	0	1	1

byte 1: CB

0	0	1	0	0	◄──r──►

byte 2

(HL)

1	1	0	0	1	0	1	1

byte 1: CB

0	0	1	0	0	1	1	0

byte 2: 26

(IX + d)

1	1	0	1	1	1	0	1

byte 1: DD

1	1	0	0	1	0	1	1

byte 2: CB

◄──────── d ────────►

byte 3: offset value

0	0	1	0	0	1	1	0

byte 4: 26

(IY + d)

1	1	1	1	1	1	0	1

byte 1: FD

1	1	0	0	1	0	1	1

byte 2: CB

◄──────── d ────────►

byte 3: offset value

0	0	1	0	0	1	1	0

byte 4: 26

r may be any one of:

A	– 111	E	– 011
B	– 000	H	– 100
C	– 001	L	– 101
D	– 010		

Description: The contents of the location determined by the specific operand are arithmetically shifted left with the contents of bit 7 being moved to the carry flag and a 0 being forced into bit 0. The final result is stored back in the original location. s is defined in the description of the similar RLC instructions.

Data Flow:

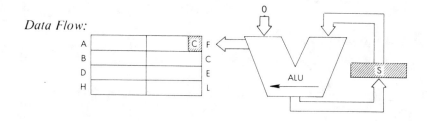

Timing:

s:	M cycles:	T states:	usec @ 2 MHz:
r	2	8	4
(HL)	4	15	7.5
(IX + d)	6	23	11.5
(IY + d)	6	23	11.5

Addressing Mode: r: implicit; (HL): indirect; (IX + d), (IY + d): indexed.

Byte Codes: SLA r

r:	A	B	C	D	E	H	L
CB-	27	20	21	22	23	24	25

Flags:

S	Z		H		P/V	N	C
●	●		○		●	○	●

C is set by bit 7 of source data.

Example: SLA (HL)

Before: After:

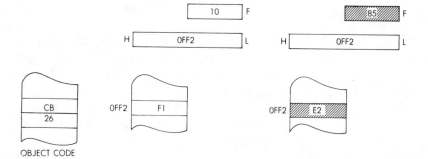

OBJECT CODE

SRA s

Shift right arithmetic s.

Function:

Format:

s:

r

| 1 | 1 | 0 | 0 | 1 | 0 | 1 | 1 | byte 1: CB |

| 0 | 0 | 1 | 0 | 1 | ← r → | | | byte 2 |

(HL)

| 1 | 1 | 0 | 0 | 1 | 0 | 1 | 1 | byte 1: CB |

| 0 | 0 | 1 | 0 | 1 | 1 | 1 | 0 | byte 2: 2E |

(IX + d)

| 1 | 1 | 0 | 1 | 1 | 1 | 0 | 1 | byte 1: DD |

| 1 | 1 | 0 | 0 | 1 | 0 | 1 | 1 | byte 2: CB |

| ← d → | | | | | | | | byte 3: offset value |

| 0 | 0 | 1 | 0 | 1 | 1 | 1 | 0 | byte 4: 2E |

(IY + d)

| 1 | 1 | 1 | 1 | 1 | 1 | 0 | 1 | byte 1: FD |

| 1 | 1 | 0 | 0 | 1 | 0 | 1 | 1 | byte 2: CB |

| ← d → | | | | | | | | byte 3: offset value |

| 0 | 0 | 1 | 0 | 1 | 1 | 1 | 0 | byte 4: 2E |

r may be any one of:

A	− 111	E	− 011
B	− 000	H	− 100
C	− 001	L	− 101
D	− 010		

Description:

The contents of the location determined by the specific operand are arithmetically shifted right. The contents of bit 0 are moved to the carry flag and the contents of bit 7 remain unchanged. The final result is stored at the original location. s is defined in the description of the similar RLC instructions.

Data Flow:

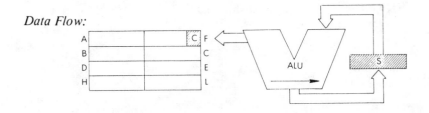

Timing:

s:	M cycles:	T states:	usec @ 2 MHz:
r	2	8	4
(HL)	4	15	7.5
(IX + d)	6	23	11.5
(IY + d)	6	23	11.5

Addressing Mode: r: implicit; (HL): indirect; (IX + d), (IY + d): indexed.

Byte Codes:

SRA r

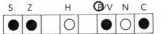

r:	A	B	C	D	E	H	L
CB-	2F	28	29	2A	2B	2C	2D

Flags:

S Z H P/V N C

C is set by bit 0 of source data.

Example: SRA A

CB
2F

OBJECT CODE

Before:

A [8B | 04] F

After:

A [C5 | 85] F

SRL s

Logical shift right s.

Function:

$$0 \rightarrow \boxed{7 \longrightarrow 0} \rightarrow \boxed{}$$

s   c

Format: s:

r

| 1 | 1 | 0 | 0 | 1 | 0 | 1 | 1 | byte 1: CB |

| 0 | 0 | 1 | 1 | 1 | ← | r | → | byte 2 |

(HL)

| 1 | 1 | 0 | 0 | 1 | 0 | 1 | 1 | byte 1: CB |

| 0 | 0 | 1 | 1 | 1 | 1 | 1 | 0 | byte 2: 3E |

(IX + d)

| 1 | 1 | 0 | 1 | 1 | 1 | 0 | 1 | byte 1: DD |

| 1 | 1 | 0 | 0 | 1 | 0 | 1 | 1 | byte 2: CB |

| ← | | | d | | | → | | byte 3: offset value |

| 0 | 0 | 1 | 1 | 1 | 1 | 1 | 0 | byte 4: 3E |

(IY + d)

| 1 | 1 | 1 | 1 | 1 | 1 | 0 | 1 | byte 1: FD |

| 1 | 1 | 0 | 0 | 1 | 0 | 1 | 1 | byte 2: CB |

| ← | | | d | | | → | | byte 3: offset value |

| 0 | 0 | 1 | 1 | 1 | 1 | 1 | 0 | byte 4: 3E |

r may be any one of:

A	– 111	E	– 011
B	– 000	H	– 100
C	– 001	L	– 101
D	– 010		

Description:

The contents of the location determined by the specific operand are logically shifted right. A zero is moved into bit 7 and the contents of bit 0 are moved into the carry flag. The final result is stored back in the original location.

Data Flow:

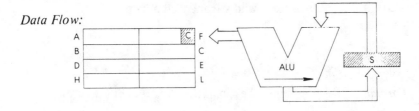

Timing:

s:	M cycles:	T states:	usec @ 2 MHz:
r	2	8	4
(HL)	4	15	7.5
(IX + d)	6	23	11.5
(IY + d)	6	23	11.5

Addressing Mode: r: implicit; (HL): indirect; (IX + d), (IY + d): indexed.

Byte Codes: SRL r

r:	A	B	C	D	E	H	L
CB	3F	38	39	3A	3B	3C	3D

Flags:

S	Z		H		P/V	N	C
●	●		○		●	○	●

C is set by bit 0 of source data.

Example: SRL E

Before: After:

OBJECT CODE

| 01 | F | → | 00 | F |
| 02 | E | → | 01 | E |

CB
3B

433

SUB s   Subtract operand s from accumulator.

Function: A ← A – s

Format: s: may be r, n, (HL), (IX + d) or (IY + d)

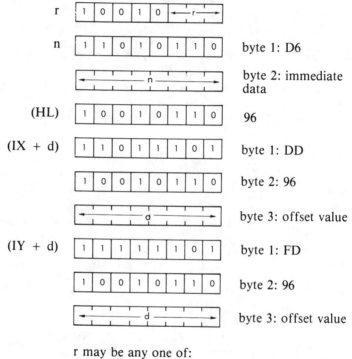

r | 1 | 0 | 0 | 1 | 0 |←—r—→|

n | 1 | 1 | 0 | 1 | 0 | 1 | 1 | 0 | byte 1: D6

     |←————— n —————→| byte 2: immediate data

(HL) | 1 | 0 | 0 | 1 | 0 | 1 | 1 | 0 | 96

(IX + d) | 1 | 1 | 0 | 1 | 1 | 1 | 0 | 1 | byte 1: DD

     | 1 | 0 | 0 | 1 | 0 | 1 | 1 | 0 | byte 2: 96

     |←————— d —————→| byte 3: offset value

(IY + d) | 1 | 1 | 1 | 1 | 1 | 1 | 0 | 1 | byte 1: FD

     | 1 | 0 | 0 | 1 | 0 | 1 | 1 | 0 | byte 2: 96

     |←————— d —————→| byte 3: offset value

r may be any one of:

A – 111   E – 011
B – 000   H – 100
C – 001   L – 101
D – 010

Description: The specified operand s is subtracted from the accumulator and the result is stored in the accumulator. The operand s is defined in the description of the similar ADD instructions.

Data Flow:

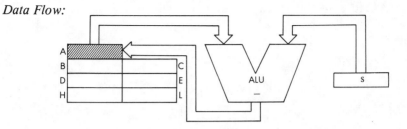

Timing:

s:	M cycles:	T states:	usec @ 2 MHz:
r	1	4	2
n	2	7	3.5
(HL)	2	7	3.5
(IX + d)	5	19	9.5
(IX + d)	5	19	9.5

Addressing Mode: r: implicit; n: immediate; (HL): indirect; (IX + d), (IY + d): indexed

Byte Codes: SUB r

r:	A	B	C	D	E	H	L
	97	90	91	92	93	94	95

Flags:

S	Z		H		P/V	N	C
●	●		●		●	1	●

Example: SUB B

Before:

A	80
B	31

After:

A	4F
B	31

90

OBJECT CODE

435

XOR s

Exclusive or accumulator and s.

Function: $A \leftarrow A \veebar s$

Format: s: may be r, n, (HL), (IX + d), or (IY + d)

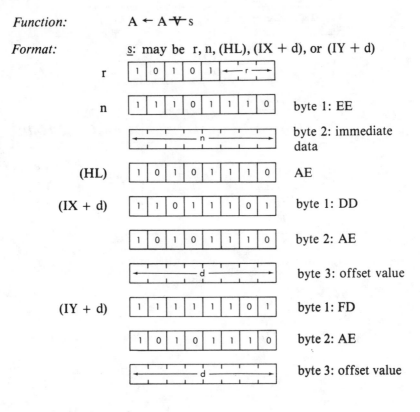

r

| 1 | 0 | 1 | 0 | 1 | ←— r —→ |

n

| 1 | 1 | 1 | 0 | 1 | 1 | 1 | 0 | byte 1: EE

| ←——————— n ———————→ | byte 2: immediate data

(HL)

| 1 | 0 | 1 | 0 | 1 | 1 | 1 | 0 | AE

(IX + d)

| 1 | 1 | 0 | 1 | 1 | 1 | 0 | 1 | byte 1: DD

| 1 | 0 | 1 | 0 | 1 | 1 | 1 | 0 | byte 2: AE

| ←——————— d ———————→ | byte 3: offset value

(IY + d)

| 1 | 1 | 1 | 1 | 1 | 1 | 0 | 1 | byte 1: FD

| 1 | 0 | 1 | 0 | 1 | 1 | 1 | 0 | byte 2: AE

| ←——————— d ———————→ | byte 3: offset value

r may be any one of:

A	– 111	E	– 011
B	– 000	H	– 100
C	– 001	L	– 101
D	– 010		

Description: The accumulator and the specified operand s are exclusive 'or'ed, and the result is stored in the accumulator. s is defined in the description of the similar ADD instructions.

Date Flow:

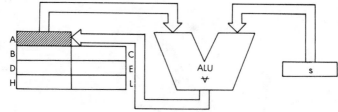

Timing:

s:	M cycles:	T states:	usec @ 2 MHz:
r	1	4	2
n	2	7	3.5
(HL)	2	7	3.5
(IX + d)	5	19	9.5
(IY + d)	5	19	9.5

Addressing Modes: r: implicit; n: immediate; (HL): indirect; (IX + d), (IY + d): indexed

Byte Codes: XOR   r

r:

A	B	C	D	E	H	L
AF	A8	A9	AA	AB	AC	AD

Flags:

S	Z		H		P/V	N	C
●	●		○		●	○	○

Example: XOR   B1H

Before:

A | 36 |

After:

A | 37 |

| EE |
| B1 |

OBJECT CODE

5

ADDRESSING TECHNIQUES

INTRODUCTION

This chapter will present the general theory of addressing and the various techniques which have been developed to facilitate the retrieval of data. In a second section, the specific addressing modes available in the Z80 will be reviewed, along with their advantages and limitations. Finally, in order to familiarize the reader with the various trade-offs possible, an applications section will demonstrate possible trade-offs between the various addressing techniques by studying specific application programs.

Because the Z80 has several 16-bit registers, in addition to the program counter, which can be used to specify an address, it is important that the Z80 user understand the various addressing modes, and in particular, the use of the index registers. Complex retrieval modes may be omitted at the beginning stage. However, all the addressing modes are useful in developing programs for this microprocessor. Let us now study the various alternatives available.

POSSIBLE ADDRESSING MODES

Addressing refers to the specification, within an instruction, of the location of the operand on which the instruction will operate. The main addressing methods will now be examined. They are all illustrated in Figure 5.1.

Implicit Addressing (or "Implied," or "Register")

Instructions which operate exclusively on registers normally use *implicit addressing*. This is illustrated in Figure 5.1. An implicit instruc-

438

tion derives its name from the fact that it does not specifically contain the address of the operand on which it operates. Instead, its opcode specifies one or more registers, usually the accumulator, or else any other register(s). Since internal registers are usually few in number (commonly eight), this will require a small number of bits. As an example, three bits within the instruction will point to one out of eight internal registers. Such instructions can, therefore, normally be encoded within eight bits. This is an important advantage, since an eight-bit instruction normally executes faster than any two- or three-byte instruction.

An example of an implicit instruction is:

LD A, B

which specifies "transfer the contents of B into A" (Load A from B.)

Immediate Addressing

Immediate addressing is illustrated in Figure 5.1. The eight-bit opcode is followed by an 8- or 16-bit literal (a constant). This type of instruction is needed, for example, to load an eight-bit value in an eight-bit register. Since the microprocessor is equipped with 16-bit registers, it may also be necessary to load 16-bit literals. An example of an immediate instruction is:

ADD A, 0H

The second word of this instruction contains the literal "0", which is added to the accumulator.

Absolute Addressing

Absolute addressing usually refers to the way in which data is retrieved from or placed in memory, in which an opcode is followed by a 16-bit address. Absolute addressing, therefore, requires three-byte instructions. An example of absolute addressing is:

LD (1234H), A

It specifies that the contents of the accumulator are to be stored at memory location "1234" hexadecimal.

The disadvantage of absolute addressing is to require a three-byte instruction. In order to improve the efficiency of the microprocessor, another addressing mode may be made available, whereby only one word is used for the address: direct addressing.

439

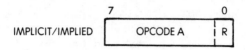

IMPLICIT/IMPLIED — OPCODE A | R (bits 7 to 0)

IMMEDIATE — OPCODE / LITERAL / LITERAL

EXTENDED/ABSOLUTE — OPCODE / FULL 16-BIT ADDRESS

DIRECT/SHORT — OPCODE / SHORT ADDRESS

INDEXED — OPCODE / OPCODE | X REG / DISPLACEMENT / OR ADDRESS

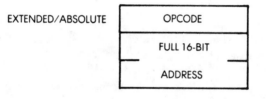

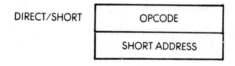

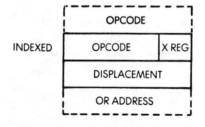

Fig. 5.1: Basic Addressing Modes

Direct Addressing (or "Short," or "Relative")

In this addressing mode, the opcode is followed by an eight-bit address. This is also illustrated in Figure 5.1. The advantage of this approach is to require only two bytes instead of three for absolute addressing. The disadvantage is to limit all addressing within this mode to addresses 0 to 255 or else − 128 to + 127. When using 0 to 255 ("page zero"), this is also called short addressing, or 0-page addressing. Whenever short addressing is available, absolute addressing is often called *extended addressing* by contrast. The range − 128 to + 127 is used with branch instructions. This is called relative addressing.

Relative Addressing

Normal jump or branch instructions require eight bits for the opcode, plus the 16-bit address to which the program has to jump. Just as in the preceding example, this mode has the disadvantage of requiring three words, i.e., three memory cycles. To provide more efficient branching, *relative addressing* uses only a two-word format. The first word is the branch specification, usually along with the test it is implementing. The second word is a displacement. Since the displacement must be positive or negative, a relative branching instruction allows a branch forward to 127 locations (seven-bits) or a branch backwards to 128 locations (usually + 129 or − 126, since PC will have been incremented by 2). Because most loops tend to be short, relative branching can be used most of the time and results in significantly improved performance for such short routines. As an example, we have already used the instruction JR NC, which specifies a "jump if no carry" to a location within 127 words of the branch instruction (more precisely + 129 to − 126).

The two advantages of relative addressing are improved performance (fewer bytes used) and program relocatability (independence from absolute addresses).

Indexed Addressing

Indexed addressing is a technique used to access the elements of a block or of a table successively. This will be illustrated by examples later in this chapter. The principle of indexed addressing is that the instruction specifies both an index register and an address. The contents of the register are added to the address to provide the final address. In this way, the address could be the beginning of a table in the memory.

The index register would then be used to access all the elements of a table successively in an efficient way. (This requires the availability of increment/decrement instructions for the index register). In practice, restrictions often exist which may limit the size of the index register, or the size of the address or displacement field.

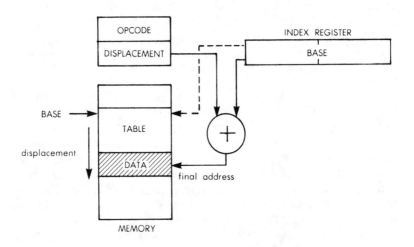

Fig. 5.2: Addressing (Pre-indexing)

Pre-Indexing and Post-Indexing

Two modes of indexing may be distinguished. Pre-indexing is the usual indexing mode in which the final address is the sum of a displacement or address and of the contents of the index register. It is shown in Figure 5.2, assuming an 8-bit displacement field and a 16-bit index register.

Post-indexing treats the contents of the displacement field like the *address* of the actual displacement, rather than the displacement itself. This is illustrated in Figure 5.3. In post-indexing, the final address is the sum of the contents of the index register plus the contents of the memory word *designated by the displacement field*. This feature utilizes, in fact, a combination of indirect addressing and pre-indexing. But we have not defined indirect addressing yet. Let us do that.

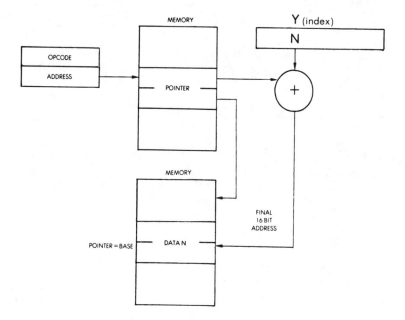

Fig. 5.3: Indirect Indexed Addressing (Post-Indexing)

Indirect Addressing

We have already seen that two subroutines may wish to exchange a large quantity of data stored in the memory. More generally, several programs, or several subroutines, may need to access a common block of information. To preserve the generality of the program, it is desirable not to keep such a block at a fixed memory location. In particular, the size of this block might grow or shrink dynamically, and it may have to reside in various areas of the memory, depending on its size. It would, therefore, be impractical to try to access this block using absolute addresses, that is without rewriting the program every time.

The solution to this problem lies in depositing the starting address of the block at a fixed memory location. This is analogous to a situation in which several persons need to get into a house, and only one key exists. By convention, the key to the house will be hidden under the mat. Every user will then know where to look (under the mat) to find the key to the house (or, perhaps, to find the address of the scheduled meeting, to propose a stricter analogy). Indirect addressing, therefore, normally uses an opcode followed by a 16-bit address. This address is used to retrieve a word from the memory. Usually, it will be a 16-bit word (in our case, two bytes) within the memory since it is an address. This is illustrated by Figure 5.4. The two bytes at the specified address A1 contain "A2". A2 is then interpreted as the actual address of the data that one wishes to access.

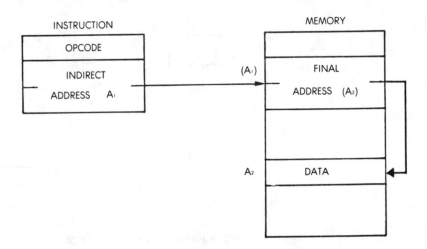

Fig. 5.4: Indirect Addressing

Indirect addressing is particularly useful any time that pointers are used. Various areas of the program can then refer to these pointers to access a word or a block of data conveniently and elegantly. The final address may also be obtained by pointing within the instruction to a 16-bit register in which it is contained. This is called "register indirect."

Combinations of Modes

The above addressing modes may be combined. In particular, it should be possible in a completely general addressing scheme to use many levels of indirection. The address A2 could be interpreted as an indirect address again, and so on.

Indexed addressing can also be combined with indirect access. This allows the efficient access to word n of a block of data, provided one knows where the pointer to the starting address is (see figure 5.2).

We have now become familiar with all usual addressing modes that can be provided in a system. Most microprocessor systems, because of the limitation on the complexity of an MPU, which must be realized within a single chip, do not provide all possible modes but only a small subset of these. The Z80 provides a good subset of possibilities. Let us examine them now.

Z80 ADDRESSING MODES

Implied Addressing (Z80)

Implied addressing is essentially used by single-byte instructions which operate on internal registers. Whenever implicit instructions operate exclusively on internal registers, they require only one machine cycle to execute.

Examples of instructions using implied (or "register") addressing are: LD r,r'; ADD A,r; ADC A,s; SUB s; SBC A,s; AND s; OR s; XOR s; CPs; INC r.

Zilog further distinguishes between "register addressing" and "implied addressing." Implied addressing is then limited, in that definition, to instructions that do not have a specific field to point to an internal register. This introduces one more addressing mode. This is one reason why the number of addressing modes is insufficient to characterize the capabilities of a microprocessor.

Immediate Addressing (Z80)

Since the Z80 has both single-length registers (eight bits), and double-length register pairs (16 bits), it provides two types of immediate addressing, both with 8-bit and 16-bit literals. Instructions are then either two or three bytes long. The second (and sometimes the third) byte contains the opcode, followed by the constant, or literal, to be loaded in a register or used for an operation. Exceptions are LD IX and LD IY, which require 16-bit opcodes.

Examples of instructions using the immediate addressing mode are:

LD r,n (two bytes)
LD dd,nn (three bytes)

and

ADD A,n (two bytes)

When the literal is two bytes long, the mode is called "immediate extended," in the case of the Z80.

445

Absolute or "Extended" Addressing (Z80)

By definition, absolute addressing requires three bytes. The first byte is the opcode and the next two bytes are the 16-bit address specifying the memory location (the "absolute address").

By contrast with "short addressing" (eight-bit address), this mode is also called "extended addressing."

Examples of instructions using extended addressing are:

LD HL, (nn) and JP nn

where nn represents the 16-bit memory address, and (nn) represents the contents of the specified location.

Modified Zero-Page Addressing (Z80)

Zero-page addressing is not available in the Z80, except through the RST instruction. The special addressing mode used by this instruction is called "modified zero-page addresing."

The RST instruction contains a 3-bit field in bit position b_5 b_4 b_3 used to pint to one of 8 locations in page 0 memory. The effective address is $b_5b_4b_3000$ and is loaded into PC. Since it requires only a single byte, this instruction executes rapidly, and is easily generated in hardware. It was generally used to respond to multiple interrupts (up to 8.) Its disadvantage is either to limit the execution sequence to 8 locations, or to require a jump eliminating the speed advantage. This is because each of the 8 branch addresses are 8-bytes apart.

Relative Addressing (Z80)

By definition, relative addressing requires two bytes. The first one is the "jump relative" opcode, whereas the second one specifies the displacement and its sign.

In order to differentiate this mode from the absolute jump instruction, it is labeled "JR".

From a timing standpoint, this instruction should be examined with caution. Whenever a test fails, i.e., whenever there is no branch, this instruction requires only seven "T cycles." This is because the next instruction to ɒe executed is already pointed to by the program counter.

However, when the test succeeds, i.e., whenever the jump takes place, this instruction requires 12 "T-states"; a new effective address must be computed and loaded into the program counter.

When computing the duration of the execution of a program segment, caution must be exercised. Whenever one is not sure whether or not the jump will succeed, one must take into consideration the fact that sometimes the jump *will require 12 T-states, (condition met), sometimes 7 (condition not met).*

When designing a loop, execution will, therefore, be faster using a JR (Jump Relative) testing a condition usually *not met*, such as a non-zero condition for the counter.

When JR's are used outside of loops, and the condition under test is unknown, an average timing value is often used for the duration of JR.

This timing problem does not apply to the unconditional jump JR e. It does not test any condition, and always lasts 12 T-states.

Indexed Addressing (Z80)

This addressing mode did not exist in the 8080, and was added to the Z80 (as well as the two index registers). As a result, it became necessary to add an extra byte to the opcode, making it a 16-bit opcode in the Z80 instruction set (LDIR is another example of a 16-bit opcode). The structure of an indexed instruction is shown on Figure 5.5.

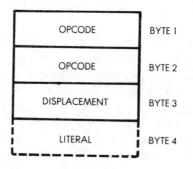

Fig. 5.5: Indexed Addressing Has 2-byte Opcode

Instructions allowing indexed addressing are:

LD, ADD, INC, RLC, BIT, SET, CP, and others.

This mode will be used extensively in the programs operating on blocks of data, tables or lists.

Indirect Addressing (Z80)

The Z80 provides a limited indirect addressing capability called "Register Indirect Addressing." In this mode, each of the 16-bit register pairs BC, DE, HL may be used as a memory address.

Whenever they point to 16-bit data, they point to the lower part. The higher part resides at the next (higher) sequential address.

Combinations of Modes

Combinations of modes are essentially non-existent, except that instructions referring to two operands may use a different type of addressing for each.

Thus, a *load* or an arithmetic instruction may access one operand in the immediate mode, and the other one through an indexed access.

Also, the bit addressing mechanism may access the eight-bit byte through one of the three addressing modes, as explained in the following paragraph. The specific addressing modes available for each instruction are indicated in the tables of the preceding chapter.

Bit Addressing

Bit addressing is generally not considered an addressing mode if addressing is defined as accessing a *byte*. However, whether defined as a mode or a group of instructions, it is a valuable facility. Since it is defined as an "addressing mode" in Zilog nomenclature, it will be so described here. It is specific to the Z80 and was not provided on the 8080.

Bit addressing refers to the access mechanism to specified bits. The Z80 is equipped with special instructions for setting, resetting and testing specified bits in a memory location or a register. The specified byte may be accessed through one of three addressing modes: register, register-indirect, and indexed. Three bits are used within the opcode to select one of eight bits.

USING THE Z80 ADDRESSING MODES

Long and Short Addressing

We have already used relative jump instructions in various programs that we have developed. They are self-explanatory. One interesting question is: What can we do if the permissible range for branching is not sufficient for our needs? On many microprocessors, the solution is to use a so called *long jump*. This is simply a jump to a location which contains an absolute or "long" jump specification:

```
JR NC, $ + 3        BRANCH TO CURRENT ADDRESS
                    + 3 IF C CLEAR
JP FAR              OTHERWISE JUMP TO FAR
(NEXT INSTRUCTION)
```

The two-line program above will result in branching to location FAR whenever the carry is set. In the case of the Z80, JP may be used instead of JR to test all conditions and removes this problem.

Use of Indexing for Sequential Block Accesses

Indexing is primarily used to address successive locations within a table. The restriction is that the maximum length must be less than 256 so that the displacement can reside in an eight-bit index register.

We have learned to check for a character. Now we will search a table of 100 elements for the presence of a '*'. The starting address for this table is called BASE. The table has only 100 elements. The program appears below: (see flowchart on Figure 5.6):

```
SEARCH    LD    IX, BASE
          LD    A, '*'
          LD    B, COUNT
TEST      CP    (IX)
          JR    Z, FOUND
          INC   IX
          DEC   B
          JR    NZ, TEST
NOTFND    ...
```

An improved program will be presented below in the section on Block Transfer, using DJ NZ.

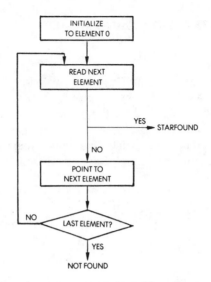

Fig. 5.6: Character Search Flowchart

A Block Transfer Routine for Fewer Than 256 Elements

We will call "COUNT" the number of elements in the block to be moved. The number is assumed to be less than 256. FROM is the base address of the block. TO is the base of the memory area where it should be moved. The algorithm is quite simple: we will move a word at a time, keeping track of which word we are moving by storing its position in the counter C. The program appears below:

```
BLKMOV    LD    IX, FROM
          LD    IY, TO
          LD    BC, COUNT
NEXT      LD    A, (IX)        GET WORD
          LD    (IY), A
          INC   IX
          INC   IY
          DEC   C
          JR    NZ, NEXT
```

Let us examine it:

```
BLKMOV    LD    IX,FROM
          LD    IY,TO
          LD    C,COUNT
```

These three instructions initialize registers IX, IY, and C respectively, as

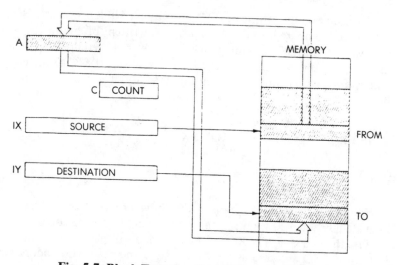

Fig. 5.7: Block Transfer: Initializing the Register

illustrated in Figure 5.7. Index register IX is used as the source pointer, and will be incremented regularly. Index register IY is used as the destination pointer, and would be incremented regularly. Register C is loaded with the maximum number of elements to be transferred (limited to 256 since this is an eight-bit register) and will be decremented regularly. Whenever C decrements to zero, all elements have been transferred. The next two instructions:

```
NEXT      LD    A, (IX)
          LD    (IY), A
```

load the contents of the memory location pointed to by IX into the accumulator, then transfer it into the memory location pointed to by register IY. In other words, these two instructions transfer an element of the source block into the destination block. The two index registers are then incremented:

```
          INC   IX
          INC   IY
```

And the counter register is decremented:

```
          DEC   C
```

Finally, as long as the counter is not 0, the program loops back to the label NEXT:

```
          JR    NZ, NEXT
```

451

This is an example of the possible utilization of index registers. However, let us compare it to the same program written for another microprocessor, the MOS Technology 6502, which is also equipped with an indexing capability, but uses different conventions (i.e., has different limitations on a general-purpose indexing facility). The program appears below:

```
          LDX    #NUMBER
NEXT      LDA     FROM, X
          STA     TO, X
          DEX
          BNE     NEXT
```

Without going into the details of the above program, the reader will immediately notice how much shorter it is than the previous one. This is because the index register X is used as a variable displacement, whereas FROM and TO are used as the fixed source and destination addresses.

This example should point out that although in theory indexing is a powerful facility, it does not necessarily lead to efficient coding, due to the addressing limitations imposed on it in the case of various microprocessors. Truly general-purpose indexing requires the possibility of a 16-bit displacement or address field as well as a 16-bit index register.

However, it should be noted that this specific problem is solved, in the Z80 by the presence of specialized instructions. A general-purpose block transfer will now be described which can be implemented in just four instructions. However, to be fair to the Z80, let us suggest additional exercises for the reader:

Exercise 5.1: Write the block transfer program for the Z80 in the style of the above program for the 6502, i.e., assuming that the index register contains a displacement. Assume that the source and the destination block are located in page 0, i.e., at addresses 0 to 256. Naturally, it will be assumed that the number of elements within each block is small enough that they do not overlap.

Exercise 5.2: Assume now that the source and the destination blocks are located anywhere in the memory, except that they are both within the same page. Rewrite the above program in that case. (Is there a difference, i.e., does page zero play any role for the Z80?)

Generalized Block Transfer Routine (More Than 256 Elements)

The register allocation and the memory map are shown in Figure 5.8.

452

The program is shown below:

```
LD BC, COUNT        NUMBER OF BYTES
LD DE, TO           DESTINATION ADDRESS
LD HL, FROM         START ADDRESS
LDIR                TRANSFER ALL BYTES
```

Memory used: 11 bytes
Timing: 21 cycles/byte transferred

The first instruction is:

```
LD    BC, COUNT
```

It loads the number of elements to be transferred (a 16-bit value) into the register pair BC. The next two instructions initialize the register pair DE and the register pair HL respectively:

```
LD    DE, TO
LD    HL, FROM
```

Finally the fourth instruction:

```
LDIR
```

performs the complete transfer.

LDIR is an *automated block-transfer* instruction. Its power should be obvious from this example. LDIR results in the following sequence: The contents of the memory location pointed to by H and L are transferred into the memory location pointed to by DE: (DE) = (HL). Next, DE is incremented: DE = DE + 1. Then, HL is incremented: HL = HL + 1. Next, BC is decremented: BC = BC − 1. If BC becomes 0, the instruction is terminated. Otherwise, the instruction is repeated.

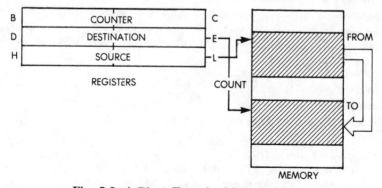

Fig. 5.8: A Block Transfer-Memory Map

The value and power of the LDIR instruction should be apparent at this point without further comments. Similarly, our search for the character "star" can be improved by the use of an automated instruction, CPIR, special to the Z80. The corresponding program appears below:

```
              LD A, '*'
              LD BC, COUNT
              LD HL, STRING
STAR          CPIR
              JR Z, STAR
NOSTAR        ---
```

The first instruction loads the accumulator with the code for the character star. Next, the register pair BC is initialized to the count of the number of words to be searched within the block:

              LD BC, COUNT

The register pair H and L is set to the starting address of the block to be searched (STRING). The automated instruction is then executed:

              LD HL, STRING
              CPIR

The CPIR instruction is an automated compare instruction. The contents of the memory location specified by the address contained in H and L is compared to the contents of the accumulator. If the comparison succeeds, then Z of the flags register will be set to 1. Then, the register pair H and L is incremented and the register pair BC is decremented. The instruction is repeated until either the pair BC goes to 0 or else the comparison succeeds. After the instruction CPIR is executed, it is therefore necessary to test the Z flag to determine whether the comparison has succeeded (the CPIR might have looped through 64K words without success in the extreme case). This is the purpose of the last instruction of the program:

              JR Z, STAR

Exercise 5.3: Rewrite the above program so that a search proceeds backwards. (Hint: Use the CPDR instruction) Continue the block transfer until '' is found.*

Let us now develop a program combining the features of the two previous ones. We will implement the block transfer from location FROM to location TO, which shall stop automatically whenever an escape character, "star", is found. The program appears below:

```
        LD   BC, COUNT
        LD   HL, FROM
        LD   DE, TO
        LD   A,'*'          DELIMITER (ESCAPE CHAR)
TEST    CP (HL)             COMPARE WITH MEMORY
                            CHARACTER
        JR   Z, END         END IF SUCCESS
        LDI                 TRANSFER CHARACTER AND
                            UPDATE POINTERS AND
                            COUNT
        JP   PE, TEST       KEEP TESTING UNLESS DONE
                            P/V INDICATES WHETHER BC  = 0
```

The first three instructions of the program perform the usual initialization, setting up the counter registers and the source and destination pointers:

```
        LD   BC, COUNT
        LD   HL, FROM
        LD   DE, TO
```

The star character is deposited, "as usual" into the accumulator, so that it can be compared to the character read from a memory location.

```
        LD   A,'*'
```

This is exactly what is done by the next instruction:

```
        TEST    CP    (HL)
```

The success or failure of the comparison is determined by testing the Z bit. The Z bit will have been set if the comparison has succeeded. This is performed by the next instruction:

```
        JR  Z, END
```

The next instruction is an *automated transfer* instruction:

```
        LDI
```

This instruction transfers the character, and updates the pointers and the *count* in a single instruction. LDI transfers the contents pointed to by H and L into the memory location pointed to by D and E: (DE) = (HL). It increments DE and HL:

```
DE = DE + 1
HL = HL + 1
```

455

Finally, it decrements BC: BC becomes BC − 1. The particularity of this instruction is that the P/V flag is cleared if BC decrements to "0" and set otherwise. This will be explicitly tested by the last instruction in the program to determine whether exit should occur:

JP   PE, TEST

Adding Two Blocks

A program will be developed here to add element by element two blocks starting respectively at addresses BLK1, and BLK2, and having equal numbers of elements, COUNT. The program is shown below:

```
BLKADD    LD    IX, BLK1
          LD    IY, BLK2
          LD    B, COUNT
          XOR   A
LOOP      LD    A, (IX + 0)
          ADC   A, (IY + 0)
          LD    (IX), A
          DEC   IX
          DEC   IY
          DEC   B
          JR    NZ, LOOP
```

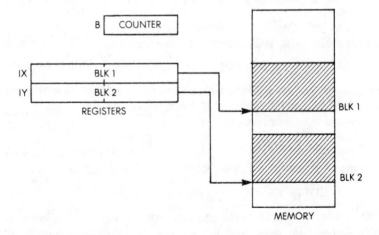

Fig. 5.9: Adding Two Blocks: BLK1 = BLK1 + BLK2

The memory layout is shown in Figure 5.9. The program is straightforward. The number of elements to be added is loaded into the counter register B, and the two index registers IX and IY are initialized to their values BLK1 and BLK2:

```
BLK ADD    LD  IX, BLK1
           LD  IY, BLK2
           LD  B, COUNT
```

The carry bit is then cleared in anticipation of the first addition:

```
XOR  A
```

The first element is loaded into the accumulator:

```
LOOP       LD  A, (IX + 0)
```

The corresponding element of BLK2 is then added to it:

```
ADC  A, (IY +0)
```

and finally saved into the element of BLK1:

```
LD  (IX), A
```

The two pointer registers X and Y are decremented:

```
DEC  IX
DEC  IY
```

as well as the counter register:

```
DEC  B
```

As long as the counter register is not 0, the addition loop is executed:

```
JR  NZ, LOOP
```

Exercise 5.4: Can you use the above program to perform a 32-bit addition?

Exercise 5.5: Can you use the above program to perform a 64-bit addition?

Exercise 5.6: Modify the above program so that the result is stored in a separate block starting at address BLK3.

Exercise 5.7: Modify the above program to perform a subtraction rather than an addition.

Exercise 5.8: Modify the original program above so that BLK1 and BLK2 are at the top of each block rather than the bottom (see Fig.5.10).

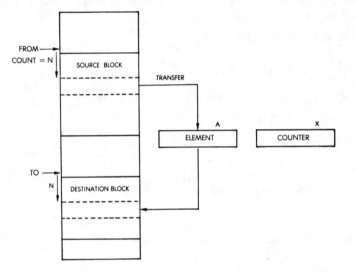

Fig. 5.10: Memory Organization for Block Transfer

SUMMARY

A complete description of addressing modes has been presented. It has been shown that the Z80 offers many possible mechanisms, and the specific addressing modes available on the Z80 have been analyzed. Finally, several application programs have been presented to demonstrate the value of the various addressing mechanisms. Programming the Z80 efficiently requires an understanding of these mechanisms. They will be used throughout the programs in the remainder of this book.

EXERCISES

5.9: Write a program to add the first 10 bytes of a table stored at location "BASE". The result will have 16 bits. (This is a checksum computation).
5.10: Can you solve the same problem without using the indexing mode?

5.11: *Reverse the order of the 10 bytes of this table. Store the result at address "REVER".*

5.12: *Search the same table for its largest element. Store it at memory address "LARGE".*

5.13: *Add together the corresponding elements of three tables, whose bases are BASE1, BASE2, BASE3. The length of these tables is stored at address "LENGTH".*

6

INPUT/OUTPUT TECHNIQUES

INTRODUCTION

We have learned so far how to exchange information between the memory and the various registers of the processor. We have learned to manage the registers and to use a variety of instructions to manipulate the data. We must now learn to communicate with the external world. This is called input/output.

Input refers to the capture of data from outside peripherals (keyboard, disk, or physical sensor). *Output* refers to the transfer of data from the microprocessor or the memory to external devices such as a printer, a CRT, a disk, or actual sensors and relays.

We will proceed in two steps. First, we will learn to perform the input/output operations required by common devices. Secondly, we will learn to manage several input/output devices simultaneously, i.e., to *schedule* them. This second part will cover, in particular, polling vs. interrupts.

INPUT/OUTPUT

In this section we will learn to sense or to generate simple signals, such as pulses. Then we will study techniques for enforcing or measuring correct timing. We will then be ready for more complex types of input/output, such as high-speed serial and parallel transfers.

The Z80 Input/Output Instructions

The Z80 is equipped with a special set of input and output instructions. Most eight-bit microprocessors are not equipped with a special set of input and output instructions, and use the general instruction set on input/output devices. The Z80, like the 8080, is equipped with basic input and output instructions. However, the Z80 is also equipped with additional I/O instructions. These will be described in more detail here in order to facilitate understanding of the programs that will be presented throughout this section.

The basic input and output instructions are respectively: IN A, (n) and OUT (n),A. These two instructions are inherited from the 8080. They will respectively read or write one byte between the selected port and the accumulator. The actual addressing process is such that the I,O device address "n" is gated on lines A0 through A7 of the address bus, while the contents of the accumulator appear on address lines A8 through A15. When only 256 devices are addressed, it may be necessary to zero the contents of the accumulator explicitly if any of the address lines A8 through A15 may be decoded by an I/O device. In the simple examples that follow, we will assume that fewer than 256 devices are present and that they are not connected to addresses A8 through A15, so that it will not be necessary to zero the contents of the accumulator explicitly, for example prior to using the IN instruction.

A special input instruction: IN r, (C), allows using the contents of register C as the I/O device address. When using this instruction, the contents of register B automatically provide the top part of the address (A8 through A15). The specified register r is loaded from the specified address. "r" may be any of the usual seven general-purpose registers.

Generate a Signal

In the simplest case, an output device will be turned off (or on) from the computer. In order to change the state of the output device, the programmer will merely change a level from a logical "0" to a logical "1", or from "1" to "0". Let us assume that an external relay is connected to bit "0" of a register called "OUT1". In order to turn it on, we will simply write a "1" into the appropriate bit position of the register. We assume here that OUT1 represents the address of this output register within our system. A program which will turn the relay on is:

```
TURNON  LD A, 00000001B      LOAD PATTERN INTO A
        OUT (OUT1), A         OUTPUT IT TO DEVICE
```

where OUT is the output instruction.

We have assumed that the state of the other seven bits of the register OUT1 is irrelevant. However, this is often not the case. These bits might be connected to other relays. Let us, therefore, improve this simple program. We want to turn the relay on, without changing the state

461

of any other bit within this register. We will assume that it is possible to read and write the contents of this register. Our improved program now becomes:

```
TURNON    IN    A, (OUT1)       READ CONTENTS OF OUT1
          OR    00000001B       FORCE BIT "0" TO "1" IN A
          OUT   (OUT1), A
```

The program first reads the contents of location OUT1, then performs an inclusive OR on its contents. This only changes bit position 0 to "1", and leaves the rest of the register intact. (For more details on the OR operation, refer to Chapter 4.) This is illustrated by Figure 6.1.

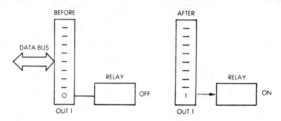

Fig. 6.1: Turning on a Relay

Pulses

Generating a *pulse* is accomplished exactly as in the case of the *level* above. An output bit is first turned on, then later turned off. This results in a pulse. This is illustrated in Figure 6.2. This time, however, an additional problem must be solved: one must generate the pulse for the correct length of time. Let us, therefore, study the generation of a computed delay.

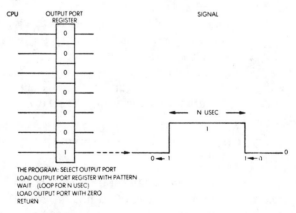

Fig. 6.2: A Programmed Pulse

Delay Generation and Measurement

A delay may be generated by software or by hardware methods. We will here study the way to perform it by program, and later show how it can also be accomplished with a hardware counter, called a programmable interval timer (PIT).

Programmed delays are achieved by counting. A counter register is loaded with a value, then is decremented. The program loops on itself and keeps decrementing until the counter reaches the value "0". The total length of time used by this process will implement the required delay. As an example, let us generate a delay of 82 clock cycles:

```
DELAY    LD    A, 5         A IS COUNTER
NEXT     DEC   A            DECREMENT
         JR    NZ,NEXT      NEXT    TEST
```

This program loads A with the value 5. The next instruction decrements A and the following instruction will cause a branch to NEXT to occur as long as A does not decrement to "0". When A finally decrements to zero, the program will exit from this loop and execute whatever instruction follows. The logic of the program is simple and appears in the flowchart of Figure 6.3.

Let us now compute the effective delay which will be implemented by the program. In Chapter 4 of the book, we will look up the number of cycles required by each of these instructions:

LD in the immediate mode requires seven clock cycles. DEC will use four cycles. Finally, JR will use 12 cycles except during the last iteration, where it will use 7 cycles. When looking up the number of cycles for JR in the table, verify that two possibilities exist: if the branch does not occur, JR will only require seven cycles. If the branch does succeed, which will usually be the case during the loop, then 12 cycles are required.

The timing is, therefore, seven cycles for the first instruction, plus 11 cycles for the next two, multiplied by the number of times the loop will be executed, minus an extra five-cycle delay for the last unsuccessful JR:

Delay $= 7 + 16 \times 5 - 5 = 82$ cycles.

Assuming a .5 microsecond cycle, this programming delay will be 41 microseconds.

463

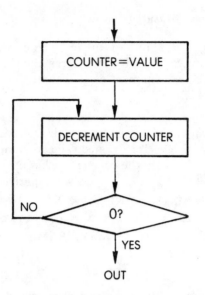

Fig. 6.3: Basic Delay Flowchart

The delay loop which has been described is used by most input/output programs. It should be well understood. Try to do the following exercises:

Exercise 6.1: *What are the maximum and the minimum delays which can be implemented with these three instructions?*

Exercise 6.2: *Modify the program to obtain a delay of about 100 microseconds.*

If one wishes to implement a longer delay, a simple solution is to add extra instructions in the program, before DEC. The simplest way to do so is to add NOP instruction. (The NOP does nothing for four cycles.)

Longer Delays

Generating longer delays by software can be achieved through using a wider counter. A register pair can be used to hold a 16-bit count. To simplify, let us assume that the lower count is "0". The lower byte will be loaded with "0", the maximum count, then go through a decrementation loop. Since the first decrementation results in 00→FF and does not affect the Z flag whenever it is decremented to "0", the upper byte of the counter will be decremented by 1. Whenever the upper byte is decremented to the value "0", the program terminates. If more precision is required in the delay generation, the lower count can have a non-null value. In this case, we would write the program just as explained and add at the end the three-line delay generation program, which has been described above.

A 24-bit delay program appears below:

```
DEL24   LD    B, COUNTH      COUNTER HIGH (8 BITS)
DEL16   LD    DE, – 1
LOOPA   LD    HL, COUNTL     COUNTER LOW
LOOPB   ADD   HL, DE         DECREMENT IT
        JR    C, LOOPB       GO ON UNTIL NULL
        DJNZ  LOOPA          DECREMENT B AND JUMP
```

Note that DE is loaded with " – 1", and used to decrement the 16-bit counter HL.

Naturally, still longer delays could be generated by using more than three words. This is analogous to the way an odometer works on a car. When the right-most wheel goes from "9" to "0", the next wheel to the left is incremented by 1. This is the general principle when counting with multiple discrete units.

However, the main disadvantage of this method is that when one is counting delays, the microprocessor will be doing nothing else for hundreds of milliseconds or even seconds. If the computer has nothing else to do, this is perfectly acceptable. However, in general the microcomputer should be available for other tasks, so that longer delays are normally not implemented by software. In fact, even short delays may be objectionable in a system if it is to provide some guaranteed response time in given situations. Hardware delays must then be used. In addition, if interrupts are used, timing accuracy may be lost if the counting loop can be interrupted.

Exercise 6.3: Write a program to implement a 100 ms delay (typical of a Teletype).

Hardware Delays

Hardware delays are implemented by using a *programmable interval timer* or "timer" in short. A register of the timer is loaded with a value.

The difference is that the timer will automatically decrement the counter periodically. The period can usually be adjusted or selected by the programmer. Whenever the timer has decremented to "0", it will normally send an interrupt to the microprocessor. It may also set a status bit which can be sensed periodically by the computer. The use of interrupts will be explained later in this chapter.

Other timer operating modes may include starting from "0" and counting the duration of the signal, or, counting the number of pulses received. When functioning as an interval timer, the timer is said to operate in a *one-shot* mode. When counting pulses, it is said to operate in a *pulse counting* mode. Some timer devices may even include multiple registers and a number of optional facilities which the programmer can select.

Sensing Pulses

The problem with sensing pulses is the reverse of that of generating pulses, and includes one more difficulty: whereas an output pulse is generated under program control, input pulses occur *asynchronously* with the program. In order to detect a pulse, two methods may be used: *polling* and *interrupts*. Interrupts will be discussed later in this chapter.

Let us now consider the polling technique. Using this technique, the program reads the value of a given input register continuously, testing a bit position, perhaps bit 0. It will be assumed that bit 0 is originally "0". Whenever a pulse is received, this bit will take the value "1". The program continuously monitors bit 0 until it takes the value "1". When a "1" is found, the pulse has been detected. The program appears below:

```
POLL    IN    A, (INPUT)    READ INPUT REGISTER
ON      BIT   0, A          TEST FOR 0
        JR    Z, POLL       KEEP POLLING IF 0
```

Conversely, let us assume that the input line is normally "1" and that we wish to detect a "0". This is the usual case for detecting a START bit, when monitoring a line connected to a Teletype. The program appears below:

```
POLL    IN    A, (INPUT)    READ INPUT REGISTER
        BIT   0, A          SET Z FLAG
        JR    NZ, POLL      TEST IS REVERSED
START   ...
```

Monitoring the Duration

Monitoring the duration of the pulse may be accomplished in the same way as computing the duration of an output pulse. Either a hardware or a software technique may be used. When monitoring a pulse by software, a counter is regularly incremented by 1, then the presence of the pulse is verified. If the pulse is still present, the program loops upon itself. Whenever the pulse disappears, the count contained in the counter register is used to compute the effective duration of the pulse. The program appears below:

```
DURTN    LD    B, 0            CLEAR COUNTER
AGAIN    IN    A, (INPUT)      READ INPUT
         BIT   0, A            MONITOR BIT 0
         JR    Z, AGAIN        WAIT FOR A "1"
LONGER   INC   B               INCREMENT COUNTER
         IN    A, (INPUT)      CHECK BIT 0
         BIT   0, A
         JR    NZ, LONGER  WAIT FOR A "0"
```

Naturally, we assume that the maximum duration of the pulse will not cause register B to overflow. If this were the case, the program would have to be changed to take that into account (or else it would be a programming error!).

Since we now know how to sense and generate pulses, let us capture or transfer larger amounts of data. Two cases will be distinguished: serial data and parallel data. Then we will apply this knowledge to actual input/output devices.

PARALLEL WORD TRANSFER

It is assumed here that eight bits of transfer data are available in parallel at address "INPUT" (see Fig. 6.4). The microprocessor must read the data word at this location whenever a status word indicates that it is valid. The status information will be assumed to be contained in bit 7 of address "STATUS". We will here write a program which will read and automatically save each word of data as it comes in. To simplify, we will assume that the number of words to be read is known in advance and is contained in location "COUNT". If this information were not available, we would test for a so-called *break character,* such as a *rubout,* or perhaps the character "*". We have learned to do this already.

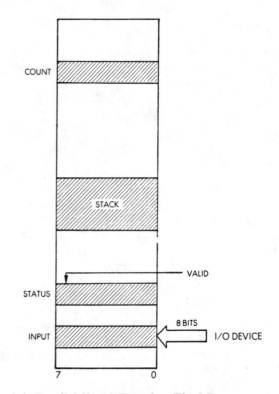

Fig. 6.4: Parallel Word Transfer - The Memory

The flowchart appears in Figure 6.5. It is quite straightforward. We test the status information until it becomes "1", indicating that a word is ready. When the word is ready, we read it and save it at an appropriate memory location. We then decrement the counter and test whether it has decremented to "0". If so, we are finished; if not, we read the next word. A simple program which implements this algorithm appears below:

```
PARAL   LD      A, (COUNT)   READ COUNT INTO A
        LD      B, A         B IS COUNTER
WATCH   IN      A, (STATUS)  LOOK FOR 'DATA READY'
                             TRUE
        BIT     7, A         BIT 7 IS "1" IF DATA READY
        JR      Z, WATCH     DATA VALID?
        IN      A, (INPUT)   READ DATA
        PUSH    AF           SAVE DATA INTO STACK
```

```
DEC   B              DECREMENT COUNT
JR    NZ, WATCH  DO IT UNTIL ZERO
```

It is assumed that the "data ready" flag is automatically cleared when STATUS is read.

The first two instructions initialize the counter register B:

```
PARAL     LD A, (COUNT)
          LD   B, A
```

Note that there is no easy way to load B only from memory. One must either load A, then transfer its contents to B, or load B and C simultaneously.

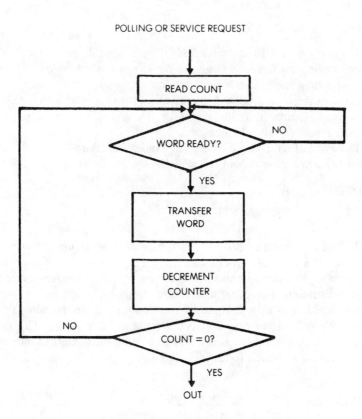

POLLING OR SERVICE REQUEST

READ COUNT

WORD READY?   NO

YES

TRANSFER WORD

DECREMENT COUNTER

COUNT = 0?   NO

YES

OUT

Fig. 6.5: Parallel Word Transfer: Flowchart

469

The next three instructions of the program read the status information and cause a loop to occur as long as bit seven of the status register is "0". (It is the sign bit, i.e., bit N.)

```
IN        A, (STATUS)
BIT       7, A            "IN" DOES NOT SET THE FLAGS
JR        Z, WATCH
```

When JP fails, data is valid and we can read it:

```
IN        A, (INPUT)
```

The word has now been read from address INPUT where it was, and must be saved. Assuming that a sufficient stack area is available, we can use:

```
PUSH      AF
```

which saves A (and F) in the stack. If the stack is full, or the number of words to be transferred is large, we could not push them on the stack and we would have to transfer them to a designated memory area, using, for example, an indexed instruction. However, this would require an extra instruction to increment or decrement the index register. PUSH is faster (only 11 clock cycles).

The word of data has now been read and saved. We will simply decrement the word counter and test whether we are finished:

```
DEC       B

JR        NZ,WATCH
```

This nine-instruction program can be called a *benchmark*. A benchmark program is a carefully optimized program designed to test the capabilities of a given processor in a specific situation. Parallel transfers are one such typical situation. This program has been designed for maximum speed and efficiency. Let us now compute the maximum transfer speed of this program. We will assume that COUNT is contained in memory. The duration of every instruction is determined by inspecting the tables in Chapter Four and is found to be the following:

PARAL	LD	A, (COUNT)	13
	LD	B, A	4
WATCH	IN	A, (STATUS)	11
	BIT	7, A	8
	JR	Z, WATCH	7/12

```
IN     A, (INPUT)    11
PUSH   AF            11
DEC    B             4
JR     NZ, WATCH     7/12
```

The minimum execution time is obtained by assuming that data is available every time that we sample STATUS. In other words, the first JP will be assumed to fail every time. Timing is then:

$$13 + 4 + (11 + 8 + 7 + 11 + 4 + 12) * COUNT$$

Neglecting the first 17 cycles necessary to initialize the counter register, the time used to transfer one word is 64 clock cycles or 32 microseconds with a 2 MHz clock.

The maximum data transfer rate is, therefore:

$$\frac{1}{32 \, (10^{-6})} = 31 \text{ K bytes per second}$$

Exercise 6.4: Assume that the number of words to be transferred is greater than 256. Modify the program accordingly and determine the impact on the maximum data transfer rate.

Exercise 6.5: Modify this program in order to try to improve its speed:
  1—using JR instead of JP
  2—using DJNZ
  3—using INI or IND
Was the above program truly optimal?

We have now learned to perform high-speed parallel transfers. Let us consider a more complex case.

BIT SERIAL TRANSFER

A serial input is one in which the bits of information (0's or 1's) come in successively on a line. These bits may come in at regular intervals. This is normally called *synchronous* transmission. Or, they may come as bursts of data at random intervals. This is called *asynchronous* transmission. We will develop a program which can work in both cases. The principle of the capture of sequential data is simple: we will watch an input line, which will be assumed to be line 0. When a bit of data is detected on this line, we will read the bit in, and shift it into a holding register. Whenever eight bits have been assembled, we will preserve the byte of data into the memory and assemble the next one. In order to simplify, we will assume that the number of bytes to be received is

471

known in advance. Otherwise, we might, for example, have to watch for a special break character, and stop the bit-serial transfer at this point. We have learned to do that. The flowchart for this program appears in Figure 6.6. The program appears below:

```
SERIAL  LD    C, 0          CLEAR INPUT WORD
        LD    A, (COUNT)    LOAD B WITH BYTE COUNT
        LD    B, A
LOOP    IN    A, (INPUT)    READ PORT
        BIT   7, A          BIT 7 IS STATUS, BIT 0 IS DATA
        JR    Z, LOOP       WAIT FOR A "1"
        SRL   A             SHIFT DATA BIT INTO CARRY
        RL    C             SAVE INPUT B INTO C
        JR    NC, LOOP      CONTINUE UNTIL 8 BITS IN
```

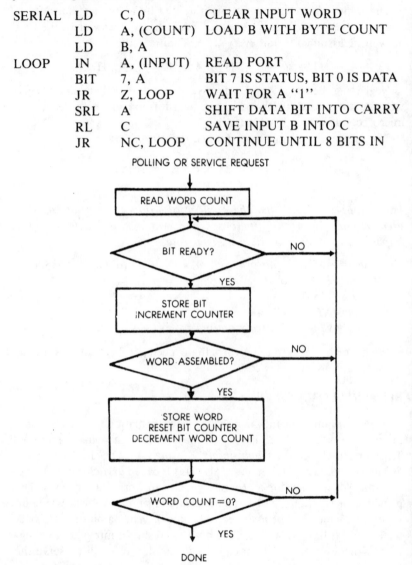

Fig. 6.6: Bit Serial Transfer—Flowchart

```
PUSH   BC              SAVE WORD IN STACK
LD     C, 01H          RESET MARKER BIT
DEC    B               DECREMENT BYTE COUNTER
JR     NZ, LOOP        ASSEMBLE NEXT WORD
```

This program has been designed for efficiency and will use new techniques which we will explain (see Fig. 6.7).

The conventions are the following: memory location COUNT is assumed to contain a count of the number of words to be transferred. Register C will be used to assemble eight consecutive bits coming in. Address INPUT refers to an input register. It is assumed that bit position 7 of this register is a status flag, or a clock bit. When it is "0", data is not valid. When it is "1", the data is valid. The data itself will be assumed to appear in bit position 0 of this same address. In many instances, the status information will appear on a different register than the data register. It should be a simple task, then, to modify this program accordingly. In addition, we will assume that the first bit of data to be received by this program is guaranteed to be a "1". It indicates that the real data follows. If this were not the case, we will later see an obvious modification to take care of it. The program corresponds exactly to the flowchart of Fig. 6.6. The first few lines of the program implement a waiting loop which tests whether a bit is ready. To determine whether a bit is ready, we read the input register, then test the zero bit (Z). As long as this bit is "0", the instruction JR will succeed, and we will branch back to the loop. Whenever the status (or clock) bit becomes true ("1"), then JR will fail and the next instruction will be executed.

This initial sequence of instructions corresponds to arrow 1 in Fig. 6.7.

At this point, the accumulator contains a "1" in bit position 7 and the actual data bit in bit position 0. The first data bit to arrive is going to be a "1". However, the following bits may be either "0" or "1". We now wish to preserve the data bit which has been collected in position 0. The instruction:

SRL A

shifts the contents of the accumulator right by one position. This causes the right-most bit of A, which is our data bit, to fall into the carry bit. We will now preserve this data bit into register C (this process is illustrated by arrows 2 and 3 in Fig. 6.7):

RL C

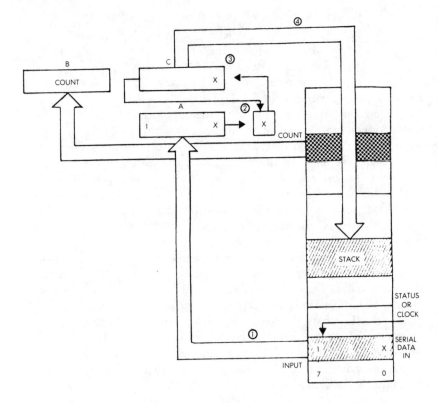

Fig. 6.7: Serial-to-Parallel: The Registers

The effect of this instruction is to read the carry bit into the right-most bit position of C. At the same time, the left-most bit of C falls into the carry bit. (If you have any doubts about the rotation operation, refer to Chapter 4!)

It is important to remember that a rotation with carry operation will both save the carry bit, here into the right-most bit position, and also recondition the carry bit with the value of bit 7 (or bit 0).

Here, a "0" will fall into the carry. The next instruction:

JR   NC, LOOP

tests the carry and branches back to address LOOP as long as the carry

474

is "0". This is our automatic bit counter. It can readily be seen that, as a result of the first RL, C will contain "00000001". Eight shifts later, the "1" will finally fall into the carry bit and stop the branching. This is an ingenious way to implement an automatic loop counter without having to waste an instruction to decrement the contents of an index register. This technique is used in order to shorten the program and improve its performance.

When JR NC finally fails, 8 bits will have been assembled into C. This value should be preserved in the memory. This is accomplished by the next instruction (arrow 4 on Fig. 6.7):

PUSH   BC

We are here saving the contents of B and C into the stack. Saving into the stack is possible only if there is enough room in the stack. Provided that this condition is met, it is usually the fastest way to preserve a word in the memory, even though we save an unnecessary register (B). The stack pointer is updated automatically. If we were not pushing a word in the stack, we would have to use one more instruction to update a memory pointer. We could equivalently perform an indexed addressing operation, but that would also involve decrementing or incrementing the index, using extra time.

After the first word of data has been saved, there is no longer any guarantee that the first data bit to come in will be a "1". It can be anything. We must, therefore, reset the contents to "00000001" so that we can keep using it as a bit counter. This is performed by the next instruction:

LD   C, 01H

Finally, we will decrement the word counter, since a word has been assembled, and test whether we have reached the end of the transfer. This is accomplished by the next two instructions:

DEC B
JR   NZ, LOOP

The above program has been designed for speed, so that one may capture a fast input stream of data bits. Once the program terminates, it is naturally advisable to immediately read away from the stack the words that have been saved there and transfer them elsewhere into the memory. We have already learned to perform such a block transfer in Chapter 2.

Exercise 6.6: Compute the maximum speed at which this program will be able to read serial bits. Look up the number of cycles required by every instruction in the table at the end of this book, then compute the time which will elapse during execution of this program. To compute the length of time which will be used by a loop, simply multiply the total duration of this loop, expressed in microseconds, by the number of times it will be executed. Also, when computing the maximum speed, assume that a data bit will be ready every time that the input location is sensed.

This program is more difficult to understand than the previous ones. Let us look at it again (refer to Fig. 6.6) in more detail, examining some trade-offs.

A bit of data comes into bit position 0 of "INPUT" from time to time. There might be, for example, three "1s" in succession. We must, therefore, *differentiate between the successive bits* coming in. This is the function of the "clock" signal.

The clock (or STATUS) signal tells us that the input bit is now valid. Before reading a bit, we will therefore first test the status bit. If the status is "0", we must wait. If it is "1", then the data bit is good.

We assume here that the status signal is connected to bit 7 of register INPUT.

Exercise 6.7: Can you explain why bit 7 is used for status, and bit 0 for data? Does it matter?

Once we have captured a data bit, we want to preserve it in a safe location, then shift it left, so that we can get the next bit.

Unfortunately, the accumulator is used to read and test both data and status in this program. If we were to accumulate data in the accumulator, bit position 7 would be erased by the status bit.

Exercise 6.8: Can you suggest a way to test status without erasing the contents of the accumulator (a special instruction)? If this can be done, could we use the accumulator to accumulate the successive bits coming in? Can you improve speed by using an "automated jump"?

Exercise 6.9: Rewrite the program, using the accumulator to store the bits coming in. Compare it to the previous one in terms of speed and number of instructions.

Let us address two more possible variations.

We have assumed that, in our particular example, the very first bit to come in would be a special signal, guaranteed to be "1". However, in general, it may be anything.

Exercise 6.10: Modify the program above, assuming that the very first bit to come in is valid data (not to be discarded), and can be "0" or "1". Hint: our "bit counter" should still work correctly, if you initialize it with the correct value.

Finally, we have been saving the assembled word in the stack, to gain time. We could naturally save it in a specified memory area.

Exercise 6.11: Modify the program above, and save the assembled word in the memory area starting at BASE.

Exercise 6.12: Modify the program above so that the transfer will stop when the character "S" is detected in the input stream.

The Hardware Alternative

As usual for most standard input/output algorithms, it is possible to implement this procedure by hardware. The chip is called a UART. It will automatically accumulate the bits. However, when one wishes to reduce the component count, this program, or a variation of it, will be used instead.

Exercise 6.13: Modify the program, assuming that data is available in bit position 0 of location INPUT, while the status information is available in bit position 0 of address INPUT + 1.

BASIC I/O SUMMARY

We have now learned to perform elementary input/output operations as well as to manage a stream of parallel data or serial bits. We are now ready to communicate with real input/output devices.

COMMUNICATING WITH INPUT/OUTPUT DEVICES

In order to exchange data with input/output devices, we will first have to ascertain whether data is available, if we want to read it; or whether the device is ready to accept data, if we want to send it. Two procedures may be used: handshaking and interrupts. Let us study handshaking first.

Handshaking

Handshaking is generally used to communicate between any two

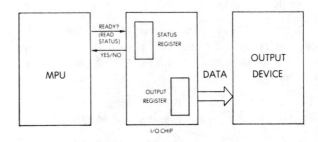

Fig. 6.8: Handshaking (Output)

asynchronous devices, i.e., between any two devices which are not synchronized. For example, if we want to send a word to a parallel printer, we must first make sure that the input buffer of this printer is available. We will, therefore, ask the printer: Are you ready? The printer will say "yes" or "no." If it is not ready we will wait. If it is ready, we will send the data (see Fig. 6.8).

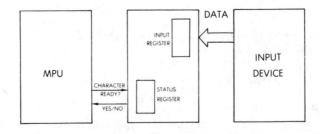

Fig. 6.8a: Handshaking (Input)

Conversely, before reading data from an input device, we will verify whether the data is valid. We will ask: "Is data valid?" And the device will tell us "yes" or "no." The "yes or no" may be indicated by status bits, or by other means (see Fig. 6.8a).

As an analogy, whenever you wish to exchange information with someone who is independent and might be doing something else at the time, you should ascertain that he is ready to communicate with you. The usual rule of courtesy is to shake his hand. Data exchange may then follow. This is the procedure normally used in communicating with input/output devices.

Let us now illustrate this procedure with a simple example.

Sending a Character To The Printer

The character will be assumed to be contained in memory location CHAR. The program to print it appears below:

```
WAIT    IN    A, (STATUS)
        BIT   7, A           TEST IF READY
        JR    Z, WAIT        OTHERWISE WAIT
        LD    A, (CHAR)      GET CHARACTER
        OUT   (PRNTD), A     PRINT IT
        JR    WAIT           GO FOR NEXT
```

The print program is straightforward and uses the handshaking procedure which has been described above. The data paths are shown in Figure 6.9.

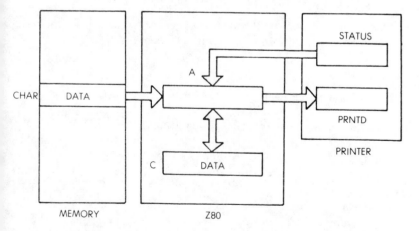

Fig. 6.9: Printer—Data Paths

The character (called DATA) is located at memory location CHAR. First, the status of the printer is checked. Whenever bit 7 of the status

479

register becomes 1, it indicates that the printer ready for input, i.e., its input buffer is available. At this point, the character is loaded into the accumulator, then output to the printer, via the accumulator. As long as the status bit remains 0, the program will remain in a loop, called WAIT in the program.

Exercise 6.14: How many instructions would be saved in the above program by loading data directly into register C as well as outputing the contents of register C directly?

Exercise 6.15: When using an actual printer, it is usually necessary to send a start order before using the device. Modify this program to generate such an order, assuming that the start command is obtained by writing a 1 in bit position 0 of the STATUS register, which is assumed to be bidirectional.

Exercise 6.16: If the BIT instruction were not available, could you use another instruction instead, in line 2 of the program? If so, explain the advantage of using the BIT instruction, if any.

Exercise 6.17: Modify the program above to print a string of n characters, where n will be assumed to be less than 255.

Exercise 6.18: Modify the above program to print a string of characters until a "carriage-return" code is encountered.

Let us now complicate the output procedure by requiring a code conversion and by outputting to several devices at a time:

Output To a Seven-Segment LED

A traditional seven-segment light-emitting diode (LED) may display the digits "0" through "9", or even "0" through "F" hexadecimal by lighting combinations of its 7 segments. A seven-segment LED is shown in Figure 6.10. The characters that may be generated with this LED appear in Figure 6.11.

The segments of an LED are labeled "a" through "g" in Figure 6.10.

For example, "0" will be displayed by lighting the segments abcdef. Let us assume, now, that bit "0" of an output port is connected to segment "a", that "1" is connected to segment "b", and so on. Bit 7 is not used. The binary code required to light up fedcba (to display "0") is, therefore, "0111111". In hexadecimal this is "3F". Do the following exercise.

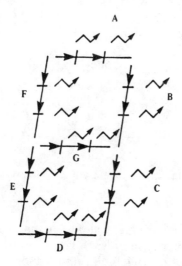

Fig. 6.10: Seven-Segment LED

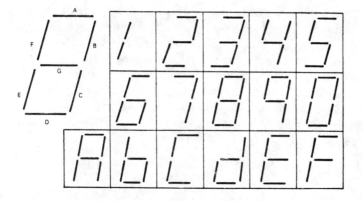

Fig. 6.11: Hexadecimal Characters Generated
with a Seven-Segment LED

481

Exercise 6.19: Compute the seven-segment equivalent for the hexadecimal digits "0" through "F". Fill out the table below:

Hex	LED code	Hex	LED code	Hex	LED code	Hex	LED code
0	3F	4		8		C	
1		5		9		D	
2		6		A		E	
3		7		B		F	

Let us now display hexadecimal values on *several* LED's.

Driving Multiple LED's

An LED has no memory. It will display the data only as long as its segment lines are active. In order to keep the cost of an LED display low, the microprocessor will display information on *each of the LED's* in turn. The rotation between the LED's must be fast enough so that there is no apparent blinking. This implies that the time spent from one LED to the next is less than 100 milliseconds. Let us design a program which will accomplish this. Register C will be used to point to the LED on which we want to display a digit. The accumulator is assumed to contain the hexadecimal value to be displayed on the LED. Our first concern is to convert the hexadecimal value into its seven-segment representation. In the preceding section, we have built the equivalence table. Since we are accessing a table, we will use the indexed addressing mode, where the displacement index will be provided by the hexadecimal value. This means that the seven-segment code for hexadecimal digit "3" is obtained by looking up the third element of the table after the base. The address of the base will be called SEGBAS. The program appears below:

```
LEDS    LD    E, A          A CONTAINS HEX DIGIT
        LD    D, 0          USE "DE" AS DISPLACEMENT
        LD    HL, SEGBAS    USE "HL" AS INDEX
        ADD   HL, DE        TABLE ADDRESS
        LD    A, (HL)       READ CODE FROM TABLE
        LD    B, 50H        DELAY VALUE = ANY
                            LARGE NBR
DELAY   OUT   (C), A        OUTPUT FOR SET DURATION
        DEC   B             DELAY COUNTER
```

```
        JR    NZ, DELAY      KEEP LOOPING
        LD    A, C           C IS PORT NUMBER
        DEC   C
        CP    MINLED         DONE FOR LAST LED?
        JR    NZ, OUT
        LD    BC, (MAXLED)   IF SO, RESET C TO TOP LED
OUT     RET
```

The program assumes that register C contains the address of the LED to be illuminated next, and that the accumulator A contains the digit to be displayed.

The program first looks up the seven-segment code corresponding to the hexadecimal value contained in the accumulator. Registers D and E are used as a displacement field, and registers H and L are used as a 16-bit index register. The hexadecimal digit is added to the base address of the table:

```
LEDS    LD    E, A           7-SEGMENT CODE
        LD    D, 0
        LD    HL, SEGBAS
        ADD   HL, DE
```

A delay loop is then implemented, so that the code obtained from the table is displayed for an appropriate duration. Here the constant "50" hexadecimal has been arbitrarily chosen:

```
        LD    A, (HL)        READ CODE FROM TABLE
        LD    B, 50H         DELAY VALUE
```

The delay is accomplished using a classic delay loop. The first instruction·

```
DELAY   OUT   (C), A
```

outputs the contents of the accumulator at the I/O port pointed to by register C (the LED number). The next two instructions implement the delay loop:

```
        DEC   B
        JR    NZ, DELAY
```

Once the delay has been implemented, we must simply decrement the LED pointer, and make sure that we loop around to the highest LED address if the smallest LED address has been reached:

```
        LD    A,C
```

```
          DEC  C
          CP   MINLED
          JR   NZ, OUT
          LD   BC, (MAXLED)
OUT       RET
```

It is assumed here that the above program has been written as a subroutine, and the last instruction is then RET: "return from subroutine"

Exercise 6.20: *It is usually necessary to turn off the segment drivers for the LED prior to displaying the digit. Modify the above program by adding the necessary instructions (output "00" as the character code prior to outputting the character).*

Exercise 6.21: *What would happen to the display if the DELAY label were moved up by one line position? Would this change the timing? Would this change the appearance of the display?*

Exercise 6.22: *You will notice that the first four instructions of the program are, in fact, performing a 16-bit indexed memory access. However, it seems clumsy, without using the indexing mechanism. Assume that the SEGBAS address is known in advance. Call SEGBSH the high-order part of this address, and SEGBSL the low part of this address. Store SEGBSH in the high-order part of the IX register. Now write the above program, using the Z80 index-addressing mechanism, and using SEGBSL as the displacement field of the instrucion. What are the advantages and disadvantages of this approach?*

Exercise 6.23: *Assuming that the above program is a subroutine, you will notice that it uses registers B, D, E, H and L internally, and modifies their contents. If the subroutine may freely use the memory area designated by address T1, T2, T3, T4, T5, could you add instructions at the beginning and at the end of this program which will guarantee that, when the subroutine returns, the contents of registers B, D, E, H and L will be the same as when the subroutine was entered?*

Exercise 6.24: *Same exercise as above, but assume that the memory area T1, etc., is not available to the subroutine. (Hint: remember that there is a built-in mechanism in every computer for preserving information in a chronological order.)*

We have now solved common input/output problems. Let us consider the case of a common peripheral: the Teletype.

Teletype Input-Output

The Teletype is a serial device. It both sends and receives words of information in a serial format. Each character is encoded in an 8-bit ASCII format (the ASCII table appears at the end of this book). In addition, every character is preceded by a "start" bit, and terminated by two "stop" bits. In the so-called 20-milliamp current loop interface, which is most frequently used, the state of the line is normally a "1". This is used to indicate to the processor that the line has not been cut. A start is a "1"-to-"0" transition. It indicates to the receiving device that data bits follow. The standard Teletype is a 10-characters-per-second device. We have just established that each character requires 11 bits. This means that the Teletype will transmit 110 bits per second. It is said to be a 110-baud device. We will design a program to serialize bits out to the Teletype at the correct speed.

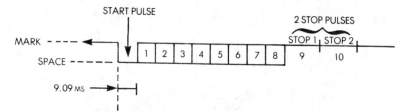

Fig. 6.12: Format of a Teletype Word

One-hundred-and-ten bits per second implies that bits are separated by 9.09 milliseconds. This will have to be the duration of the delay loop to be implemented between successive bits. The format of a Teletype word appears in Figure 6.12. The flowchart for bit input appears in Figure 6.13. The program follows:

```
TTYIN   IN    A, (STATUS)
        BIT   7, A          DATA READY?
        JR    Z, TTYIN      OTHERWISE WAIT
        CALL  DELAY1        CENTER OF PULSE
        IN    A, (TTYBIT)   START BIT
        OUT   (TTYBIT), A   ECHO IT
        CALL  DELAY9        NEXT PULSE (9 MS)
        LD    B, 08H        BIT COUNT
NEXT    IN    A, (TTYBIT)   READ DATA BIT
        OUT   (TTYBIT), A   ECHO IT
        SRL   A             SAVE IT IN CARRY
```

485

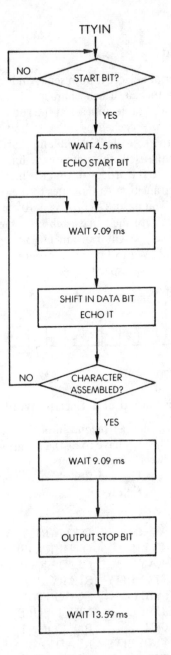

Fig. 6.13: TTY Input with Echo

```
RR     C            PRESERVE IT INTO C
CALL   DELAY9       NEXT PULSE (9 MS)
DEC    B            DECREMENT BIT COUNT
JR     NZ, NEXT
IN     A, (TTYBIT)  READ STOP BIT
OUT    (TTYBIT), A  ECHO IT
CALL   DELAY9       SKIP SECOND STOP
RET
```

Fig. 6.14: Teletype Program

Let us examine the program in detail. First, the status of the Teletype must be tested to determine if a character is available:

```
TTYIN        IN     A, (STATUS)
             BIT    7, A
             JR     Z, TTYIN
```

The "BIT" instruction is a useful Z80 facility which allows testing any bit in any data register. It does not modify the contents of the register under test. The Z flag is set if the specified bit is 0, and reset otherwise.

This program will, therefore, loop until the status finally becomes "1". It is a classic polling loop.

Note that, since the STATUS does not need to be preserved, we could also use

```
        AND    10000000B
```
instead of
```
        BIT    7, A
```

However, using the AND instruction destroys the contents of A (acceptable here).

When optimizing a program, remember that each new instruction may introduce side-effects.

Next, a 4.5 ms delay is implemented in order to sense the start bit in the middle of the pulse.

```
        CALL  DELAY1
```

where DELAY1 is the delay subroutine implementing the required delay. The first bit to come is the start bit. It should be echoed to the Teletype, but otherwise ignored. This is done by the next instructions:

```
TTYIN    IN    A, (TTYBIT)
         OUT   (TTYBIT), A
```

487

We must then wait for the first data bit. The necessary delay is equal to 9.09 milliseconds and is implemented by a subroutine:

          CALL   DELAY9

Register B is used as a counter and is loaded with the value 8 in order to capture the 8 data bits:

          LD   B, 08H

Next, each data bit will be read in turn into the accumulator, then echoed. It is assumed to arrive in bit position 0 of the accumulator. The data bit will then be preserved into register C, where it will be shifted in. The transfer from A to C is performed through the carry bit:

```
NEXT     IN     A, (TTYBIT)
         OUT    (TTYBIT), A
         SRL    A
         RR     C
```

This sequence is illustrated in Figure 6.15.

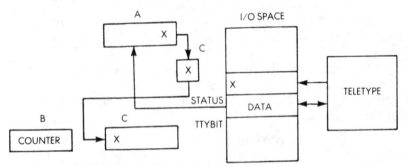

Fig. 6.15: Teletype Input

Next, the usual 9 millisecond delay is implemented, the bit-counter is decremented, and the loop is entered again as long as the eight bits have not been captured:

```
         CALL   DELAY9
         DEC    B
         JR     NZ, NEXT
```

Finally, the STOP bit is captured, and echoed. It is usually sufficient to send a single STOP bit, however both could be sent back using two more instructions:

```
         IN     A, (TTYBIT)
         OUT    (TTYBIT), A
         CALL   DELAY9
         RET
```

The program should be examined with attention. The logic is quite simple. The new fact is that whenever a bit is read from the Teletype (at address TTYBIT), it is echoed back to the Teletype. This is a standard feature of the Teletype. Whenever a user presses a key, the information is transmitted to the processor and then back to the printing mechanism of the Teletype. This verifies that the transmission lines are working and that the processor is operating when a character is, indeed, printing correctly on the paper.

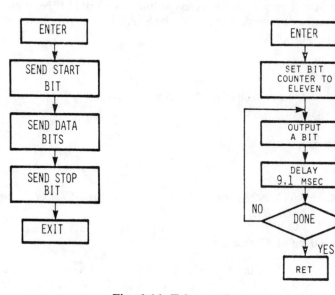

Fig. 6.16: Teletype Output

Exercise 6.25: Write the delay routine which results in the 9.09 millisecond delay. (DELAY subroutine)

Exercise 6.26: Using the example of the program developed above, write a PRINTC program which will print on the Teletype the contents of memory location CHAR (see Fig. 6.15).

The answer appears below:

```
PRINTC  LD    B, 11        COUNTER = 11 BITS
        LD    A, (CHAR)    GET CHARACTER
        OR    A            CLEAR CARRY = START BIT
        RLA                CARRY INTO A
```

```
NEXT    OUT    (TTYBIT), A    OUTPUT
        CALL   DELAY
        RRA                   NEXT BIT
        SCF                   CARRY = 1 (STOP BIT)
        DEC    B              BIT COUNT
        JR     NZ, NEXT
        RET
```

Register B is used as a bit counter for the transmission. The contents of bit 0 of A will be sent to the Teletype line ("TTYBIT"). Note how the carry is used to provide a ninth bit (the START bit). Also, note that the carry is cleared by:

```
        OR     A
```

At the end of the program, the carry is set to one by:

```
        SCF
```

in order to generate a stop bit.

Exercise 6.27: Modify the program so that it waits for a START bit instead of a STATUS bit.

Printing a String of Characters

We will assume that the PRINTC routine (see Exercise 6.26) takes care of printing a character on our printer, or display, or any output device. We will here print the contents of memory locations (START) to (START + N).

The program is straightforward (see Figure 6.17):

```
PSTRING LD     B, NBR         LENGTH OF STRING
        LD     HL, START      BASE ADDRESS
NEXT    LD     A, (HL)        GET CHARACTER
        CALL   PRINTC         PRINT IT
        INC    HL             NEXT ELEMENT
        DEC    B
        JR     NZ, NEXT       DO IT AGAIN
        RET
```

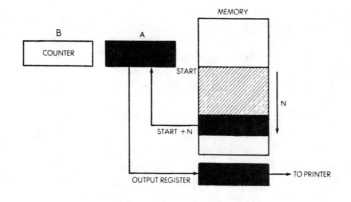

Fig. 6.17: Printing a Memory Block

PERIPHERAL SUMMARY

We have now described the basic programming techniques used to communicate with typical input/output devices. In addition to the data transfer, it will be necessary to condition one or more control registers within each I/O device in order to condition the transfer speeds, the interrupt mechanism, and the various other options correctly. The manual for each device should be consulted. (For more details on the specific algorithms for exchanging information with all the usual peripherals, the reader is referred to our book, C207, *Microprocessor Interfacing Techniques.*)

We have now learned to manage single devices. However, in a real system, all peripherals are connected to the buses, and may request service simultaneously. How are we going to schedule the processor's time?

INPUT/OUTPUT SCHEDULING

Since input/output requests may occur simultaneously, a scheduling mechanism must be implemented in every system to determine in which order service will be granted. Three basic input/output techniques are used, which can be combined with each other. They are: polling, interrupt, DMA. Polling and interrupts will be described here. DMA is purely a hardware technique, and as such will not be described here. (It is covered in the reference books C201 and C207.)

Polling

Conceptually, polling is the simplest method for managing multiple peripherals. With this strategy, the processor interrogates the devices connected to the buses in turn. If a device requests service, the service is granted. If it does not request service, the next peripheral is examined. Polling is used not just for the devices, but for *any device service routine.*

As an example, if the system is equipped with a Teletype, a tape recorder, and a CRT display, the polling routine would interrogate the Teletype: "Do you have a character to transmit?" It would interrogate the Teletype *output routine,* asking: "Do you have a character to send?" Then, assuming that the answers are negative so far, it would interrogate the tape-recorder routines, and finally the CRT display. If only one device is connected to a system, polling will be used as well to determine whether it needs service. As an example, the flowcharts for reading a paper-tape reader and for printing on a printer appear in Figures 6.20 and 6.21.

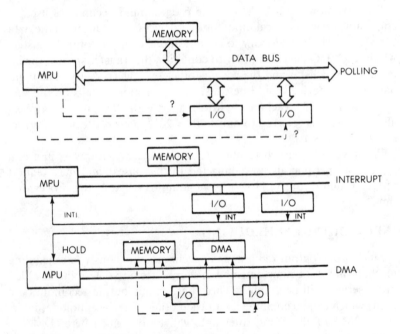

Fig. 6.18: Three Methods of I/O Control

Example: a polling loop for devices 1, 2, 3, 4 (see Fig. 6.19):

```
POLL4  IN    A, (STATUS 1)   GET STATUS OF DEVICE 1
       BIT   7, A            SERVICE REQUEST?
       CALL  NZ, ONE         BIT 7 = 1?
       IN    A, (STATUS2)    DEVICE 2
       BIT   7, A
       CALL  NZ, TWO
       IN    A, (STATUS3)    DEVICE 3
       BIT   7, A
       CALL  NZ, THREE
       IN    A, (STATUS4)    DEVICE 4
       BIT   7, A
       CALL  NZ, FOUR
       JR    POLL4           NO REQUEST, TRY AGAIN
```

Bit 7 of the status register for each device is "1" when it wants service. When a request is sensed, this program branches to the device handler, at address ONE for device 1, TWO for device 2, etc.

A fine point is worth noting here. For each instruction, it is important to verify carefully the way in which it affects the condition codes. It should be noted that the IN A instruction does not change the flags. If an IN r instruction has been used instead of an IN A instruction, bit 7 of the input would automatically be reflected as the SIGN bit in the flags register. The special instruction "BIT 7,A" would become unnecessary. However, because the IN A instruction does not change the flags, this extra test must be included in the program.

In some hardware implementations, input/output devices may be treated as memory devices for purposes of addressing. This is called memory-mapped input/output. In this case, the IN instruction would be replaced by an LD instruction and the rest of the program would be as above, since LD does not affect the flags.

The advantages of polling are obvious: it is simple, does not require any hardware assistance, and keeps all input/output synchronous with the program operation. Its disadvantage is just as obvious: most of the processor's time is wasted looking at devices that do not need service. In addition, by wasting so much time, the processor might give service to a device too late.

Another mechanism is, therefore, desirable in order to guarantee that the processor's time can be used to perform useful computations rather than polling devices needlessly all the time. However, let us stress that polling is used extensively whenever a microprocessor has nothing bet-

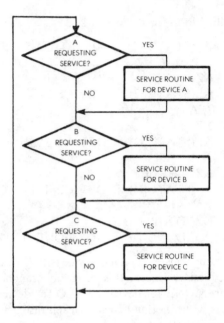

Fig. 6.19: Polling Loop Flowchart

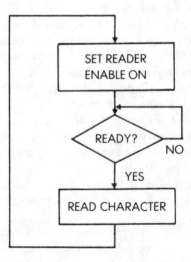

Fig. 6.20: Reading from a Paper-Tape Reader

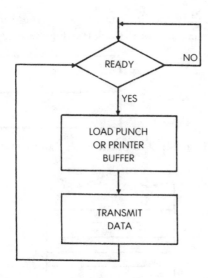

Fig. 6.21: Printing on a Punch or Printer

ter to do, as it keeps the overall organization simple. Let us examine the essential alternative to polling: interrupts.

Interrupts

The concept of interrupts is illustrated in Figure 6.18. A special hardware line, the interrupt line, is connected to a specialized pin of the microprocessor. Multiple input/output devices may be connected to this interrupt line. When any one of them needs service, it sends a level or a pulse on this line. An interrupt signal is the service request from an input/output device to the processor. Let us examine the response of the processor to this interrupt.

In any case, the processor completes the instruction that it was currently executing; otherwise, this would create chaos inside the microprocessor. Next, the microprocessor should branch to an interrupt-handling routine which will process the interrupt. Branching to such a subroutine implies that the contents of the program counter must be saved on the stack. *An interrupt must, therefore, cause the automatic preservation of the program counter on the stack.* In addition, the flag register F should be also preserved automatically, as its contents will be altered by any subsequent instruction. Finally, if the interrupt-handling routine should modify any internal registers, these internal registers should also be preserved on the stack (see Figures 6.22 and 6.23).

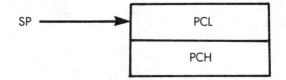

Fig. 6.22: Z80 Stack After Interruption

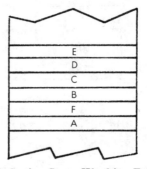

Fig. 6.23: Saving Some Working Registers

After all these registers have been preserved, one can branch to the appropriate interrupt-handling address. At the end of this routine, all the registers should be restored, and a special interrupt return should be executed so that the main program will resume execution. Let us examine in more detail the interrupt lines of the Z80.

Z80 Interrupts

An interrupt is a signal sent to the microprocessor, which may request service at any time and is asynchronous to the program. Whenever a program branches to a subroutine, such branching is *synchronous* to program execution, i.e., scheduled by the program. An interrupt, however, may occur at any time, and will generally suspend the execution of the current program (without the program knowing it). Because it may happen at any time relative to program execution, it is called *asynchronous*.

Three interruption mechanisms are provided on the Z80: the bus request (BUSRQ), the non-maskable interrupt (NMI) and the usual interrupt (INT).

Let us examine these three types.

The Bus Request

The bus request is the highest priority interrupt mechanism on the Z80. The interrupt sequence for the Z80 is shown in Figure 6.24. As a general rule, no interrupt will be sensed by the Z80 until the current machine cycle is completed. The NMI and INT interrupts will not be taken into account until the current instruction is finished. However, the BUSRQ will be handled at the end of the current machine cycle, without necessarily waiting for the end of the instruction. It is used for

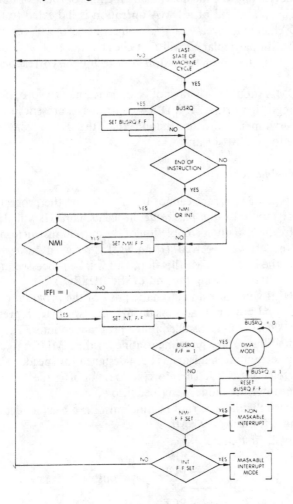

Fig. 6.24: Interrupt Sequence

a direct memory access (DMA), and will cause the Z80 to go into DMA mode (see ref. C201 for an explanation of the DMA mechanism). If the end of an instruction has been reached, and if any NMI or INT were pending, they would be memorized internally in the Z80 by setting specialized flip-flops: the NMI flip-flop, and the INT flip-flop. In DMA mode, the Z80 suspends operation and releases its data-bus and address-bus in the high-impedance state. This mode is normally used by a DMA controller to perform transfers between a high-speed input-output device and the memory, using the microprocessor data-bus and address-bus. The end of a DMA operation is indicated to the Z80 by BUSRQ changing levels. At this point, the Z80 will resume normal operation. In particular, it will first check whether its internal NMI or INT flip-flops had been set and, if so, execute the corresponding interrupts.

The DMA should normally not be of concern to the programmer, unless timing is important. If a DMA controller is present in the system, the programmer must understand that the DMA may delay the response to an NMI or an INT.

The Non-Maskable Interrupt

This type of interrupt cannot be inhibited by the programmer. It is therefore said to be *non-maskable,* hence its name. It will always be accepted by the Z80 upon completion of the current instruction, assuming no bus request was received. (If an NMI is received during a BUSRQ, it will set the internal NMI flip-flop, and will be processed at the end of the instruction following the end of the BUSRQ.)

The NMI will cause an automatic push of the program counter into the stack and branch to address 0066H: the two bytes representing the address 0066H will be installed in the program counter. They represent the start address of the handling routine for the NMI (see figure 6.25).

This interrupt mechanism has been designed for speed, as it is used in case of "emergencies". Therefore, it does not offer the flexibility of the maskable interrupt mode, described below.

Note also that an interrupt routine must have been loaded at address 0066H prior to using the NMI.

NMI will first cause:

$$
\left.
\begin{array}{l}
\text{SP} \leftarrow \text{SP} - 1 \\
(\text{SP}) \leftarrow \text{PCH} \\
\text{SP} \leftarrow \text{SP} - 1 \\
(\text{SP}) \leftarrow \text{PCL}
\end{array}
\right\} \quad \text{push PC}
$$

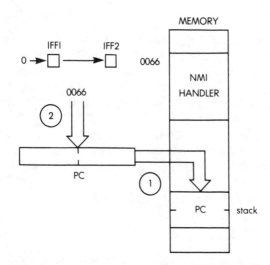

Fig. 6.25: NMI Forces Automatic Vectoring

Then, NMI causes an automatic restart at location 0066H. The complete sequence of events is the following:

PC $\longrightarrow$ STACK	(preserve program counter)
IFF1 $\longrightarrow$ IFF2	(preserve IFF)
0 $\longrightarrow$ IFF1	(reset IFF)
JUMP TO 0066H	(execute interrupt handler)

Also, the status of interrupt-mask-bit flip-flop (IFF1) at the time that NMI was received is preserved automatically into IFF2. Then, IFF1 is reset in order to prevent any further interrupts. This feature is important to prevent the loss of lower-priority INT's and simplifies the external hardware: the status of a pending INT is preserved internally in the Z80.

The NMI interrupt is normally used for high priority events such as a real-time clock or a power failure.

The return from an NMI is accomplished by a special instruction, RETN: "return from non-maskable interrupt." The contents of IFF1 are restored from IFF2, and the contents of the program counter PC are restored from their location in the stack. Since IFF1 had been reset during execution of the NMI, no external INT's could be accepted during the NMI (unless the programmer uses an EI instruction within the NMI routine): there has been no loss of information.

Upon termination of the interrupt handler, the sequence is:

IFF2 $\longrightarrow$ IFF1	(restore IFF)
STACK $\longrightarrow$ PC	(restore program counter)

Note that, once IFF1 is restored, maskable interrupt enable status is restored.

499

Interrupt

The ordinary, maskable, interrupt INT may operate in one of three modes. They are specific to the Z80, as the 8080 is equipped with only a single interrupt mode. The ordinary interrupt INT may also be masked selectively by the programmer. Setting the interrupt flip-flops IFF1 and IFF2 to a "1" will authorize interruptions. Setting them to a "0" (masking them) will prevent detection of INT. The EI instruction is used to set them, and the DI instruction is used to reset them. IFF1 and IFF2 are set or reset simultaneously. During execution of the EI and DI instructions, INT's are disabled in order to prevent any loss of information.

Let us now examine the three interrupt modes:

Interrupt Mode 0

This mode is identical to the 8080 interrupt mode. The Z80 will operate in interrupt mode 0 either when initially started (when the RE-SET signal has been applied) or else when an IM0 instruction has been executed. Once mode 0 has been set, an interrupt will be recognized if the interrupt enable flip-flop IFF1 is set to 1, provided no bus-request or non-maskable interrupt occurs at the same time. The interrupt will be detected only at the end of an instruction. Essentially, the Z80 will respond to the interrupt by generating an IORQ (and an M1 signal), and then do nothing, except wait.

It is the responsibility of an *external device* to recognize the IORQ and M1 (this is called an *interrupt acknowledge* or INTA) and to place an instruction on the data-bus. The Z80 expects an instruction to be placed on its data bus by the external device within the next cycle. Typically, an RST or a CALL instruction is placed on the bus. Both of these instructions automatically preserve the program-counter in the stack, and cause branching to a specific address. The advantage of the RST instruction is that it resides within a single byte, i.e., it executes rapidly. Its disadvantage is to branch to only one of eight possible locations in page zero (addresses 0 through 255). The advantage of the CALL instruction is that it is a general-purpose branch instruction which specifies a full 16-bit address. However, it requires three bytes and therefore executes less rapidly.

Note that once the interrupt processing starts, all further interrupts are disabled. IFF1 and IFF2 are automatically set to "0". It is then the responsibility of the programmer to insert an EI instruction (Enable Interrupts) at the appropriate location within his program if he wishes to enable interrupts, and, in any case, before returning from the interrupt.

The detailed sequence corresponding to the mode 0 interrupt is shown in Figure 6.26.

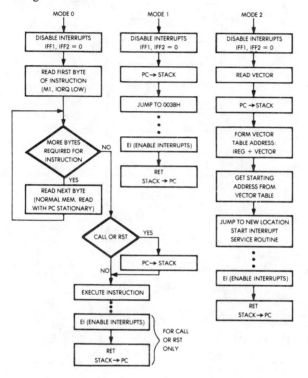

Fig. 6.26: Interrupt Modes

The return from the interrupt is accomplished by an RETI instruction. Let us remind the programmer at this point that he/she is usually responsible for explicitly clearing the interrupt which has been serviced on the I/O device, and always for restoring the interrupt disable flag inside the Z80. However, the peripheral controller may use the INTA signal to clear the INT request, thus freeing the programmer of this chore.

In addition, should the interrupt-handling routine modify the contents of any of the internal registers, the programmer is specifically responsible for preserving these registers in the stack prior to executing the interrupt-handling routine. Otherwise, the contents of these registers will be destroyed, and when the interrupted program resumes execution, it will fail. For example, assuming that registers A, B, C, D, E, H and L will be used within the interrupt handler, they will have to be saved (see Figure 6.27).

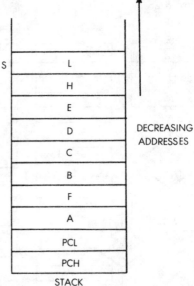

Fig. 6.27: Saving the Registers

The corresponding program is:

```
SAVREG    PUSH   AF
          PUSH   BC
          PUSH   DE
          PUSH   HL
```

Upon completion of the interrupt-handling routine, these registers must be restored. The interrupt handler will terminate with the following sequence of instructions:

```
          POP    HL
          POP    DE
          POP    BC
          POP    AF
          EI                      (unless EI was used earlier in
                                  the routine)
```

Additionally, if registers IX and IY are used by the routine they must also be preserved, then restored.

Interrupt Mode 1

This interrupt mode is set by executing the IM1 instruction. It is an automated interrupt handler which causes an automatic branch to location 0038H. It is therefore essentially analogous to the NMI interrupt mechanism except that it may be masked. The Z80 automatically preserves the contents of PC into the stack (see Figure 6.28).

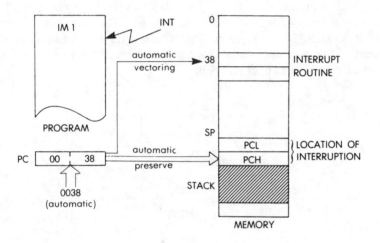

Fig. 6.28: Mode 1 Interrupt

This automated interrupt response, which "vectors" all interrupts to memory location 38H, stems from the early 8080's requirement to minimize the amount of external hardward necessary for using interrupts. Its possible disadvantage is to cause a branch to a *single* memory location. In case several devices are connected to the INT line, the program starting at location 38H will be responsible for determining which device requested service. This problem will be addressed below.

One precaution must be taken with respect to the timing of this interrupt: when performing programmed input/output transfers, the Z80 will ignore any data that may be present in the data bus during the cycle which follows the interrupt (the interrupt acknowledge cycle).

Interrupt Mode 2 (Vectored Interrupts)

This mode is set by executing an IM2 instruction. It is a powerful mode which allows automatic vectoring of interrupts. The interrupt vector is an address supplied by the peripheral device which generated the interrupt, and used as a memory pointer to the start address of the interrupt-handling routine. The addresssing mechanism provided by the Z80 in mode 2 is indirect, rather than direct. Each peripheral supplies a seven-bit branching address which is appended to the 8-bit address contained in the special I register in the Z80. The right-most bit of the final 16-bit address bit 0 is set to "0". This resulting address points to an entry in a table anywhere in the memory. This table may contain up to 128 double-word entries. Each of these double words is the address of the interrupt handler for the corresponding device. This is illustrated in Figures 6.29 and 6.30.

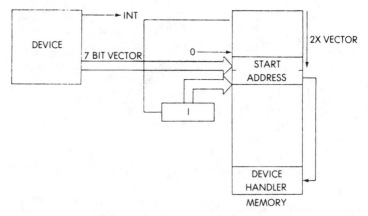

Fig. 6.29: Mode 2 Interrupt

The interrupt table may have up to 128 double-word entries.

In this mode, the Z80 also automatically pushes the contents of the program counter into the stack. This is obviously necessary, since PC will be reloaded with the contents of the interrupt table entry corresponding to the vector provided by the device.

Interrupt Overhead

For a graphic comparison of the polling process vs. the interrupt process, refer to Figure 6.18, where the polling process is illustrated on the top, and the interrupt process underneath. It can be seen that in the polling technique the program wastes a lot of time waiting.

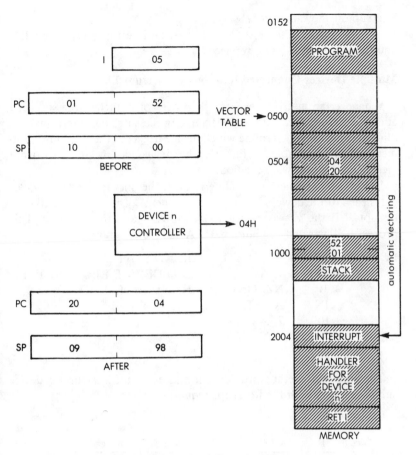

Fig. 6.30: Mode 2 - A Practical Example

Using interrupts, the program is interrupted, the interrupt is serviced, then the program resumes. However, the obvious disadvantage of an interrupt is to introduce several additional instructions at the beginning and at the end, resulting in a delay before the first instruction of the device handler can be executed. This is additional overhead.

Exercise 6.28: *Using the tables indicating the number of cycles per instruction, in Chapter 4, compute how much time will be lost to save and then restore registers A, B, D, H.*

Having clarified the operation of the interrupt lines, let us now consider two important remaining problems:

1—How do we resolve the problem of multiple devices triggering an interrupt at the same time?

2—How do we resolve the problem of an interrupt occurring while another interrupt is being serviced?

Multiple Devices Connected to a Single Interrupt Line

Whenever an interrupt occurs, the processor branches to a specified address. Before it can do any effective processing, the interrupt handling routine must determine which device triggered the interrupt. Two methods are available to identify the device, as usual: a software method and a hardware method.

In the software method, polling is used: the microprocessor interrogates each of the devices in turn and asks them, "Did you trigger the interrupt?" If the answer is negative, it interrogates the next one. This process is illustrated in Figure 6.31. A sample program is:

```
POLINT   IN    A, (STATUS1)  READ STATUS
         BIT   7, A          DID DEVICE REQUEST INT?
         JP    NZ, ONE       HANDLE IT IF SO
         IN    A, (STATUS2)
         BIT   7, A
         JP    NZ, TWO
         etc.  ---
```

The hardward method provides the address of the interrupting device simultaneously with the interrupt request.

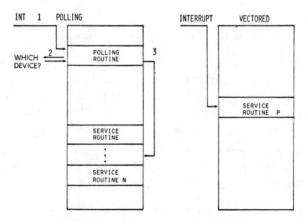

Fig. 6.31: Polled vs. Vectored Interrupt

To be more precise, when operating in mode 0, the peripheral device controller will supply a one-byte RST or a three-byte CALL on the data bus in response to the interrupt acknowledge, thus automating the interrupt vectoring, and minimizing the overhead.

Note that a subroutine call instruction is required as the Z80 does not save the PC when operating in mode 0.

In most cases, the speed of reaction to an interrupt is not crucial, and a polling approach is used. If response time is a primary consideration, a hardware approach must be used.

Simultaneous Interrupts

The next problem which may occur is that a new interrupt can be triggered during the execution of an interrupt-handling routine. Let us examine what happens and how the stack is used to solve the problem. We have indicated in Chapter 2 that this was another essential role of the stack, and the time has come now to demonstrate its use. We will refer to Figure 6.33 to illustrate multiple interrupts. Time elapses from left to right in the illustration. The contents of the stack are shown at the bottom of the illustration. Looking at the left, at time T0, program P is in execution. Moving to the right, at time T1, interrupt I1 occurs. We will assume that the interrupt mask was enabled, authorizing I1. Program P will be suspended. This is shown at the bottom of the illustration. The stack will contain the program counter and the status register of program P, at least, plus any optional registers that might be saved by the interrupt handler or I1 itself.

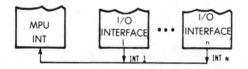

Fig. 6.32: Several Devices May Use the Same Interrupt Line

At time T1, interrupt I1 starts executing until time T2. At time T2, interrupt I2 occurs. We will assume that interrupt I2 has a higher priority than interrupt I1. If it had a lower priority, it would be ignored until I1 had been completed. At time T2, the registers for I1 are stacked, and this appears at the bottom of the illustration. Again, the contents of the program counter and AF are pushed into the stack. In addition, the routine for I2 might decide to save an additional few registers. I2 will now execute to completion at time T3.

When 12 terminates (with an RETI), the contents of the stack are automatically popped back into the Z80, and this is illustrated at the bottom of Figure 6.33. Thus, automatically I1 resumes execution. Unfortunately, at time T4, an interrupt 13 of higher priority occurs again. We can see at the bottom of the illustration that again the registers for I1 are pushed into the stack. Interrupt 13 executes from T4 to T5 and

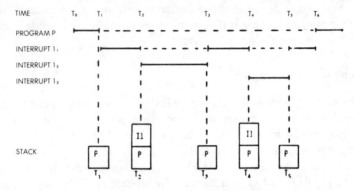

Fig. 6.33: Stack Contents During Multiple Interrupts

terminates at T5. At that time, the contents of the stack are popped into Z80, and interrupt I1 resumes execution. This time it runs to completion and terminates at T6. At T6, the remaining registers that have been saved in the stack are popped into Z80, and progam P may resume execution. The reader will verify that the stack is empty at this point. In fact, the number of dashed lines indicating program suspension indicates at the same time how many levels there are in the stack.

Exercise 6.29: Assume that the area available to the stack is limited to 300 locations in a specific program. Assume that all the registers must always be saved and that the programmer allows interrupts to be nested, i.e., to interrupt each other. Which is the maximum number of simultaneous interrupts that can be handled? Will any other factor contribute to still reduce further the maximum number of simultaneous interrupts?

It must be stressed, however, that, in practice, microprocessor systems are normally connected to a small number of devices using interrupts. It is, therefore, unlikely that a high number of simultaneous interrupts will occur in such a system.

We have now solved all the problems usually associated with interrupts. Their use is, in fact, simple and they should be employed to advantage even by the novice programmer.

508

SUMMARY

In this chapter we have presented the range of techniques used to communicate with the outside world. From elementary input/output routines to more complex programs for communication with actual peripherals, we have learned to develop all the usual programs and have even examined the efficiency of benchmark programs in the case of a parallel transfer and a parallel-to-serial conversion. Finally, we have learned to schedule the operation of multiple peripherals by using polling and interrupts. Naturally, many other exotic input/output devices might be connected to a system. With the array of techniques which have been presented so far, and with an understanding of the peripherals involved, it should be possible to solve most common problems.

In the next chapter, we will examine the actual characteristics of the input/output interface chips usually connected to a Z80. Then, we will consider the basic data structures that the programmer may use.

Exercise 6.30: Compute the overhead when operating in mode 0, assuming that all registers are saved, and that an RST is received in response to the interrupt acknowledge. The overhead is defined as the total delay incurred, exclusive of the instructions required to implement the interrupt processing proper.

Exercise 6.31: A 7-segment LED display can also display digits other than the hex alphabet. Compute the codes for: H, I, J, L, O, P, S, U, Y, g, h, i, j, l, n, o, p, r, t, u, y.

Exercise 6.32: The flowchart for interrupt management appears in Figure 6.34 Answer the following questions:
a—What is done by hardware, what is done by software?
b—What is the use of the mask?
c—How many registers should be preserved?
d—How is the interrupting device identified?
e—What does the RETI instruction do? How does it differ from a subroutine return?
f—Suggest a way to handle a stack overflow situation.
g—What is the overhead ("lost time") introduced by the interrupt mechanism?

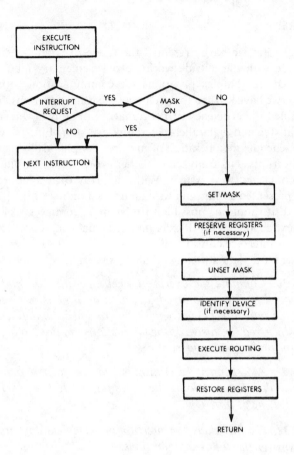

Fig. 6.34: Interrupt Logic

7

INPUT/OUTPUT DEVICES

INTRODUCTION

We have learned how to program the Z80 microprocessor in most usual situations. However, we should make a special mention of the input/output chips normally connected to the microprocessor. Because of the progress in LSI integration, new chips have been introduced which did not exist before. As a result, programming a system requires, naturally, first to program a microprocessor itself, and then *to program the input/output chips.* In fact, it is often more difficult to remember how to program the various control options of an input/output chip than to program the microprocessor itself! This is not because the programming in itself is more difficult, but because each of these devices has its own idiosyncrasies. We are going to examine here first the most general input/output device, the programmable input/output chip (in short a "PIO"), then some Zilog I/O devices.

The "Standard PIO"

There is no "standard PIO". However, each PIO device is essentially analogous in function to all similar PIO's produced by other manufacturers for the same purpose. The purpose of a PIO is to provide a multiport connection for input/output devices. (A "port" is simply a set of 8 input/output lines.) Each PIO provides at least two sets of 8-bit lines for I/O devices. Each I/O device needs a *data buffer* in order to stabilize the contents of the data bus on output at least. Our PIO will, therefore, be equipped at a minimum with a buffer for each port.

In addition, we have established that the microcomputer will use a *handshaking* procedure, or else *interrupts* to communicate with the

I/O device. The PIO will also use a similar procedure to communicate with the peripheral. Each PIO must, therefore, be equipped with at least *two control lines per port* to implement the handshaking function.

The microprocessor will also need to be able to read the status of each port. Each port must be equipped with one or more *status bits.* Finally, a number of options will exist within each PIO to configure its resources. The programmer must be able to access a special register within the PIO to specify the programming options. This is the *control-register.* In some cases the status information is part of the control register.

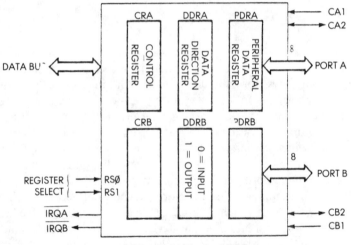

Fig. 7.1: Typical PIO

One essential faculty of the PIO is the fact that each line may be configured as either an input or an output line. The diagram of a PIO appears in illustration 7.1. The programmer may specify whether any line will be input or output. In order to program the direction of the lines, a *data-direction register* is provided for each port. On many PIO's, "0" in a bit position of the data-direction register specifies an input. A "1" specifies an output. Zilog uses the reverse convention.

It may be surprising to see that a "0" is used for input and a "1" for output when really "0" should correspond to output and "1" to input. This is quite deliberate: whenever power is applied to the system, it is of great importance that all the I/O lines be configured as *input.* Otherwise, if the microcomputer is connected to some dangerous peripheral, it might activate it by accident. When a reset is applied, all registers are normally zeroed and that will result in configuring all input lines of the PIO as inputs. The connection to the microprocessor appears on the left of the illustration. The PIO naturally connects to the 8-bit data bus, the microprocessor address bus, and the microprocessor control-bus. The programmer will simply specify the address of any register that it wishes to access within the PIO.

The Internal Control Register

The Control Register of the PIO provides a number of options for generating or sensing interrupts, or for implementing automatic handshake functions. The complete description of the facilities provided is not necessary here. Simply, the user of any practical system which uses a PIO will have to refer to the data-sheet showing the effect of setting the various bits of the control register. Whenever the system is initialized, the programmer will have to load the control register of the PIO with the correct contents for the expected application.

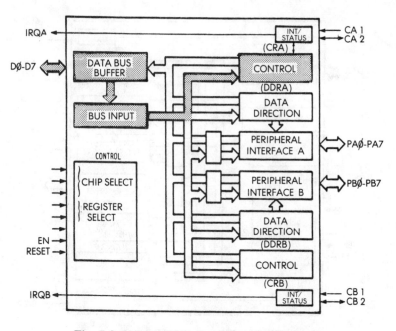

Fig. 7.2: Using a PIO–Load Control Register

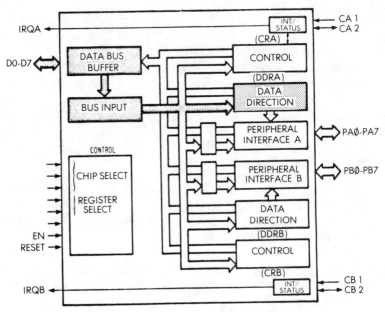

Fig. 7.3: Using a PIO-Load Data Direction

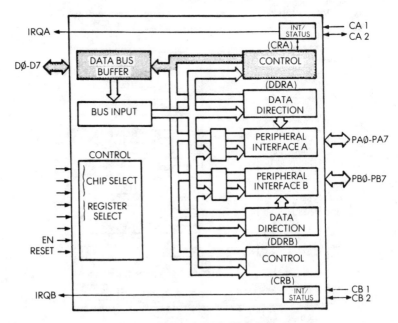

Fig. 7.4: Using a PIO-Read Status

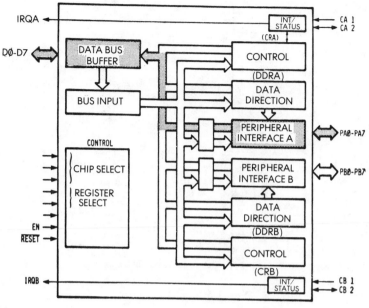

Fig. 7.5: Using a PIO Read INPUT

Programming a PIO

A typical sequence, when using a PIO channel, is the following (assuming an input):

Load the control register
This is accomplished by a programmed transfer between a Z80 register (usually the accumulator) and the PIO control register. This sets the options and operating mode of the PIO (see Figure 7. 2). It is normally done only once at the beginning of a program.

Load the direction register
This specifies the direction in which the I/O lines will be used. (See Figure 7.3.)

Read the status
The status register indicates whether a valid byte is available on input. (See Figure 7.4).

Read the port
The byte is read into the Z80. (See Figure 7.5).

515

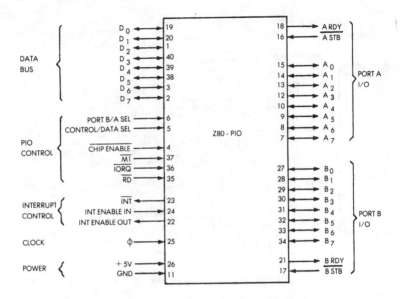

Fig. 7.6: Z80 PIO pinout

The Zilog Z80 PIO

The Z80 PIO is a two-port PIO whose architecture is essentially compatible with the standard model we have described. The actual pinout is shown in Figure 7.6, and a block diagram is shown in Figure 7.7.

Each PIO port has six registers: an 8-bit input register, an 8-bit output register, a 2-bit mode-control register, an 8-bit mask register, an 8-bit input/output select (direction register), and a 2-bit mask-control register. The last three registers are used only when the port is programmed to operate in the bit mode.

Each port may operate in one of four modes, as selected by the contents of the mode-control registers (2 bits). They are: byte output, byte input, byte bidirectional bus, and bit mode.

The two bits of the mask control register are loaded by the programmer, and specify the high or low state of a peripheral device which is to be monitored, and conditions for which an interrupt can be generated. generated.

The 8-bit input/output select register allows any pin to be either an input or an output when operating in the bit mode.

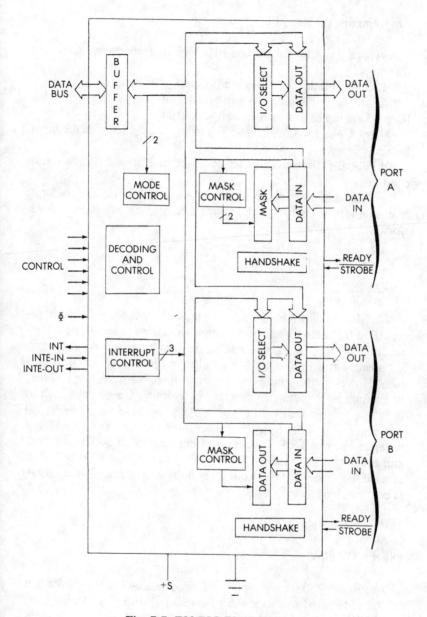

Fig. 7.7: Z80 PIO Block Diagram

517

Programming the Zilog PIO

A typical sequence for using a PIO, say in bit mode, would be the following:

Load the mode control register to specify the bit mode.

Load the input/output select register of port A to specify that lines 0-5 are inputs and lines 6 and 7 are outputs.

Then a word would be read by reading the contents of the input buffer.

Additionally, the mask register could be used to specify the status conditions.

For a detailed description of the operation of the PIO, the reader is referred to the companion volume in this series, the *Z80 Applications Book*.

The Z80 SIO

The SIO (Serial Input/Output) is a dual-channel peripheral chip designed to facilitate asynchronous communications in serial form. It includes a UART, i.e., a universal asynchronous receiver-transmitter. Its essential function is serial-to-parallel and parallel-to-serial conversion. However, this chip is equipped with sophisticated capabilities, like automatic handling of complex byte-oriented protocols, such as IBM bisync as well as HDLC and SDLC, two bit-oriented protocols.

Additionally, it can operate in synchronous mode like a USRT, and generate and check CRC codes. It offers a choice of polling, interrupt, and block-transfer modes. The complete description of this device is beyond the scope of this introductory book and appears in the *Z80 Applications Book*.

Other I/O Chips

Because the Z80 is commonly used as a replacement for the 8080, it has been designed so that it can be associated with almost any of the usual 8080 input/output chips, as well as the specific I/O chips manufactured by Zilog. All the 8080 input/output chips may be considered for use in a Z80 system.

SUMMARY

In order to make effective use of input/output components it is necessary to understand in detail the function of every bit, or group of bits, within the various control registers. These complex new chips automate a number of procedures that had to be carried out by software or special logic before. In particular, a good deal of the handshaking procedures are automated within components such as an SIO. Also, interrupt handling and detection may be internal. With the information that has been presented in the preceding chapter, the reader should be able to understand what the functions of the basic signals and registers are. Naturally, still newer components are going to be introduced which will offer a hardware implementation of still more complex algorithms.

8
APPLICATION EXAMPLES

INTRODUCTION

This chapter is designed to test your new programming skills by presenting a collection of utility programs. These programs or "routines" are frequently encountered in applications, and are generally called "utility routines." They will require a synthesis of the knowledge and techniques presented so far.

We are going to fetch characters from an I/O device and process them in various ways. But first, let us clear an area of the memory (this may not be necessary—each of these programs is only presented as a programming example).

CLEARING A SECTION OF MEMORY

We want to clear (zero) the contents of the memory from address BASE to address BASE ± LENGTH, where LENGTH is less than 256.

The program is:

```
ZEROM    LD    B, LENGTH    LOAD B WITH LENGTH
         LD    A,0          CLEAR A
         LD    HL, BASE     POINT TO BASE
CLEAR    LD    (HL), A      CLEAR A LOCATION
         INC   HL           POINT TO NEXT
         DEC   B            DECREMENT COUNTER
         JR    NZ, CLEAR    END OF SECTION?
         RET
```

In the above program, the length of the section of memory is assumed to be equal to LENGTH. The register pair HL is used as a pointer to the current word which will be cleared. Register B is used, as usual, as a counter.

The accumulator A is loaded only once with the value 0 (all zeros), then copied into the successive memory locations.

In a memory test program, for example, this utility routine could be used to zero the contents of a block. Then the memory test program would usually verify that its contents remained 0.

The above was a straightforward implementation of a clearing routine. Let us improve on it.

The improved program appears below.

```
ZEROM    LD     B, LENGTH
         LD     HL, BASE
LOOP     LD     (HL), 0
         INC    HL
         DJNZ   LOOP
         RET
```

The two improvements were obtained by eliminating the LD A, 0 instruction and loading a "zero" directly into the location pointed to by H and L, and also by using the special Z80 instruction DJNZ.

This improvement example should demonstrate that *every time a program is written, even though it may be correct, it can usually be improved by examining it carefully.* Familiarity with the complete instruction set is essential for bringing about such improvements. These improvements are not just cosmetic. They improve the execution time of the program, require fewer instructions and therefore less memory space, and also generally improve the readability of the program and, therefore, its chances of being correct.

Exercise 8.1: Write a memory test program which zeroes a 256-word block, then verifies that each location is 0. Then, it will write all 1's and verify the contents of the block. Then it will write 01010101 and verify the contents. Finally, it will write 10101010, and verify the contents.

Exercise 8.2: Modify the above program so that it will fill the memory section with alternating 0's and 1's (all 0's, then all 1's).

Let us now poll our I/O devices to find which one needs service.

POLLING I/O DEVICES

We will assume that those I/O devices are connected to our system. Their status registers are located at addresses STATUS1, STATUS2, STATUS3. The program is:

```
TEST      IN      A, (STATUS1)  READ IO STATUS1
          BIT     7, A          TEST "READY" BIT (BIT 7)
          JP      NZ, FOUND1    JUMP TO HANDLER 1
          IN      A, (STATUS2)  SAME FOR DEVICE 2
          BIT     7, A
          JP      NZ, FOUND2
          IN      A, (STATUS3)  SAME FOR DEVICE 3
          BIT     7, A
          JP      NZ, FOUND3
          (failure exit)
```

As a result of the BIT instruction, the Z bit of the status flags will be set to 1 if STATUS is zero. The JP NZ instruction (jump if non-equal to zero) will then result in a branch to the appropriate FOUND routine.

GETTING CHARACTERS IN

Assume we have just found that a character is ready at the keyboard. Let us accumulate characters in a memory area called BUFFER until we encounter a special character called SPC, whose code has been previously defined.

The subroutine GETCHAR will fetch one character from the keyboard (see Chapter 6 for more details) and leave it in the accumulator. We assume that 256 characters maximum will be fetched before an SPC character is found.

```
STRING  LD    HL, BUFFER   POINT TO BUFFER
NEXT    CALL  GETCHAR      GET A CHARACTER
        CP    SPC          CHECK FOR SPECIAL CHAR
        JR    Z, OUT       FOUND IT?
        LD    (HL), A      STORE CHAR IN BUFFER
        INC   HL           NEXT BUFFER LOCATION
        JR    NEXT         GET NEXT CHAR
OUT     RET
```

Exercise 8.3: Let us improve this basic routine:
a—Echo the character back to the device (for a Teletype, for example).
b—Check that the input string is no longer than 256 characters.

We now have a string of characters in a memory buffer. Let us process them in various ways.

TESTING A CHARACTER

Let us determine if the character at memory location LOC is equal to 0, 1, or 2:

```
ZOT    LD     A, (LOC)    GET CHARACTER
       CP     00          IS IT A ZERO?
       JP     Z, ZERO     JUMP TO ROUTINE
       CP     01          A ONE?
       JP     Z, ONE
       CP     02          A TWO?
       JP     Z, TWO
       JP     NOTFND      FAILURE
```

We simply read the character, then use the CP instruction to check its value.

Let us run a different test now.

BRACKET TESTING

Let us determine if the ASCII character at memory location LOC is a digit between 0 and 9:

```
BRACK  LD     A, (LOC)    GET CHARACTER
       AND    7FH         MASK OUT PARITY BIT
       CP     30H         ASCII 0
       JR     C, OUT      CHAR TOO LOW?
       CP     39H         ASCII 9
       JR     NC, OUT     CHAR TOO HIGH?
       CP     A           FORCE ZERO FLAG
OUT    RET    EXIT
```

ASCII "0" is represented in hexadecimal by "30" or by "B0", depending upon whether the parity bit is used or not. Similarly, ASCII "9" is represented in hexadecimal by "39" or by "B9".

The purpose of the second instruction of the program is to delete bit 7, the parity bit, in case it was used, so that the program is applicable to both cases. The value of the character is then compared to the ASCII values for "0" and "9". When using a comparison instruction, the Z flag is set if the comparison succeeds. The carry bit is set in the case of borrow, and reset otherwise. In other words, when using the CP instruction, the carry bit will be set if the value of the literal that appears in the instruction is greater than the value contained in the accumulator. It will be reset ("0") if less than or equal.

The last instruction, CP A, forces a "1" into the Z flag. The Z flag is used to indicate to the calling routine that the character in CHAR was indeed in the interval (0, 9). Other conventions can be used, such as loading a digit in the accumulator in order to indicate the result of the test.

Exercise 8.4: Is the following program equivalent to the one above?:

```
LD    A, (CHAR)
SUB   30H
JP    M, OUT
SUB   10
JP    P, OUT
ADD   10
```

Exercise 8.5: Determine if an ASCII character contained in the accumulator is a letter of the alphabet.

When using an ASCII table, you will notice that parity is often used. For example, the ASCII for "0" is "0110000", a 7-bit code. However, if we use odd parity, for example, we guarantee that the total number of ones in a word is odd; then the code becomes: "10110000". An extra "1" is added to the left. This is "B0" in hexadecimal. Let us therefore develop a program to generate parity.

PARITY GENERATION

This program will generate an even parity with bit position 7:

```
PARITY LD    A, (CHAR)    GET CHARACTER
       AND   7FH          CLEAR PARITY BIT
       JP    PE, OUT      CHECK IF PARITY
                          ALREADY EVEN
       OR    80H          SET PARITY BIT
OUT    LD    (LOC), A     STORE RESULT
```

The program uses the internal parity detection circuit available in the Z80.

The third instruction: JP PE, OUT checks whether parity of the word in the accumulator is already even. This instruction will succeed if the parity is even, "PE", and will exit.

If the parity is not even, i.e., if the jump instruction failed, then the parity is odd, and a "1" must be written in bit position 7. This is the purpose of the fourth instruction:

OR   80H

Finally, the resulting value is saved in memory location LOC.

Exercise 8.6: *The above problem was too simple to solve, using the internal parity detection circuitry. As an exercise, you are requested to solve the same problem without using this circuitry. Shift the contents of the accumulator, and count the number of 1's in order to determine which bit should be written into the parity position.*

Exercise 8.7: *Using the above program as an example, verify the parity of a word. You must compute the correct parity, then compare it to the one expected.*

CODE CONVERSION: ASCII TO BCD

Converting ASCII to BCD is very simple. We will observe that the hexadecimal representation of ASCII characters 0 to 9 is 30 to 39 or B0 to B9, depending on parity. The BCD representation is simply obtained by dropping the "3" or the "B", i.e., masking off the left nibble (4 bits):

```
ASCBCD  CALL  BRACK         CHECK THAT CHAR IS 0 TO 9
        JP    NZ, ILLEGAL   EXIT IF ILLEGAL CHAR
        AND   OFH           MASK HIGH NIBBLE
        LD    (BCDCHAR), A  STORE RESULT
```

Exercise 8.8: *Write a program to convert BCD to ASCII.*

Exercise 8.9: *Write a program to convert BCD to binary (more difficult).*
Hint: $N_3 N_2 N_1 N_0$ in BCD is $(((N_3 \times 10) + N_2) \times 10 + N_1) \times 10 + N_0$ in binary.

To multiply by 10, use a left shift ($= \times 2$), another left shift ($= \times 4$), an ADC ($= \times 5$), another left shift ($= \times 10$).

In full BCD notation, the first word may contain the count of BCD digits, the next nibble contain the sign, and every successive nibble contain a BCD digit (we assume no decimal point). The last nibble of the block may be unused.

CONVERT HEX TO ASCII

"A" contains one hexadecimal digit. We simply need to add a "3" (or a

525

"B") into the left nibble:

```
AND    0FH           ZERO LEFT NIBBLE (optional)
ADD    A, 30H        ASCII
CP     3AH           CORRECTION NECESSARY?
JP     M, OUT
ADD    A, 7          CORRECTION FOR A TO F
```

Exercise 8.10: Convert HEX to ASCII, assuming a packed format (two hex digits in A).

FINDING THE LARGEST ELEMENT OF A TABLE

The beginning address of the table is contained at memory address BASE. The first entry of the table is the number of bytes it contains. This program will search for the largest element of the table. Its value will be left in A, and its position will be stored in memory location INDEX.

This program uses registers A, F, B, H and L, and will use indirect addressing, so that it can search a table anywhere in the memory (see Figure 8.1).

```
MAX          LD   HL, BASE          TABLE ADDRESS
             LD   B, (HL)           NBR OF BYTES IN TABLE
             LD   A, 0              CLEAR MAXIMUM VALUE
             INC  HL                INITIALIZE INDEX
             LD   (INDEX), HL       NEXT ENTRY
LOOP         CP   (HL)              COMPARE ENTRY
             JR   NC, NOSWITCH      JUMP IF LESS THAN MAX
             LD   A, (HL)           LOAD NEW MAX VALUE
             LD   (INDEX), HL       LOAD NEW MAX VALUE
NOSWITCH     INC  HL                POINT TO NEXT ENTRY
             DEC  B                 DECREMENT COUNTER
             JR   NZ, LOOP          KEEP GOING IF NOT ZERO
             RET
```

This program tests the nth entry first. If it is greater than 0, the entry goes in A, and its location is remembered into INDEX. The (n-1)st entry is then tested, etc.

This program works for positive integers.

Exercise 8.11: Modify the program so that it works also for negative numbers in two's complement.

Exercise 8.12: Will this program also work for ASCII characters?

Exercise 8.13: Write a program which will sort n numbers in ascending

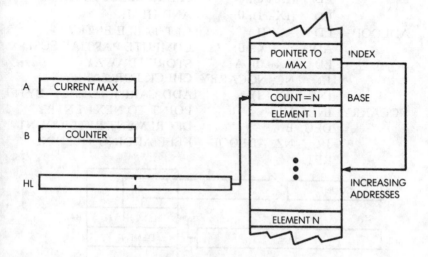

Fig. 8.1: Largest Element in a Table

order.

Exercise 8.14: Write a program which will sort n names (3 characters each) in alphabetical order.

SUM OF N ELEMENTS

This program will compute the 16-bit sum of N positive entries of a table. The starting address of the table is contained at memory address BASE. The first entry of the table contains the number of elements N. The 16-bit sum will be left in memoy locations SUMLO and SUMHI. If the sum should require more than 16 bits, only the lower 16 will be kept. (The high order bits are said to be truncated.)

This program will modify registers A, F, B, H, L, IX. It assumes 256 elements maximum (see Figure 8.2).

SUMN	LD	HL, BASE	POINT TO TABLE BASE
	LD	B, (HL)	READ LENGTH INTO COUNTER
SUMIG	INC	HL	POINT TO FIRST ENTRY
	LD	IX, SUMLO	POINT TO RESULT, LOW

527

```
                LD    (IX + 0), 0      CLEAR RESULT LOW
                LD    (IX + 1), 0      AND HIGH
ADLOOP     LD    A, (HL)           GET TABLE ENTRY
                ADD   A, (IX + 0)    COMPUTE PARTIAL SUM
                LD    (IX + 0), A      STORE IT AWAY
                JR     NC, NOCARRY  CHECK FOR CARRY
                INC   (IX + 1)         ADD CARRY TO HIGH BYTE
NOCARRY  INC   HL                 POINT TO NEXT ENTRY
                DEC   B                 DECREMENT BYTE COUNT
                JR     NZ, ADLOOP    KEEP ADDING TILL END
                RET
```

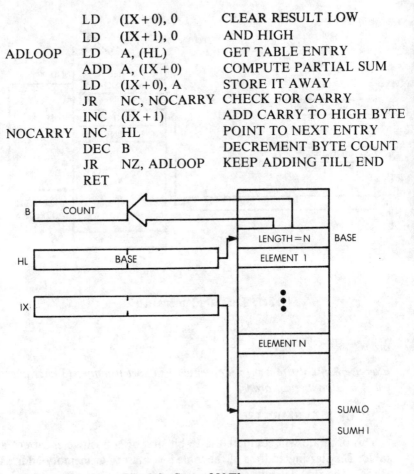

Fig. 8.2: Sum of N Elements

This program is straightforward and should be self-explanatory.

Exercise 8.15: Modify this program to:
a—compute a 24-bit sum
b—compute a 32-bit sum
c—detect any overflow.

A CHECKSUM COMPUTATION

A checksum is a digit or set of digits computed from a block of successive characters. The checksum is computed at the time the data is stored and put at the end. In order to verify the integrity of the data, the data is read, then the checksum is recomputed and compared against the stored value. A discrepancy indicates an error or a failure.

Several algorithms are used. Here, we will exclusive-OR all bytes in a table of N elements, and leave the result in the accumulator. As usual, the base of the table is stored at address BASE. The first entry of the table is its number of elements N. The program modifies A, F, B, H, L. N must be less than 256

```
CHKSUM    LD   HL, BASE      LOAD ADDRESS OF TABLE
                            INTO HL
          LD   B, (HL)       GET N = LENGTH
          XOR  A             CLEAR CHECKSUM
          INC  HL            POINT TO FIRST ELEMENT
CHLOOP    XOR  (HL)          COMPUTE CHECKSUM
          INC  HL            POINT TO NEXT ELEMENT
          DEC  B             DECREMENT COUNTER
          JR   NZ, CHLOOP    DO IT AGAIN IF NOT END
          LD   (CHECKSUM),A  PRESERVE CHECKSUM
          RET
```

COUNT THE ZEROES

This program will count the number of zeroes in our usual table, and leave it in location TOTAL. It modifies A, B, C, H, L, F.

```
ZEROS  LD   HL, BASE     POINT TO TABLE
       LD   B, (HL)      READ LENGTH INTO COUNTER
       LD   C, 0         ZERO TOTAL
       INC  HL           POINT TO FIRST ENTRY
ZLOOP  LD   A, (HL)      GET ELEMENT
       OR   0            SET ZERO FLAG
       JR   NZ, NOTZ     IS IT A ZERO?
       INC  C            IF SO, INCREMENT ZERO COUNT
NOTZ   INC  HL           POINT TO NEXT ENTRY
       DEC  B            DECREMENT LENGTH COUNTER
       JR   NZ, ZLOOP
       LD   A,C
       LD   (TOTAL), A   SAVE IT
```

Exercise 8.16: Modify this program to count
a—the number of stars (the character "")*
b—the number of letters of the alphabet
c—the number of digits between "0" and "9"

BLOCK TRANSFER

Let us pick up every third entry in the source block at address FROM and store it into a block at address TO:

```
FER3   LD    HL, FROM
       LD    DE, TO        SET UP POINTERS
       LD    BC, SIZE
LOOP   LDI                 AUTOMATED TRANSFER
       INC   HL
       INC   HL            SKIP 2 ENTRIES
       JP    PE, LOOP
```

BCD BLOCK TRANSFER

We will push up BCD digits in the memory, i.e, shift 4-bit nibbles (see Figure 8 .3).   The program appears below:

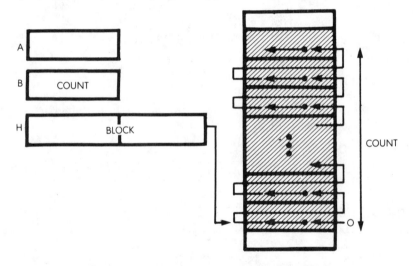

Fig. 8.3: BCD Block Transfer - The Memory

```
DMOV   LD    B, COUNT
       LD    HL, BLOCK
       XOR   A          A = 0
LOOP   RLD
       DEC   HL         POINT TO NEXT BYTE
       DJNZ  LOOP       DEC COUNT LOOP UNTIL ZERO
```

The program uses the RLD instruction, which we have not used yet. RLD rotates a BCD digit left between A and (HL). (HL) or M designate the contents of the memory location pointed to by H and L.

M LOW goes into M HIGH
M HIGH goes into A LOW
A LOW goes into M LOW

Here, "low" and "high" refer to a 4-bit nibble.

In order to use the powerful DJNZ instruction, register B is used as the digit counter. HL is set to point to the beginning of the block.

A is used to store the left digit displaced by each rotation between two successive accesses to the block.

By convention, "0" will be entered at the bottom of the block.

COMPARE TWO SIGNED 16-BIT NUMBERS

IX points to the first number N1.
IY points to N2 (see Figure 8.4).

The program sets the carry bit if N1< N2, and the Z bit if N1 = N2.

COMP	LD	B, (IX + 1)	GET SIGN OF N1
	LD	A, B	
	AND	80H	TEST SIGN, CLEAR CY
	JR	NZ, NEGM1	N1 IS NEG
	BIT	7, (IY + 1)	
	RET	NZ	N2 IS NEG
	LD	A, B	
	CP	(IY + 1)	SIGNS ARE BOTH POS
	RET	NZ	
	LD	A, (IX)	
	CP	(IY)	
	RET		
NEGM1	XOR	(IY + 1)	
	RLA		SIGN BIT INTO CY
	RET	C	SIGNS DIFFERENT
	LD	A, B	
	CP	(IY + 1)	BOTH SIGNS NEG
	RET	NZ	
	LD	A, (IX)	
	CP	(IY)	
	RET		

The program first tests the signs of N1 and N2. If N1 is negative, a

531

jump occurs to NEGM\. Otherwise, the top of the program is executed.

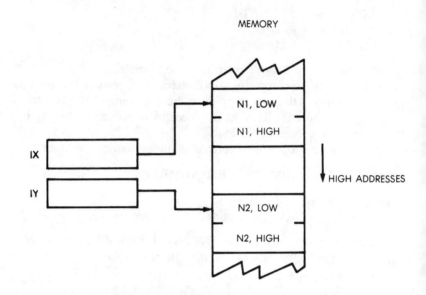

Fig. 8.4: Comparing Two Signed Numbers

Note that the BIT instruction is used in the 5th line to test directly the sign bit of N2 in the memory:

> BIT   7, (IY + 1)

The same could have been done for N1, except that we will need the value of N1 shortly. It is therefore simpler to read N1 from memory and preserve it into B:

COMP   LD   B, (IX + 1)

It is necessary to preserve N1 into B because the AND may destroy the contents of A:

> LD   A, B
> AND   80H

Note also that a conditional return is used (line 6):

> RET   NZ

This is a powerful feature of the Z80 which simplifies programming.

Note that the comparison instruction executes directly on the contents of memory, in indexed mode:

CP   (IY + 1)

When comparing the two numbers, the most significant byte is compared first, the least significant one second.

Note the extensive use of the indexing mechanism in this program, which results in efficient code.

BUBBLE-SORT

Bubble-sort is a sorting technique used to arrange the elements of a table in ascending or descending order. The bubble-sort technique derives its name from the fact that the smallest element "bubbles up" to the top of the table. Every time it "collides" with a "heavier" element, it jumps over it.

A practical example of a bubble-sort is shown on Figure 8.5 The list to be sorted contains: (10, 5, 0, 2, 100), and must be sorted in descending order ("0" on top). The algorithm is simple, and the flowchart is shown on Figure 8.7

The top two (or else bottom two) elements are compared. If the lower one is less ("lighter") than the top one, they are exchanged. Otherwise not. For practical purposes, the exchange, if it occurs, will be remembered in a flag called "EXCHANGED". The process is then repeated on the next pair of elements, etc., until all elements have been compared two by two.

This first pass is illustrated by steps 1, 2, 3, 4, 5, 6 on Figure 8.5, going from the bottom up. (Equivalently we could go from the top down.)

If no elements have been exchanged, the sort is complete. If an exchange has occurred, we start all over again.

Looking at Figure 8.6, it can be seen that four passes are necessary in this example.

The process is simple, and is widely used.

One additional complication resides in the actual mechanism of the exchange.

When exchanging A and B, one may not write

A = B
B = A

as this would result in the loss of the previous value of A (try it on an example).

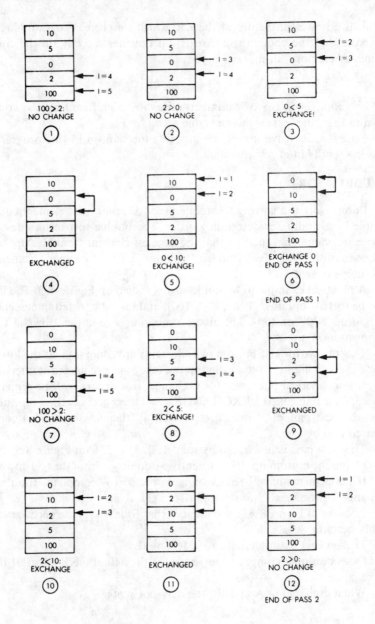

Fig. 8.5: Bubble-Sort Example: Phases 1 to 12

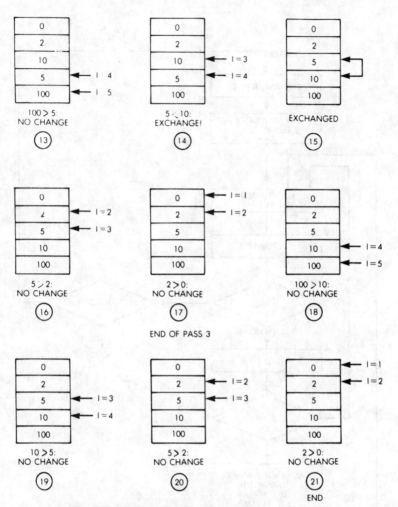

Fig. 8.6: Bubble-Sort Example: Phases 13 to 21

The correct solution is to use a temporary variable or location to preserve the value of A:

$$
\begin{aligned}
\text{TEMP} &= \text{A} \\
\text{A} &= \text{B} \\
\text{B} &= \text{TEMP}
\end{aligned}
$$

It works (try it on an example). This is called a circular permutation.

This is the way all programs implement the exchange. This technique is illustrated on the flowchart of Figure 8.7.

535

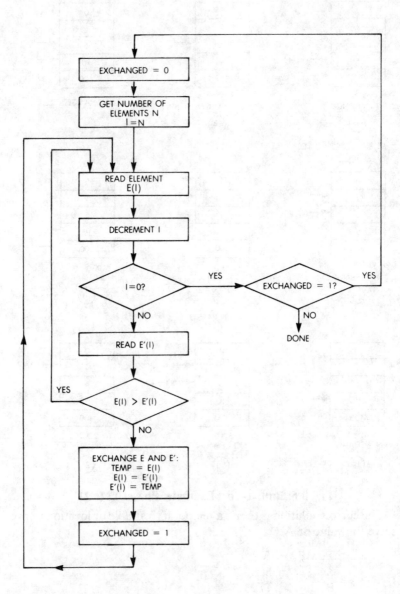

Fig. 8.7: Bubble-Sort Flowchart

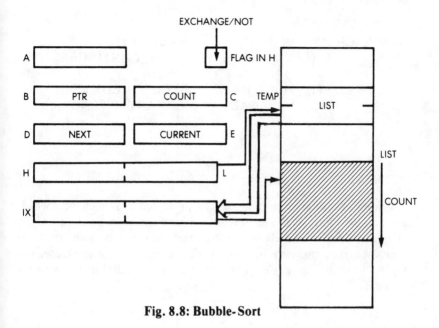

Fig. 8.8: Bubble-Sort

The register and memory assignments are shown on Figure 8.8, and the program is:

```
BUBBLE   LD    (TEMP), HL      TEMP = (HL)
AGAIN    LD    IX, (TEMP)      IX = (HL)
         RES   FLAG, H         EXCHANGED FLAG = 0
         LD    B, C
         DEC   B
NEXT     LD    A, (IX)
         LD    D, A            D = CURRENT ENTRY
         LD    E, (IX + 1)     E = NEXT ENTRY
         CP    E               COMPARE
         JR    NC, NOSWITCH    GO TO NOSWITCH IF
                               CURRENT ⩾ NEXT
XCHANGE  LD    (IX), E         STORE NEXT INTO
                               CURRENT
         LD    (IX + 1), D     STORE CURRENT INTO
                               NEXT
         SET   FLAG, H         EXCHANGED FLAG = 1
```

537

```
NOSWITCH INC   IX                NEXT ENTRY
          DJNZ    NEXT           DEC B, CONTINUE UNTIL
                                 ZERO
          BIT   FLAG, H          EXCHANGED = 1?
          JR    NZ, AGAIN        RESTART IF FLAG = 1
          RET
```

SUMMARY

Common utility routines have been presented in this chapter which use combinations of the techniques we have described in the previous chapters. They should allow you to start designing your own programs now. Many of these routines have used a special data structure, the table. Other possibilities exist for structuring data, and will now be reviewed.

9

DATA STRUCTURES

PART I — THEORY

INTRODUCTION

The design of a good program involves two tasks: *algorithm design* and *data structures design*. In most simple programs, no significant data structures are involved, so the main objective in learning programming is designing algorithms and coding them efficiently in a given machine language. This is what we have accomplished here. However, designing more complex programs also requires an understanding of data structures. Two data structures have already been used throughout the book: the table and the stack. The purpose of this chapter is to present other, more general, data structures that you may want to use. This chapter is completely independent of the microprocessor, or even the computer, selected. It is theoretical and involves the logical organization of data in the system. Specialized books exist on the topic of data structures, just as specialized books exist on the subject of efficient multiplication, division or other usual algorithms. This chapter, therefore, will be limited to essentials only. It does not claim to be complete. The most common data structures will now be reviewed.

POINTERS

A pointer is a number which is used to designate the location of the actual data. Every pointer is an address. However, every address is not necessarily called a pointer. An address is a pointer only if it points at some type of data or at structured information. We have already encountered a typical pointer: the stack pointer, which points to the top of the stack (or usually just over the top of the stack). We will see that the stack is a common data structure, called an LIFO structure.

As another example, when using indirect addressing, the indirect address is always a pointer to the data that one wishes to retrieve.

Exercise 9.1: Examine Fig. 9.1. At address 15 in the memory, there is a pointer to Table T. Table T starts at address 500. What are the actual contents of the pointer to T?

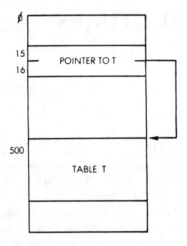

Fig. 9.1: An Indirection Pointer

LISTS

Almost all data structures are organized as lists of various kinds.

Sequential Lists

A sequential list, or table, or block, is probably the simplest data structure, and is one that we have already used. Tables are normally ordered in function of a specific criterion, such as alphabetical ordering or numerical ordering. It is then easy to retrieve an element in a table, using, for example, indexed addressing, as we have done. A block normally refers to a group of data which has definite limits but whose contents are not ordered. It may contain a string of characters; it may be a sector on a disk; or it may be some logical area (called segment) of the memory. In such cases, it may not be easy to access a random element of the block.

In order to facilitate the retrieval of blocks of information, directories are used.

Directories

A directory is a list of tables or blocks. For example, the file system will normally use a directory structure. As a simple example, the master directory of the system may include a list of the users' names. This is illustrated in Figure 9.2. The entry for user "John" points to John's file directory. The file directory is a table which contains the names of all of John's files and their location. This is, again, a table of pointers. In this case, we have just designed a two-level directory. A flexible directory system will allow the inclusion of additional intermediate directories, as may be found convenient by the user.

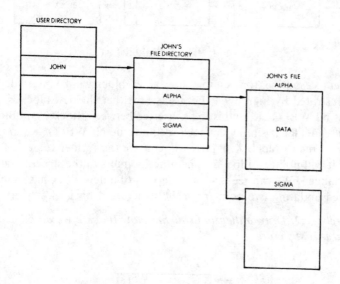

Fig. 9.2: A Directory Structure

Linked List

In a system there are often blocks of information which represent data, events, or other structures which cannot be moved around easily. If they could, we would probably assemble them in a table in order to sort or structure them. The problem now is that we wish to leave them where they are and still establish an ordering among them such as first, second, third, fourth. A linked list will be used to solve this problem. The concept of a linked list is illustrated by Figure 9.3. On the illustration, we see that a list pointer, called FIRSTBLOCK, points to the beginning of the first block. A dedicated location within Block 1 such as, perhaps, the first or the last word in it, contains a pointer to Block 2, called PTR1. The process is then repeated for Block 2 and Block 3. Since Block 3 is the last entry in the list, PTR3, by convention, either contains a special "nil" value, or points to itself, so that the end of the list can be detected. This structure is economical, as it requires only a few pointers (one per block) and frees the user from having to physically move the blocks in the memory.

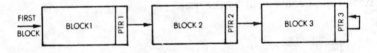

Fig. 9.3: A Linked List

Let us examine, for example, how a new block will be inserted. This is illustrated by Figure 9.4. Let us assume that the new block is at address NEWBLOCK, and is to be inserted between Block 1 and Block 2. Pointer PTR1 is simply changed to the value NEWBLOCK, so that it now points to Block X. PTRX will contain the former value of PTR1, i.e., it will point to Block 2. The other pointers in the structure are left unchanged. We can see that the insertion of a new block has simply required updating two pointers in the structure. This is clearly efficient.

Exercise 9.2: *Draw a diagram showing how Block 2 would be removed from this structure.*

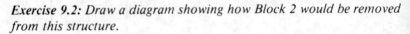
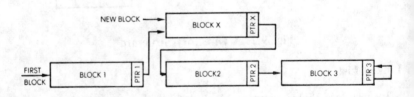

Fig. 9.4: Inserting a New Block

Several types of lists have been developed to facilitate specific types of access, insertions, and deletions to and from the list. Let us examine some of the most frequently used types of linked lists.

Queue

A queue is formally called a FIFO, or first-in-first-out list. A queue is illustrated in Figure 9.5. To clarify the diagram, we can assume, for example, that the block on the left is a service routine for an output device, such as a printer. The blocks appearing on the right are the request blocks from various programs or routines, to print characters. The order in which they will be serviced is the order established by the waiting queue. It can be seen that the first event which will obtain service is Block 1, the next one is Block 2, and the following one is Block 3. In a queue, the convention is that any new event arriving in the queue will be inserted at the end. Here it will be inserted after PTR3. This guarantees that the first block to be inserted in the queue will be the first one to be serviced. It is quite common in a computer system to have queues for a number of events whenever they must wait for a scarce resource, such as the processor or some input/output device.

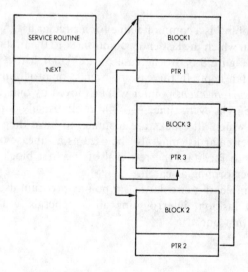

Fig. 9.5: A Queue

Stack

The stack structure has already been studied in detail throughout the book. It is a last-in-first-out structure (LIFO). The last element deposited on top is the first one to be removed. A stack may either be implemented as a sorted block, or it may be implemented as a list. Because most stacks in microprocessors are used for high-speed events, such as subroutines and interrupts, a continuous block is usually allocated to the stack instead of using a linked list.

Linked List vs. Block

Similarly, the queue could be implemented as a block of reserved locations. The advantage of using a continuous block is fast retrieval and the elimination of the pointers. The disadvantage is that it is usually necessary to dedicate a fairly large block to accommodate the worst-case size of the structure. Also, it makes it difficult or impractical to insert or remove elements from within the block. Since memory is traditionally a scarce resource, blocks have usually been reserved for fixed-size structures or structures requiring the maximum speed of retrieval, such as the stack.

Circular List

"Round robin" is a common name for a circular list. A circular list is a linked list in which the last entry points back to the first one. This is illustrated in Figure 9.6. In the case of a circular list, a *current-block* pointer is often kept. In the case of events, or programs, waiting for service, the *current-event* pointer will be moved by one position to the left or to the right every time. A round robin usually corresponds to a structure in which all blocks are assumed to have the same priority. However, a circular list may also be used as a subcase of other structures simply to facilitate the retrieval of the first block after the last one, when performing a search.

As an example of a circular list, a polling program usually goes in a round robin fashion, interrogating all peripherals and then coming back to the first one.

Trees

Whenever a logical relationship exists among all elements of a structure (this is usually called a syntax), a tree structure may be used. A simple example of a tree structure is a descendant, or genealogical, tree.

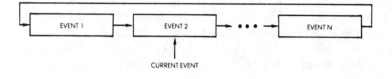

Fig. 9.6: Round Robin is Circular List

This is illustrated in Figure 9.7. It can be seen that Smith has two children: a son, Robert, and a daughter, Jane. Jane, in turn, has three children: Liz, Tom and Phil. Tom, in turn, has two more children: Max and Chris. However, Robert, on the left of the illustration, has no descendants.

This is a structured tree. We have, in fact, already encountered an example of a simple tree in Figure 9.2. The directory structure is a two-level tree. Trees are used to advantage whenever elements may be classified according to a fixed structure. This facilitates insertion and retrieval. In addition, they may establish groups of information in a structured way which may be required for later processing, such as in a compiler or interpreter design.

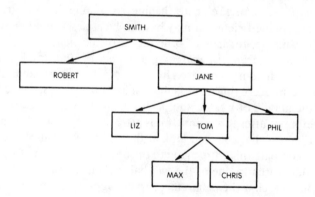

Fig. 9.7: Genealogical Tree

Doubly-Linked Lists

Additional links may be established between elements of a list. The simplest example is the doubly-linked list. This is illustrated in Figure 9.8. We can see that we have the usual sequence of links from left to right, plus another sequence of links from right to left. The goal is to allow easy retrieval of the element just before the one which is being processed, as well as just after it. This costs an extra pointer per block.

Fig. 9.8: Doubly-Linked List

SEARCHING AND SORTING

Searching and sorting elements of a list depends directly on the type of structure which has been used for the list. Many searching algorithms have been developed for the most frequently used data structures. We have already used indexed addressing. This is possible whenever the elements of a table are ordered in function of a known criterion. Such elements may then be retrieved by their numbers.

Sequential searching refers to the linear scanning of an entire block. This is clearly inefficient but may have to be used when no better technique is available, for lack of ordering of the elements.

Binary, or *logarithmic, searching* attempts to find an element in a sorted list by dividing the search interval in half at every step. Assuming that we are searching an alphabetical list, one might start, for example, in the middle of a table and determine if the name we are looking for is before or after this point. If it is after this point, we will eliminate the first half of the table and look at the middle element of the second half. We compare this entry again to the one we are looking for, and we restrict our search to one of the two halves, and so on. The maximum length of a search is then guaranteed to be $\log_2 n$, where n is the number of elements in the table.

Many other search techniques exist.

SECTION SUMMARY

This section was intended as only a brief presentation of usual data structures which may be used by a programmer. Although most common data structures have been organized in types and given a name, the overall organization of data in a complex system may use any combination of them, or require the programmer to invent more appropriate structures. The array of possibilities is only limited by the imagination of the programmer. Similarly, a number of well-known sorting and searching techniques have been developed for coping with the usual data structures. A comprehensive description is beyond the scope of this book. The contents of this section were intended to stress the importance of designing appropriate section structures for the data to be manipulated and to provide the basic tools to that effect.

Actual programming examples will now be presented in detail.

PART II — DESIGN EXAMPLES

INTRODUCTION

Actual design examples will be presented here for typical data structures: table, sorted list, linked list. Practical searching and insertion and deletion algorithms will be programmed for these structures.

The reader interested in these advanced programming techniques is encouraged to analyze in detail the programs presented in this section.

However, the beginning programmer may skip this section initially, and come back to it when he feels ready for it.

A good understanding of the concepts presented in the first part of this chapter is necessary to follow the design examples. Also, the programs will use all of the addressing modes of the Z80, and integrate many of the concepts and techniques presented in the previous chapters.

Three structures will now be introduced: a simple list, an alphabetical list and a linked-list plus directory. For each structure, three programs will be developed: search, enter and delete.

DATA REPRESENTATION FOR THE LIST

Both the simple list and the alphabetic list will use a common representation for each list element:

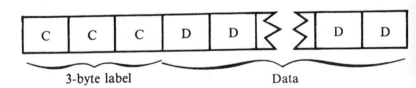

3-byte label   Data

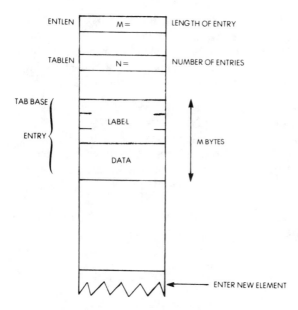

Fig. 9.9: The Table Structure

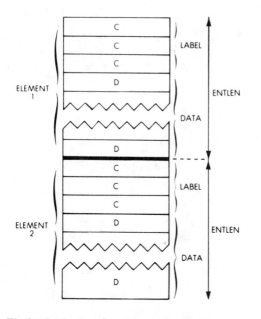

Fig 9.10: Typical List Entries in the Memory

Each element, or "entry", includes a 3-byte label, and an n-byte block of data, with n between 1 and 253. Thus, at most, each entry uses one page (256 bytes). Within each list, all elements have the same length (see Figure 9.10). The programs operating on these two simple lists use some common variable conventions:

ENTLEN is the length of an element. For example, if each element has 10 bytes of data, ENTLEN = 3 + 10 = 13

TABASE   is the base of the list or table in the memory
POINTR   is a running pointer to the current element
OBJECT   is the current entry to be located, inserted or deleted
TABLEN   is the number of entries.

All labels are assumed to be distinct. Changing this convention would require a minor change in the programs.

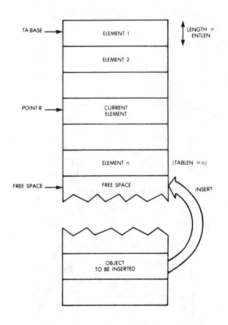

Fig. 9.11: The Simple List

A SIMPLE LIST

The simple list is organized as a table of n elements. The elements are not sorted (see Figure 9.11). When searching, one must scan through the list until an entry is found or the end of the table is reached. When inserting, new entries are appended to the existing ones. When an entry is deleted, the entries in higher memory locations, if any, will be shifted up to keep the table continuous.

Searching

A serial search technique is used. Each entry's label field is compared in turn to the OBJECT's label, letter by letter.

The running pointer POINTR is initialized to the value of TABASE.

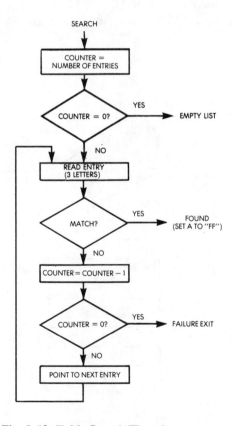

Fig. 9.12: Table Search Flowchart

The search proceeds in the obvious way, and the corresponding flow-chart is shown on Figure 9.12. The program appears on Figure 9.16 at the end of this section (program "SEARCH"). A sample run of the program is shown in Figure 9.17.

Inserting

When inserting a new element, the first available memory block of (ENTLEN) bytes at the end of the list is used (see Figure 9.11).

The program first checks that the new entry is not already in the list (all labels are assumed to be distinct in this example). If not, it increments the list length TABLEN, and moves the OBJECT to the end of the list. The corresponding flowchart is shown in Figure 9.13.

The program is shown in Figure 9.16. It is called "NEW" and resides at memory locations 0135 to 015E.

The index register IY points to the source. HL and DE are destination pointers.

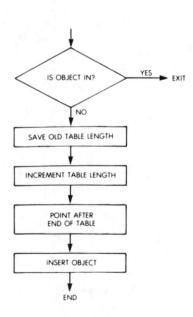

Fig. 9.13: Table Insertion Flowchart

Deleting

In order to delete an element from the list, the elements following it in the list at higher addresses are merely moved up by one element position. The length of the list is decremented. This is illustrated on Figure 9.14.

The corresponding program is straightforward and appears on Figure 9.16. It is called "DELETE", and resides at memory addresses 015F to 0187. The flowchart is shown in Figure 9.15.

Memory location TEMPTR is used as a temporary pointer pointing to the element to be moved up.

During the transfer, POINTR always points to the "hole" in the list, i.e., the destination of the next block transfer.

The Z flag is used to indicate a successful deletion upon exit.

Note how the LDIR instruction is used for efficient automated block transfer (refer to address 0178 in Figure 9.16).

```
            LD      A, B            BLOCK COUNTER
NEWBLOC     LD      BC, (ENTLEN)    BLOCK LENGTH
            LDIR
            DEC     A
            JP      NZ, NEWBLOC
```

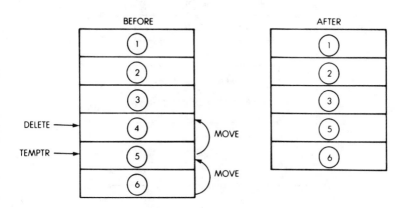

Fig. 9.14: Deleting an Entry (Simple List)

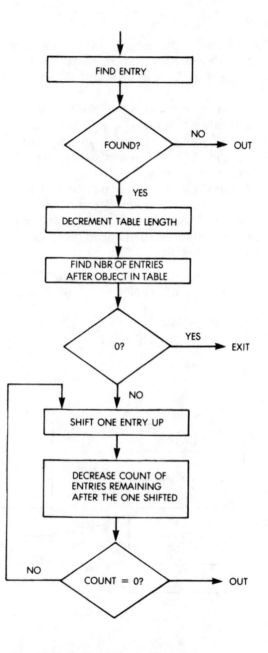

Fig. 9.15: Table Deletion Flowchart

554

```
0000                     ORG    0100H
        (0187)  ENTLEN   DL     ENDER
        (0189)  TABLEN   DL     ENDER+2
        (018A)  TABASE   DL     ENDER+3
        (018C)  TEMP     DL     ENDER+5
                         ;
0100  1600       SEARCH  LD     D,0
0102  3A8901             LD     A,(TABLEN)     ;CHECK FOR A ZERO TABLE LENGTH
0105  A7                 AND    A              ;SET FLAGS
0106  C8                 RET    Z
0107  47                 LD     B,A            ;STORE TABLE LENGTH
0108  DD2A8A01           LD     IX,(TABASE)    ;PUT BASE ADDR. IN IX
010C  DD7E00     LOOP    LD     A,(IX+0)       ;CHECK FIRST LETTER OF ENTRY
010F  FDBE00             CP     (IY+0)
0112  C22701             JP     NZ,NEXTONE
0115  DD7E01             LD     A,(IX+1)       ;CHECK 2ND LETTER
0118  FDBE01             CP     (IY+1)
011B  C22701             JP     NZ,NEXTONE
011E  DD7E02             LD     A,(IX+2)       ;CHECK 3RD LETTER
0121  FDBE02             CP     (IY+2)
0124  CA3201             JP     Z,FOUND        ;EXIT IF ALL LETTERS MATCH
0127  05         NEXTONE DEC    B              ;DECREMENT TABLE LENGTH COUNTER
0128  C8                 RET    Z              ;EXIT IF AT END OF TABLE
0129  ED5B8701           LD     DE,(ENTLEN)    ;SET IX TO NEXT ENTRY ADDR.
012D  DD19               ADD    IX,DE
012F  C30C01             JP     LOOP           ;TRY AGAIN
0132  16FF       FOUND   LD     D,0FFH         ;SET D TO SHOW IX CONTAINS ADDR.
0134  C9                 RET                   ;..OF ENTRY IN TABLE
                         ;
                         ;
                         ;
0135  CD0001     NEW     CALL   SEARCH         ;SEE IF OBJECT IS THERE
0138  14                 INC    D
0139  CA5E01             JP     Z,OUTE         ;IF D WAS FF, EXIT
013C  3A8901             LD     A,(TABLEN)
013F  5F                 LD     E,A            ;LOAD E WITH TABLE LENGTH
0140  3C                 INC    A
0141  328901             LD     (TABLEN),A     ;INCREMENT TABLE LENGTH
0144  1600               LD     D,0
0146  2A8A01             LD     HL,(TABASE)
0149  ED4B8701           LD     BC,(ENTLEN)    ;SET B TO LENGTH OF AN ENTRY
014D  41                 LD     B,C
014E  19         LOOPE   ADD    HL,DE
014F  10FD               DJNZ   LOOPE          ;ADD HL TO (ENTLEN×TABLEN)
0151  ED4B8701           LD     BC,(ENTLEN)
0155  FDE5               PUSH   IY             ;MOVE IY TO DE
0157  D1                 POP    DE
0158  EB                 EX     DE,HL
0159  EDB0               LDIR                  ;MOVE MEMORY FROM OBJECT TO END
015B  01FFFF             LD     BC,0FFFFH      ;..OF TABLE
015E  C9         OUTE    RET
                         ;
                         ;
                         ;
015F  CD0001     DELETE  CALL   SEARCH         ;FIND ENTRY TO BE DELETED
0162  14                 INC    D              ;SEE IF IT WAS FOUND
0163  C28601             JP     NZ,OUT
0166  3A8901             LD     A,(TABLEN)     ;DECREMENT TABLE LENGTH
0169  3D                 DEC    A
016A  328901             LD     (TABLEN),A
016D  05                 DEC    B              ;B NOW=# OF ENTRIES LEFT IN TABLE
016E  CA8301             JP     Z,EXIT         ;..AFTER ONE TO BE DELETED
0171  DDE5               PUSH   IX             ;MOVE IX TO DE
0173  D1                 POP    DE
0174  2A8701             LD     HL,(ENTLEN)    ;SET HL ONE ENTRY AHEAD OF DE
0177  19                 ADD    HL,DE
0178  78                 LD     A,B            ;SET BLOCK COUNTER
0179  ED4B8701   NEWBLOC LD     BC,(ENTLEN)    ;SET BLOCK LENGTH COUNTER
017D  EDB0               LDIR                  ;SHIFT 1 ENTRY OF TABLE
017F  3D                 DEC    A
0180  C27901             JP     NZ,NEWBLOC     ;SHIFT ANOTHER BLOCK
0183  01FFFF     EXIT    LD     BC,0FFFFH      ;SHOW THAT IT WAS DONE
0186  C9         OUT     RET
                         ;
0187  (0000)     ENDER   END
```

Fig. 9.16: Simple List— The Programs

```
SYMBOL TABLE

DELETE   015F     ENDER   0187     ENTLEN  0187     EXIT    0183     FOUND   0132
LOOP     010C     LOOPE   014E     NEW     0135     NEWBLO  0179     NEXTON  0127
OUT      0186     OUTE    015E     SEARCH  0100     TABASE  018A     TABLEN  0189
TEMP     018C
```

Fig. 9.16: Simple List — The Programs (cont.)

Display Memory

Listing of Objects
with their locations
in memory

```
-DM300
0300  53 4F 4E 31 31 31 31 31-31 31 31 31 31 00 00 00   SON1111111111...
0310  44 41 44 32 32 32 32 32-32 32 32 32 32 00 00 00   DAD2222222222...
0320  4D 4F 4D 33 33 33 33 33-33 33 33 33 33 00 00 00   MOM3333333333...
0330  55 4E 43 34 34 34 34 34-34 34 34 34 34 00 00 00   UNC4444444444...
0340  41 4E 54 35 35 35 35 35-35 35 35 35 35 00 00 00   ANT5555555555...
0350  00 00 00 00 00 00 00 00-00 00 00 00 00 00 00 00   ...............
0360  00 00 00 00 00 00 00 00-00 00 00 00 00 00 00 00   ...............
0370  00 00 00 00 00 00 00 00-00 00 00 00 00 00 00 00   ...............

-SY
Y=0000 300   Set IY to 0300H (pointer to OBJECT)

-G193/196

P=0196 0196'  Run 'INSERT'
```

Table configuration
after program run

```
-DM400
0400  53 4F 4E 31 31 31 31 31-31 31 31 31 31 00 00 00   SON1111111111...
0410  00 00 00 00 00 00 00 00-00 00 00 00 00 00 00 00   ...............
0420  00 00 00 00 00 00 00 00-00 00 00 00 00 00 00 00   ...............
0430  00 00 00 00 00 00 00 00-00 00 00 00 00 00 00 00   ...............
0440  00 00 00 00 00 00 00 00-00 00 00 00 00 00 00 00   ...............
0450  00 00 00 00 00 00 00 00-00 00 00 00 00 00 00 00   ...............
0460  00 00 00 00 00 00 00 00-00 00 00 00 00 00 00 00   ...............
0470  00 00 00 00 00 00 00 00-00 00 00 00 00 00 00 00   ...............

-SY
Y=0300 310   Set IY to 0310H (next OBJECT)

-G193/196

P=0196 0196'  Run 'INSERT'
```

Table configuration
after second insert

```
-DM400
0400  53 4F 4E 31 31 31 31 31-31 31 31 31 31 44 41 44   SON1111111111DAD
0410  32 32 32 32 32 32 32 32-32 32 00 00 00 00 00 00   2222222222......
0420  00 00 00 00 00 00 00 00-00 00 00 00 00 00 00 00   ...............
0430  00 00 00 00 00 00 00 00-00 00 00 00 00 00 00 00   ...............
0440  00 00 00 00 00 00 00 00-00 00 00 00 00 00 00 00   ...............
0450  00 00 00 00 00 00 00 00-00 00 00 00 00 00 00 00   ...............
0460  00 00 00 00 00 00 00 00-00 00 00 00 00 00 00 00   ...............
0470  00 00 00 00 00 00 00 00-00 00 00 00 00 00 00 00   ...............
```

· · · (More insertions) · · ·

Table configuration
after several inserts

```
-DM400
0400  53 4F 4E 31 31 31 31 31-31 31 31 31 31 44 41 44   SON1111111111DAD
0410  32 32 32 32 32 32 32 32-32 32 55 4E 43 34 34 34   2222222222UNC444
0420  34 34 34 34 34 34 4D-4F 4D 33 33 33 33 33 33   4444444MOM333333
0430  33 33 33 33 41 4E 54 35-35 35 35 35 35 35 35 35   3333ANT555555555
0440  35 00 00 00 00 00 00 00-00 00 00 00 00 00 00 00   5...............
0450  00 00 00 00 00 00 00 00-00 00 00 00 00 00 00 00   ...............
0460  00 00 00 00 00 00 00 00-00 00 00 00 00 00 00 00   ...............
0470  00 00 00 00 00 00 00 00-00 00 00 00 00 00 00 00   ...............
```

Fig. 9.17: Simple List—A Sample Run

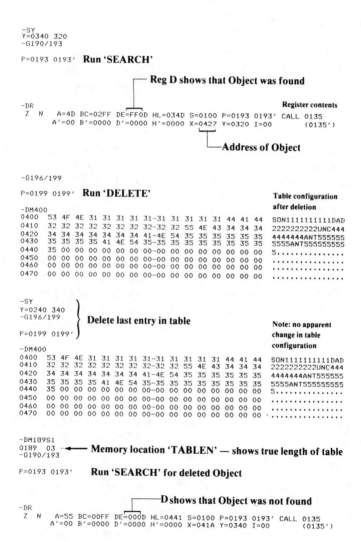

```
-SY
Y=0340 320
-G190/193
```

P=0193 0193' **Run 'SEARCH'**

┌── **Reg D shows that Object was found**

```
-DR                                                        Register contents
 Z  N    A=4D BC=02FF DE=FF0D HL=034D S=0100 P=0193 0193' CALL 0135
         A'=00 B'=0000 D'=0000 H'=0000 X=0427 Y=0320 I=00       (0135')
```

└──**Address of Object**

```
-G196/199
```

P=0199 0199' **Run 'DELETE'**   Table configuration
                                      after deletion
```
-DM400
0400   53 4F 4E 31 31 31 31 31-31 31 31 31 31 44 41 44   SON1111111111DAD
0410   32 32 32 32 32 32 32 32-32 32 55 4E 43 34 34 34   2222222222UNC444
0420   34 34 34 34 34 34 34 41-4E 54 35 35 35 35 35 35   4444444ANT555555
0430   35 35 35 35 41 4E 54 35-35 35 35 35 35 35 35 35   5555ANT555555555
0440   35 00 00 00 00 00 00 00-00 00 00 00 00 00 00 00   5...............
0450   00 00 00 00 00 00 00 00-00 00 00 00 00 00 00 00   ................
0460   00 00 00 00 00 00 00 00-00 00 00 00 00 00 00 00   ................
0470   00 00 00 00 00 00 00 00-00 00 00 00 00 00 00 00   ................
```

```
-SY
Y=0240 340
-G196/199
```
} **Delete last entry in table**

P=0199 0199'   Note: no apparent
                                      change in table
                                      configuration
```
-DM400
0400   53 4F 4E 31 31 31 31 31-31 31 31 31 31 44 41 44   SON1111111111DAD
0410   32 32 32 32 32 32 32 32-32 32 55 4E 43 34 34 34   2222222222UNC444
0420   34 34 34 34 34 34 34 41-4E 54 35 35 35 35 35 35   4444444ANT555555
0430   35 35 35 35 41 4E 54 35-35 35 35 35 35 35 35 35   5555ANT555555555
0440   35 00 00 00 00 00 00 00-00 00 00 00 00 00 00 00   5...............
0450   00 00 00 00 00 00 00 00-00 00 00 00 00 00 00 00   ................
0460   00 00 00 00 00 00 00 00-00 00 00 00 00 00 00 00   ................
0470   00 00 00 00 00 00 00 00-00 00 00 00 00 00 00 00   ................
```

```
-DM189S1
0189  03 ──◄── Memory location 'TABLEN' — shows true length of table
-G190/193
```

P=0193 0193' **Run 'SEARCH' for deleted Object**

┌──**D shows that Object was not found**

```
-DR
 Z  N    A=55 BC=00FF DE=000D HL=0441 S=0100 P=0193 0193' CALL 0135
         A'=00 B'=0000 D'=0000 H'=0000 X=041A Y=0340 I=00       (0135')
```

Fig. 9.17: Simple List— A Sample Run (cont.)

ALPHABETIC LIST

The alphabetic list, or "table," unlike the previous one, keeps all its elements sorted in alphabetic order. This allows the use of faster search techniques than the linear one. A binary search is used here.

Searching

The search algorithm is a classic binary search. Let us recall that the technique is essentially analogous to the one used to find a name in a telephone book. One usually starts somewhere in the middle of the book, and then, depending on the entries found there, goes either backwards or forward to find the desired entry. This method is fast and reasonably simple to implement.

The binary seach flowchart is shown in Fig. 9.18, and the program is shown in Fig. 9.23.

This list keeps the entries in alphabetical order and retrieves them by using a binary or "logarithmic" search. An example is shown in Figure 9.19. The search is somewhat complicated by the need to keep track of several conditions. The major problem to be avoided is searching for an object that is not there. In such a case, the entries with immediately higher and lower alphabetic values could be alternately tested forever. To avoid this, a flag is maintained in the program to preserve the value of the carry flag after an unsuccessful comparison. When the INCMNT value, which shows by how much the pointer will next be incremented reaches a value of "1", another flag called "CLOSENOW", which we will abbreviate to "CLOSE", is set to the value of the COMPRES flag Thus, since all further increments will be "1", if the pointer goes past the point where the object should be, COMPRES will no longer equal CLOSE and the search will terminate. This feature also enables the NEW routine to determine where the logical and physical pointers are located, relative to where the object will go.

Thus, if the OBJECT searched for is not in the table, and the running pointer is incremented by one, the CLOSE flag will be set. On the next pass of the routine, the result of the comparison will be opposite to the previous one. The two flags will no longer match, and the program will exit indicating "not found".

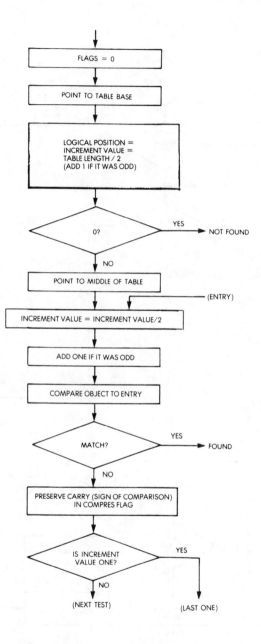

Fig. 9.18: Binary Search Flowchart

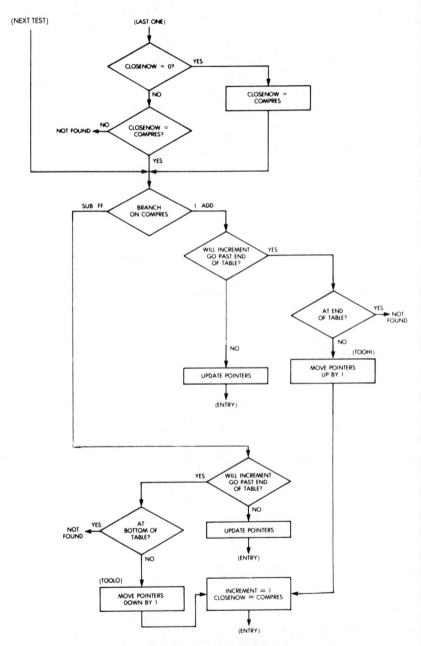

Fig. 9.18: Binary Search Flowchart (cont.)

The other major problem that must be dealt with is the possibility of running off one end of the table when adding or subtracting the increment value. This is solved by performing a test "add" or "subtract" using the logical pointer and length value which record the actual number of entries, not the physical positions in memory used by the physical pointers.

In summary, two flags are used by the program to memorize infor-

```
(0121)          LD        A,  C
                SRL       A
                ADC       0
                LD        C,  A
```

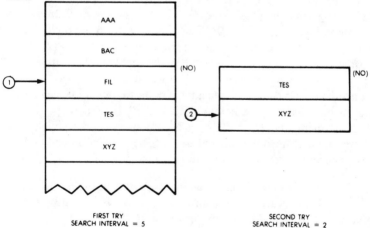

Fig. 9.19: A Binary Search

mation: COMPRES and CLOSE. The COMPRES flag is used to preserve the fact that the carry was either "0" or "1" after the most recent comparison. This determines if the element under test was larger or smaller than the one with which it was compared. The C indicates the relation. Whenever the carry C was "1", and the element was smaller than the object COMPRES is set to "1". Whenever the carry C was "0", indicating that the element was greater than the object, COMPRES will be set to "FF".

The second flag used by the program is CLOSE. This flag is set equal to COMPRESS when the search increment INCMNT becomes equal to "1". It will detect the fact that the element has not been found if COMPRES is not equal to CLOSE the next time around.

Other variables used by the program are:

LOGPOS   which indicates the logical position in the table (element number)

INCMNT   which represents the value by which the running pointer will be incremented or decremented if the next comparison fails

TABLEN   represents as usual the total length of the list.

LOGPOS and INCMNT will be compared to TABLEN in order to assure that the limits of the list are not exceeded.

The program called "SEARCH" is shown on Figure 9.23. It resides at memory locations 0100 to 01CF, and deserves to be studied with care, as it is much more complex than in the case of a linear search.

An additional complication is due to the fact that the search interval may at times be either even or odd. When it is odd, a correction must be introduced. (It cannot, for instance, point to the middle element of a four-element list.) When it is odd, a "trick" is used to point to the middle element: the division by 2 is accomplished by a right shift. The bit "falling off" into the carry after the SRL instruction will be "1" if the interval was odd. It is merely added to the pointer.

The OBJECT is then matched against the entry in the middle of the new search interval. If the comparison succeeds, the program exits. Otherwise ("NOGOOD"), the carry is set to "0" if the OBJECT is less than the entry. Whenever the INCMNT becomes "1", the CLOSE flag (which had been initialized to "0") is then checked to see if it was set. If it was not, it gets set. If it was set, a check is run to determine whether we passed the location where the OBJECT should have been but is not.

Also note that when the carry was "1", the running pointer will point to the entry below the OBJECT.

Element Insertion

In order to insert a new element, a binary search is conducted. If the element is found in the table, it does not need to be inserted. (We assume here that all elements are distinct). If the element was not found in the table, it must be inserted immediately before or immediately after the last element to which it was compared. The value of the COMPRES flag after the search indicates whether it should be inserted immediately before or immediately afterwards. All the elements following the new location where it is going to be placed are moved down by one block position, and the new element is inserted.

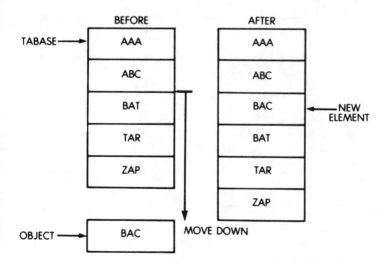

Fig. 9.20: Insert: "BAC"

The insertion process is illustrated in Figure 9.20, and the corresponding program appears in Figure 9.23.

The program is called NEW, and starts at memory location 01D0. Note that the automated Z80 instructions LDDR and LDIR are used for efficient block transfers.

Element Deletion

Similarly, a binary search is conducted to find the object. If the search fails, it does not need to be deleted. If the search succeeds, the element is deleted, and all the following elements are moved up by one block position. A corresponding example is shown in Figure 9.21, and the program appears in Figure 9.23. The flowchart is shown in Fig. 9.22.

The program is called "DELETE" and resides at address 0221.

A sample run of the above programs is shown in Fig. 9.24.

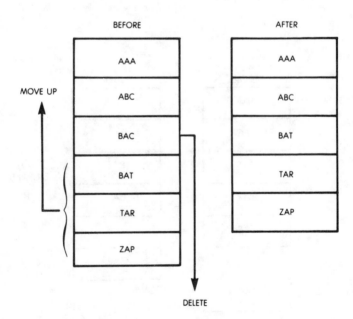

Fig. 9.21: Delete "BAC"

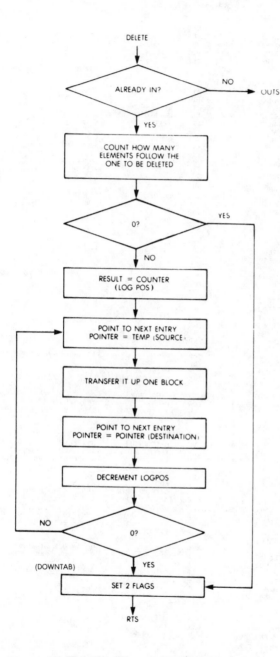

Fig. 9.22: Deletion Flowchart (Alphabetic List)

```
0000                        ORG     0100H
        (024A)    CLOSENOW  DL      ENDED
        (024B)    COMPRES   DL      ENDED+1
        (024C)    TABLEN    DL      ENDED+2
        (024D)    TABASE    DL      ENDED+3
        (024F)    ENTLEN    DL      ENDED+5
                  ;
0100    3E00      SEARCH    LD      A,0
0102    324A02              LD      (CLOSENOW),A    ;ZERO FLAG LOCATIONS
0105    324B02              LD      (COMPRES),A
0108    57                  LD      D,A
0109    2A4D02              LD      HL,(TABASE)     ;INITIALIZE HL
010C    3A4C02              LD      A,(TABLEN)
010F    CB3F                SRL     A               ;DIVIDE BY 2
0111    CE00                ADC     0               ;ADD 1'S BIT BACK IN
0113    4F                  LD      C,A             ;STORE AS INCREMENT VALUE
0114    47                  LD      B,A             ;STORE AS LOGICAL POSITION VALUE
0115    CABA01              JP      Z,NOTFOUND      ;CHECK IF LENGTH IS ZERO
0118    5F                  LD      E,A             ;MULTIPLY (E-1)×ENTLEN
0119    1D                  DEC     E
011A    CDBD01              CALL    MULT
011D    19                  ADD     HL,DE           ;SET HL TO MIDDLE OF TABLE
011E    E5        ENTRY     PUSH    HL              ;LOAD HL INTO IX
011F    DDE1                POP     IX
0121    79                  LD      A,C             ;DIVIDE INCREMENT VALUE BY TWO
0122    CB3F                SRL     A
0124    CE00                ADC     0
0126    4F                  LD      C,A
0127    DD7E00              LD      A,(IX+0)        ;COMPARE FIRST LETTER
012A    FDBE00              CP      (IY+0)
012D    C24201              JP      NZ,NOGOOD
0130    DD7E01              LD      A,(IX+1)        ;COMPARE 2ND LETTER
0133    FDBE01              CP      (IY+1)
0136    C24201              JP      NZ,NOGOOD
0139    DD7E02              LD      A,(IX+2)        ;COMPARE 3RD LETTER
013C    FDBE02              CP      (IY+2)
013F    CABC01              JP      Z,FOUND
0142    3E01      NOGOOD    LD      A,1             ;SET COMPARE RESULT FLAG TO
0144    DA4901              JP      C,TESTS         ;..RESULT OF COMPARE (1,FF)
0147    3EFF                LD      A,0FFH
0149    324B02    TESTS     LD      (COMPRES),A
014C    79                  LD      A,C             ;IS INCREMENT VALUE 1?
014D    3D                  DEC     A
014E    C26901              JP      NZ,NEXTEST
0151    3A4A02              LD      A,(CLOSENOW)    ;YES, IS CLOSE FLAG SET?
0154    A7                  AND     A
0155    CA6301              JP      Z,NOTCLOSE      ;YES,SEE IF HAVE PASSED WHERE
0158    57                  LD      D,A             ;..ENTRY SHOULD BE BUT ISN'T
0159    3A4B02              LD      A,(COMPRES)
015C    92                  SUB     D
015D    CA6901              JP      Z,NEXTEST
0160    C3BA01              JP      NOTFOUND
0163    3A4B02    NOTCLOSE  LD      A,(COMPRES)     ;SET CLOSE FLAG TO DIRECTION OF
0166    324A02              LD      (CLOSENOW),A    ;..SEARCH TO PREVENT REPETITION
0169    DDE5      NEXTEST   PUSH    IX              ;PREPARE HL AND DE FOR ADD OR
016B    E1                  POP     HL              ;..SUB OF INCREMENT VALUE
016C    59                  LD      E,C
016D    CDBD01              CALL    MULT
0170    3A4B02              LD      A,(COMPRES)     ;TEST IF WANT TO ADD OR SUB
0173    3C                  INC     A
0174    C29601              JP      NZ,ADDIT
0177    78                  LD      A,B             ;TEST TO SEE IF SUB WILL RUN
0178    91                  SUB     C               ;..OFF BOTTOM OF TABLE
0179    CA8501              JP      Z,TOOLOW
017C    DA8501              JP      C,TOOLOW
017F    47                  LD      B,A             ;SET NEW LOGICAL POSITION VALUE
0180    ED52                SBC     HL,DE           ;CHANGE ADDRESS ITSELF
0182    C31E01              JP      ENTRY
0185    78        TOOLOW    LD      A,B             ;SEE IF POSITION IS 1
0186    3D                  DEC     A
0187    CABA01              JP      Z,NOTFOUND      ;IF SO, EXIT
018A    ED5B4F02            LD      DE,(ENTLEN)     ;JUST SUB 1 ENTRY POSITION
018E    37                  SCF
018F    3F                  CCF
0190    ED52                SBC     HL,DE
0192    05                  DEC     B               ;CHANGE LOGICAL POSITION
0193    C3AF01              JP      REALCLOS
```

Fig. 9.23: Binary Search Program

```
0196   3A4C02   ADDIT      LD    A,(TABLEN)    ;TEST TO SEE IF CURRENT POSITION
0199   90                  SUB   B             ;..PLUS INCREMENT WILL GO PAST
019A   91                  SUB   C             ;....END OF THE TABLE
019B   DAA501              JP    C,TOOHIGH
019E   19                  ADD   HL,DE         ;IS OK, CHANGE ACTUAL ADDRESS
019F   78                  LD    A,B           ;CHANGE LOGICAL POS. VALUE
01A0   81                  ADD   C
01A1   47                  LD    B,A
01A2   C31E01              JP    ENTRY
01A5   81       TOOHIGH    ADD   C             ;SEE IF POSITION IS AT TOP OF
01A6   CABA01              JP    Z,NOTFOUND    ;..TABLE (SAME AS TABLEN-B)
01A9   ED5B4F02            LD    DE,(ENTLEN)   ;ADD 1 ENTRY POSITION
01AD   19                  ADD   HL,DE
01AE   04                  INC   B             ;INCREMENT LOGICAL POSITION
01AF   0E01     REALCLOS   LD    C,1           ;SET INCREMENT TO 1
01B1   3A4B02              LD    A,(COMPRES)   ;SET CLOSE FLAG TO COMPARE
01B4   324A02              LD    (CLOSENOW),A  ;..RESULT
01B7   C31E01              JP    ENTRY
01BA   16FF     NOTFOUND   LD    D,0FFH
01BC   C9       FOUND      RET
                 ;
01BD   E5       MULT       PUSH  HL            ;MULTIPLIES E BY (ENTLEN),
01BE   C5                  PUSH  BC            ;..VALUE IN DE ON EXIT
01BF   1600                LD    D,0
01C1   210000              LD    HL,0000
01C4   ED4B4F02            LD    BC,(ENTLEN)
01C8   41                  LD    B,C
01C9   19       ADDEM      ADD   HL,DE
01CA   10FD                DJNZ  ADDEM
01CC   C1                  POP   BC
01CD   EB                  EX    DE,HL
01CE   E1                  POP   HL
01CF   C9                  RET
                 ;
                 ;
                 ;
01D0   CD0001   NEW        CALL  SEARCH        ;SEE IF OBJECT IS ALREADY THERE
01D3   14                  INC   D
01D4   C22002              JP    NZ,OUT
01D7   3A4C02              LD    A,(TABLEN)    ;CHECK FOR 0 TABLE
01DA   A7                  AND   A
01DB   CA0C02              JP    Z,INSERT
01DE   3A4B02              LD    A,(COMPRES)
01E1   3C                  INC   A
01E2   CAED01              JP    Z,HISIDE
01E5   ED5B4F02            LD    DE,(ENTLEN)   ;COMPRES=1, SET HL ABOVE WHERE
01E9   19                  ADD   HL,DE         ;..OBJECT SHOULD GO
01EA   C3EE01              JP    SETUP
01ED   05       HISIDE     DEC   B             ;COMPRES=0, SET B FOR SUBTRACT
01EE   3A4C02   SETUP      LD    A,(TABLEN)    ;SEE HOW MANY ENTRES ARE LEFT
01F1   90                  SUB   B
01F2   CA0C02              JP    Z,INSERT
01F5   5F                  LD    E,A           ;SET HL TO LAST POSITION IN LAST
01F6   CDBD01              CALL  MULT          ;..ENTRY
01F9   19                  ADD   HL,DE
01FA   2B                  DEC   HL
01FB   EB                  EX    DE,HL         ;SET DE 1 ENTRY ABOVE HL
01FC   2A4F02              LD    HL,(ENTLEN)
01FF   19                  ADD   HL,DE
0200   EB                  EX    DE,HL
0201   ED4B4F02 MOVEM      LD    BC,(ENTLEN)   ;SHIFT UP ONE ENTRY OF MEMORY
0205   EDB8                LDDR
0207   3D                  DEC   A
0208   C20102              JP    NZ,MOVEM      ;REPEAT IF NECCESSARY
020B   23                  INC   HL            ;HL IS FRONT OF NOW EMPTY SPACE
020C   FDE5     INSERT     PUSH  IY            ;LOAD OBJECT INTO EMPTY SPACE
020E   D1                  POP   DE
020F   EB                  EX    DE,HL
0210   ED4B4F02            LD    BC,(ENTLEN)
0214   EDB0                LDIR
0216   3A4C02              LD    A,(TABLEN)    ;INCREMENT TABLE LENGTH
0219   3C                  INC   A
021A   324C02              LD    (TABLEN),A
021D   01FFFF              LD    BC,0FFFFH     ;SHOW THAT IT WAS DONE
0220   C9       OUT        RET
                 ;
                 ;
                 ;
```

Fig. 9.23: Binary Search Program (cont.)

567

```
0221  CD0001   DELETE    CALL    SEARCH          ;GET ADDRESS OF OBJECT
0224  14                 INC     D               ;SEE IF OBJECT IS THERE
0225  CA4902             JP      Z,OUTE
0228  ED5B4F02           LD      DE,(ENTLEN)
022C  EB                 EX      DE,HL
022D  19                 ADD     HL,DE           ;DE IS LOC. OF OBJECT, HL IS
022E  3A4C02             LD      A,(TABLEN)      ;..ONE ENTRY OBOVE
0231  90                 SUB     B               ;SEE HOW MANY ENTRIES ARE LEFT
0232  CA3F02             JP      Z,DOWNTAB
0235  ED4B4F02 SHIFTIN   LD      BC,(ENTLEN)
0239  EDB0               LDIR                    ;SHIFT DOWN 1 ENTRY LENGTH
023B  3D                 DEC     A
023C  C23502             JP      NZ,SHIFTIN
023F  3A4C02   DOWNTAB   LD      A,(TABLEN)      ;DECREMENT TABLE LENGTH
0242  3D                 DEC     A
0243  324C02             LD      (TABLEN),A
0246  01FFFF             LD      BC,OFFFFH       ;SHOW THAT ACTION WAS TAKEN
0249  C9       OUTE      RET
                         ;
024A  (0000)   ENDED     END

SYMBOL TABLE

ADDEM    01C9    ADDIT    0196    CLOSEN   024A    COMPRE   024B    DELETE   0221
DOWNTA   023F    ENDED    024A    ENTLEN   024F    ENTRY    011E    FOUND    01BC
HISIDE   01ED    INSERT   020C    MOVEM    0201    MULT     01BD    NEW      01D0
NEXTES   0169    NOGOOD   0142    NOTCLO   0163    NOTFOU   01BA    OUT      0220
OUTE     0249    REALCL   01AF    SEARCH   0100    SETUP    01EE    SHIFTI   0235
TABASE   024D    TABLEN   024C    TESTS    0149    TOOHIG   01A5    TOOLOW   0185
```

Fig. 9.23: Binary Search Program (cont.)

LINKED LIST

The linked list is assumed to contain, as usual, the three alphanumeric characters for the label, followed by one to 250 bytes of data, followed by a two-byte pointer which contains the starting address of the next entry, and lastly followed by a one-byte marker. Whenever this one-byte marker is set to "1", it will prevent the insert-routine from substituting a new entry in the place of the existing one.

Further, a directory contains a pointer to the first entry for each letter of the alphabet, in order to facilitate retrieval. It is assumed in the program that the labels are ASCII alphabetic characters. All pointers at the end of the list are set to a NIL value which has been chosen here to be equal to the table base, as this value should never occur within the linked list.

The insertion and the deletion programs perform the obvious pointer manipulations. They use the flag INDEXED to indicate if a pointer pointing to an object came from a previous entry in the list or from the directory table. The corresponding programs are shown in Figure 9.29.

The data structure is shown in Figure 9.25.

```
-DM400                                                   Initial table
0400  00 00 00 00 00 00 00 00-00 00 00 00 00 00 00 00    ..............
0410  00 00 00 00 00 00 00 00-00 00 00 00 00 00 00 00    ..............
0420  00 00 00 00 00 00 00 00-00 00 00 00 00 00 00 00    ..............
0430  00 00 00 00 00 00 00 00-00 00 00 00 00 00 00 00    ..............
0440  00 00 00 00 00 00 00 00-00 00 00 00 00 00 00 00    ..............
0450  00 00 00 00 00 00 00 00-00 00 00 00 00 00 00 00    ..............
0460  00 00 00 00 00 00 00 00-00 00 00 00 00 00 00 00    ..............
0470  00 00 00 00 00 00 00 00-00 00 00 00 00 00 00 00    ..............
```

Listing of Objects
and their locations
in memory

```
-DM300
0300  53 4F 4E 31 31 31 31 31-31 31 31 31 31 00 00 00    SON1111111111...
0310  44 41 44 32 32 32 32 32-32 32 32 32 32 00 00 00    DAD2222222222...
0320  4D 4F 4D 33 33 33 33 33-33 33 33 33 33 00 00 00    MOM3333333333...
0330  55 4E 43 34 34 34 34 34-34 34 34 34 34 00 00 00    UNC4444444444...
0340  41 4E 54 35 35 35 35 35-35 35 35 35 35 00 00 00    ANT5555555555...
0350  00 00 00 00 00 00 00 00-00 00 00 00 00 00 00 00    ..............
0360  00 00 00 00 00 00 00 00-00 00 00 00 00 00 00 00    ..............
0370  00 00 00 00 00 00 00 00-00 00 00 00 00 00 00 00    ..............
```

```
-SY
Y=0000 320
-G263/266        }  Run 'INSERT'

P=0266 0266'     }
```

```
-DM400                                                   Table after insertion
0400  4D 4F 4D 33 33 33 33 33-33 33 33 33 33 00 00 00    MOM3333333333...
0410  00 00 00 00 00 00 00 00-00 00 00 00 00 00 00 00    ..............
0420  00 00 00 00 00 00 00 00-00 00 00 00 00 00 00 00    ..............
0430  00 00 00 00 00 00 00 00-00 00 00 00 00 00 00 00    ..............
0440  00 00 00 00 00 00 00 00-00 00 00 00 00 00 00 00    ..............
0450  00 00 00 00 00 00 00 00-00 00 00 00 00 00 00 00    ..............
0460  00 00 00 00 00 00 00 00-00 00 00 00 00 00 00 00    ..............
0470  00 00 00 00 00 00 00 00-00 00 00 00 00 00 00 00    ..............
```

```
-SY
Y=0320 310       }
-G263/266        }  Run 'INSERT' on another Object

P=0266 0266'     }
```

Listing of table after
insertion. Note: table
is kept alphabetic

```
-DM400
0400  44 41 44 32 32 32 32 32-32 32 32 32 32 4D 4F 4D    DAD2222222222MOM
0410  33 33 33 33 33 33 33 33-33 33 00 00 00 00 00 00    3333333333......
0420  00 00 00 00 00 00 00 00-00 00 00 00 00 00 00 00    ..............
0430  00 00 00 00 00 00 00 00-00 00 00 00 00 00 00 00    ..............
0440  00 00 00 00 00 00 00 00-00 00 00 00 00 00 00 00    ..............
0450  00 00 00 00 00 00 00 00-00 00 00 00 00 00 00 00    ..............
0460  00 00 00 00 00 00 00 00-00 00 00 00 00 00 00 00    ..............
0470  00 00 00 00 00 00 00 00-00 00 00 00 00 00 00 00    ..............
```

• • • (additional inserts) • • •

Fig. 9.24: Alphabetic List—A Sample Run

Table configuration
after all Objects
have been inserted

```
-DM400
0400    41 4E 54 35 35 35 35 35-35 35 35 35 35 44 41 44    ANT5555555555DAD
0410    32 32 32 32 32 32 32 32-32 32 4D 4F 4D 33 33 33    2222222222MOM333
0420    33 33 33 33 33 33 33 53-4F 4E 31 31 31 31 31 31    3333333SON111111
0430    31 31 31 31 55 4E 43 34-34 34 34 34 34 34 34 34    1111UNC444444444
0440    34 00 00 00 00 00 00 00-00 00 00 00 00 00 00 00    4...............
0450    00 00 00 00 00 00 00 00-00 00 00 00 00 00 00 00    ................
0460    00 00 00 00 00 00 00 00-00 00 00 00 00 00 00 00    ................
0470    00 00 00 00 00 00 00 00-00 00 00 00 00 00 00 00    ................
```

```
-SY
Y=0340 300
-G260/263
                                            }    Run 'SEARCH' for "SON" (at address 0300)
P=0263 0263'
```

```
                                ┌───── Found
-DR
Z  N    A=4E BC=0401 DE=000D HL=0427 S=0100.P=0263 0263'  CALL 01D0
        A'=00 B'=0000 D'=0000 H'=0000 X=0427 Y=0300 I=00           (01D0')
                                        └───── Address of Object in table
```

(verify in Table above that it is "SON")

```
-G266/269
                    Run 'DELETE' on "SON"
P=0269 0269'
```

Table configuration
after deletion. Note:
that UNC was shifted
up. The last UNC
entry must be
disregarded

```
-DM400
0400    41 4E 54 35 35 35 35 35-35 35 35 35 35 44 41 44    ANT5555555555DAD
0410    32 32 32 32 32 32 32 32-32 32 4D 4F 4D 33 33 33    2222222222MOM333
0420    33 33 33 33 33 33 33 55-4E 43 34 34 34 34 34 34    3333333UNC444444
0430    34 34 34 34 55 4E 43 34-34 34 34 34 34 34 34 34    4444UNC444444444
0440    34 00 00 00 00 00 00 00-00 00 00 00 00 00 00 00    4...............
0450    00 00 00 00 00 00 00 00-00 00 00 00 00 00 00 00    ................
0460    00 00 00 00 00 00 00 00-00 00 00 00 00 00 00 00    ................
0470    00 00 00 00 00 00 00 00-00 00 00 00 00 00 00 00    ................
```

```
-G260/263       Try run of "SEARCH" again (on "SON")
P=0263 0263'
```

```
                                ┌───── Not found
-DR
S  N    A=FE BC=0401 DE=FF0D HL=0427 S=0100 P=0263 0263'  CALL 01D0
        A'=00 B'=0000 D'=0000 H'=0000 X=0427 Y=0300 I=00           (01D0')
-G263/266       Re-insert Object ("SON")
P=0266 0266'
```

Current table
configuration.
Compare to the one
prior to the
DELETE

```
-DM400
0400    41 4E 54 35 35 35 35 35-35 35 35 35 35 44 41 44    ANT5555555555DAD
0410    32 32 32 32 32 32 32 32-32 32 4D 4F 4D 33 33 33    2222222222MOM333
0420    33 33 33 33 33 33 33 53-4F 4E 31 31 31 31 31 31    3333333SON111111
0430    31 31 31 31 55 4E 43 34-34 34 34 34 34 34 34 34    1111UNC444444444
0440    34 00 00 00 00 00 00 00-00 00 00 00 00 00 00 00    4...............
0450    00 00 00 00 00 00 00 00-00 00 00 00 00 00 00 00    ................
0460    00 00 00 00 00 00 00 00-00 00 00 00 00 00 00 00    ................
0470    00 00 00 00 00 00 00 00-00 00 00 00 00 00 00 00    ................
```

```
                ┌───── Shows that action was executed
-DR
        A=05 BC=FFFF DE=0434 HL=030D S=0100 P=0266 0266'  CALL 0221
        A'=00 B'=0000 D'=0000 H'=0000 X=0427 Y=0300 I=00           (0221')
```

Fig. 9.24: Alphabetic List—A Sample Run (cont.)

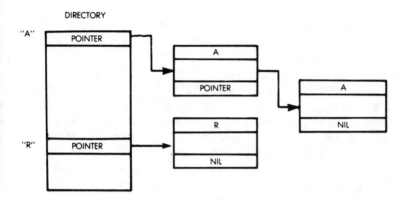

Fig. 9.25: Linked List Structure

An application for this data structure would be a computerized address book, where each person is represented by a unique three-letter code (perhaps the usual initials) and the data field contains a simplified address, plus the telephone number (up to 250 characters). Let us examine the structure in more detail. The entry format is:

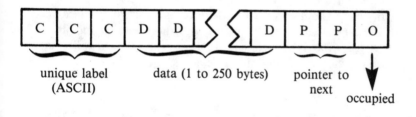

As usual the conventions are:

ENTLEN: total element length (in bytes)
TABASE: address of base of list

The address of the OBJECT is always assumed to reside in the IY register prior to entering the program. Here, REFBASE points to the base address of the directory, or "reference table."

Each two-byte address within this directory points to the first occurrence of the letter to which it corresponds in the list. Thus, each group

571

of entries with an identical first letter in their labels actually forms a separate list within the whole structure. This feature facilitates searching and is analogous to an address book. Note that no data are moved during an insert or delete. Only pointers are changed, as in every well-behaved linked list structure.

If no entry starting with a specific letter is found, or if there is no entry alphabetically following an existing one, their pointers will point to the beginning of the table (= "NIL"). At the bottom of the table, by convention a value is stored such that the absolute value of the difference between it and "Z" is greater than the difference between "A" and "Z". This represents an End Of Table (EOT) marker. The EOT value is assumed here to occupy the same amount of memory as a normal entry but could be just one byte if desired. The letters are assumed to be alphabetic letters in ASCII code. Changing this would require changing the constant in the PRETAB routine.

The end-of-table marker is set to the value of the beginning of the table ("NIL").

By convention, the "NIL pointers", found at the end of a string, or within a directory location which does not point to a string, are set to the value of the table base to provide a unique identification. Another convention could be used. In particular, a different marker for EOT results in some space savings, as no NIL entries need be kept for non-existing entries.

Insertion and deletion are performed in the usual way (see Part I of this chapter) by merely modifying the required pointers. The INDEXED flag is used to indicate if the pointer to the object is in the reference table or another string element.

Searching

The SEARCH program resides at memory locations 0100 to 0155 an uses subroutine PRETAB at address 01D2.

The search principle is straightforward:

1—Get the directory entry corresponding to the letter of the alphabet in the first position of the OBJECT's label.

2—Get the pointer. Access the element. If NIL, the entry does not exist.

3—If not NIL, match the element against the OBJECT. If a match is found, the search has succeeded. If not, get the pointer to the next entry down the list.

4—Go back to 2.

An example is shown in Figure 9.26.

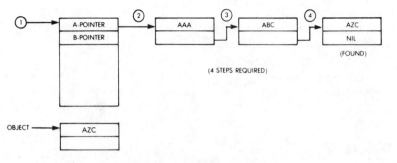

Fig. 9.26: Linked List—A Search

Inserting

The insertion is essentially a search followed by an insertion once a "NIL" has been found.

A block of storage for the new entry is allocated past the EOT marker by looking for an occupancy marker set at "available".

The program is called "NEW" in Figure 9.29 and resides at addresses 0156 to 1A3. An example is shown in Figure 9.27.

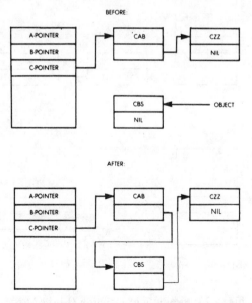

Fig. 9.27: Linked List: Example of Insertion

Deleting

The element is deleted by setting its occupancy marker to "available" and adjusting the pointer to it from the directory or else the previous element.

The program is called "DELETE", and resides at addresses 01A4 to 01D1.

An example of a deletion is shown in Figure 9.28.

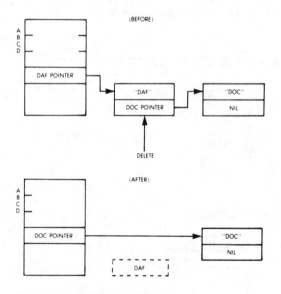

NOTE DAF IS NOT ERASED, BUT "INVISIBLE"

Fig. 9.28: Example of Deletion (Linked List)

```
0000'                       ORG    0100H
        (01E7)  INDEXED  DL    ENDER
        (01E8)  TABASE   DL    ENDER+1
        (01EA)  REFBASE  DL    ENDER+3
        (01EC)  ENTLEN   DL    ENDER+5
                ;
0100    3E00    SEARCH   LD    A,0           ;INITIALIZE FLAGS
0102    47               LD    B,A
0103    3C               INC   A
0104    32E701           LD    (INDEXED),A
0107    CDD201           CALL  PRETAB        ;GET ADDR OF INDEX POINTER
010A    1A               LD    A,(DE)        ;MOVE POINTER CONTENTS TO HL
010B    6F               LD    L,A
010C    13               INC   DE
010D    1A               LD    A,(DE)
010E    67               LD    H,A
010F    E5               PUSH  HL
0110    DDE1             POP   IX
0112    DD7E00  COMPARE  LD    A,(IX+0)      ;LOOK AT FIRST LETTER OF ENTRY
0115    FE7C             CP    7CH           ;SEE IF IS EOT MARKER
0117    D25501           JP    NC,NOTFOUND
011A    DD7E00           LD    A,(IX+0)      ;COMPARE FIRST LETTERS
011D    FDBE00           CP    (IY+0)
0120    DA3E01           JP    C,NOGOOD
0123    C25501           JP    NZ,NOTFOUND
0126    DD7E01           LD    A,(IX+1)      ;COMPARE 2ND LETTERS
0129    FDBE01           CP    (IY+1)
012C    DA3E01           JP    C,NOGOOD
012F    C25501           JP    NZ,NOTFOUND
0132    DD7E02           LD    A,(IX+2)      ;COMPARE 3RD LETTERS
0135    FDBE02           CP    (IY+2)
0138    CA5301           JP    Z,FOUND
013B    D25501           JP    NC,NOTFOUND
013E    DDE5    NOGOOD   PUSH  IX
0140    D1               POP   DE
0141    2AEC01           LD    HL,(ENTLEN)   ;JUMP TO POINTER OF ENTRY
0144    19               ADD   HL,DE
0145    4E               LD    C,(HL)        ;PUT POINTER VALUE IN BC
0146    23               INC   HL
0147    46               LD    B,(HL)
0148    C5               PUSH  BC            ;LOAD IX WITH POINTER
0149    DDE1             POP   IX
014B    3E00             LD    A,0
014D    32E701           LD    (INDEXED),A   ;RESET FLAG
0150    C31201           JP    COMPARE
0153    06FF    FOUND    LD    B,0FFH
0155    C9      NOTFOUND RET
                ;
                ;
                ;
0156    CD0001  NEW      CALL  SEARCH        ;SEE WHERE OBJECT SHOULD GO
0159    04               INC   B
015A    CAA301           JP    Z,OUT
015D    D5               PUSH  DE            ;STORE ADDR. OF PREVIOUS ENTRY
015E    2AE801           LD    HL,(TABASE)   ;FIND SPACE IN TABLE FOR NEW
0161    EB      NEXTONE  EX    DE,HL         ;MOVE TO END OF NEXT ENTRY
0162    2AEC01           LD    HL,(ENTLEN)
0165    23               INC   HL            ;ADD 3 FOR REAL LENGTH OF ENTRY
0166    23               INC   HL
0167    23               INC   HL
0168    19               ADD   HL,DE
0169    7E               LD    A,(HL)
016A    3D               DEC   A
016B    CA6101           JP    Z,NEXTONE     ;IF SOMETHING IS THERE, TRY AGAIN
016E    13               INC   DE
016F    D5               PUSH  DE            ;SAVE POSITION OF EMPTY SPACE
0170    FDE5             PUSH  IY            ;MOVE IY TO HL
0172    E1               POP   HL
0173    ED4BEC01         LD    BC,(ENTLEN)   ;MOVE OBJECT INTO TABLE
0177    EDB0             LDIR
0179    DDE5             PUSH  IX            ;PUT ADDR OF ENTRY AFTER OBJECT
017B    E1               POP   HL            ;..AT POINTER POSITION
017C    EB               EX    DE,HL
017D    73               LD    (HL),E
017E    23               INC   HL
017F    72               LD    (HL),D
0180    23               INC   HL
0181    3601             LD    (HL),1        ;SET OCCUPANCY MARKER
```

Fig. 9.29: Linked List—The Programs

575

```
0183   E1                    POP     HL              ;GET ADDR OF WHERE THIS SPACE IS
0184   3AE701                LD      A,(INDEXED)     ;SEE WHAT PREVIOUS POINTERS MUST
0187   3D                    DEC     A               ;..BE SET
0188   CA9801                JP      Z,SETINX
018B   E3                    EX      (SP),HL         ;GET ADDR OF ENTRY PREVIOUS TO
018C   ED5BEC01              LD      DE,(ENTLEN)     ;..OBJECT & MOVE TO POINTER AREA
0190   19                    ADD     HL,DE
0191   D1                    POP     DE              ;RETRIEVE ADDR OF OBJECT
0192   73                    LD      (HL),E          ;PUT IT AT POINTER POSITION
0193   23                    INC     HL
0194   72                    LD      (HL),D
0195   C3A001                JP      FINISH
0198   C1        SETINX      POP     BC              ;CLEAR OUT STACK
0199   CDD201                CALL    PRETAB          ;GET INDEX ADDRESS
019C   EB                    EX      DE,HL           ;LOAD HL INTO IT
019D   73                    LD      (HL),E
019E   23                    INC     HL
019F   72                    LD      (HL),D
01A0   01FFFF    FINISH      LD      BC,0FFFFH       ;SHOW THAT IT WAS DONE
01A3   C9                    OUT     RET
                             ;
                             ;
                             ;
01A4   CD0001    DELETE      CALL    SEARCH          ;GET ADDRESS OF OBJECT
01A7   04                    INC     B               ;SEE IF IT IS THERE
01A8   C2D101                JP      NZ,OUTE
01AB   DDE5                  PUSH    IX              ;SET HL TO POINTER AREA OF OBJECT
01AD   E1                    POP     HL
01AE   ED4BEC01              LD      BC,(ENTLEN)
01B2   09                    ADD     HL,BC
01B3   4E                    LD      C,(HL)          ;RETRIEVE POINTER
01B4   23                    INC     HL
01B5   46                    LD      B,(HL)
01B6   23                    INC     HL
01B7   3600                  LD      (HL),0          ;REMOVE OCCUPANCY MARKER
01B9   3AE701                LD      A,(INDEXED)     ;SEE IF INDEX NEEDS CHANGING
01BC   3D                    DEC     A
01BD   C2C701                JP      NZ,CHANGEM
01C0   CDD201                CALL    PRETAB          ;YES,PUT ADDR INTO HL
01C3   EB                    EX      DE,HL
01C4   C3CB01                JP      MOVIN
01C7   2AEC01    CHANGEM     LD      HL,(ENTLEN)     ;SET HL TO POINTER OF PREVIOUS
01CA   19                    ADD     HL,DE
01CB   71        MOVIN       LD      (HL),C          ;PUT ADDR OF NEXT INTO WHATEVER
01CC   23                    INC     HL              ;..(EITHER INDEX OR ENTRY)
01CD   70                    LD      (HL),B
01CE   01FFFF                LD      BC,0FFFFH
01D1   C9        OUTE        RET
                             ;
                             ;
                             ;
01D2   E5        PRETAB      PUSH    HL
01D3   FD7E00                LD      A,(IY+0)        ;GET FIRST LETTER OF OBJECT
01D6   3D                    DEC     A               ;REMOVE ASCII LEADER
01D7   D640                  SUB     40H
01D9   CB27                  SLA     A               ;MULTIPLY BY 2
01DB   2AEA01                LD      HL,(REFBASE)
01DE   85                    ADD     L
01DF   6F                    LD      L,A
01E0   D2E401                JP      NC,FIXUP
01E3   24                    INC     H
01E4   EB        FIXUP       EX      DE,HL
01E5   E1                    POP     HL
01E6   C9                    RET
                             ;
01E7   (0000)    ENDER       END
```

```
SYMBOL TABLE

CHANGE   01C7    COMPAR   0112    DELETE   01A4    ENDER    01E7    ENTLEN   01EC
FINISH   01A0    FIXUP    01E4    FOUND    0153    INDEXE   01E7    MOVIN    01CB
NEW      0156    NEXTON   0161    NOGOOD   013E    NOTFOU   0155    OUT      01A3
OUTE     01D1    PRETAB   01D2    REFBAS   01EA    SEARCH   0100    SETINX   0198
TABASE   01E8
```

Fig. 9.29: Linked List—The Programs (cont.)

The Objects in memory

Listing of Objects
and their locations
in memory

```
DM300
0300   53 4F 4E 31 31 31 31 31-31 31 31 31 31 00 00 00    SON1111111111...
0310   44 41 44 32 32 32 32 32-32 32 32 32 32 00 00 00    DAD2222222222...
0320   4D 4F 4D 33 33 33 33 33-33 33 33 33 33 00 00 00    MOM3333333333...
0330   55 4E 43 34 34 34 34 34-34 34 34 34 34 00 00 00    UNC4444444444...
0340   41 4E 54 35 35 35 35 35-35 35 35 35 35 00 00 00    ANT5555555555...
0350   41 41 41 36 36 36 36 36-36 36 36 36 36 00 00 00    AAA6666666666...
0360   41 5A 5A 37 37 37 37 37-37 37 37 37 37 00 00 00    AZZ7777777777...
0370   53 49 44 38 38 38 38 38-38 38 38 38 38 00 00 00    SID8888888888...
```

EOT character in
initial table

```
-DM400
0400   7B 00 00 00 00 00 00 00-00 00 00 00 00 00 00 00    {..............
0410   00 00 00 00 00 00 00 00-00 00 00 00 00 00 00 00    ...............
0420   00 00 00 00 00 00 00 00-00 00 00 00 00 00 00 00    ...............
0430   00 00 00 00 00 00 00 00-00 00 00 00 00 00 00 00    ...............
0440   00 00 00 00 00 00 00 00-00 00 00 00 00 00 00 00    ...............
0450   00 00 00 00 00 00 00 00-00 00 00 00 00 00 00 00    ...............
0460   00 00 00 00 00 00 00 00-00 00 00 00 00 00 10 04 01    ...............
0470   00 00 00 00 00 00 00 00-00 00 00 00 00 00 00 00    ...............
```

Initial Directory

```
-DM500
0500   00 04 00 04 00 04 00 04-00 04 00 04 00 04 00 04    ...............
0510   00 04 00 04 00 04 00 04-00 04 00 04 00 04 00 04    ...............
0520   00 04 00 04 00 04 00 04-00 04 00 04 00 04 00 04    ...............
0530   00 04 00 04 00 00 00 00-00 00 00 00 00 00 00 00    ...............
0540   00 00 00 00 00 00 00 00-00 00 00 00 00 00 00 00    ...............
0550   00 00 00 00 00 00 00 00-00 00 00 00 00 00 00 00    ...............
0560   00 00 00 00 00 00 00 00-00 00 00 00 00 00 00 00    ...............
0570   00 00 00 00 00 00 00 00-00 00 00 00 00 00 00 00    ...............
```

Occupancy markers ―┐

Pointers ―

Table configuration
after several
insertions.

```
DM400
0400   7B 00 00 00 00 00 00 00-00 00 00 00 00 00 00 00    {..............
0410   41 4E 54 35 35 35 35 35-35 35 35 35 35 70 04 01    ANT5555555555P..
0420   44 41 44 32 32 32 32 32-32 32 32 32 32 00 04 01    DAD2222222222...
0430   41 41 41 36 36 36 36 36-36 36 36 36 36 00 04 01    AAA6666666666...
0440   53 4F 4E 31 31 31 31 31-31 31 31 31 31 00 04 01    SON1111111111...
0450   4D 4F 4D 33 33 33 33 33-33 33 33 33 33 00 04 01    MOM3333333333...
0460   53 49 44 38 38 38 38 38-38 38 38 38 38 40 04 01    SID8888888888@..
0470   41 5A 5A 37 37 37 37 37-37 37 37 37 37 00 04 01    AZZ7777777777...
```

```
-SY
Y=0360 310
-6226/229         } Delete an entry
P=0229 0229'
```

Only change

```
-DM400
0400   7B 00 00 00 00 00 00 00-00 00 00 00 00 00 00 00    {..............
0410   41 4E 54 35 35 35 35 35-35 35 35 35 35 70 04 01    ANT5555555555P..
0420   44 41 44 32 32 32 32 32-32 32 32 32 32 00 04 00    DAD2222222222...
0430   41 41 41 36 36 36 36 36-36 36 36 36 36 10 04 01    AAA6666666666...
0440   53 4F 4E 31 31 31 31 31-31 31 31 31 31 00 04 01    SON1111111111...
0450   4D 4F 4D 33 33 33 33 33-33 33 33 33 33 00 04 01    MOM3333333333...
0460   53 49 44 38 38 38 38 38-38 38 38 38 38 40 04 01    SID8888888888@..
0470   41 5A 5A 37 37 37 37 37-37 37 37 37 37 00 04 01    AZZ7777777777...
```

Fig. 9.30: Linked List—A Sample Run

```
-G220/223          Run 'SEARCH' for deleted entry
P=0223 0223'

                        —Not found
-DR
   N    A=37  BC=00FF  DE=0400  HL=0000  S=0100  P=0223 0223'  CALL  0171
        A'=00  B'=0000  D'=0000  H'=0000  X=0400  Y=0310  I=00           (0171')
-SY
Y=0310 340     ⎫
-              ⎬  Run "SEARCH" for an existent entry
-G220/223      ⎭

P=0223 0223'
                  ┌—Entry found
-DR
  Z   N   A=54  BC=FF10  DE=0430  HL=043E  S=0100  P=0223 0223'  CALL  0171
          A'=00  B'=0000  D'=0000  H'=0000  X=0410  Y=0340  I=00           (0171')
-G226/229                                              └—Address of entry in table
              Delete
P=0229 0229'
```

Note: Changes in
pointers.

```
-DM400
0400   7B 00 00 00 00 00 00 00-00 00 00 00 00 00 00 00   (................
0410   41 4E 54 35 35 35 35 35-35 35 35 35 35 70 04 00   ANT5555555555p..
0420   44 41 44 32 32 32 32 32-32 32 32 32 32 00 04 00   DAD2222222222...
0430   41 41 41 36 36 36 36 36-36 36 36 36 36 70 04 01   AAA6666666666p..
0440   53 4F 4E 31 31 31 31 31-31 31 31 31 31 00 04 01   SON1111111111...
0450   4D 4F 4D 33 33 33 33 33-33 33 33 33 33 00 04 01   MOM3333333333...
0460   53 49 44 38 38 38 38 38-38 38 38 38 38 40 04 01   SID8888888888@..
0470   41 5A 5A 37 37 37 37 37-37 37 37 37 37 00 04 01   AZZ7777777777...
```

Fig. 9.30: Linked List— A Sample Run (cont.)

SUMMARY

The beginning programmer need not concern himself yet with the details of data structures implementation and management. However, efficient programming of non-trivial algorithms requires a good understanding of data structures. The actual examples presented in this chapter should help the reader achieve such an understanding and solve all the common problems encountered with reasonable data structures.

10

PROGRAM DEVELOPMENT

INTRODUCTION

All the programs we have studied and developed so far have been developed by hand without the aid of any software or hardware resource. The only improvement over straight binary coding has been the use of mnemonic symbols, those of the assembly language. For effective software development, it is necessary to understand the range of hardware and software development aids. It is the purpose of this chapter to present and evaluate these aids.

BASIC PROGRAMMING CHOICES

Three basic alternatives exist: writing a program in binary or hexadecimal, writing it in assembly-level language, or writing it in a high-level language. Let us review these alternatives.

Hexadecimal Coding

The program will normally be written using assembly language mnemonics. However, most low-cost, one-board computer systems do not provide an assembler. The assembler is the program which will automatically translate the mnemonics used for the program into the required binary codes. When no assembler is available, this translation from mnemonics into binary must be performed by hand. Binary is *unpleasant* to use and error-prone, so that hexadecimal is normally used. It has been shown in Chapter 1 that one hexadecimal digit will represent four binary bits. Two hexadecimal digits will, therefore, be used to represent the contents of every byte. As an example, the table showing the hexadecimal equivalent of the Z80 instructions appears in the Appendix.

In short, whenever the resources of the user are limited and no assembler is available, he will have to translate the program by hand into hexadecimal. This can reasonably be done for a small number of instructions, such as, perhaps, 10 to 100. For larger programs, this process is tedious and error-prone, so that it tends not to be used. However, nearly all single-board microcomputers require the entry of programs in hexadecimal mode. They are not equipped with an assembler and a full alphanumeric keyboard, in order to limit their cost.

In summary, hexadecimal coding is not a desirable way to enter a program in a computer. It is simply an economical one. The cost of an assembler and the required alphanumeric keyboard is traded-off against increased labor required to enter the program in the memory. However, this does not change the way the program itself is written. *The program is still written in assembly-level language* so that it can be examined by the human programmer and be meaningful.

Assembly Language Programming

Assembly-level programming covers both programs that may be entered in hexadecimal and those that may be entered in symbolic assembly-level form in the system. Let us now examine the entry of a program directly in its assembly language representation. An assembler program must be available. The assembler will read each of the mnemonic instructions of the program and translate it into the required bit pattern using 1 to 5 bytes, as specified by the encoding of the instructions. In addition, a good assembler will offer a number of additional facilities for writing the program. These will be reviewed in the section on the assembler below. In particular, *directives* are available which will modify the value of symbols. Symbolic addressing may be used and a branch to a symbolic location may be specified. During the debugging phase, when a user may remove or add instructions, it will not be necessary to rewrite the entire program if an extra instruction is inserted between a branch and the point to which it branches, as long as symbolic labels are used. The assembler will take care of automatically adjusting all the labels during the translation process. In addition, an assembler allows the user to debug his program in symbolic form. A disassembler may be used to examine the contents of a memory location and reconstruct the assembly-level instruction that it represents. The various software resources normally available on a system will be reviewed below. Let us now examine the third alternative.

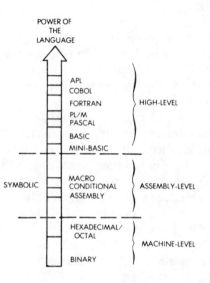

Fig. 10.1: Programming Levels

High-Level Language

A program may be written in a high-level language such as BASIC, APL, PASCAL, or others. Techniques for programming in these various languages are covered by specific books and will not be reviewed here. We will, therefore, only briefly review this mode of programming. A high-level language offers powerful instructions which make programming much easier and faster. These instructions must then be translated by a complex program into the final binary representation that a microcomputer can execute. Typically, each high-level instruction will be translated into a large number of individual binary instructions. The program which performs this automatic translation is called a *compiler* or an *interpreter*. A compiler will translate all the instructions of a program in sequence into object code. In a separate phase, the resulting code will then be executed. By contrast, an interpreter will interpret a single instruction, then execute it, then "translate" the next one, then execute it. An interpreter offers the advantage of interactive response, but results in low efficiency compared to a compiler. These topics will not be studied further here. Let us revert to the programming of an actual microprocessor in the assembly-level language.

581

SOFTWARE SUPPORT

We will review here the main software facilities which are (or should be) available in the complete system for convenient software development. Some of the definitions have already been introduced. They will be summarized here and the rest of the important programs will be defined before we proceed.

The *assembler* is the program which translates the mnemonic representation of instructions into their binary equivalent. It normally translates one symbolic instruction into one binary instruction (which may occupy 1, 2 or 3 bytes). The resulting binary code is called *object code*. It is directly executable by the microcomputer. As a side effect, the assembler will also produce a complete symbolic listing of the program, as well as the equivalence tables to be used by the programmer and the symbol occurrence list in the program. Examples will be presented later in this chapter.

In addition, the assembler will list syntax errors such as instructions misspelled or illegal, branching errors, duplicate labels or missing labels.

It will not delete *logical* errors (this is *your* problem).

A *compiler* is the program which translates high-level language instructions into their binary form.

An *interpreter* is a program similar to a compiler, which also translates high-level instructions into their binary form but does not keep the intermediate representation and executes them immediately. In fact, it often does not even generate any intermediate code, but rather executes the high-level instructions directly.

A *monitor* is the basic program which is indispensable for using the hardware resources of this system. It continuously monitors the input devices for input and manages the rest of the devices. As an example, a minimal monitor for a single-board microcomputer, equipped with a keyboard and with LED's, must continuously scan the keyboard for a user input and display the specified contents on the light-emitting diodes. In addition, it must be capable of understanding a number of limited commands from the keyboard, such as START, STOP, CONTINUE, LOAD MEMORY, EXAMINE MEMORY. On a large system, the monitor is often qualified as the *executive* program, when complex file management or task scheduling is also provided. The overall set of facilities is called an *operating system*. If files are residing on a disk, the operating system is qualified as the *disk operating system,* or DOS.

582

An *editor* is the program designed to facilitate the entry and the modification of text or progams. It allows the user to enter characters conveniently, append them, insert them, add lines, remove lines, search for characters or strings. It is an important resource for convenient and effective text entry.

A *debugger* is a facility necessary for debugging programs. When a program does not work correctly, there may typically be no indication whatsoever of the cause. The programmer, therefore, wishes to insert breakpoints in his program in order to suspend the execution of the program at specified addresses, and to be able to examine the contents of registers or memory at this point. This is the primary function of a debugger. The debugger allows for the possibility of suspending a program, resuming execution, examining, displaying and modifying the contents of registers or memory. A good debugger will be equipped with a number of additional facilities, such as the ability to examine data in symbolic form, hex, binary, or other usual representations, as well as to enter data in this format.

A *loader,* or *linking loader,* will place various blocks of object code at specified positions in the memory and adjust their respective symbolic pointers so that they can reference each other. It is used to relocate programs or blocks in various memory areas. A *simulator* or an *emulator* program is used to simulate the operation of a device, usually the microprocessor, in its absence, when developing a program on a simulated processor prior to placing it on the actual board. Using this approach, it becomes possible to suspend the program, modify it, and keep it in RAM memory. The disadvantages of a simulator are that:

1—It usually simulates only the processor itself, not input/output devices

2—The execution speed is slow, and one operates in simulated time. It is therefore not possible to test real-time devices, and synchronization problems may still occur even though the logic of the program may be found correct.

An *emulator* is essentially a simulator in real time. It uses one processor to simulate another one, and simulates it in complete detail.

Utility routines are essentially all the routines which are necessary in most applications and that the user wishes the manufacturer had provided!

They may include multiplication, division and other arithmetic operations, block move routines, character tests, input/output device handlers (or "drivers"), and more.

THE PROGRAM DEVELOPMENT SEQUENCE

We will now examine a typical sequence for developing an assembly-level program. We will assume that all the usual software facilities are available in order to demonstrate their value. If they should not be available in a particular system, it will still be possible to develop programs, but the convenience will be decreased and, therefore, the amount of time necessary to debug the program is likely to be increased.

The normal approach is to first design an algorithm and define the data structures for the problem to be solved. Next, a comprehensive set of flowcharts is developed which represents the program flow. Finally, the flowcharts are translated into the assembly-level language for the microprocessor; this is the coding phase.

Next, the program has to be entered on the computer. We will examine in the next section the hardware options to be used in this phase.

The program is entered in RAM memory of the system under the control of the editor. Once a section of the program, such as one or more subroutines, has been entered, it will be tested.

First, the assembler will be used. If the assembler did not already reside in the system, it would be loaded from an external memory, such as a disk. Then, the program will be assembled, i.e., translated into a binary code. This results in the object program, ready to be executed.

One does not normally expect a program to work correctly the first time. To verify its correct operation, a number of breakpoints will normally be set at crucial locations where it is easy to test whether the intermediate results are correct. The debugger will be used for this purpose. Breakpoints will be specified at selected locations. A "Go" command will then be issued so that program execution is started. The program will automatically stop at each of the specified breakpoints. The programmer can then verify, by examining the contents of the registers, or memory, that the data so far is correct. If it is correct, we proceed until the next breakpoint. Whenever we find incorrect data, an error in the program has been detected. At this point, the programmer normally refers to his program listing and verifies whether his coding has been correct. If no error can be found in the programming, the error might be a logical one and one might refer to the flowchart. We will assume here that the flowcharts have been checked by hand and are assumed to be reasonably correct. The error is likely to come from the coding. It will, therefore, be necessary to modify a section of the program. If the symbolic representation of the program is still in the memory, we will simply re-enter the editor and modify the required lines, then go through the preceding sequence again. In some systems, the memory available may not be large enough, so that it is necessary to flush out the symbolic representation of the program onto a disk or cassette prior to executing the object code. Naturally, in such a case, one would have to reload the symbolic representation of the program from its support medium prior to entering the editor again.

The above procedure will be repeated as long as necessary until the results of the program are correct. Let us stress that prevention is much more effective than cure. A correct design will typically result in a program which runs correctly very soon after the usual typing mistakes or obvious coding errors have been removed. However, sloppy design may result in programs which will take an extremely long time to be debugged. The debugging time is generally considered to be much longer than the actual design time. In short, it is always worth investing more time in the design in order to shorten the debugging phase.

However, using this approach, it is possible to test the overall organization of the program, but not to test it in real time with input/output devices. If input/output devices are to be tested, the direct solution consists of transferring the program onto EPROM's and installing it on the board and then watching whether it works.

There is a better solution. It is the use of an *in-circuit emulator*. An in-circuit emulator uses the Z80 microprocessor (or any other one) to emulate a Z80 in (almost) real time. It emulates the Z80 physically. The emulator is equipped with a cable terminated by a 40-pin connector, exactly identical to the pin-out of a Z80. This connector can then be inserted on the real application board that one is developing. The signals generated by the emulator will be exactly those of the Z80, only perhaps a little slower. The essential advantage is that the program under test will still reside in the RAM memory of the development system. It will generate the real signals which will communicate with the real input/output devices that one wishes to use. As a result, it becomes possible to keep developing the program using all the resources of the development system (editor, debugger, symbolic facilities, file system) while testing input/output in real time.

In addition, a good emulator will provide special facilities, such as a *trace*. A trace is a recording of the last instructions or status of various data busses in the system prior to a breakpoint. In short, a trace provides the film of the events that occurred prior to the breakpoint or the malfunction. It may even trigger a scope at a specified address or upon the occurrence of a specified combination of bits. Such a facility is of great value, since when an error is found it is usually too late. The instruction, or the data, which caused the error has occurred prior to the detection. The availability of a trace allows the user to find which segment of the program caused the error to occur. If the trace is not long enough, we will simply set an earlier breakpoint.

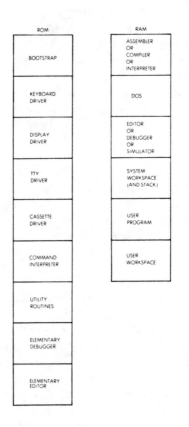

Fig. 10.2: A Typical Memory Map

This completes our description of the usual sequence of events involved in developing a program. Let us now review the hardware alternatives available for developing programs.

HARDWARE ALTERNATIVES

Single-Board Microcomputer

The single-board microcomputer offers the lowest cost approach to program development. It is normally equipped with a hexadecimal keyboard, plus some function keys, plus 6 LED's which can display address and data. Since it is equipped with a small amount of memory, an assembler is not usually available. At best, it has a small monitor and virtually no editing or debugging facilities, except for a very few commands. All programs must, therefore, be entered in hexadecimal form. They will also be displayed in hexadecimal form on the LED's. A single-board microcomputer has, in theory, the same hardware power as any other computer. Simply because of its restricted memory size and keyboard, it does not support all the usual facilities of a larger system and makes program development much longer. Because it is tedious to develop programs in hexadecimal format, a single board microcomputer is best suited for education and training where programs of limited length have to be developed and their short length is not an obstacle to programming. Single-boards are probably the cheapest way to learn programming by doing. However, they cannot be used for complex program development unless additional memory boards are attached and the usual software aids are made available.

The Development System

A development system is a microcomputer system equipped with a significant amount of RAM memory (32K, 48K) as well as the required input/output devices, such as a CRT display, a printer, disks, and, usually, a PROM programmer, as well as, perhaps, an in-circuit emulator. A development system is specifically designed to facilitate program development in an industrial environment. It normally offers all, or most, of the software facilities that we have mentioned in the preceding section. In principle, it is the ideal software development tool.

The limitation of a microcomputer development system is that it may not be capable of supporting a compiler or an interpreter. This is because a compiler typically requires a very large amount of memory, often more than is available on the system. However, for developing programs in assembly-level language, it offers all the required facilities. But because development systems sell in relatively small numbers compared to hobby computers, their cost is significantly higher.

Hobby-Type Microcomputers

The hobby-type microcomputer hardware is naturally exactly analogous to that of a development system. The main difference lies in the fact that it is normally not equipped with the sophisticated software development aids which are available on an industrial development system. As an example, many hobby-type microcomputers offer only elementary assemblers, minimal editors, minimal file systems, no facilities to attach a PROM programmer, no in-circuit emulator, no powerful debugger. They represent, therefore, an intermediate step between the single-board microcomputer and the full microprocessor development system. For a user who wishes to develop programs of modest complexity, they are probably the best compromise, since they offer the advantage of low cost and a reasonable array of software development tools, even though they are quite limited as to their convenience.

Time-Sharing System

It is possible to rent terminals from several companies which will connect to time-sharing networks. These terminals share the time of the larger computer and benefit from all the advantages of large installations. *Cross assemblers* are available for all microcomputers on virtually all commercial time-sharing systems. A cross assembler is simply an assembler for, say, a Z80 which resides, for example, in an IBM370. Formally, a cross assembler is an assembler for microprocessor X, which resides on processor Y. The nature of the computer being used is irrelevant. The user still writes a program in Z80 assembly-level language, and the cross assembler translates it into the appropriate binary pattern. The difference, however, is that the program cannot be executed at this point. It can be executed by a simulated processor, if one is available, provided it does not use any input/output resources. This solution is used, therefore, only in industrial environments.

In-House Computer

Whenever a large in-house computer is available, cross assemblers may also be available to facilitate program development. If such a computer offers time-shared service, this option is essentially analogous to the one above. If it offers only batch service, this is probably one of the most inconvenient methods of program development, since submitting programs in batch mode at the assembly level for a microprocessor results in a very long development time.

Front Panel or No Front Panel?

The front panel is a hardware accessory often used to facilitate program debugging. It has traditionally been a tool for conveniently displaying the binary contents of a register or of memory. However, all the functions of the control panel may be accomplished from a terminal, and the dominance of CRT displays now offers a service almost equivalent to the control panel by displaying the binary value of bits. The additional advantage of using the CRT display is that one can switch at will from binary representation to hexadecimal, to symbolic, to decimal (if the appropriate conversion routines are available, naturally). The disadvantage of the CRT is that one must hit several keys to obtain the appropriate display rather than turn a knob. However, since the cost of providing a control panel is quite substantial, most recent microcomputers have abandoned this debugging tool. The value of the control panel is often considered more on the basis of emotional arguments influenced by one's own past experience than by the use of reason. It is not indispensable.

Summary of Hardware Resources

Three broad cases may be distinguished. If you have only a minimal budget and if you wish to learn how to program, buy a single-board microcomputer. Using it, you will be able to develop all the simple programs in this book and many more. Eventually, however, when you want to develop programs of more than a few hundred instructions, you will feel the limitations of this approach.

If you are an industrial user, you will need a full development system. Any solution short of the full development system will cause a significantly longer development time. The trade-off is clear: hardware resources vs. programming time. Naturally, if the programs to be developed are quite simple, a less expensive approach may be used. However, if complex programs are to be developed, it is difficult to justify any hardware savings when buying a development system, since the programming costs will be by far the dominant cost of the project.

For a personal computerist, a hobby-type microcomputer will typically offer sufficient, although minimal, facilities. Good development software is still to come for many of the hobby computers. The user will have to evaluate his system in view of the comments presented in this chapter.

Let us now analyze in more detail the most indispensable resource: the assembler.

THE ASSEMBLER

We have used assembly-level language throughout this book without presenting the formal syntax or definition of assembly-level language. The time has come to present this definition. An assembler is designed to allow the convenient symbolic representation of the user program, and yet to make it simple for the assembler program to convert these mnemonics into their binary representation.

Assembler Fields

When typing in a program for the assembler, we have seen that fields are used. They are:

The label field, optional, which may contain a symbolic address for the instruction that follows.

The instruction field, which includes the opcode and any operands. (A separate operand field may be distinguished.)

The comment field, far to the right, which is optional and is intended to clarify the program.

These fields are shown on the programming form in Figure 10.3.

Once the program has been fed to the assembler, the assembler will produce a *listing* of it. When generating a listing, the assembler will provide three additional fields, usually on the left of the page. An example appears on Figure 10.4. On the far left is the line number. Each line which has been typed by the programmer is assigned a symbolic line number.

The next field to the right is the actual address field, which shows in hexadecimal the value of the program counter which will point to that instruction.

Moving still further to the right, we find the hexadecimal representation of the instruction.

This shows one of the possible uses of an assembler. Even if we are designing programs for a single-board microcomputer which accepts only hexadecimal, we should still write the program in assembly-level language, providing we have access to a system equipped with an assembler. We can then run the programs on the system, using the assembler. The assembler will automatically generate the correct hexadecimal codes on our system. This shows, in a simple example, the value of additional software resources.

Fig. 10.3: Microprocessor Programming Form

Tables

When the assembler translates the symbolic program into its binary representation, it performs two essential tasks:

1—It translates the mnemonic instructions into their binary encoding.

2—It translates the symbols used for constants and addresses into their binary representation.

In order to facilitate program debugging, the assembler shows at the end of the listing the equivalence between the symbol used and its hexadecimal value. This is called the symbol table.

Some symbol tables will not only list the symbol and its value, but also the line numbers where the symbol occurs, thereby providing an additional facility.

Error Messages

During the assembly process, the assembler will detect syntax errors and include them as part of the final listing. Typical diagnostics include: undefined symbols, label already defined, illegal opcode, illegal address, illegal addressing mode. Many more detailed diagnostics are naturally desirable and are usually provided. They vary with each assembler.

The Assembly Language

Opcodes have already been defined. We will here define the symbols, constants and operators which may be used as part of the assembler syntax.

Symbols

Symbols are used to represent numerical values, either data or addresses. Symbols may include up to six characters, and must start with an alphabetical character. The characters are restricted to letters of the alphabet and numbers. Also, the user may not choose names identical to the opcodes utilized by the Z80, the names of registers such as A,B, C,D,E,H,L, BC, DE, HL, AF, BC, DE, IX, IY, SP, as well as the various short names used as pseudo-operators by the assembler. The names of these assembler "directives" are listed below in the corresponding sections. Also, the abbreviations used to designate the flags should not be used as symbols: C,Z,N,PE,NC,P,PO,NZ,M.

Assigning a Value to a Symbol

Labels are special symbols whose values do not need to be defined by the programmer. The value will automatically be defined by the assembler program whenever it finds that label. The label value thus automatically corresponds to the address of the instruction generated at the line where it appears. Special pseudo-instructions are available to force a new starting value for labels, or to assign them a specific value.

```
CROMEMCO CDOS Z80 ASSEMBLER version 02.15                    PAGE 0001

0000'            0001              ORG     0100H
       (0200)    0002 MPRAD        DL      0200H
       (0202)    0003 MPDAD        DL      0202H
       (0204)    0004 RESAD        DL      0204H
                 0005 ;
0100  ED4B0002   0006 MP488        LD      BC,(MPRAD)    ;LOAD MULTIPLIER INTO C
0104  0608       0007              LD      B,8           ;B IS BIT COUNTER
0106  ED5B0202   0008              LD      DE,(MPDAD)    ;LOAD MUTIFLICAND INTO E
010A  1600       0009              LD      D,0           ;CLEAR D
010C  210000     0010              LD      HL,0          ;SET RESULT TO 0
010F  CB39       0011 MULT         SRL     C             ;SHIFT MULTIPLIER BIT INTO CARRY
0111  3001       0012              JR      NC,NOADD      ;TEST CARRY
0113  19         0013              ADD     HL,DE         ;ADD MPD TO RESULT
0114  CB23       0014 NOADD        SLA     E             ;SHIFT MPD LEFT
0116  CB12       0015              RL      D             ;SAVE BIT IN D
0118  05         0016              DEC     B             ;DECREMENT SHIFT COUNTER
0119  C20F01     0017              JP      NZ,MULT       ;DO IT AGAIN IF COUNTER <> 0
011C  220402     0018              LD      (RESAD),HL    ;STORE RESULT
011F  (0000)     0019              END

Errors           0
```

Fig. 10.4: Assembler Output—An Example

However, other symbols used for constants or memory addresses must be defined by the programmer prior to their use.

A special assembler *directive* may be used to assign a value to any symbol. A *directive* is essentially an instruction to the assembler which will not be translated into an executable statement. For example, the constant LOG will be defined as:

LOG   EQU   3002H

This assigns the value 3002 hexadecimal to the variable LOG. The assembler directives will be examined in detail in a later section.

Constants or Literals

Constants may traditionally be expressed either in decimal, in hexadecimal, in octal, or in binary, or as alphanumeric strings. In order to differentiate between the base used to represent the number, a symbol must be used. To load "0" into the accumulator, we will simply write:

LD   A, 0

Optionally a "D" may be used at the end of the constant.

A hexadecimal number will be terminated by the symbol "H". To load the value "FF" into the accumulator, we will write:

LD   A, 0FFH

An octal symbol is terminated by the symbol "O" or "Q". A binary symbol is terminated by "B".

For example, in order to load the value "11111111" into the accumulator, we will write:

LD   A,   11111111B

Literal ASCII characters may also be used in the literal field. The ASCII symbol must be enclosed in single quotes.

For example, in order to load the symbol "S" into the accumulator, we will write:

LD   A,   'S'

Exercise 10.1: Will the following two instructions load the same value in the accumulator: LD A, '5', and LD A, 5H?

Note that in the Zilog convention, parentheses denote an address. For example:

LD   A,   (10)

specifies that the accumulator is loaded from the contents of memory location 10 (decimal).

Operators

In order to further facilitate the writing of symbolic programs, assemblers allow the use of operators. At a minimum, they should allow plus and minus so that one can specify, for example:

LD   A, (ADDRESS)
LD   A, (ADDRESS + 1)

It is important to understand that the expression ADDRESS + 1 will be computed by the assembler in order to determine the actual memory address which must be inserted as the binary equivalent. It will be computed *at assembly time,* not at program-execution time.

In addition, more operators may be available, such as multiply and divide, a convenience when accessing tables in memory. More specialized operators may be also available, such as greater than and less than, which truncate a two-byte value respectively into its high and low byte.

Naturally, an expression must *evaluate* to a positive value. Negative numbers may normally not be used and should be expressed in a hexadecimal format.

Finally, a special symbol is traditionally used to represent the current value of the address of the line: "$". This symbol should be interpreted as "current location" (value of PC).

Exercise 10.2: What is the difference between the following instructions?

LD   A, 10101010B
LD   A, (10101010B)

Exercise 10.3: What is the effect of the following instruction?

JR   NC, $ − 2

Expressions

The Z80 assembler specifications allow a wide range of expressions with arithmetic and logical operations. The assembler will evaluate the expressions in a left-to-right manner, using the priorities specified by the table in Figure 10.5. Parentheses may be used to enforce a specific order of evaluation. However, the outermost parentheses will denote that the contents are to be treated as an address.

Assembler Directives

Directives are special orders given by the programmer to the assembler, which result either in storing values into symbols or into the memory, or in controlling the execution or printing modes of the assembler. The set of commands which specifically controls the printing modes of the assembler is also called "commands" and is described in a separate section.

To provide a specific example, let us review here the 11 assembler directives available on the Zilog development system:

ORG nn

This directive will set the assembler address counter to the value nn. In other words, the first executable instruction encountered after this directive will reside at the value nn. It can be used to locate different segments of a program at different memory locations.

EQU nn

This directive is used to assign a value to a label.

DEFL nn

This directive also assigns a value nn to a label, but may be repeated within the program with different values for the same label, whereas EQU may be used only once.

DEFB n

This directive assigns eight-bit contents to a byte residing at the current reference counter.

DEFB 'S'

assigns the ASCII value of "S" to the byte.

DEFW nn

This assigns the value nn to the two-byte word residing at the current reference counter and the following location.

OPERATOR	FUNCTION	PRIORITY
+	UNARY PLUS	1
−	UNARY MINUS	1
.NOT. or \	LOGICAL NOT	1
.RES.	RESULT	1
**	EXPONENTIATION	2
*	MULTIPLICATION	3
/	DIVISION	3
.MOD.	MODULO	3
.SHR.	LOGICAL SHIFT RIGHT	3
.SHL.	LOGICAL SHIFT LEFT	3
+	ADDITION	4
-	SUBTRACTION	4
.AND. or &	LOGICAL AND	5
.OR. or 1	LOGICAL OR	6
.XOR.	LOGICAL XOR	6
.EQ. or =	EQUALS	7
.GT. or >	GREATER THAN	7
.LT. or <	LESS THAN	7
.UGT.	UNSIGNED GREATER THAN	7
.ULT.	UNSIGNED LESS THAN	7

Fig. 10.5: Operator Precedence

DEFS nn

reserves a block of memory size nn bytes, starting at the current value of the reference counter.

DEFM 'S'

stores into memory the string 'S' starting at the current reference counter. It must be less than 63 in length.

MACRO P0 P1...Pn

is used to define a label as a macro, and to define its formal parameter list. Macros are defined in another section below.

END

indicates the end of the program. Any other statements following it will be ignored.

ENDM

is used to mark the end of a macro definition.

Assembler Commands

Commands are used to modify the format of the listing to control the printing modes of the assembler. All commands start with a star in column one. Seven commands are provided by the Z80 assembler. Typical examples are:

EJECT

which causes the listing to move to the top of the next page; and

LIST OFF

which causes the printing to be suspended, effective with this command. The others are: "*HEADING S", "*LIST ON", "*MACLIST ON", "*MACLIST OFF", "*INCLUDE FILENAME".

Macros

A macro is simply a name assigned to a group of instructions. It is a convenience to the programmer. If a group of instructions is used several times in a program, we could define a macro to represent them, instead of always having to write this group of instructions.

As an example, we could write:

```
SAVREG MACRO
       PUSH AF
       PUSH BC
       PUSH DE
       PUSH HL
       ENDM
```

then simply write the name "SAVREG" instead of the above instructions. Any time that we write SAVREG, the five corresponding lines will get substituted instead of the name. An assembler equipped with a macro facility is called a macro-assembler. When the macro assembler encounters a SAVREG, it performs a mere physical substitution of equivalent lines.

Macro or Subroutine?

At this point, a macro may seem to operate in a way analogous to a subroutine. This is not the case. When the assembler is used to produce the object code, any time that a macro name is encountered, it will be replaced by the actual instructions that it stands for. At execution time, the group of instructions will appear as many times as the name of the macro did.

By contrast, a subroutine is defined only once, and then it can be used repeatedly; the program will jump to the subroutine address. A macro is called an *assembly-time* facility. A subroutine is an *execution-time* facility. Their operation is quite different.

Macro Parameters

Each macro may be equipped with a number of parameters. As an example, let us consider the following macro:

```
SWAP   MACRO   #M, #N, #T
       LD      A, #M      ; M INTO A
       LD      #T, A      ; A INTO T (=M)
       LD      A, #N      ; N INTO A
       LD      #M, A      ; A INTO M (=N)
       LD      A, #T      ; T INTO A
       LD      #N, A      ; A INTO N (=T)
       END     M
```

This macro will result in swapping (exchanging) the contents of memory locations M and N. A swap between two registers, or two memory locations, is an operation which is not provided by the Z80. A macro may be used to implement it. "T" in this instance is simply the name for a temporary storage location required by the program. As an example, let us swap the contents of memory locations ALPHA and BETA. The instruction which does this appears below:

SWAP (ALPHA), (BETA), (TEMP)

In this instruction, TEMP is the name of some temporary storage location, which we know to be available and which can be used by the macro. The resulting expansion of the macro appears below:

```
LD   A, (ALPHA)
LD   (TEMP), A
LD   A, (BETA)
LD   (ALPHA), A
LD   A, (TEMP)
LD   (BETA), A
```

The value of a macro should now be apparent: it is convenient for the programmer to use pseudo-instructions, which have been defined with macros. In this way, the apparent instruction set of the Z80 can be expanded at will. Unfortunately, one must bear in mind that each macro directive will expand into whatever number of instructions were used. A macro will, therefore, run more slowly than any single instruction. Because of its convenience for the development of any long program, a macro facility is highly desirable for such applications.

Additional Macro Facilities

Many other directives and syntactic facilities may be added to a simple macro facility; macros may be *nested,* i.e., a macro call may appear within a macro definition. Using this facility, a macro may modify itself with a nested definition! A first call will produce one expansion, whereas subsequent calls will produce a modified expansion of the same macro. This is allowed by the Z80 assembler, but nested definitions are not allowed.

CONDITIONAL ASSEMBLY

Conditional assembly is another facility provided in the Z80 assembly. With a conditional assembly facility, the programmer can devise programs for a variety of cases, and then conditionally assemble the segments of codes required by a specific application. As an example, an industrial user might design programs to take care of any number of traffic lights at an intersection, for a variety of control algorithms. He will then receive the specifications from the local traffic engineer, who specifies how many traffic lights there should be and which algorithms should be used. The programmer will then simply set parameters in his program and assemble conditionally. The conditional assembly will result in a "customized" program which will retain only those routines which are necessary for the solution to the problem.

Conditional assembly is, therefore, of specific value to industrial program generation in an environment where many options exist and where the programmer wishes to assemble portions of programs quickly and automatically in response to external parameters.

Only two conditional pseudo-OPs are provided in the standard micro-assembler version supplied by Zilog. They are respectively:

COND NN and ENDC

where NN represents an expression. The pseudo-OP "COND NN" will result in the evaluation of the expression NN. As long as the expression evaluates to a true value (non-zero), the statement following the COND will be assembled. However, if the expression should be false, i.e., evaluate to a zero value, the assembly of all subsequent statements will be disabled up to the ENDC instruction.

ENDC is used to terminate a COND, so that the assembly of subsequent statements is re-enabled. The COND pseudo-OP's cannot be nested.

In theory, more powerful conditional assembly facilities could exist, with "IF" and "ELSE" specification. They may become available in future versions of the assembler.

SUMMARY

This chapter has presented the techniques and the hardware and software tools required to develop a program, along with the various trade-offs and alternatives.

These range at the hardware level from the single-board microcomputer to the full development system; at the software level, from binary coding to high-level programming.

You will have to select them on the basis of your goals and resources.

601

CHAPTER 11

CONCLUSION

We have now covered all important aspects of programming, from definitions and basic concepts to the internal manipulation of the Z80 registers, to the management of input/output devices, as well as the characteristics of software development aids. What is the next step? Two views can be offered, the first one relating to the development of technology, the second one relating to the development of your own knowledge and skill. Let us address these two points.

TECHNOLOGICAL DEVELOPMENT

The progress of integration in MOS technology makes it possible to implement more and more complex chips. The cost of implementing the processor function itself is constantly decreasing. The result is that many of the input/output chips or the peripheral-controller chips used in a system now incorporate a simple processor. This means that most LSI chips in the system are becoming *programmable*. An interesting conceptual dilemma is now developing. In order to simplify the software design task, as well as to reduce the component count, the new I/O chips now incorporate sophisticated programmable capabilities: many programmed algorithms are now integrated within the chip. However, as a result, the development of programs is complicated by the fact that all these input/output chips are radically different and need to be studied in detail by the programmer! *Programming the system is no longer programming the microprocessor alone, but also programming all the other chips attached to it*. The learning time for every chip can be significant.

Naturally, this is only an apparent dilemma. If these chips were not available, the complexity of the interface to be realized, as well as of the corresponding programs, would be still greater. The new complexity that is introduced is the need to program more than just a processor, and to learn the various features of the different chips in a system. However, it is hoped that the techniques and concepts presented in this book will make this a reasonably easy task.

THE NEXT STEP

You have now learned the basic techniques required to program simple applications on paper. That was the goal of this book. The next step is actual practice for which there is no substitute. It is impossible to learn programming completely on paper; experience is required. You should now be in a position to start writing your own programs. It is hoped that this journey will be a pleasant one.

APPENDIX A

HEXADECIMAL CONVERSION TABLE

HEX	0	1	2	3	4	5	6	7	8	9	A	B	C	D	E	F	00	000
0	0	1	2	3	4	5	6	7	8	9	10	11	12	13	14	15	0	0
1	16	17	18	19	20	21	22	23	24	25	26	27	28	29	30	31	256	4096
2	32	33	34	35	36	37	38	39	40	41	42	43	44	45	46	47	512	8192
3	48	49	50	51	52	53	54	55	56	57	58	59	60	61	62	63	768	12288
4	64	65	66	67	68	69	70	71	72	73	74	75	76	77	78	79	1024	16384
5	80	81	82	83	84	85	86	87	88	89	90	91	92	93	94	95	1280	20480
6	96	97	98	99	100	101	102	103	104	105	106	107	108	109	110	111	1536	24576
7	112	113	114	115	116	117	118	119	120	121	122	123	124	125	126	127	1792	28672
8	128	129	130	131	132	133	134	135	136	137	138	139	140	141	142	143	2048	32768
9	144	145	146	147	148	149	150	151	152	153	154	155	156	157	158	159	2304	36864
A	160	161	162	163	164	165	166	167	168	169	170	171	172	173	174	175	2560	40960
B	176	177	178	179	180	181	182	183	184	185	186	187	188	189	190	191	2816	45056
C	192	193	194	195	196	197	198	199	200	201	202	203	204	205	206	207	3072	49152
D	208	209	210	211	212	213	214	215	216	217	218	219	220	221	222	223	3328	53248
E	224	225	226	227	228	229	230	231	232	233	234	235	236	237	238	239	3584	57344
F	240	241	242	243	244	245	246	247	248	249	250	251	252	253	254	255	3840	61440

5		4		3		2		1		0	
HEX	DEC	HEX	DEC	HEX	DEC	HEX	DEC	HEX	DEC	HEX	DEC
0	0	0	0	0	0	0	0	0	0	0	0
1	1,048,576	1	65,536	1	4,096	1	256	1	16	1	1
2	2,097,152	2	131,072	2	8,192	2	512	2	32	2	2
3	3,145,728	3	196,608	3	12,288	3	768	3	48	3	3
4	4,194,304	4	262,144	4	16,384	4	1,024	4	64	4	4
5	5,242,880	5	327,680	5	20,480	5	1,280	5	80	5	5
6	6,291,456	6	393.216	6	24,576	6	1,536	6	96	6	6
7	7,340,032	7	458,752	7	28,672	7	1,792	7	112	7	7
8	8,388,608	8	524,288	8	32,768	8	2,048	8	128	8	8
9	9,437,184	9	589,824	9	36,864	9	2,304	9	144	9	9
A	10,485,760	A	655,360	A	40,960	A	2,560	A	160	A	10
B	11,534,336	B	720,896	B	45,056	B	2,816	B	176	B	11
C	12,582,912	C	786,432	C	49,152	C	3,072	C	192	C	12
D	13,631,488	D	851,968	D	53,248	D	3,328	D	208	D	13
E	14,680,064	E	917,504	E	57,344	E	3,584	E	224	E	14
F	15,728,640	F	983,040	F	61,440	F	3,840	F	240	F	15

APPENDIX B

ASCII CONVERSION TABLE

HEX	MSD	0	1	2	3	4	5	6	7
LSD	BITS	000	001	010	011	100	101	110	111
0	0000	NUL	DLE	SPACE	0	@	P	`	p
1	0001	SOH	DC1	!	1	A	Q	a	q
2	0010	STX	DC2	"	2	B	R	b	r
3	0011	ETX	DC3	#	3	C	S	c	s
4	0100	EOT	DC4	$	4	D	T	d	t
5	0101	ENQ	NAK	%	5	E	U	e	u
6	0110	ACK	SYN	&	6	F	V	f	v
7	0111	BEL	ETB	'	7	G	W	g	w
8	1000	BS	CAN	(	8	H	X	h	x
9	1001	HT	EM	)	9	I	Y	i	y
A	1010	LF	SUB	*	:	J	Z	j	z
B	1011	VT	ESC	+	;	K	[	k	{
C	1100	FF	FS	,	<	L	\	l	--
D	1101	CR	GS	--	=	M	]	m	}
E	1110	SO	RS	.	>	N	∧	n	~
F	1111	SI	US	/	?	O	←	o	DEL

THE ASCII SYMBOLS

NUL	— Null	DLE	— Data Link Escape
SOH	— Start of Heading	DC	— Device Control
STX	— Start of Text	NAK	— Negative Acknowledge
ETX	— End of Text	SYN	— Synchronous Idle
EOT	— End of Transmission	ETB	— End of Transmission Block
ENQ	— Enquiry	CAN	— Cancel
ACK	— Acknowledge	EM	— End of Medium
BEL	— Bell	SUB	— Substitute
BS	— Backspace	ESC	— Escape
HT	— Horizontal Tabulation	FS	— File Separator
LF	— Line Feed	GS	— Group Separator
VT	— Vertical Tabulation	RS	— Record Separator
FF	— Form Feed	US	— Unit Separator
CR	— Carriage Return	SP	— Space (Blank)
SO	— Shift Out	DEL	— Delete
SI	— Shift In		

APPENDIX C

RELATIVE BRANCH TABLES

FORWARD RELATIVE BRANCH TABLE

LSD / MSD	0	1	2	3	4	5	6	7	8	9	A	B	C	D	E	F
0	0	1	2	3	4	5	6	7	8	9	10	11	12	13	14	15
1	16	17	18	19	20	21	22	23	24	25	26	27	28	29	30	31
2	32	33	34	35	36	37	38	39	40	41	42	43	44	45	46	47
3	48	49	50	51	52	53	54	55	56	57	58	59	60	61	62	63
4	64	65	66	67	68	69	70	71	72	73	74	75	76	77	78	79
5	80	81	82	83	84	85	86	87	88	89	90	91	92	93	94	95
6	96	97	98	99	100	101	102	103	104	105	106	107	108	109	110	111
7	112	113	114	115	116	117	118	119	120	121	122	123	124	125	126	127

BACKWARD RELATIVE BRANCH TABLE

LSD / MSD	0	1	2	3	4	5	6	7	8	9	A	B	C	D	E	F
8	128	127	126	125	124	123	122	121	120	119	118	117	116	115	114	113
9	112	111	110	109	108	107	106	105	104	103	102	101	100	99	98	97
A	96	95	94	93	92	91	90	89	88	87	86	85	84	83	82	81
B	80	79	78	77	76	75	74	73	72	71	70	69	68	67	66	65
C	64	63	62	61	60	59	58	57	56	55	54	53	52	51	50	49
D	48	47	46	45	44	43	42	41	40	39	38	37	36	35	34	33
E	32	31	30	29	28	27	26	25	24	23	22	21	20	19	18	17
F	16	15	14	13	12	11	10	9	8	7	6	5	4	3	2	1

APPENDIX D

DECIMAL TO BCD CONVERSION

DECIMAL	BCD	DEC	BCD	DEC	BCD
0	0000	10	00010000	90	10010000
1	0001	11	00010001	91	10010001
2	0010	12	00010010	92	10010010
3	0011	13	00010011	93	10010011
4	0100	14	00010100	94	10010100
5	0101	15	00010101	95	10010101
6	0110	16	00010110	96	10010110
7	0111	17	00010111	97	10010111
8	1000	18	00011000	98	10011000
9	1001	19	00011001	99	10011001

APPENDIX E

Z80 INSTRUCTION CODES

(The literal d is shown as 05 in the object code.)

OBJ CODE	SOURCE STATEMENT		OBJ CODE	SOURCE STATEMENT	
8E	ADC	A,(HL)	E620	AND	n
DD8E05	ADC	A,(IX+d)	CB46	BIT	0,(HL)
FD8E05	ADC	A,(IY+d)	DDCB0546	BIT	0,(IX+d)
8F	ADC	A,A	FDCB0546	BIT	0,(IY+d)
88	ADC	A,B	CB47·	BIT	0,A
89	ADC	A,C	CB40	BIT	0,B
8A	ADC	A,D	CB41	BIT	0,C
8B	ADC	A,E	CB42	BIT	0,D
8C	ADC	A,H	CB43	BIT	0,E
8D	ADC	A,L	CB44	BIT	0,H
CE20	ADC	A,n	CB45	BIT	0,L
ED4A	ADC	HL,BC	CB4E	BIT	1,(HL)
ED5A	ADC	HL,DE	DDCB054E	BIT	1,(IX+d)
ED6A	ADC	HL,HL	FDCB054E	BIT	1,(IY+d)
ED7A	ADC	HL,SP	CB4F	BIT	1,A
86	ADD	A,(HL)	CB48	BIT	1,B
DD8605	ADD	A,(IX+d)	CB49	BIT	1,C
FD8605	ADD	A,(IY+d)	CB4A	BIT	1,D
87	ADD	A,A	CB4B	BIT	1,E
80	ADD	A,B	CB4C	BIT	1,H
81	ADD	A,C	CB4D	BIT	1,L
82	ADD	A,D	CB56	BIT	2,(HL)
83	ADD	A,E	DDCB0556	BIT	2,(IX+d)
84	ADD	A,H	FDCB0556	BIT	2,(IY+d)
85	ADD	A,L	CB57	BIT	2,A
C620	ADD	A,n	CB50	BIT	2,B
09	ADD	HL,BC	CB51	BIT	2,C
19	ADD	HL,DE	CB52	BIT	2,D
29	ADD	HL,HL	CB53	BIT	2,E
39	ADD	HL,SP	CB54	BIT	2,H
DD09	ADD	IX,BC	CB55	BIT	2,L
DD19	ADD	IX,DE	CB5E	BIT	3,(HL)
DD29	ADD	IX,IX	DDCB055E	BIT	3,(IX+d)
DD39	ADD	IX,SP	FDCB055E	BIT	3,(IY+d)
FD09	ADD	IY,BC	CB5F	BIT	3,A
FD19	ADD	IY,DE	CB58	BIT	3,B
FD29	ADD	IY,IY	CB59	BIT	3,C
FD39	ADD	IY,SP	CB5A	BIT	3,D
A6	AND	(HL)	CB5B	BIT	3,E
DDA605	AND	(IX+d)	CB5C	BIT	3,H
FDA605	AND	(IY+d)	CB5D	BIT	3,L
A7	AND	A	CB66	BIT	4,(HL)
A0	AND	B	DDCB0566	BIT	4,(IX+d)
A1	AND	C	FDCB0566	BIT	4,(IY+d)
A2	AND	D	CB67	BIT	4,A
A3	AND	E	CB60	BIT	4,B
A4	AND	H	CB61	BIT	4,C
A5	AND	L	CB62	BIT	4,D

OBJ CODE	SOURCE STATEMENT	
CB63	BIT	4,E
CB64	BIT	4,H
CB65	BIT	4,L
CB6E	BIT	5,(HL)
DDCB056E	BIT	5,(IX+d)
FDCB056E	BIT	5,(IY+d)
CB6F	BIT	5,A
CB68	BIT	5,B
CB69	BIT	5,C
C86A	BIT	5,D
CB6B	BIT	5,E
CB6C	BIT	5,H
CB6D	BIT	5,L
CB76	BIT	6,(HL)
DDCB0576	BIT	6,(IX+d)
FDCB0576	BIT	6,(IY+d)
CB77	BIT	6,A
CB70	BIT	6,B
CB71	BIT	6,C
CB72	BIT	6,D
CB73	BIT	6,E
CB74	BIT	6,H
CB75	BIT	6,L
CB7E	BIT	7,(HL)
DDCB057E	BIT	7,(IX+d)
FDCB057E	BIT	7,(IY+d)
CB7F	BIT	7,A
CB78	BIT	7,B
CB79	BIT	7,C
CB7A	BIT	7,D
CB7B	BIT	7,E
CB7C	BIT	7,H
CB7D	BIT	7,L
DC8405	CALL	C,nn
FC8405	CALL	M,nn
D48405	CALL	NC,nn
C48405	CALL	NZ,nn
F48405	CALL	P,nn
EC8405	CALL	PE,nn
E48405	CALL	PO,nn
CC8405	CALL	Z,nn
CD8405	CALL	nn
3F	CCF	
BE	CP	(HL)
DDBE05	CP	(IX+d)
FDBE05	CP	(IY+d)
BF	CP	A
B8	CP	B
B9	CP	C
BA	CP	D
BB	CP	E
BC	CP	H
BD	CP	L
FE20	CP	n
EDA9	CPD	
EDB9	CPDR	

OBJ CODE	SOURCE STATEMENT	
EDB1	CPIR	
EDA1	CPI	
2F	CPL	
27	DAA	
35	DEC	(HL)
DD3505	DEC	(IX+d)
FD3505	DEC	(IY+d)
3D	DEC	A
05	DEC	B
0B	DEC	BC
0D	DEC	C
15	DEC	D
1B	DEC	DE
1D	DEC	E
25	DEC	H
2B	DEC	HL
DD2B	DEC	IX
FD2B	DEC	IY
2D	DEC	L
3B	DEC	SP
F3	DI	
102E	DJNZ	e
FB	EI	
E3	EX	(SP),HL
DDE3	EX	(SP),IX
FDE3	EX	(SP),IY
08	EX	AF,AF'
EB	EX	DE,HL
D9	EXX	
76	HALT	
ED46	IM	0
ED56	IM	1
ED5E	IM	2
ED78	IN	A,(C)
ED40	IN	B,(C)
ED48	IN	C,(C)
ED50	IN	D,(C)
ED58	IN	E,(C)
ED60	IN	H,(C)
ED68	IN	L,(C)
34	INC	(HL)
DD3405	INC	(IX+d)
FD3405	INC	(IY+d)
3C	INC	A
04	INC	B
03	INC	BC
0C	INC	C
14	INC	D
13	INC	DE
1C	INC	E
24	INC	H
23	INC	HL
DD23	INC	IX
FD23	INC	IY
2C	INC	L
33	INC	SP
DB20	IN	A,(n)

OBJ CODE	SOURCE STATEMENT	
EDAA	IND	
EDBA	INDR	
EDA2	INI	
EDB2	INIR	
C38405	JP	nn
E9	JP	(HL)
DDE9	JP	(IX)
FDE9	JP	(IY)
DA8405	JP	C,nn
FA8405	JP	M,nn
D28405	JP	NC,nn
C28405	JP	NZ,nn
F28405	JP	P,nn
EA8405	JP	PE,nn
E28405	JP	PO,nn
CA8405	JP	Z,nn
382E	JR	C,e
302E	JR	NC,e
202E	JR	NZ,e
282E	JR	Z,e
182E	JR	e
02	LD	(BC),A
12	LD	(DE),A
77	LD	(HL),A
70	LD	(HL),B
71	LD	(HL),C
72	LD	(HL),D
73	LD	(HL),E
74	LD	(HL),H
75	LD	(HL),L
3620	LD	(HL),n
DD7705	LD	(IX+d),A
DD7005	LD	(IX+d),B
DD7105	LD	(IX+d),C
DD7205	LD	(IX+d),D
DD7305	LD	(IX+d),E
DD7405	LD	(IX+d),H
DD7505	LD	(IX+d),L
DD360520	LD	(IX+d),n
FD7705	LD	(IY+d),A
FD7005	LD	(IY+d),B
FD7105	LD	(IY+d),C
FD7205	LD	(IY+d),D
FD7305	LD	(IY+d),E
FD7405	LD	(IY+d),H
FD7505	LD	(IY+d),L
FD360520	LD	(IY+d),n
328405	LD	(nn),A
ED438405	LD	(nn),BC
ED538405	LD	(nn),DE
228405	LD	(nn),HL
DD228405	LD	(nn),IX
FD228405	LD	(nn),IY
ED738405	LD	(nn),SP
0A	LD	A,(BC)
1A	LD	A,(DE)
7E	LD	A,(HL)

OBJ CODE	SOURCE STATEMENT	
DD7E05	LD	A,(IX+d)
FD7E05	LD	A,(IY+d)
3A8405	LD	A,(nn)
7F	LD	A,A
78	LD	A,B
79	LD	A,C
7A	LD	A,D
7B	LD	A,E
7C	LD	A,H
ED57	LD	A,I
7D	LD	A,L
3E20	LD	A,n
ED5F	LD	A,R
46	LD	B,(HL)
DD4605	LD	B,(IX+d)
FD4605	LD	B,(IY+d)
47	LD	B,A
40	LD	B,B
41	LD	B,C
42	LD	B,D
43	LD	B,E
44	LD	B,H
45	LD	B,L
0620	LD	B,n
ED4B8405	LD	BC,(nn)
018405	LD	BC,nn
4E	LD	C,(HL)
DD4E05	LD	C,(IX+d)
FD4E05	LD	C,(IY+d)
4F	LD	C,A
48	LD	C,B
49	LD	C,C
4A	LD	C,D
4B	LD	C,E
4C	LD	C,H
4D	LD	C,L
0E20	LD	C,n
56	LD	D,(HL)
DD5605	LD	D,(IX+d)
FD5605	LD	D,(IY+d)
57	LD	D,A
50	LD	D,B
51	LD	D,C
52	LD	D,D
53	LD	D,E
54	LD	D,H
55	LD	D,L
1620	LD	D,n
ED5B8405	LD	DE,(nn)
118405	LD	DE,nn
5E	LD	E,(HL)
DD5E05	LD	E,(IX+d)
FD5E05	LD	E,(IY+d)
5F	LD	E,A
58	LD	E,B
59	LD	E,C
5A	LD	E,D

OBJ CODE	SOURCE STATEMENT		OBJ CODE	SOURCE STATEMENT	
5B	LD	E,E	EDB3	OTIR	
5C	LD	E,H	ED79	OUT	(C),A
5D	LD	E,L	ED41	OUT	(C),B
1E20	LD	E,n	ED49	OUT	(C),C
66	LD	H,(HL)	ED51	OUT	(C),D
DD6605	LD	H,(IX+d)	ED59	OUT	(C),E
FD6605	LD	H,(IY+d)	ED61	OUT	(C),H
67	LD	H,A	ED69	OUT	(C),L
60	LD	H,B	D320	OUT	(n),A
61	LD	H,C	EDAB	OUTD	
62	LD	H,D	EDA3	OUTI	
63	LD	H,E	F1	POP	AF
64	LD	H,H	C1	POP	BC
65	LD	H,L	D1	POP	DE
2620	LD	H,n	E1	POP	HL
2A8405	LD	HL,(nn)	DDE1	POP	IX
218405	LD	HL,nn	FDE1	POP	IY
ED47	LD	I,A	F5	PUSH	AF
DD2A8405	LD	IX,(nn)	C5	PUSH	BC
DD218405	LD	IX,nn	D5	PUSH	DE
FD2A8405	LD	IY,(nn)	E5	PUSH	HL
FD218405	LD	IY,nn	DDE5	PUSH	IX
6E	LD	L,(HL)	FDE5	PUSH	IY
DD6E05	LD	L,(IX+d)	CB86	RES	0,(HL)
FD6E05	LD	L,(IY+d)	DDCB0586	RES	0,(IX+d)
6F	LD	L,A	FDCB0586	RES	0,(IY+d)
68	LD	L,B	CB87	RES	0,A
69	LD	L,C	CB80	RES	0,B
6A	LD	L,D	CB81	RES	0,C
6B	LD	L,E	CB82	RES	0,D
6C	LD	L,H	CB83	RES	0,E
6D	LD	L,L	CB84	RES	0,H
2E20	LD	L,n	CB85	RES	0,L
ED4F	LD	R,A	CB8E	RES	1,(HL)
ED7B8405	LD	SP,(nn)	DDCB058E	RES	1,(IX+d)
F9	LD	SP,HL	FDCB058E	RES	1,(IY+d)
DDF9	LD	SP,IX	CB8F	RES	1,A
FDF9	LD	SP,IY	CB88	RES	1,B
318405	LD	SP,nn	CB89	RES	1,C
EDA8	LDD		CB8A	RES	1,D
EDB8	LDDR		CB8B	RES	1,E
EDA0	LDI		CB8C	RES	1,H
EDB0	LDIR		CB8D	RES	1,L
ED44	NEG		CB96	RES	2,(HL)
00	NOP		DDCB0596	RES	2,(IX+d)
B6	OR	(HL)	FDCB0596	RES	2,(IY+d)
DDB605	OR	(IX+d)	CB97	RES	2,A
FDB605	OR	(IY+d)	CB90	RES	2,B
B7	OR	A	CB91	RES	2,C
B0	OR	B	CB92	RES	2,D
B1	OR	C	CB93	RES	2,E
B2	OR	D	CB94	RES	2,H
B3	OR	E	CB95	RES	2,L
B4	OR	H	CB9E	RES	3,(HL)
B5	OR	L	DDCB059E	RES	3,(IX+d)
F620	OR	n	FDCB059E	RES	3,(IY+d)
ED8B	OTDR				

OBJ CODE	SOURCE STATEMENT	
CB9F	RES	3,A
CB98	RES	3,B
CB99	RES	3,C
CB9A	RES	3,D
CB9B	RES	3,E
CB9C	RES	3,H
CB9D	RES	3,L
CBA6	RES	4,(HL)
DDCB05A6	RES	4,(IX+d)
FDCB05A6	RES	4,(IY+d)
CBA7	RES	4,A
CBA0	RES	4,B
CBA1	RES	4,C
CBA2	RES	4,D
CBA3	RES	4,E
CBA4	RES	4,H
CBA5	RES	4,L
CBAE	RES	5,(HL)
DDCB05AE	RES	5,(IX+d)
FDCB05AE	RES	5,(IY+d)
CBAF	RES	5,A
CBA8	RES	5,B
CBA9	RES	5,C
CBAA	RES	5,D
CBAB	RES	5,E
CBAC	RES	5,H
CBAD	RES	5,L
CBB6	RES	6,(HL)
DDCB05B6	RES	6,(IX+d)
FDCB05B6	RES	6,(IY+d)
CBB7	RES	6,A
CBB0	RES	6,B
CBB1	RES	6,C
CBB2	RES	6,D
CBB3	RES	6,E
CBB4	RES	6,H
CBB5	RES	6,L
CBBE	RES	7,(HL)
DDCB05BE	RES	7,(IX+d)
FDCB05BE	RES	7,(IY+d)
CBBF	RES	7,A
CBB8	RES	7,B
CBB9	RES	7,C
CBBA	RES	7,D
CBBB	RES	7,E
CBBC	RES	7,H
CBBD	RES	7,L
C9	RET	
D8	RET	C
F8	RET	M
D0	RET	NC
C0	RET	NZ
F0	RET	P
E8	RET	PE
E0	RET	PO
C8	RET	Z

OBJ CODE	SOURCE STATEMENT	
ED4D	RETI	
ED45	RETN	
CB16	RL	(HL)
DDCB0516	RL	(IX+d)
FDCB0516	RL	(IY+d)
CB17	RL	A
CB10	RL	B
CB11	RL	C
CB12	RL	D
CB13	RL	E
CB14	RL	H
CB15	RL	L
17	RLA	
CB06	RLC	(HL)
DDCB0506	RLC	(IX+d)
FDCB0506	RLC	(IY+d)
CB07	RLC	A
CB00	RLC	B
CB01	RLC	C
CB02	RLC	D
CB03	RLC	E
CB04	RLC	H
CB05	RLC	L
07	RLCA	
ED6F	RLD	
CB1E	RR	(HL)
DDCB051E	RR	(IX+d)
FDCB051E	RR	(IY+d)
CB1F	RR	A
CB18	RR	B
CB19	RR	C
CB1A	RR	D
CB1B	RR	E
CB1C	RR	H
CB1D	RR	L
1F	RRA	
CB0E	RRC	(HL)
DDCB050E	RRC	(IX+d)
FDCB050E	RRC	(IY+d)
CB0F	RRC	A
CB08	RRC	B
CB09	RRC	C
CB0A	RRC	D
CB0B	RRC	E
CB0C	RRC	H
CB0D	RRC	L
0F	RRCA	
ED67	RRD	
C7	RST	00H
CF	RST	08H
D7	RST	10H
DF	RST	18H
E7	RST	20H
EF	RST	28H
F7	RST	30H
FF	RST	38H
DE20	SBC	A,n

OBJ CODE	SOURCE STATEMENT	
9E	SBC	A,(HL)
DD9E05	SBC	A,(IX+d)
FD9E05	SBC	A,(IY+d)
9F	SBC	A,A
98	SBC	A,B
99	SBC	A,C
9A	SBC	A,D
9B	SBC	A,E
9C	SBC	A,H
9D	SBC	A,L
ED42	SBC	HL,BC
ED52	SBC	HL,DE
ED62	SBC	HL,HL
ED72	SBC	HL,SP
37	SCF	
CBC6	SET	0,(HL)
DDCB05C6	SET	0,(IX+d)
FDCB05C6	SET	0,(IY+d)
CBC7	SET	0,A
CBC0	SET	0,B
CBC1	SET	0,C
CBC2	SET	0,D
CBC3	SET	0,E
CBC4	SET	0,H
CBC5	SET	0,L
CBCE	SET	1,(HL)
DDCB05CE	SET	1,(IX+d)
FDCB05CE	SET	1,(IY+d)
CBCF	SET	1,A
CBC8	SET	1,B
CBC9	SET	1,C
CBCA	SET	1,D
CBCB	SET	1,E
CBCC	SET	1,H
CBCD	SET	1,L
CBD6	SET	2,(HL)
DDCB05D6	SET	2,(IX+d)
FDCB05D6	SET	2,(IY+d)
CBD7	SET	2,A
CBD0	SET	2,B
CBD1	SET	2,C
CBD2	SET	2,D
CBD3	SET	2,E
CBD4	SET	2,H
CBD5	SET	2,L
CBD8	SET	3,B
CBDE	SET	3,(HL)
DDCB05DE	SET	3,(IX+d)
FDCB05DE	SET	3,(IY+d)
CBDF	SET	3,A
CBD9	SET	3,C
CBDA	SET	3,D
CBDB	SET	3,E
CBDC	SET	3,H
CBDD	SET	3,L
CBE6	SET	4,(HL)

OBJ CODE	SOURCE STATEMENT	
DDCB05E6	SET	4,(IX+d)
FDCB05E6	SET	4,(IY+d)
CBE7	SET	4,A
CBE0	SET	4,B
CBE1	SET	4,C
CBE2	SET	4,D
CBE3	SET	4,E
CBE4	SET	4,H
CBE5	SET	4,L
CBEE	SET	5,(HL)
DDCB05EE	SET	5,(IX+d)
FDCB05EE	SET	5,(IY+d)
CBEF	SET	5,A
CBE8	SET	5,B
CBE9	SET	5,C
CBEA	SET	5,D
CBEB	SET	5,E
CBEC	SET	5,H
CBED	SET	5,L
CBF6	SET	6,(HL)
DDCB05F6	SET	6,(IX+d)
FDCB05F6	SET	6,(IY+d)
CBF7	SET	6,A
CBF0	SET	6,B
CBF1	SET	6,C
CBF2	SET	6,D
CBF3	SET	6,E
CBF4	SET	6,H
CBF5	SET	6,L
CBFE	SET	7,(HL)
DDCB05FE	SET	7,(IX+d)
FDCB05FE	SET	7,(IY+d)
CBFF	SET	7,A
CBF8	SET	7,B
CBF9	SET	7,C
CBFA	SET	7,D
CBFB	SET	7,E
CBFC	SET	7,H
CBFD	SET	7,L
CB26	SLA	(HL)
DDCB0526	SLA	(IX+d)
FDCB0526	SLA	(IY+d)
CB27	SLA	A
CB20	SLA	B
CB21	SLA	C
CB22	SLA	D
CB23	SLA	E
CB24	SLA	H
CB25	SLA	L
CB2E	SRA	(HL)
DDCB052E	SRA	(IX+d)
FDCB052E	SRA	(IY+d)
CB2F	SRA	A
CB28	SRA	B
CB29	SRA	C
CB2A	SRA	D

OBJ CODE	SOURCE STATEMENT	
CB2B	SRA	E
CB2C	SRA	H
CB2D	SRA	L
CB3E	SRL	(HL)
DDCB053E	SRL	(IX+d)
FDCB053E	SRL	(IY+d)
CB3F	SRL	A
CB38	SRL	B
CB39	SRL	C
CB3A	SRL	D
CB3B	SRL	E
CB3C	SRL	H
CB3D	SRL	L
96	SUB	(HL)
DD9605	SUB	(IX+d)
FD9605	SUB	(IY+d)
97	SUB	A
90	SUB	B
91	SUB	C
92	SUB	D
93	SUB	E
94	SUB	H
95	SUB	L
D620	SUB	n
AE	XOR	(HL)
DDAE05	XOR	(IX+d)
FDAE05	XOR	(IY+d)
AF	XOR	A
A8	XOR	B
A9	XOR	C
AA	XOR	D
AB	XOR	E
AC	XOR	H
AD	XOR	L
EE20	XOR	n

(Courtesy of Zilog Inc.)

APPENDIX F

Z80 to 8080 EQUIVALENCE

Z80	8080	Z80	8080	Z80	8080
ADC A, (HL)	ADC M	EX (SP), HL	XTHL	OR n	ORI [B2]
ADC A, n	ACI [B2]	HALT	HLT	OR r	ORA r
ADC A, r	ADC r	IN A, (n)	IN [B2]	OR (HL)	ORA M
ADD A, (HL)	ADD M	INC BC	INX B	OUT (n), A	OUT [B2]
ADD A, n	ADI [B2]	INC DE	INX D	POP AF	POP PSW
ADD A, r	ADD r	INC HL	INX H	POP BC	POP B
ADD HL, BC	DAD B	INC r	INR r	POP DE	POP D
ADD HL, DE	DAD D	INC SP	INX SP	POP HL	POP H
ADD HL, HL	DAD H	INC (HL)	INR M	PUSH AF	PUSH PSW
ADD HL, SP	DAD SP	JP C, nn	JC [B2] [B3]	PUSH BC	PUSH B
AND n	ANI [B2]	JP M, nn	JM [B2][B3]	PUSH DE	PUSH D
AND r	ANA r	JP NC, nn	JNC [B2] [B3]	PUSH HL	PUSH H
AND (HL)	ANA M	JP nn	JMP [B2] [B3]	RET	RET
CALL C, nn	CC [B2] [B3]	JP NZ, nn	JNZ [B2] [B3]	RET C	RC
CALL M, nn	CM [B2] [B3]	JP P, nn	JP [B2] [B3]	RET M	RM
CALL NC, nn	CNC [B2] [B3]	JP PE, nn	JPE [B2][B3]	RET NC	RNC
CALL nn	CALL	JP PO, nn	JPO [B2][B3]	RET NZ	RNZ
CALL NZ, nn	CNZ [B2] [B3]	JP Z, nn	JZ [B2] [B3]	RET P	RP
CALL P, nn	CP [B2] [B3]	JP (HL)	PCHL	RET PE	RPE
CALL PE, nn	CPE [B2] [B3]	LD A, (DE)	LDAX	RET PO	RPO
CALL PO, nn	CPO [B2] [B3]	LDA, (nn)	LDA [B2] [B3]	RET Z	RZ
CALL Z, nn	CZ [B2] [B3]	LD DE, nn	LXID, [B2] [B3]	RLA	RAL
CCF	CMC	LD SP, nn	LXI SP, [B2] [B3]	RLCA	RLC
CP r	CMP r	LD (BC), A	STAX B	RRA	RAR
CP (HL)	CMP M	LD (DE), A	STAX D	RRCA	RRC
CPL	CMA	LD (HL), r	MOV M, r	RST P	RST P
CP n	CPI [B2]	LD (nn), A	STA [B2] [B3]	SBC A, (HL)	SBB M
DAA	DAA	LD (nn), HL	SHLD [B2] [B3]	SBC A, n	SBI [B2]
DEC BC	DCX B	LD A, (BC)	LDAX B	SBC A, r	SBB r
DEC DE	DCX D	LD BC, nn	LXIB, [B2] [B3]	SCF	STC
DEC HL	DCX H	LD HL, (nn)	LHLD [B2] [B3]	SUB n	SUI [B2]
DEC r	DCR r	LD HL, nn	LXI H [B2] [B3]	SUB r	SUB r
DEC SP	DCX SP	LD r, (HC)	MOV 1, M	SUB (HL)	SUB M
DEC (HL)	DCR M	LD r, n	MVI r, [B2]	XOR n	XRI [B2]
DI	DI	LD r, r¹	MOV r1, r2	XOR r	XRA r
EI	EI	LD SP, HL	SPHL	XOR (HL)	XRA M
EX DE, HL	XCHG	NOP	NOP		

APPENDIX G

8080 to Z80 EQUIVALENCE

8080	Z80	8080	Z80	8080	Z80
ACI [B2]	ADC A, n	IN [B2]	IN A, (n)	POP H	POP HL
ADC M	ADC A, (HL)	INR M	INC (HL)	POP PSW	POP AF
ADC r	ADC A, r	INR r	INC r	PUSH B	PUSH BC
ADD M	ADD A, (HL)	INX B	INC BC	PUSH D	PUSH DE
ADD r	ADD A, r	INX D	INC DE	PUSH H	PUSH HL
ADI [B2]	ADD A, n	INX H	INC HL	PUSH PSW	PUSH AF
ANA M	AND (HL)	INX SP	INC SP	RAL	RLA
ANA r	AND r	JC [B2] [B3]	JP C, nn	RAR	RRA
ANI [B2]	AND n	JM [B2] [B3]	JP M, nn	RC	RET C
CALL	CALL nn	JMP [B2] [B3]	JP nn	RET	RET
CC [B2] [B3]	CALL C, nn	JNC [B2] [B3]	JP NC, nn	RLC	RLCA
CM [B2] [B3]	CALL M, nn	JNZ [B2] [B3]	JP NZ, nn	RM	RET M
CMA	CPL	JP [B2] [B3]	JP P, nn	RNC	RET NC
CMC	CCF	JPE [B2] [B3]	JP PE, nn	RNZ	RET NZ
CMP M	CP (HL)	JPO [B2] [B3]	JP PO, nn	RP	RET P
CMP r	CP r	JZ [B2] [B3]	JP Z, nn	RPE	RET PE
CNC [B2] [B3]	CALL NC, nn	LDA [B2] [B3]	LD A, (nn)	RPO	RET PO
CNZ [B2] [B3]	CALL NZ, nn	LDAX B	LD A, (BC)	RRC	RRCA
CP [B2] [B3]	CALL P, nn	LDAX D	LD A, (DE)	RST	RST P
CPE [B2] [B3]	CALL PE, nn	LH LD [B2] [B3]	LD HL, (nn)	RZ	RET Z
CPI [B2]	CP n	LXI B [B2] [B3]	LD BC, nn	SBB M	SBC A, (HL)
CPO [B2] [B3]	CALL PO, nn	LDID [B2] [B3]	LD DE, nn	SBB r	SBC A, r
CZ [B2] [B3]	CALL Z, nn	LXI H [B2] [B3]	LD HL, nn	SBI [B2]	SBC A, n
DAA	DAA	LXI SP [B2] [B3]	LD SP, nn	SHLD [B2] [B3]	LD (nn), HL
DAD B	ADD HL, BC	MOV M, r	LD (HL), r	SPHL	LD SP, HL
DAD D	ADD HL, DE	MOV r, M	LD r, (HL)	STA [B2] [B3]	LD (nn), A
DAD H	ADD HL, HL	MOV r1, r2	LD r, r¹	STAX B	LD (BC), A
DAD SP	ADD HL, SP	MVI M	LD (HL), n	STAX D	LD (DE), A
DCR M	DEC (HL)	MVI r [B2]	LD r, n	STC	SCF
DCR r	DEC r	NOP	NOP	SUB M	SUB (HL)
DCX B	DEC BC	ORA M	OR (HL)	SUB r	SUB r
DCX D	DEC DE	ORA r	OR r	SUI [B2]	SUB n
DCX H	DEC HL	ORI [B2]	OR n	XCHG	EX DE, HL
DCX SP	DEC SP	OUT [B2]	OUT (n), A	XRA M	XOR (HL)
DI	DI	PCHL	JP (HL)	XRA r	XOR r
EI	EI	POP B	POP BC	XRI [B2]	XOR n
HALT	HLT	POP D	POP DE	XTHL	EX (SP), HL

INDEX

The SYBEX Library

BASIC PROGRAMS FOR SCIENTISTS AND ENGINEERS
by Alan R. Miller 340 pp., 120 illustr., Ref. B240
This second book in the "Programs for Scientists and Engineers" series provides a library of problem solving programs while developing proficiency in BASIC.

INSIDE BASIC GAMES
by Richard Mateosian
350 pp., 240 Illustr., Ref. B245
Teaches interactive BASIC programming through games. Games are written in Microsoft BASIC and can run on the TRS-80, APPLE II and PET/CBM.

FIFTY BASIC EXERCISES
by J.P. Lamoitier 240 pp., 195 Illustr., Ref. B250
Teaches BASIC by actual practice using graduated exercises drawn from everyday applications. All programs written in Microsoft BASIC.

EXECUTIVE PLANNING WITH BASIC
by X.T. Bui 192 pp., 19 illustr., Ref. B380
An important collection of business management decision models in BASIC, including Inventory Management (EOQ), Critical Path Analysis and PERT, Financial Ratio Analysis, Portfolio Management, and much more.

BASIC FOR BUSINESS
by Douglas Hergert
250 pp., 15 illustr., Ref. B390
A logically organized, no-nonsense introduction to BASIC programming for business applications. Includes many fully explained accounting programs, and shows you how to write them.

BASIC EXERCISES FOR THE APPLE
by J.P. Lamoitier 230 pp., 80 illustr., Ref. B500
For all Apple users, this learn-by-doing book is written in APPLESOFT II BASIC. Exercises have been chosen for their educational value and application to math, physics, games, business, accounting, and statistics.

YOUR FIRST COMPUTER
by Rodnay Zaks 260 pp., 150 Illustr., Ref. C200A
The most popular introduction to small computers and their peripherals: what they do and how to buy one.

DON'T
(or How to Care for Your Computer)
by Rodnay Zaks 220 pp., 100 Illustr., Ref. C400
The correct way to handle and care for all elements of a computer system including what to do when something doesn't work.

INTRODUCTION TO WORD PROCESSING
by Hal Glatzer 200 pp., 70 illustr., Ref. W101
Explains in plain language what a word processor can do, how it improves productivity, how to use a word processor and how to buy one wisely.

INTRODUCTION TO WORDSTAR
by Arthur Naiman 200 pp., 30 illustr., Ref. W105
Makes it easy to learn how to use WordStar, a powerful word processing program for personal computers.

FROM CHIPS TO SYSTEMS: AN INTRODUCTION TO MICROPROCESSORS
by Rodnay Zaks 560 pp., 255 illustr., Ref. C201A
A simple and comprehensive introduction to microprocessors from both a hardware and software standpoint: what they are, how they operate, how to assemble them into a complete system.

MICROPROCESSOR INTERFACING TECHNIQUES
by Rodnay Zaks and Austin Lesea
460 pp., 400 Illustr., Ref. C207
Complete hardware and software interconnect techniques including D to A conversion, peripherals, standard buses and troubleshooting.

PROGRAMMING THE 6502
by Rodnay Zaks 390 pp., 160 Illustr., Ref. C202
Assembly language programming for the 6502, from basic concepts to advanced data structures.

6502 APPLICATIONS BOOK
by Rodnay Zaks 280 pp., 205 Illustr., Ref. D302
Real life application techniques: the input/output book for the 6502.